The life of a prisoner of war (POW) is not easy. One endures the shock, trauma and fear of death during the shoot-down and capture. It is a monumental and unforgettable experience. Resistance to interrogation and refusal to give the enemy propaganda, as long as you are there, is followed by torture. Cruel and agonizing punishments are widespread. There is barely adequate food, if not starvation, and medical care is lacking. There is excessive harassment, isolation, and loneliness. Years pass slowly and the future is uncertain. Many survive with religion, for family or patriotism but all survive on hope. However, the bright side of this misery is that most POW's come home to fight another day.

A Story of the Fifth Longest Held POW in US History

First POW Released from North Vietnam

Ray Vohden

authorHOUSE®

AuthorHouse™
1663 Liberty Drive, Suite 200
Bloomington, IN 47403
www.authorhouse.com
Phone: 1-800-839-8640

First published by AuthorHouse 6/22/2009

ISBN: 978-1-4389-5095-2 (sc)

Library of Congress Control Number: 2009900919

Printed in the United States of America
Bloomington, Indiana

This book is printed on acid-free paper.

CONTENTS

PROLOGUE

On 12 February 1973, after nearly eight years as a prisoner of war in North Vietnam, I became a free man. Although I still had to serve a couple of years at stateside hospitals to salvage a badly wounded leg, my new quarters seemed princely compared to my squalid prison cells. Furloughed from the Navy hospital in Memphis, Tennessee, and facing a long, solitary drive to my parents' home in New Jersey, I decided to bring a tape recorder along and recount my experiences while the memories were still fresh. Maybe someday I would write a book.

I knew I had a unique vantage point and a story to tell. As the fourth U.S. pilot shot down in North Vietnam, I was one of the oldest of the old-timers among the POWs. During my captivity, the number of Americans killed in the war grew from sixty to nearly sixty thousand, and the treatment of POWs shifted from neglectful to brutal to halfway humane. Moreover, of the nearly six hundred Americans held prisoner in North Vietnam, I may have had the widest range of experiences:

1) I sustained serious injuries and endured horrific medical care, which caused me to walk with crutches for nearly eight years;

2) I was the senior man in the Cuban Program and the first to be tortured by the mysterious Caucasian known as Fidel;

3) Because my injured leg made me particularly vulnerable to torture, I had to resist the enemy through guile, rather than confrontation, which led some of my fellow POWs to misinterpret my polite façade as a sign of weakness;

4) During the early, difficult years, when the high-ranking POWs were isolated, I was one of ten or twelve mid-level officers with daily responsibility for leading many of the men;

5) After the senior officers joined the majority of the POWs in late 1970, their chaotic leadership caused our treatment to worsen, and the improvements the mid-grade officers had worked for years to attain went down the drain (either the senior officers misjudged the reason for the improved treatment or they were unable to adjust to it, but chaos resulted from their actions);

6) I served on the panel that conducted the only court martial of a POW in North Vietnam;

7) I prevented my men from taking drastic action against some POWs who were improperly slated for early release after collaborating with the enemy; and

8) I was the first POW to be released from North Vietnam after the signing of the Paris peace accords.

Although my book contains familiar POW lore, including torture, leg irons, and tap codes, the prison routine serves merely as a backdrop for the clashes and tenderness, competition and compassion, pettiness and sacrifices of ordinary men who survived a remarkable ordeal. My aim is to show us as we really were, with our foibles as well as our strengths. We weren't as heroic as we wished – or in some cases claimed – to be, but most of us did the best we could, and our whole story deserves to be heard. I believe that my perspective will help complete the record and that my experience could help future POWs to survive.

CHAPTER 1 - CAPTURE

U.S.S. Hancock
CVA-19

U.S. Navy Photo courtesy of Robert M. Ciera, via NavSource (www.navsource.org)

3 April 1965. A balmy Saturday morning with good visibility and light winds. A fine day to chalk up my fourth combat mission as a Navy carrier pilot. After too many sixteen-hour days of planning targets and preparing the aircraft, only to have Lyndon Johnson change his mind and cancel the missions, I was raring to get back into action.

Our target was the Dong Phuong Bridge, a small span across the Nam Ma River sixty-five miles south of Hanoi on Route One, the vital north-south road and rail link for ammo and troops heading south into battle. As a thirty-four-year-old lieutenant commander and operations officer of the *U.S.S. Hancock's* jet attack squadron VA 216, I had helped to plan and coordinate the mission, which would strike farther north than any raid since the Tonkin Gulf retaliation in August 1964. Unlike the ammunition depots/ grain silos, army barracks, radar installations, and triple-A (anti-aircraft artillery) sites we had hit before, the bridge was used by both military personnel and civilians.

At 0700, we assembled for the mission briefing in the air intelligence center on the second deck. I lit my first El Producto of the day and smoked contentedly, while Lt. j.g. Jack Hannon gave the intelligence briefing. No triple-A or other target defenses had been sighted.

Acting as honcho for our mission was Cmdr. Boyd Muncie, commanding officer of our sister squadron VA 212, a veteran of the Korean conflict and a legendary poker player, who had once fulfilled a promise to kiss a shipmate's bare ass upon losing a showdown at seven-card stud. With his ever-present red beanie on his bald head, Cmdr. Muncie outlined our strategy. An airwing from the *U.S.S. Coral Sea* would hit the bridge first, and we would be on target moments later to finish the job with twelve propeller-driven Al-bombers, which could tote their weight in ordnance, and twenty-four A4-Skyhawks, each carrying four 500-pound bombs. Eighteen F8-Crusaders would fly cover and knock out any enemy defenses.

After laying out the tactics we would follow, Cmdr. Muncie closed with an admonition. "From time to time in Korea, a pilot would release his bombs early, so he wouldn't have to worry about being shot down over the target. That's not going to happen today, gentlemen. Hold your bombs for the bridge. Good hunting."

I walked down the passageway to the ready room for an additional briefing from my squadron's executive officer. Standing by the mapcases and blackboard at the front of the room, Cmdr. Charles "Tex" Birdwell, assigned our roles. A tall, cool, Have-Gun-Will-Travel type with a pencil moustache and a tightly packed frame, he would lead his division of four aircraft over the target, and I would lead the second division. A third division would follow mine. By the time we were through with that bridge, nobody would be able to ride so much as a bicycle over it.

At 0830, we received the order to man our aircraft. I zipped up my G-suit—nylon pants that fit over my flight suit and automatically inflated to prevent the blood from rushing out of my brain when I pulled heavy Gs—and put on my Mae West, then picked up the kneeboard with the info I'd need for the flight. I grabbed my hardhat from a hook on the grey wall and took the escalator up to the flight deck.

The slower AI-bombers had already taken off when I buckled myself into an A4-Skyhawk, the Navy's all-weather light attack bomber, affectionately called the Tinker Toy. Each man in the squadron had his name painted on an aircraft, but the assignments were randomly made, and we rarely flew in our namesakes. Today, by coincidence, I had been assigned number 683, the Skyhawk with my name on it.

At 0855, the flight-deck's public-address system blared. "Start engines." The Crusaders were launched first, and we followed in the Skyhawks. After climbing to angels twenty (pilot jargon for 20,000 feet), we flew in a loose-V formation over the Tonkin Gulf. Within half an hour, we cleared the coastline at the mouth of the narrow, winding Nam Ma River and turned toward the target. As we began our descent to 5,000 feet for the final ten miles inland to the bridge, the divisions separated. Below me, a dark quilt of rice paddies spread out from the pearl-lipped shore and indigo sea.

I was not insensitive to the moral ambiguities of the war or to the faint stirring of opposition to it back home. Just the other day, I had read an article setting out the intellectuals' antiwar position. But as a career military officer, I believed in doing my duty and upholding the honor of my country. Nine months ago, Vietnam had been just a red blob on a map to me, another assignment on my way to retirement. I hadn't chosen to come here, but I couldn't deny that dive-bombing enemy targets was exciting.

From his orbit at 7,000 feet over the target, Cmdr. Muncie radioed a warning to expect heavy, gusting winds from the west. We'd have to adjust our air speeds, dive angles, and flight paths. The fighters had done their jobs well, hosing down the entire area with rockets and 20-millimeter cannon fire. The bridge looked like any railroad trestle in the States. An easy mark. But the gusts took our bombs and tossed them all over the terrain. Coming off the target, I heard something pop behind me, and a needle on my instrument panel jumped, indicating that my cockpit-pressurization system had malfunctioned. I tightened my oxygen mask and kicked the oxygen up to 100 percent. "Diamondback One." Cmdr. Muncie's voice crackled in my headset, as he radioed Cmdr. Birdwell. "This is Red Dog One. You've got two MiGs at nine o'clock."

"Diamondback One, Roger," came my squadron leader's laconic response.

And then, out of the corner of my eye, I spotted them. MiGs at five miles! This was the first time they had been sighted over a North Vietnamese target.

I pushed the stick forward and hauled ass down to 3,500 feet. The MiGs could give a Skyhawk trouble, but I wasn't really worried. They were no match for our faster, more manueverable Crusaders. These boys were probably on a dry run, just taking a look. Nonetheless, I shivered as they streaked upward through the clouds and disappeared.

Back aboard the ship, I rode the escalator down to the ready room and shed my flight gear. I hung my G-suit and hard hat on a hook and stowed my kneeboard in the drawer under my padded leather seat, then walked down the passageway to the wardroom for lunch. Admiral Eddy Outlaw, an old combat pilot and the commander of our carrier division, was probably raising hell about our performance. Still disappointed at my own failure, I retrieved my napkin from its cubbyhole and placed it on one of the long tables, before entering the cafeteria line.

"How about those winds?" said Lt. j.g. Ralph Tallent, my young wing man.

I shook my head in disgust. "I'll bet we didn't lay one damned bomb on the target."

"Did you see Meyers? His bombs landed on that bridge five miles downriver."

"No shit?" I grabbed a couple of grilled cheese sandwiches and a salad.

The squadron duty officer approached us with welcome news. "We're going back for another shot at the bridge. We brief in twenty minutes."

Great. Maybe we could nail it this time.

The briefing for the afternoon strike was like the morning one, only shorter. "Cmdr. Muncie will lead his squadron in first, then he'll go upstairs and call out where our bombs are dropping. Same tactics as this morning. When it's our squadron's turn, I'll take my division in first," said Cmdr. Birdwell. "Same order as before. Two-minute intervals between divisions."

The weather forecast hadn't changed, so we discussed ways to compensate for the gusting winds. Intelligence still reported no triple-A.

"Maintain radio silence until we reach the target," Birdwell added, as the briefing drew to a close. "Heads up, guys. Let's lay some bombs on that bridge."

Before taking the escalator topside to my aircraft, I picked up a code sheet for verifying radio communications, along with a small medical kit, and a blood chit—a white silk rectangle embossed with the American flag and a message in six languages, including Vietnamese, saying that anyone who helped the bearer of the flag to the nearest Allied lines would be rewarded for his humanitarian efforts.

This might have worked in World War I or II, but I doubted that it would work here. What Vietnamese peasant would put me on the handlebars of his bicycle and pedal four hundred miles, dodging his comrades and our bombs just to deliver me to his enemies for a few lousy bucks? Then again, you never knew.

The Seventh Fleet had lost six or seven planes in the past few weeks, but most of the pilots had ejected over water and been rescued. One guy had drifted on a raft for a few days before they found him, but he survived. The North Vietnamese had captured two Navy pilots and one Air Force pilot. Lt. j.g. Everett Alvarez, whom I had met while serving on the *U.S.S. Constellation* in 1963, had been shot down last August, and Lt. Cmdr. Bob Shumaker, from the *Coral Sea*, had gone down in early February. Air Force First Lt. Hayden Lockhart had been shot down in March.

The A1-bombers had already launched, and the brown-shirted mechanics were still trying to repair the malfunctioning pressure system on my aircraft. If they didn't fix it soon, the plane would be grounded, and I'd be sidelined with it. Furious, I ran through the exterior pre-flight check, then climbed into the cockpit. I strapped myself in, connected my G-suit's hose, and methodically performed the rest of the pre-flight routine.

Ten minutes before launch time, the blueshirts began positioning the box-shaped huffer units, mobile compressors that blew air into the aircrafts' compressors to get the engines turning. At zero minus five minutes and counting, the command to start the engines came over the loudspeaker. My anxiety was building. I badly wanted this flight.

One by one, the engines roared to life. The redshirts were still loading bombs under the wings of the last few Skyhawks. The ship had completed its turn into the wind, and the Crusaders slowly paraded toward the catapult, unfolding their wings as they moved into position. Caught up in the psychic momentum of the launch, I would be mightily frustrated if I had to abort my mission now. I looked down at my mechanic. With his oversized goggles, he looked like a wise old owl. A smiling owl. He raised both thumbs skyward. I was on. If the bastard went out on me again, it would be his ass. I pulled the canopy down and locked myself in. I looked to wing-man Ralph Tallent, on my left, and gave him thumbs up. He returned the gesture.

Once the blueshirts had removed my chocks and tie-down cables, the yellow-shirted flight director beckoned with upturned palms, and I taxied onto the catapult track. The director signaled a halt with closed fists, and the greenshirts attached the bridle and installed the holdback bar. The director gave me the tension signal. As the shuttle moved forward, locking me onto the catapult sled, I took my feet off of the brakes, pushed the throttle forward, and verified that my tachometer registered 100 percent.

With the Skyhawk straining against the holdback cable, I sat back in my seat, double checked my tach, and gave the cat officer a sharp salute. Grasping the stick loosely in my right hand, I waited for the catapult to fling my ten-ton plane down three hundred feet of runway in two seconds flat.

Whoosh! The G-force drove me straight back into the padded seat, and I was airborne.

I climbed left away from the ship and rendezvoused with the rest of my division, while ascending to angels twenty. At 18,000 feet, the seal on my cockpit-pressurization valve broke again. My ears popped, and my stomach growled, as the gasses expanded. When I got back, I would pluck that wise old owl's tail-feathers. I had enough to do without worrying about passing out from anoxia. I set the oxygen output at 100 percent and pressed on. When I reached the coast, I descended to 5,000 feet and found the haze thicker than I had expected.

"Diamondback One. This is Red Dog One. We still have strong winds from the west over the target. Estimate 35 to 40 knots, gusting to 50. Make corrections for your run. No triple-A in the target area. Over." Cmdr. Muncie was telling Cmdr. Birdwell not to screw up the job this time. The airwing from the *Coral Sea* must have missed again.

Suddenly, through the haze, I saw the bridge. The approaches were empty. A thin wisp of smoke from a village to the north was the only sign of life—or the sign of a bomb that had missed its target.

Cmdr. Birdwell and his division made their bombing runs and pulled off. The bridge remained untouched.

"Diamondback Five, this is Red Dog One," radioed Cmdr. Muncie to me. "Ordnance is still wide of the mark. High and to the left. Make your corrections."

"Red Dog One. Diamondback Five. Roger," I answered as coolly as possible.

I was not the best stick-and-rudder man in the squadron, but few guys had my combination of recklessness and will power. Determined to be the first to hit the damned bridge, I decided to go for a shallow, flatter dive angle than the one I had used this morning. I would be more vulnerable to enemy fire, but releasing the bombs at a lower altitude would boost my accuracy.

I gave Tallent thumbs up and rolled in on the target. The altimeter unwound faster and faster as I dove. At 2,000 feet, I had my bombsight right where I wanted it. I moved my thumb lightly over the bomb-release button on the stick. Closer, closer. Now! I pickled once, twice. That ought to do it.

As I pulled back on the stick to climb away from the target, I blacked out. (Unknown to me, the fusing had malfunctioned, and my bombs had detonated prematurely, exploding beneath my plane.)

When I regained consciousness, the fire-warning lights were glowing on my instrument panel. Smoke filled the cockpit, and heat lapped me from behind. I tried to send a Mayday message, but as soon as I began speaking, I knew the mike was dead.

My plane was banking to the right at an altitude of 2,800 feet, my airspeed was dropping from 300 knots, and the rudder pedals and stick were frozen. With no way to control the plane, I saw no need to hang around and wait for it to explode or crash. I fumbled between my legs for my ejection seat's D-ring. As I yanked it, I blacked out again.

When I came to, my parachute had blossomed above me. I looked right then left, trying to orient myself, hoping to land near water. I saw only rice paddies stretching endlessly in all directions.

This was my first experience punching out, and I felt great. The sensation of floating silently and serenely through the air was exhiliarating. The sky was a blue plate heaped with vanilla clouds. The terrain below looked soft— nice spongy vegetation or rice paddies to cushion my fall.

My watch and kneeboard had apparently flown off when I ejected. My hard hat had twisted around, and the strap was digging into my chin. I unfastened the strap and took off the five-pound helmet. What did I need this thing for? I let go, and it plummeted out of sight. If it landed on a peasant sloshing through a rice paddy, I hoped I didn't land nearby.

As I got closer to the ground, I realized that the same damned winds that had been protecting the bridge were blowing me across the countryside at 35 or 40 knots. I was heading straight for a butte that thrust up from the land like a limestone fist. I tugged at my shroud lines, but my direction didn't change.

Before I had time to panic, I slammed into the rocky top of the butte and pitched forward. My chute instantly collapsed. Dazed, I sat up and noticed that the flight boot on my right foot had flopped over at a ninety-degree angle from my leg. I pulled my pants away from the foot and raised my leg to get a better look at the damage. The big boot hung down, and I saw the jagged ends of two pinkish-white bones sticking out of my G-suit. Strangely, there was no blood on them.

I closed my eyes and tried to control my breathing. I was going to lose my foot! I lay down again, trying to slow my heartbeat. As I struggled to erase the image of the shattered bones, I was transported back a few years to the *Constellation*, where a cable for catching incoming aircraft had snapped, whipped across the flight deck, and hit a door I had just passed through. I had reopened the door and gone back outside to find an appalling array of severed legs and feet scattered on the blood-spattered deck. Ten or twelve men lay motionless, far from their limbs. The wind blew silently across the deck, and not a single murmur issued from the crumpled men.

Now my foot, still encased in its boot, looked just as many of theirs had looked. Dropping bombs from my air-conditioned cockpit had been fun, but I sure as shit didn't want to lose my foot or my leg. Hell, I might even die. I'd heard that the chances of a prisoner's remaining alive were considerably higher if he was healthy and able to walk. When the North Vietnamese saw my broken leg, they might decide to finish me off on the spot and save themselves the trouble of hauling me to a doctor. I took off my parachute. The adrenalin was pumping into my blood, as I stuck the ends of my bones into my boot. I had to hide or get away. I stood up and began hopping on my left foot, but after falling twice in the first five hops, I realized that escape was impossible. There was no place to go, no hope of getting there.

My pantleg was now saturated with blood. I needed a tourniquet. From the sleeve of my flight suit, I cut a strip of cloth and tied it tightly around my right leg above the knee. I felt no pain, but it

11

would surely come as soon as the shock wore off. I fumbled for the medical kit in the shoulder pocket of my flight suit. I pulled out a tube of morphine, attached a needle, and jabbed it into my upper left arm. Sweat streamed from my face and body. This rocky hilltop was as hot as New York City in August.

Five minutes after landing, I spotted a pair of peasants crouched on the lip of the butte, about sixty yards away. Brandishing machetes, the men crept toward me. When they were ten yards away, the wiry one on the right stood up and stared at me. The one on the left hung back somewhat, watching my every move. Dressed in baggy, tattered, grey pants and matching short-sleeved shirts, the barefooted men gracefully crossed the rocky ground. They spread apart and moved in sync, cautiously, like hunters closing in on a wounded animal.

If they were going to kill me, I couldn't stop them, but I wasn't going to do anything to piss them off. I raised my hands over my head. When the men were three yards from me, they crouched again, resting their machetes on their thighs. The wiry one looked to be about thirteen years old. His companion, who had a wispy goatee and a bit more meat on his thin frame, was older. As they sized me up, I suddenly realized that they were afraid of me. Me, with my dangling foot. Hoping they didn't bear any grudges about the bombing, I lifted my hands higher.

With raised machetes, the men silently approached. Was this the end? They pointed their machetes at my neck, and a foul, fishy odor swept over me. With it came the full realization that I had been shot down and badly wounded in a country I had just bombed. I was alone with my enemies.

CHAPTER 2 - IMPRISONMENT

3 April 1965. Once they saw that I was injured, my captors laid their machetes on the ground, out of my reach, and began emptying my pockets. The men were not particularly rough, but when they reached the pocket on my right leg, I couldn't help but flinch. They stopped. A good omen, I hoped. I showed them how to work the zippers to remove my sweltering G-suit.

A Skyhawk roared overhead at strafing altitude, and the men scurried for cover near a cliff. I squinted at the number painted on the nose: It was Cmdr. Birdwell's plane. He rocked his wings to show that he saw me, and I waved him off. Nobody could rescue me from this fix. I would have to take my chances with the Vietnamese.

When Cmdr. Birdwell flew away, the men returned and continued stripping me of my gear. They removed my left boot, but I persuaded them with gestures not to touch the right one. My broken bones needed all the support they could get.

Seeing my handkerchief and wallet lying on the rocks, I realized that I had left my Armed Forces I.D. and Geneva Convention card on the ship. Hell, I wasn't even wearing my dog tags. I had never thought I'd be in a position to need them—or that they'd do any good if I did get shot down. I hadn't said a thing, and already I'd violated the rules.

Within minutes, twenty-five or thirty people had climbed the hill and gathered around to stare at me. Shaking their heads and chattering quietly in words I didn't understand, they seemed more curious than hostile. Probably didn't have many foreigners dropping in on them. As I looked at these shaggy-haired men, emaciated women, and scrawny children in bare feet and rags, I despaired. If they had so little for themselves, what kind of medical care could I expect? How could they possibly save my foot?

For perhaps half an hour, I sat and watched the people gawking and pointing at me. Eventually, their discussion became more animated. A couple of the men departed briefly and returned with six or seven 3-1/2-foot sticks. Were they going to kill me in some barbaric ritual?

Several people approached and pushed me down flat on my back, while shoving the sticks under my neck, back, rump, and knees to form a crude stretcher. I couldn't believe it. Not one of these people weighed more than a hundred pounds. Did they think they could carry my two-hundred-pound six-foot frame down this steep slope with nothing more than a few sticks? Apparently so. Twelve volunteers, including an elderly woman, surrounded me. One man held my good foot, another held my bad leg and foot, and the rest grabbed the ends of the sticks and hoisted me into the air.

With much shouting and grunting, they inched down the precipitous hillside. They paused often, waiting for someone to find a solid foothold. Occasionally, one or two of them slipped and fell, and others grabbed the sticks in time to keep me from tumbling off. With each torturous step, the sticks bit into my spine. I felt like Gulliver being hauled away by a party of Lilliputians. What a primitive country this was! How could they even consider waging war against the United States?

After half an hour, we reached the bottom of the hill. They carried me another thirty-five or forty yards and laid me on the grass beside a raised dirt road, which ran like a dike between open fields and rice paddies. A few thatched houses sat in the fields, and small buildings clustered in the distance. The sun beat down onto a treeless landscape. A glass of water would be nice, but unless I wanted to drink out of the rice paddy, I was out of luck.

I lay on the ground for an hour or so, as a crowd quietly gathered. Nearly two hundred people had come to see me. None of them wore the black pajamas we had heard so much about. Their clothes were made of dirty grey cloth that reminded me of the laundry bags we used aboard ship.

The morphine was still working, or maybe I was in shock. The only pain I felt was in my heart. What would Bonnye do when they told her? I'd been on sea duty for so much of the time, she was used to having me gone. And the kids were too young—Ray was barely four, Connie was not quite three—to know the difference. Even so, how many months would pass before I could see them again? It was bound to be tough on Bonnye, but she'd be cool. I could see her laughing, the dimples in her pale cheeks playing peekaboo with her dark hair, as she shook her head at the kids' antics. Yeah, Bonnye would be cool. A Navy wife had to be cool.

Behind me, an old man began yelling, and others seemed to be trying to calm him. He stepped into view and pointed a pistol at me. I didn't need to understand Vietnamese to interpret the rage in his voice. We must have bombed his hooch or killed his cattle—or maybe even his family. He wanted retribution, and I couldn't stop him. As he continued to rail at me, I lay still and watched the gun in his quivering hand.

A young man in khaki pants and a white shirt appeared and spoke softly to the old man, who turned at once and departed. Maybe captured American pilots were too valuable to kill. For now, at least.

The young man, whose neatly combed hair and clean clothes set him apart from the others, said something to the onlookers, and they moved back. He left without a word to me.

I waited and waited, wondering what would become of me. I'd heard that French prisoners from Dien Bien Phu were still being held in Hanoi. Intelligence had plied us with tales of how the North and

South Vietnamese had brutalized each other. One magazine picture showed South Vietnamese soldiers parading through a village with the head of a Viet Cong on a stick. But maybe it was just propaganda, like the stuff I had heard about Germans during World War II. The propagandists in those days hadn't bothered to distinguish between the Nazis, who *were* monsters, and the Germans like Oma, my dear, sweet grandmother, who was tarred by the same brush. I hoped the North Vietnamese were more like Oma than like Hitler. Failing that, I hoped they'd go easy on me because of my broken leg.

Eventually, someone brought a piece of canvas tied to two poles and helped me onto it. It was not exactly a Red Cross ambulance, but it beat riding on the sticks. More spectators lined the road, as a new set of volunteers carried me about half a mile to a row of four crude one-story buildings with tile roofs.

We entered one of the faded brown structures, which resembled adobe huts in the southwestern United States. Late-afternoon sunlight slanting through two glassless windows provided the only illumination in the one narrow room. My bearers put the stretcher next to a wooden table and helped me scoot onto it. The only other furniture was a wooden cabinet with bandages and bottles on its open shelves. The room had a dirt floor. Dehydrated from the loss of blood and perspiration, I desperately needed water. I put my hand to my mouth in a drinking motion and tipped my head back. The people surrounding my table ignored me. I said, "Water?" and repeated the motion periodically, but no water came.

As I lay there, looking up at the underside of the roof, a boy no more than ten years old approached me. He smiled and pointed at my wedding band. Nearly five years had passed since I stood in my white uniform in a Memphis church and exchanged rings with

Bonnye. I still remembered the yellow dress she had changed into for our honeymoon trip to New Orleans. Man, she was gorgeous.

The boy pointed at my ring again, then pointed at himself. Someone would undoubtedly take the ring sooner or later, so this sorry-looking kid in tattered clothes might as well have it. I nodded. He tried to remove the ring, but it was too tight. I pulled it off of my finger and gave it to him. He smiled and disappeared into the crowd.

I had been staring at the roof beams for fifteen minutes, when the man in the white shirt came in and ordered most of those present to leave the room. People still gaped at me through the open windows.

A few minutes later, a man wearing a dingy, white apron entered. He cut off the lower part of my right pantleg and examined my wound, then left briefly and returned with three pieces of wood. After splinting my leg with the wood, he wrapped it with gauze. My leg hurt now, but not as much as I would have thought.

At last, someone brought me a small cup of hot tea, and I eagerly took a sip. It contained enough sugar to gag a maggot. I pointed to the cup and shook my head, then made the drinking motion again and said, "Water!" They didn't seem to understand. Or maybe they didn't have any potable water.

The medic gave me five small pills to take with the tea. I hesitated. Could they be cyanide? What the hell— if they were going to kill me, I couldn't stop them. I swallowed the pills and choked down the tea.

By now, shadows filled the room. A vehicle rumbled up outside, and five men in green uniforms entered. They put me onto a stretcher and carried me out to a large army truck with a tarp over the back. After loading me into the truckbed, they wrapped my torso and the stretcher together with wire and attached the stretcher to the truck. The soldiers sat on wooden benches along the sides. The truck started with a lurch, and we drove off into the darkness.

One of the soldiers pulled out a pack of cigarettes and offered me one. I usually stuck to cigars, but I took a cigarette anyway. Why risk offending him? Pretending to smoke, I puffed away on the cigarette without inhaling. Maybe these guys weren't so bad, after all. We drove for half an hour, and then stopped. As the soldiers climbed out of the truck, one man stayed behind to blindfold me with a piece of khaki cloth. He detached the wire from the truck, and the others lifted me down and carried me on the stretcher up a steep hill.

I peeked out of the side of my blindfold and saw people with torches lining the path and shouting at me. Like a trophy, I was borne through the mob. Now I understood the soldier's apparent generosity: He had been offering me a last cigarette. They were going to throw me off a cliff! I was about to be sacrificed to some pagan god. I would never see Bonnye again; never see Ray and Connie grow up.

I envisioned myself floating endlessly in space without light, without sound, without a body. Would it hurt when I hit the ground? What were the guys on the ship saying about me? What wouldn't I give to start the day over and be back in the wardroom, sitting at one of the long tables with a clean white tablecloth, eating a sirloin steak and a baked potato, and looking forward to a few hands of bridge after dinner?

We climbed for ten minutes before the ground leveled off. The mob was louder now, perhaps exhorted by the authoritative voice that stood out above the roar. Instead of tossing me off the cliff, however, the soldiers took me to another truck.

They left my blindfold on and drove for half an hour or more. When the truck finally stopped, they carried me into a darkened building. Light from their small flashlights was visible through my blindfold, as we moved down a long hall. They took me into a dark room, put me onto a table, and removed my blindfold. For what seemed like the five-hundredth time, I asked for water and made the drinking gesture. This time, they brought me a small cup of it. Aboard ship, I drank only ice-cold water, but this lukewarm liquid felt as good as a frosty beer sliding down my parched throat.

I lay in the room for a quarter of an hour, trying to empty my mind. The door opened, and a man in a white smock entered, followed by a man in street clothes. Pointing to himself, the man in white said in barely recognizable English, "Doctor...operation."

His assistant picked up a piece of paper and a pencil and said, "Name?"

"Ray Vohden."

Frowning, he asked me to repeat it. He still didn't understand. After asking me several times, he finally handed me the pencil and paper.

Was he trying to trick me? Would they attach my signature to a typewritten confession of some horrendous deed? Or did they just want my name for their records? The Code of Conduct required me to give my name, rank, serial number, and date of birth, but I was not supposed to write anything down. My mind jumped back to the jagged bones poking out of my pant leg on the butte. If I refused to write my name, they might withhold medical treatment. I knew it was wrong, but I gripped the pencil and printed my name where the flashlight beam indicated. If you could be court-martialed for violating the code without being tortured, I was done for.

As I grappled with my conscience, a man brought in a pair of blast lamps, which lighted up the room almost as well as a sixty-watt electric bulb would have. The doctor washed his hands and donned a mask. His assistant covered my face with a loose wad of large handkerchiefs and dripped ether onto it. I felt as if my whole body were glued to a huge rubber membrane, which sprang back and forth, faster and faster, until I passed out.

A few minutes later, I came to. Pain knifed through my leg. They had cut off my right pantleg just below the crotch, and someone was holding my foot so that it wouldn't flop over. Noticing that I was awake, the doctor said, "More operation." His assistant rubbed alcohol on my right arm and emptied a large syringe of clear fluid into my vein. Before I could think *sodium pentathol,* I was out.

The next morning, I woke up in a clean room with two Vietnamese men watching over me from chairs pulled close to my bed. A plaster cast encased my leg from the upper thigh to the sole of my foot. My foot was still there! My leg ached, but the cast meant that the doctor had set the bones. I'd be able to walk again, once they healed.

Sunlight streamed into the room, and tall trees rose beyond the window. Soon I heard the distant roar of Skyhawks rolling in and bombs exploding like thunder. As the planes pulled away from the target, rifle shots popped, and a soldier outside my window pointed his puny weapon skyward. Reports of the Vietnamese taking on jet planes with small-arms fire had always seemed too cartoonish to be true, but now I realized that the joke was on us. The planes continued their runs, and I found myself wishing that they wouldn't bomb so close to me. More death and destruction from the sky would hardly improve the hospitality my hosts had to offer a downed pilot.

Later, one of my overseers brought me three bananas and a half-pint of condensed milk. The syrupy liquid made me gag, but I kept the can in case my appetite returned. I slipped in and out of consciousness, driven awake by the throbbing in my leg. Again and again, I asked for morphine, hoping that its painkilling properties were internationally known, but the men never seemed to understand what I wanted. At dusk, they finally gave me a shot of something that dulled the pain, and I drifted off.

A few hours later, they woke me, put me onto a stretcher, and carried me outdoors into the glare of bright torches. Three or four hundred people had assembled to see me displayed on the front porch. A man stood beside me and talked for an hour, gesturing in my direction from time to time. The crowd listened quietly. The arrival of a small jeep signaled the end of the lecture.

Several soldiers carried the stretcher to the jeep and helped me maneuver into the tiny back seat. A soldier took the wheel, and a medic sat in the passenger seat. With blankets hung over the windows and between the front and back seats, we jounced along a cobbled road. I repeatedly asked for water and morphine, to no avail.

After a few hours, the medic said in English, "We take boat now."

My heart leaped. Maybe these guys had brought me to the coast and were about to row me out to a U.S. destroyer and collect the reward. I had read newspaper and magazine articles saying that Ho Chi Minh was a ruthless dictator with little support from the Vietnamese people. We probably had spies and sympathizers all over the place. Maybe my companions were members of the underground.

Alas, we stopped by a river. Peeping through a small hole in one of the blankets, I saw a long line of vehicles stretching down to the riverbank. Beyond them stood a bridge, its girders twisted, pieces of wood and metal dangling below. Could this be Dong Phuong?

Had our bombs found their mark? That would be something—held up by my own squadron's handiwork.

We waited about fifteen minutes, then drove onto a small ferry, which carried four vehicles, two abreast. The boat took us to a sandbar in the middle of the river. After a half-hour's wait, we boarded another ferry and crossed to the far bank.

Onward we rode, through the night. My leg was still throbbing, and every joint in my body ached. Wedged into this jolting jeep, my bones absorbed the shock from each bump and hole in the road. Despite my pleas, I got no morphine and, consequently, no sleep.

As the sun rose, I peeked out onto open fields and scattered hamlets. An hour after dawn, the jeep stopped, and the medic alighted to make a telephone call. The phone jangled as he dialed each number. Buildings crowded the roadside. We must have entered a city. Hanoi? When the medic returned, he blindfolded and handcuffed me. Did he think I was going to make a break for it? How far would I get with this cast on my leg?

The jeep started up again and followed a circuitous route through the awakening city. An occasional car or truck growled past us now. Bicycle bells tinkled. Motor bikes buzzed. Trolleys clanged. Policemen whistled. Schoolchildren chattered. Vendors yelled. We stopped for red lights. Eventually, we slowed down, made a final turn, and came to a halt. The driver spoke to someone outside, and a heavy metal gate opened with a rusty groan. The jeep rolled forward a short distance, and the driver killed the engine.

My escorts opened their doors and climbed out. After more talk outside, the medic removed the blankets and untied my blindfold. We had driven through a tunnel into a large courtyard surrounded by one- and two-story stuccoed buildings whose paint had long-since faded. A trellis laden with grapevines shaded part of the courtyard.

The medic motioned for me to get out of the jeep, but even the smallest movement sent pain ripping through my leg. He summoned reinforcements, and several men in tan uniforms pried me out of the jeep and laid me on a stretcher. The sun beamed down on me, and the cool morning air felt good. Another beautiful day.

They carried me through a set of large French doors into a small room and set the stretcher down beside a low bed—a wooden board forty inches wide and seven feet long supported by a metal frame and topped with a thin straw mat. Four poles, the size of broom handles, protruded from holes in the corners of the board. Across from the bed sat two desks and a couple of filing cabinets piled with papers and office supplies. A table stood in the middle of the room.

With help, I managed to slide onto the bed. This wasn't the bridal suite at the Plaza, but it beat the hell out of the back seat of that damned jeep. At least I could stretch out. Now, if only I could get a drink! I went through my mime routine again and croaked, "Water!"

The men shook their heads, mumbled something in Vietnamese, and departed.

I had been lying there in my skivvies for about an hour, when three or four men dressed in rumpled, dingy white smocks and rubber-tire sandals entered, accompanied by two guys in street clothes. One of the civilians—a young man in khaki pants and a white shirt—stepped forward and said, "I speak English." Gesturing toward a chubby, balding man with wire-rimmed glasses and refined features, the interpreter said, "Tell doctor what happen to leg."

Little by little, through the interpreter, I described my injury and the treatment I had received.

The men listened intently, then discussed the matter in Vietnamese for several minutes. Finally, the interpreter turned to me and said, "We take you to hospital for X-ray tonight. You rest today."

Relief washed over me. Conditions here might have been primitive by American standards, but these people obviously had had some medical training, and they wanted to help me. If they had an X-ray machine, they couldn't be too backward.

When they left, I lay on the bed and stared at the naked light bulb hanging from the ceiling. The bulb wasn't lit, but the sunlight shining through a transom over the French doors was enough for now. The transom was open to the air—did the Vietnamese ever use glass in their windows? In the courtyard beyond, rats scampered across the grapevines.

Things could have been a lot worse—I could have been in a dungeon or a jungle camp. I might be a prisoner of war with a busted leg, but I was alive. This conflict couldn't last more than a few months, and then I'd be home. No matter what, I could hold my breath for that long.

A short guard in a tan uniform came into the room with two small blankets for me. One was red, the other green. Both were threadbare. He soon brought other gifts: a large grey ceramic pitcher full of water; an enameled cup with a handle; an aluminum scoop-like spoon; a wash cloth; a red toothbrush with well-worn bristles; a tube of Vietnamese toothpaste; and a pair of blue hand-me-down pajamas three sizes too small.

I grabbed the brimming pitcher immediately, but the water was only one degree shy of boiling. Was this a cruel joke? A cultural tradition? A sanitary measure? I poured myself a steaming cupful and reluctantly set it aside to cool. I killed time by slipping one blanket under my body for extra padding and folding the other one around the pajamas to make a pillow. When I could wait no longer, I picked up the small yellow cup and gulped the water, cringing with each scalding sip.

My first meal arrived at mid-morning. After one taste of the unidentifiable swill, I abandoned it in favor of the stale slice of crusty bread. Much better. I topped off lunch with the remainder of the water, which was still quite warm.

Periodically, men in uniform or civilian dress wandered into my room, looked me over, talked among themselves, then left without attempting to communicate with me. Just wanted to check out the freak, I guessed.

In the early afternoon, a gong sounded. Presently, the guard took away my dirty dishes and returned with a mosquito net. He tied it to the tops of the poles rising from my bed.

"Bzzzz," he said, lightly pinching my arm to simulate an insect bite. He showed me how to let the net down and tuck it in at night and how to raise it in the daytime, when the mosquitoes went off duty.

By now, my bladder was full, but I didn't have the proverbial pot to piss in. I put the water pitcher between my thighs and said, "Pee?"

The guard went out and found me a two-gallon can, then left me to make the most of it. I placed the bulky can between my legs as best I could and promptly peed all over the bed and myself. Only half of the urine made it into the can. In the late afternoon, the guard brought me a bowl of fish soup and a slice of fairly fresh bread. This time, I ate everything.

The room was hot, and I lay there trying not to notice the throbbing in my leg. After dark, the interpreter from this morning arrived with three or four green-uniformed soldiers. One of the soldiers produced a blindfold, and the interpreter said, "We go to hospital now for X-ray."

When they removed my blindfold ten minutes later, I was lying on a stretcher in a dim room. Grime coated the walls. My escorts helped me slide onto a narrow wooden table, which sat in the middle of the room, alongside what must have been the oldest X-ray machine in existence. The technician, who wore the standard rumpled medical smock, took X-rays of my leg in five or six positions. Each time I changed to a new position, the pain intensified.

Back in my room, my leg was burning, and I asked the interpreter for morphine.

He said, "I ask doctor."

Alone again, I looked at the worn toothbrush. My mouth felt scummy, but I sure as hell didn't want to pick up TB, polio, or any other disease the former owner might have had. In the end, I figured I had more important things than germs to worry about. The toothpaste tasted like soap, but my mouth felt 100 percent better. I wished I could say as much for my leg.

I was in luck. The interpreter brought me a couple of pills and says, "Swallow these."

Still wary, I hesitated, but only for a second. A little cyanide would certainly take my mind off of my leg. The pills quickly took effect, and for the next two or three hours, I felt pretty good. By midnight, however, the pain had returned.

I tried to block out the sensation by thinking about my family, but that only made me feel worse. I remembered our last hours together in California, before I left on the cruise in September. The four of us had taken a train to Oakland from Lemore, where I was stationed. After renting a car and a room in a motel on the outskirts of Alameda, we ate dinner in an Italian restaurant, walked around Fisherman's Wharf, and went to a wax museum. Because Ray and Connie were with us, we skipped the party thrown by the other members of my squadron and their wives.

Although I had requested shore duty so Bonnye and the kids could be with me, a pal who thought he was looking out for my career had assigned me to sea duty again. I was disappointed but took the assignment in stride.

I had always dreaded leaving, and this time was no exception. I woke up at 0530 and got ready to go. Bonnye threw a terrycloth bathrobe over her nightgown and put sweaters over the children's pajamas. We bundled Ray and Connie into the back seat, and Bonnye took the wheel for the drive to my ship.

"Be sure to write more often," she said.

"Sure." I just wanted to get the ordeal over with, before I lost my cool.

She stopped the car at the gangplank, and I got out and walked around to her window. I kissed her and leaned into the back window for pecks on the cheek from the kids.

"I'll see you," I said, then turned and walked up the gangway without looking back. I had been cool, all right. Cool to the point of cold.

Somehow, I managed to get through the night. As the early morning sunlight filtered through the grapevines outside my transom, a feminine voice humming a Vietnamese folk song wafted through a window that connected my room with the one next to it.

Soon, a young woman appeared at my door, wearing a relatively clean white dress with a surgical mask hanging from her neck. I liked her smile and the way her short black hair brushed her shoulders

28

when she nodded hello. She removed my dishes and returned with a folding chair, which she placed next to my bed. She brought in a pan of cold water and handed me a rock-hard bar of light-brown soap. The pain of moving prevented me from taking a full-fledged sponge bath, but it felt great to wash my hands and face for the first time in nearly three days.

An hour later, the medical team came in. The balding doctor was not with them. A dark-haired man of about my age was now in charge. Through the interpreter, the new doctor said both bones were broken, and the cast would have to come off, so they could treat the wound. "Doctor say break very bad, but we fix. Leg heal quick."

As a child, I had had casts removed from my arms and legs with a little circular saw whose rubber blade cut plaster but not skin. The process took about five minutes. Here in Hoa Lo Prison, the method was somewhat different: A medic with a strong arm took a six-inch knife with a dull blade and spent twenty minutes sawing, hacking, and yanking the cast until it came off. I did my part by entertaining everyone in the vicinity with an aria of groans and howls.

I didn't argue when the interpreter told me to lie back. "Bad wound. You no look. Doctor fix."

One of the medics brought in an open wooden box about thirty inches long. As the doctor changed my bandage, the medic padded the bottom of this contraption with cotton. Together, they helped me place my leg in the box, and then the medic wrapped the entire thing with gauze. Although it didn't immobilize my leg, as the cast had done, the box kept my foot from flopping around and allowed the medics to change the bandage without having to change the cast each time.

I asked the interpreter whether the doctor would prescribe morphine for me to take at bedtime each night.

They talked in Vietnamese awhile, and the interpreter said, "Doctor want to know if you are drug addict."

Startled, I said, "No, it's for my leg." Maybe people here had a higher tolerance for pain than I did. Or perhaps drugs were in short supply—not to be liberally doled out to American fighter pilots and other enemies of the people.

After further discussion in Vietnamese, the interpreter said they would look into getting me some drugs, They left, locking the French doors behind them.

With my leg in the box, my ability to move diminished considerably. I could either sit up or lie on my back, but I couldn't get comfortable. It was impossible to roll on my side. If I so much as thought about rolling onto my side, the broken bones ground against each other. Taking a piss was really going to be a challenge now. And what in the world would I do when my bowels were ready to move?

As I lay flat on my back, pondering such weighty questions, a voice called out from no more than a hundred feet away.

"Cigarette, please."

My heart beat wildly. Another American!

"Cigarette, please."

Would I be punished if I spoke to him? I couldn't afford to antagonize my captors before my leg healed, but I desperately wanted to talk to him.

"Cigarette, please."

Screw it. "Hey, Yank," I yelled. "Air Force or Navy?"

No answer.

I called out again.

Silence.

Why didn't the bastard respond? I was taking the risk. Why couldn't he? I waited a few minutes and called out two or three times more.

Nothing.

He must have had his reasons for not answering, but I felt as though he'd held out his hand only to swat me with it. Pinned to my bed, I was as fragile as a butterfly. And more alone than ever.

CHAPTER 3 - INTERROGATION

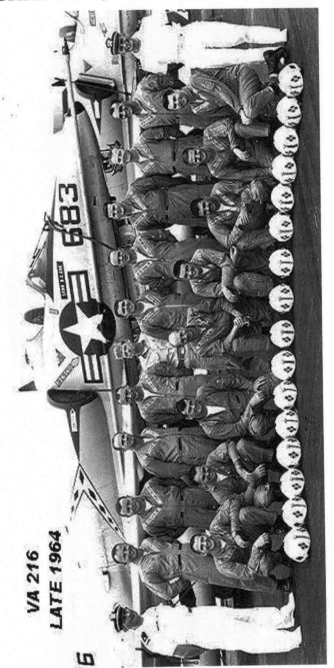

PHOTO OF VA 216 SQUADRON MATES

7 April 1965. After a painful, restless night, I awoke early to what sounded like someone banging a tire iron against a car bumper suspended from a tree. Sounding somewhat similar to a musical triangle, this was much louder and far less pleasing to the ear. The time between each hit was initially about five seconds, then it decreased for about a minute until the final ten seconds, when the bangs came as fast as possible. This sound–which the POWs came to call the gong–rang out four times a day, signaling when to sleep and when to wake up.

The Vietnamese anthem came next, followed by the sounds of people exercising– mot, hai, ba, bon" (one, two, three, four)–in the courtyard. The next hour was devoted to Vietnamese folk music and exhortations about the war and the revolutionary spirit of the people. Although the music sounded Asian, the first time I heard it, it reminded me of the accompaniment to the voice of John McCormack, a popular Irish tenor in America during the 1920s. McCormack sang years before I was born, but I remembered the music from records my grandmother had given me when I was growing up.

By 0600, the sounds from the courtyard had ceased. An hour and a half later, the same nurse as yesterday removed my dishes and brought me a pan of water with a small washrag. She also filled my water jug. I decided to enlist her help in the problem I was having with trying to urinate into the two-gallon can from a semi-prone position without getting it all over myself. Whenever I sat and tilted the can in front of me, half of it spilled out before I could put any in. I still had the small can of condensed milk I had received the day after I was shot down. I quickly drank the remainder of the milk and, after several attempts to explain my predicament, convinced the nurse to get the top of the can cut off. After that, it was just a matter of transferring fluid from the small can to the bigger one. It wasn't exactly simple, but it was a major improvement.

Around 1015, the first of two meals arrived. They usually consisted of a hunk of stale bread, pigskin with hair on it, and– if I was lucky–some watery pumpkin, cabbage or swamp green soup. Later in the morning, the local radio station played instrumental music that sounded like Japanese kabuki with cymbals and chimes. This was the signal that I had three and half more hours of isolation before the guard or nurse would come again and another twelve hours of daydreaming and talking to myself before another day was done.

At 0430 in the afternoon, the nurse would bring the second meal. Then she turned on the light, and closed the door for the night. When the door shut, the room closed in, the air suddenly thickened, making it impossible to breathe deeply. I felt caught in a giant vice slowly squeezing the life out of me.

9 April 1965. In place of the nurse, a male turnkey came to the room. He wore a light tan uniform and had the demeanor of Manners the butler. He never showed one quiver of emotion no matter what I said or did. Months later, when I got my first roommate and we compared notes about the various guards, he only had to mention "Stoneface" and I instantly knew whom he was talking about. I found out later that Stoneface was one of the regular prison guards and not part of the Army group that eventually took charge of the POWs. Stoneface would turn out to be one of the most decent guards I had during my entire stay in Hanoi.

I learned very quickly, as most people in my situation did, that the mind was both a blessing and a curse. With it, you could travel back in time; relive the most joyous or erotic moments of your life. You could taste the food you always savored at your favorite restaurant, could feel the warmth of your wife's bare body against yours and the trembling ecstasy of those final moments of making love. It was like watching a video replay of the moments in your life when it couldn't have been any better. The downside of these head games was coming back to earth. Being thrust back into reality, particularly in a North Vietnamese prison, had a way of slamming shut the fantasy of moments before. The result was being driven even deeper into depression.

10 April 1965. In the evening, I heard voices outside my door. Instinctively, I knew why they were there. The door opened, and two Vietnamese came into the room. The younger one, who was in civilian clothes, was about 32 years old. I had met him previously when he translated for the medic tending to my leg. He seemed quite pleasant and never gave me a hard time. He had a very round face and large, dark, beady eyes that seemed to glisten with energy when he spoke. He became known to the POWs as The Owl. The other man was about 40. He was shorter, had a large hooked nose, high cheekbones, and some grey hair. He wore army khaki pants and an oversized, wrinkled white shirt with the sleeves rolled up to the elbow. He talked with a nasal twang and out of the side of his mouth like a movie gangster. This man was obviously the interrogator and seemed to have a better understanding of flying and military tactics than the translator did, but his English was poor. He would become known as the Eagle. He sat on the desk, his short legs dangling over the side, chain smoking foul-smelling Vietnamese cigarettes to the bitter end.

They came on slow and friendly that first night. They inquired about my leg, to which I replied, "Not well. Can you give me some morphine tonight?" I knew it wasn't right to ask, but I was hurting. The Owl said, "We'll see." Then they made small talk and offered me a cigarette, which I refused. I knew any conversation with the Vietnamese, except for giving name, rank, service number, and date of birth, was forbidden by the code of conduct. I figured there was no harm in listening to them to find out what they wanted and exactly how much they knew. That first session lasted about an hour. It beat lying on my back staring up at the lightbulb and listening to mosquitoes buzz around my netting. Fortunately, the only thing on the agenda was a monologue: propaganda about the determination of the Vietnamese people to win the war and reunify their country.

Later that night someone brought two pills for the pain. I knew now that I was getting into dangerous territory. Surely, the next time I saw the Eagle and the Owl, they would start asking military questions.

11 April 1965. The pills lasted about an hour. My leg still throbbed, and the pain of the ends of the bones rubbing against each other kept me awake most of the time. It was not a good night. I thought hard about how I should handle interrogations. Like every man who became a POW, I was in a dicey situation, and the broken bones in my leg made it even worse. They weren't following the Geneva Convention, or I would have seen other POWs. I didn't want to violate the Code of Conduct, but my leg hurt badly, and I would need medical help to survive. I decided to talk but to only pretend to be helpful and to give harmless and inaccurate information. I prayed and crossed my fingers that the Vietnamese would buy my stories.

12 April 1965. I didn't have to wait very long to find out. That night the Eagle and the Owl wasted no time on propaganda. They started with questions about what kind of plane I was flying when I was shot down, what its performance capabilities were, how many bombs it carried, and so forth. I gave them the name of my aircraft and then fudged the other information.

"What is name of ship you on?" asked the Owl. "How long is it? How high? How many catapults has it?"

I gave them a mixture of lies and other information that was true but which I was certain was not even close to being classified.

The Eagle mumbled to the Owl, and the Owl translated: "What name of squadron you in?"

"Fighter Squadron 74," I said with a straight face, giving them the squadron I had flown with ten years before.

Then came questions about my squadron commander and the other guys I flew with, to which I responded with more bullshit. I gave them names of previous commanding officers and guys I had flown with back on my first cruise in the mid-1950s. I knew my squadron was rotating back to the U.S. several days after I had been shot down, so the chances of any of my mates winding up here was pretty slim.

15 April 1965. When the door to my room opened tonight, a boyish looking Vietnamese was with the Owl. The new man was no more than 20 years old, wore civilian clothes, and had the appearance of a freshly scrubbed university graduate. He spoke English fairly well and had floppy ears that stuck out. He reminded me of Mad Magazine's Alfred E. Neuman, but he would become known as the Rabbit. He and the Owl would sit upright on folding chairs near my bed waiting for my answers. Sometimes I had to bite the inside of my mouth to avoid laughing at their questions and the line of crap I was giving them. Of the three interrogators, the Rabbit was the most naive and ignorant of air warfare and military tactics in general. Yet, he was the only one who remained in contact with the POWs over the next eight years. As the war intensified, and the torture in the camps began, he would lose his innocence and naivete. Although many POWs hated him for his part in the torture, I never felt that he took particular delight in it. He had a job to do: extract information. My job was to withhold that information as long as humanly possible.

16 April 1965. Although I had solved my urinating problem, bowel movements were much trickier. The first time, it took me thirty minutes to inch my leg box onto the top of a chair next to my bed and then line my cheeks up over the target–a tin can nine inches high with a diameter of twelve inches. I missed it by a good six inches. Then I spent another half hour cleaning up the mess, all from the horizontal position, using one free arm and a rag. It took me three or four tries before I hit that particular target. It reminded me of the problems I'd had trying to hit the goddamn bridge, without the wind. Each time nature called during the next five months, I went through the same acrobatics.

19 April 1965. Nighttime with the Rabbit. After the usual amenities about how I was feeling, he said they wanted to know about the tactics that Navy pilots used in attacking a target. This was obviously intelligence they could use to position their triple A and knock our planes down. I wasn't about to give them the real poop, but my problem as always was how to lie and make it sound believable. "Well," I finally told him after clearing my throat and rubbing my bad leg as long as possible, "the Navy attacks targets in a very democratic fashion. The pilots sort of do anything they want in order to get the job done. Some guys use a ten-degree dive angle, while others might use an angle of seventy-five degrees. Everybody drops their bombs in any fashion they want, just as long as they hit the target."

After I spoke, I figured I'd really screwed up this time. No way they would buy that bullshit, I thought, trying to keep a straight face. I looked quickly at the Rabbit and, by God, he was nodding and writing it all down, evidently proud of himself for eliciting such valuable information. For the first few months or so, interrogations were like that: garbage in, garbage out. The Vietnamese simply didn't know the difference between an A-4 and an F-4. That particular honeymoon would eventually end.

20 April 1965. I spent most of the time during these first few weeks lying flat on my back, staring up at the faded grey plaster ceiling trying to remember every happy moment of my past life in order to blot out the present. In those moments when I could no longer handle my predicament, I ran away in my mind, back to dinners with my wife at a steakhouse called the Embers in Memphis. I would savor each mouthful of T-bone, the smell of the baked potato steaming hot and dripping with butter and sour cream, the fresh taste of the lettuce from the salad bar with all the trimmings–bits of bacon, toasted garlic croutons, and Roquefort dressing–hot rolls, and strong black coffee.

23 April 1965. The Eagle and the Rabbit were occasional after-dinner companions through April. And the game intensified: They became more persistent in extracting accurate intelligence from me; and I had to stay one step ahead of them, giving feasible but cockeyed data. In many ways, I no longer felt like a Navy pilot, but more like an undercover spy, living by my wits, trying to keep my interrogators off the trail of the real treasure. But I found it exhausting mentally and emotionally. There was no room for error. And ironically, I was learning a new trade–that of the actor, learning how to play many roles, becoming adept at lying with an expression that seemed to radiate truth. It was not one of the skills covered in Navy survival school. And not mentioned in the Code of Conduct. But as time dragged on, it became one of the most critical skills for surviving.

One night the Rabbit started asking me about targets. He prefaced the question by telling me there was a list of targets on a wall in the air intelligence space on an aircraft carrier. When I heard this, I died a little inside. Apparently another Navy POW had told them more than he should have, or maybe his lies were my truth. As an operations officer, I had planned at least fifty targets. Knowing that I was a lieutenant commander, they assumed I was of high enough rank to know about those target lists. Thus far, I had done a good job of gaining their confidence. But this was no little white lie. They grilled me pretty hard on the subject, and I kept telling them I didn't know anything about it. I denied that we had pre-planned targets. I said the targets were assigned the day or hours before we hit them, sometimes we never knew what the targets were until we were in the air.

For the first time, the Eagle and the Rabbit weren't buying my lies.

I tried another one: "Perhaps you're referring to lists of practice targets in the Philippines."

They shook their heads in unison. "We know you not tell the truth now," said the Rabbit.

"No, no. That's the truth, I swear it."

They bought it. The Eagle wrote everything down, which always made me a little nervous. Eventually, they would start asking repeat questions, checking my original responses with the new ones.

Then they asked a question that reflected their ignorance of aviation technology. Is in-flight refueling difficult? I really didn't know the answer. Maybe it was hard for some and easy for others. I told them it was easy. Later on, my first roommate said he told them it was difficult. Fortunately, they weren't savvy enough technically to confront us with our lies. Not yet.

28 April 1965. I was alone again in the evenings, left to think about the answers I gave. I was unlucky to be shot down in the

40

early part of the war but lucky that the Vietnamese knew so little about military affairs that it was easy to lie to them. I never did or said any thing that would harm a fellow prisoner. But I knew that I had violated the Code of Conduct, even if the only information I gave them was already in the public domain. I knew that by just talking to them, I could have accidentally provided information of value. Guilt was a messy emotion to deal with, especially when I had no one to talk to about it. It made me think and act like a ten-year-old who had decided his life was over before it began. It was a paralyzing, sickening tightness in the chest that never lightened up, but grew inside me like a tumor, quietly, painlessly eating me up moment by moment.

2 May 1965. May finally arrived. A month had passed since I sat on a rocky hillside staring incredulously at two white pinkish stumps of bone sticking out of my leg. At first, I experienced the novelty and some excitement along with my disbelief at what had happened, but now I had passed from the denial stage to acceptance. I was a POW, and the cavalry wasn't coming to my rescue.

I was going downhill physically. The shattered ends of the bones in my right leg floated just below the surface of the bandage that grew darker and ranker with each passing day. Fortunately, I'd gotten so used to the odor that I no longer noticed it. I still could not lie on either of my sides because my leg was in the wooden box. Even when I wanted to move, I tried not to because the more I moved the longer my leg would take to heal. But when I could no longer endure either sitting or lying down and had to change from one position to the other, I moved as slowly as possible to avoid the dull pain from the bones rubbing against each other. If I moved too quickly, the sharp ends of the bones grinding against each other ignited the pain like the frayed ends of bare electrical wires suddenly touching.

Now there was new problem to deal with: At the base of my spine was a huge bedsore that felt like a large, wet hole. The nurse gave me some medicine that controlled the open wound from growing larger but did nothing for the discomfort. A propped-up blanket eased my problem but didn't solve it.

For the first week, the only respite from the pain was the medicine they gave me at night in response to my constant requests. Whatever it was, the relief it brought always ended before midnight. There weren't any more pills. So now I dozed off and woke up again and again throughout the night. In those moments when I lapsed into exhausted sleep, my waking misery was replaced by nightmares.

I laughed at the memory of the Navy survival training I had gone through years ago. The toughest part of it had been being stuffed in a small "box," with no room to spare for no more than a half hour. Several guys had washed out of the training because they couldn't take it for more than a few minutes. I had lasted the required amount of time and thought it was a piece of cake. Now, a terrifying thought often came to me: My captors had not even lifted a hand against me, and I was already reduced to raw meat. How would I fare when things started getting heavy?

5 May 1965. This afternoon a young-looking doctor came to my room with his assistant to inspect my leg and change the bandage. The assistant handled the dirty work, and his bedside manner earned him the sobriquet the Butcher, an observation about where he might have received his medical training. After a few words, the Butcher ripped and yanked off the bandages, indifferent to the pain he was causing. Then he left a small piece of cotton wadded into a lump under the ankle tendon when he redressed the leg wound. Within moments after the Butcher and the doctor left the room, my ankle felt as if someone was sticking a white-hot poker into the tendon.

After about ten minutes, I began to make noise to attract attention. "Help! Help! Someone, please, help! Pain! I'm in pain! Someone, goddamnit, help me! Help me!"

It occurred to me as I was screaming for help at the top of my lungs that I could be dying, and no one would understand what I was saying. As the pain worsened, I stopped trying to speak and simply made as much noise as possible. It finally worked. The door opened, and a Vietnamese I had never seen before came into the room. I was shocked and relieved to find that he spoke excellent English. I explained the problem with my leg and told him that it had something to do with what the Butcher had done when he put the fresh dressing on the wound. Without another word, the Vietnamese told me to lie down. He lifted the dressing, looked at the wound and nodded. He told me he would be back in a few moments, and for the first time in my experience here, I trusted someone. Within minutes, he was back in the room. He lifted the dressing again and removed the cotton pad the Butcher had left in the wound. The feeling of relief was indescribable. I thanked him profusely.

"You do not speak any Vietnamese?" he asked.

"Not a word," I said.

"O.K. If you have pain again and you want someone to come, you say *'Joop toy voy,'* which means 'Please help me,' and *'tau dau lam,'* which is 'I hurt very much.'"

"What is the word for 'thank you?'"

"*Cam an.*"

"*Cam an,*" I said, meaning it sincerely. I found out later that he was one of the highest-ranking officers within the prison system. He would become known as the Dog.

43

11 May 1965. The Butcher and the doctor came to my room to change the dressing again. It had been more than a month since I was shot down. It seemed like years since that last morning aboard ship, getting ready for the mission. My eyes started to well up. With great effort I put those thoughts out of my mind. The doctor left, and a few minutes later, returned with another man, evidently another doctor. This new man examined my leg, and after some conversation, the first doctor told me in halting English what I had already suspected: The bones in my leg were not mending and the tibia, the larger of the two bones, had become infected and was starting to rot. They had to cut away the dead part of the bone or the infection would spread. The doctor tried to assure me that this was not a serious problem and that once the bones had healed, a bone graft would be a simple procedure.

It didn't sound simple to me, but I knew I had no choice. If they had given me one, I don't know what I would have said. This was my body they were messing with, the one and only, not some used car with a five-year/50,000-mile warrantee. This baby had no return clause. I didn't even want to consider the idea that they were going to start cutting parts of it away. But I also knew my leg was in bad shape, probably gangrenous. Even Stoneface left my meals on a chair now, not wanting to get near the smell. It was the odor of death, small but terrifying. I had no choice and no opportunity for a second opinion. If they waited, I could lose my foot or possibly my leg. I nodded and shrugged my shoulders.

15 May 1965. The Owl came into my room very early and told me I would have the operation this evening. He smiled at me, making it clear that this visit had no connection to an interrogation. At this point, I would prefer answering questions to a session with a scalpel. The morning meal was unreal: two fried eggs and a small hamburger patty with lots of gristle, but the first real meat and eggs

I'd had since I was captured. It felt like a condemned man's last meal.

And then, something beyond my wildest expectations. The Owl came back to my room later that morning, grinning broadly. "Because you going to have operation tonight," he said, "you be allowed to meet one of your fellows."

At first, I didn't understand the word *fellows*. But thirty seconds later, the door opened again and a tall, blond, curly haired, handsome kid in grey-striped pants and shirt came bouncing into the room. He was obviously an American, but I couldn't believe my eyes. This guy was smiling at me like we were about to party, and I figured maybe it was a set-up by the Vietnamese, a new wrinkle in the game of information gathering. While I was trying to recover from the shock of seeing the first American in more than five weeks, the Owl quietly left the room, closing the door behind him. For a moment, I was speechless and still a trifle suspicious. But the American seemed as genuinely glad to see me as I was to see him.

Bubbling over with enthusiasm, he said, "How're you doing, Ray? It's great to see you."

I was still wary about all this. I wondered what the Vietnamese were up to. Was this some sort of a trick? Had they put this guy in here to get me to lower my guard? I'd never laid eyes on him before and wondered how he knew my name. I sat up.

"Hi. How're you doing? What's your name?"

"Phil Butler."

We shook hands, and I relaxed a little. He told me he was a Navy Lt. j.g. from VA 22, shot down April 20. I figured the Owl was standing outside the door listening, and I kept the conversation very general, giving away no more information than the Vietnamese already had on me.

"I heard you were going to have an operation tonight, and I wanted to wish you luck," he said. "How's your leg?"

"I guess it's not coming along very well. They told me they're going to cut out a piece of my shinbone. It's become infected and has started to rot."

Butler shook his head with concern. "Hey, maybe afterwards they'll move me in with you, and I can help you get along," he said.

"That would be great."

I was just getting used to the idea that I was having a conversation with another POW when the door opened, and the Owl motioned to Butler that visiting time was up. I tried to hide my disappointment. Butler grimaced and then he smiled.

"See you, Ray. Good luck."

"Thanks, Phil."

Within seconds, Butler was gone. But my mood was up. Despite the fact that I was about to have a piece of my leg cut out, I was actually feeling a little giddy. If they had let me see this guy, perhaps they really might let us room together. It was another case of my letting my expectations out-distance the reality. In the next seven and a half years, I would see Phil Butler only twice more, and that was in New Guy Village, when he emptied our *bo*, and on the plane coming home.

After quiet hour in the early afternoon, the Rabbit and the Butcher came to prepare my leg to take me downtown. In order to move me, they had to replace the box with a full-length cast. Before the Rabbit left the room, he asked me if I was allergic to any medicines. Then he asked, "How is your sex?"

I laughed. "Not so terrific lately."

The Rabbit was not amused by my answer. I realized he was asking if I had any venereal disease, but he didn't know the word for it. The Rabbit stared at me silently while waiting for an answer. As I shook my head no, I thought to myself, wouldn't it be a real bitch to have caught some venereal disease a few days before getting bagged. That would really put a guy behind the eight ball, wouldn't it? The Rabbit grunted and left the room.

Now that my leg was out of the box and in a cast and I could roll on my side, I said a silent prayer of thanks. What a feeling of relief. I could have cried, but I didn't. When I lay on my side, I felt like I was floating on air. For the first time since I'd been here, I was excited, wired with anticipation. With any luck, this operation would cause my leg to heal more quickly, making me more mobile and getting me off the rack. I was pumped up because I was going to get out of my room for the first time in what seemed like an eternity. But more than that, maybe my leg would come out of the box after the operation.

They came for me just after dark, the heavy keys jingling in the old French door lock. It was the Rabbit with Stoneface and some other guards, who had brought with them a World War I-type canvas stretcher. Once I was on the stretcher, they handcuffed my hands loosely in front, blindfolded me, and covered my entire body with a blanket. Fortunately, the truck they took me downtown in was open in the back, and as I lay there, I was able to nudge the blindfold away from my eyes. Wow! My heart quickened at the sight of a huge, silver, full moon. My mind raced with memories of other full moons, and I was struck by how something as mundane as this act of nature had the power to jerk my emotions like a yo-yo. Within a few minutes it seemed, the truck stopped and they carried me into the hospital. As my blindfold was removed, about a dozen photographers came into the room and began snapping pictures.

I supposed I should cover my face, but I didn't. I wanted to get this over with. Two medical assistants helped take off my clothes, preparing me for another special treat. I got to take a sponge bath with honest-to-God warm water. I swore to myself that I would never take anything for granted again. I realized that the bath was probably as much for the sake of the doctors and nurses who would operate on me as for following ordinary sanitary procedures. I surely smelled like diseased meat after being locked up in a room for 40 days straight in temperatures well over 100 degrees.

The next thing that happened was vintage Vietnam. Four more assistants put me back on the stretcher and carried me to an empty hallway. They put me down and two of them took me from the stretcher and laid me on the cold stone floor. One of the men grunted and nodded as if to explain that they needed the stretcher for someone else. I was sitting there wondering what was next when five little guys suddenly appeared in the hallway and tried to pick me up to carry me to the operating room. They seemed strong, but their size was against them, and several times they almost dropped me. "Forget it," I shouted. "Put me down, goddamnit. Put me down." They obliged, not so gently. One of them pointed to a door about forty feet down the hall, the operating room. There was no other choice but to get there under my own damaged power. I pushed myself to a sitting position and inched my way down the hall to the door, now held open by yet another assistant. As I made my way slowly down the floor, I wondered how they would lift me onto the operating table. Or would I also have to manage that. As it turned out, I pulled myself up partway onto the operating table, and the orderlies, who were grunting and groaning, somehow got the rest of me up there. They left me alone in the operating room, which resembled one from the turn of the century that I had seen in the Smithsonian Institution on a class trip to Washington once.

The room was painted a dull green and smelled like it had not been cleaned in months. The operating light overhead had a large bulb protruding from a shiny metal reflecting disk. It was identical to the light used in the hospital where I had my tonsils out in 1938.

I lay back on the table, closed my eyes for a moment, and said another mumbled prayer to a God I wasn't not sure was listening anymore. The emotion I had was not fear but rather burned-out exhaustion. I opened my eyes as I heard footsteps on the hall floor. Large windows were open. Sounds from the city and a warm breeze passed through. Geckos ran in and out the windows and across the ceiling. I hoped they wouldn't defecate into my open wound as the infected bone was cut out.

A nurse smiled at me and started to assemble the operating instruments next to the table. Then a familiar face: The Butcher came in with his trusty knife to cut off the cast again. More theater of the absurd. A few minutes later, a man dressed in green operating room garb indicated he was going to put me to sleep. He wiped my arm with alcohol, and I barely felt the needle go in before I started to drop away. My last thought was that they'd given me sodium pentathol, and that the Rabbit would start extracting the truth from me while they operated.

I woke up from the operation as I was being carried through the prison courtyard. The Rabbit was walking beside me. The moon was still large and high in the night sky, and I could see the grapevines growing along the sidewalk. I realized back in my room that my leg was back in the box again. I was conscious of enormous pain in my right ankle, which only drove me deeper into melancholy. The worst part of it was the feeling that no one was listening, no one cared. I finally fell asleep, praying that I would not wake up to this misery.

16 May 1965. The Voice of Vietnam radio was the next thing I heard, as I awoke. I was so weak that I could barely move a muscle or speak above a whisper. My leg back in the box, back in my cell! My spirit was like a run-down battery barely able to generate a peep out of a car horn.

"How you feeling, Ray?" It was the voice of another POW, an Air Force pilot named Smitty Harris. He had called to me from a cell in Heartbreak Hotel once before.

"O.K.," I answer. His voice took the edge off the sense of isolation. But I couldn't muster even a word of appreciation until days later.

CHAPTER 4 - DESPAIR

16 May 1965. Later that morning, the Rabbit told me that the doctor had removed a two-inch piece of shinbone just above the ankle, and that had they wired the other broken bone in the back together. If only they had put my leg in a cast, life would have at least been tolerable. But anyway, thank God, the bones in the leg didn't rub against each other when I moved.

I was soon able to sit up again, but life was no better.

4 June 1965. The Rabbit unveiled the propaganda hour. Twice a week for about an hour or more he came to my room, sat on the edge the desk, his feet dangling above the floor, and told me the story of Vietnam. The centerpiece of the story was about Ho Chi Minh, the architect and spiritual force behind the country's goal of reuniting north and south. The Rabbit was not a great storyteller, partly because of his halting English but mostly because he lacked the animation necessary to bring the story to life. Nevertheless, the sessions were a form of entertainment.

The best part of these sessions was when I had my chance to talk. I was permitted to speak frankly about the war, communism, democracy, and the everyday miracles of capitalism. And I gave it my stem-winding best. The United States was in South Vietnam to help people who wanted to remain free. We were a friend and ally of South Vietnam, just doing what any friend would do for another. Communism was not about equality, but rather the subjugation of the spirits of people who had no say in their destiny.

The Rabbit listened patiently without interruption. Then he countered with more arguments about the evils of democracy and capitalism. I finally silenced him with an exquisitely detailed description of what it was like to go shopping in an American super-market. He listened with an expression of amazement, like a child hearing about Santa Claus and The Night Before Christmas. When I finished reliving the sentient experience of two hours wandering the aisles of Safeway, the Rabbit stood abruptly and left. When he returned for the next session, he brought more arguments about the merits of communism, like a sophomore arguing for a higher grade on a term paper.

12 June 1965. Time was my greatest enemy now. The only thing that kept me from going over the edge was my memory. My mind had a superhuman ability to recall the most minute details from the past. No matter how often I escaped, however, I could never run far enough. My situation was always there waiting for me, quietly, patiently. Ready to take me down to ground zero, where I died by seconds, praying for a resolution one way or the other. Mostly, I thought about my wife and the kids and regretted all the things I should have done but hadn't.

Friday nights were particularly bad. I needed neither clock nor calendar to tell me the exact date. It was a symptom of my deprived state that I knew the day of the week. Friday nights reminded me of our last home together, a house in Lemore, California, where we had lived for about a year before I left on cruise, and Bonnye went back to live with her parents in Memphis. I remembered having dinner with my family and my two year old daughter, Connye, sat at the table in her highchair. The summer was sweltering, and Connye would sit there in the nude, a glass of milk in front of her. Halfway through the meal, she would begin to fuss. My wife would say, "Connye, don't knock your milk over." Then, sure enough, the milk would go on the floor. Connye would look at me, then at Bonnye, who would say, "Connye, now look what you did." And the tears would start. She would stick out her lower lip and begin to cry like her heart was breaking.

22 June 1965. As time passed, I entered a twilight zone of horror every night. I was often afraid to close my eyes because the dreams seemed so terribly real. Three nightmares occurred almost in sequence. The first was a replay of my capture. I would be picked up by a mob of men and women, laid on a bed of sticks, the pain in my leg forcing me to scream out, "Don't drop me, please, don't drop me." Instead of putting me into a jeep bound for Hanoi, however, they blindfolded me, placed me on the stretcher of sticks, and carried down a hill and through the jungle. I was sweating, slapping the soldier ants that gathered on my bare arms and neck. Guys up front with machetes slashed a path through the dense foliage. We would cross a stream so deep that I could feel the water flowing around me as we moved through it. I feared that they would drop me in the rapid current, and I would drown. We would climb one hill and then another. And all the time, I was being jostled, and my leg was burning with pain. I would ask them not to drop me, and I would tell them that I was tired and needed to rest. But they continued on, never answering, never speaking, and never looking back. We seemed to move on this forced march forever, until I woke up exhausted and screaming, with my heart beating so hard that I felt it was about to stop.

The second nightmare was the worst. The dream began back aboard ship. I was sleeping in my bunk in my stateroom, and I would dream that I was shot down. The circumstances followed the reality perfectly. I relived the shoot down, saw the two pieces of bone sticking out of my right leg, and gave myself the shots of morphine before the pain hit. I experienced the two peasants coming for me with their machetes raised over their heads and the entire episode of my capture and incarceration, including the trip to Hanoi. Then, suddenly I would wake up back aboard ship and sit straight up in my bunk, trembling with a fear I had never known before. I would look around my room, reassure myself that it was only a dream and thank God that I was high and dry in my bunk. The relief and happiness I felt that it was only a dream was incredible. Then, as I tried to go back to sleep, I would open my eyes see the light bulb in my cell in Hanoi.

At first, I refused to believe where I was. I would tell myself I was still dreaming. But as many times as I closed my eyes and opened them, the bare bulb was still there, casting a small round shadow on the faded ceiling. I would begin to smell the foulness of the thick dungeon-like air. I felt the sweat running down my neck and chest. I heard the ubiquitous mosquitoes buzzing around the netting that shrouded the light, and made me feel like I was sitting at the bottom of a well.

At that point, I began to wonder if I was losing it, going mad. Each time I woke up after that particular dream, I would ask myself, sometimes aloud, "Am I awake? Am I really here in Hanoi, or am I still dreaming?" I would wonder if I had died and was languishing in limbo. This dream occurred frequently now–often two or three times a night.

The first two dreams were clearly tricks of the mind, the result of the pain and psychological deprivation of solitary confinement. I was never sure, however, that the third dream was a dream at all.

After the last meal of the day, the guard would turn the overhead light on, leave, and lock the door. My standard routine was to eat and put the dishes on the chair alongside the bed. The room was infested with cockroaches and rats, and I knew they would start their nightly forage for food as soon as darkness fell outside. So I would push the chair holding the dishes as far away from the bed as possible. The brazenness of the rats was what astounded me, almost as if they knew I couldn't stop them from making their nightly forays. When they would start to go for the crumbs under the chair and beside the bed, I would shout at them, bang my hand on the wooden board that was my mattress, to scare them away.

Sometimes in the night, I would awaken and hear or see the rats on top of the chair, trying to find any crumbs I might have left. But I seemed powerless to make a sound that would scare them away. I felt my body stiffen, as if I had suddenly become paralyzed. I knew at that moment that the rats were about to attack me. They had put me in some sort of trance, rendering every muscle in my body still as ice. I was completely defenseless. I had visions of them feasting on the rotting wound on my leg and the weeping bedsore on my spine. When the rats began their final assault on me, jumping from the chair to the bed, sticking their snouts into the mosquito netting and starting to gnaw through, I made one final mental effort to break free, summoning all the strength and energy in my body. Finally, I was able to barely move a finger or some other part of my body, and that would shatter the spell that had me paralyzed. Now free, I would slap my hand as hard as possible on the bed board and scare the rats away. Many times after I awoke, I saw the rats jumping off the bed and running away.

The problem with the rats (dream or reality) stayed with me longer than any of the other nightmares. Often over the next seven years, whether I was solo or with another POW, I would get a return visit from the rats. When it happened, I would go through the same feeling of powerlessness, finally, desperately stopping the attack. Years later, far removed from Hanoi, I wondered whether Freud could provide a psychological explanation of that episode. But when it was happening to me night after night, hour after hour, as I lay anchored to a hard wood bed in a small fetid place, cut off from everything and everyone I'd ever known, I could find no way to rationalize or explain it away.

29 June 1965. The doctor and the Butcher came to look at my leg. The verdict was in my favor. The leg had improved, and the doctor ordered it put into a full leg cast. The past eleven weeks had been like an eternity. The pain in my leg was still there but not nearly so bad. The bedsore was the main problem now. But finally my leg was out of the box and I could lie on my sides as well as my back. The relief was indescribable.

1 July 1965. With the beginning of July came a heat hotter than any hell imaginable. Nothing stirred. The sounds from outside my room were strangely absent, as if the camp had been shut down and the guards sent home. Inside the room, the heat was suffocating. Even the cockroaches and geckos slowed down. My body was constantly bathed in sweat, which caked the dust to my skin like a thin layer of cosmetic cream. I passed the time scraping the dirt from my skin with my fingernails until they were as grimy as those of an auto mechanic. I received a pan of water for washing twice a week.

7 July 1965. The nurse brought me an old, rusty safety razor, and a pan of water. She pointed to my beard and gestured that it was time to shave. She also brought me a tiny shard of mirror with which to see myself. As I picked up the piece of mirror and looked into it, the eyes were the first thing that seemed unfamiliar. Mostly shot with red, the whites looked rheumy, sick. They were the eyes of an old man. My beard, a black bush specked with grey, only accentuated the aged look. But there was something else I didn't recognize: the emptiness in the eyes. It was the look of man with no inner torque–the wheels of the mind frozen, ground to a halt. God, this was a stranger. Had I disappeared before my very eyes, slipped away into some emotional fugue, waiting for the end?

I put the mirror down, picked up the razor, and ran the edge along my finger. It was sharp enough for anything I had in mind, shaving or otherwise. I looked up and saw the door ajar. The nurse had ducked out. She'd be back in a few minutes. This was my chance to stop the nightmare. I pictured Bonnye and the kids. I remembered the mornings lying in bed with Bonnye, hearing the children in their cribs laughing and talking with each other. I would get up, go to their room, stand by the door, and watch them for a while. They were so happy, without a care in the world, and I was part of that world. I could not give that up. I wanted those days again. If it took forever, I was not willing to throw away the chance to be with them again.

The nurse was back in the room, gesturing to me to hurry up. She had better things to do than wait around here all day. I'd become sort of attached to my beard, but I shaved it off, scraping my face raw with the cold water and not-so-sharp-after-all blade. From here on, the shaving ritual would be about twice a month or less, depending on whether the guards or the nurse remembered. More important was the twice-weekly pan of water, but there was no laundry service at this hotel, and even I began to gag at the smell of my t-shirt, skivvies, and pajama top, which quickly changed from blue to charcoal.

9 July 1965. Another hot day. The temperature inside the room felt like it was over a hundred degrees. The nurse told me to take off my clothes and indicated that she was going to wash them. I was stunned at this new room service and quickly obliged. The day went by, and when Stoneface brought my food, I was still in the buff, covered only with a thin blanket. I asked him to check on my clothes. With his best Manners the butler demeanor, he nodded, grunted, and disappeared for several minutes. He returned, holding my clothes, which were still as filthy as when I had taken them off.

Room service wasn't so great after all. Later, the Rabbit informed me that the nurse had asked another POW to wash my clothes, and he had refused, saying the responsibility to provide that service belonged to the Vietnamese, not the POWs. I chuckled to myself and put on my dirty clothes again. Give em hell, boys.

13 July 1965. A new turnkey showed up. I call him Rudolph because of his red nose. He was a little friendlier than Stoneface, but he was lazy and slovenly. Stoneface always brought my food when it was still warm, and I never had to remind him about toilet paper. Not so with Rudolph. Stoneface had even left the door open for several hours one particularly hot night. Rudolph was far less sensitive to creature comfort.

14 July 1965. The boredom and nothingness caused me to search for ways to keep my sanity. Every night after the last meal, I fished for cockroaches. I pulled a two-and-a-half-foot piece of cotton string from my blanket and tied one end around a piece of pig fat. Holding one end of the string, I laid the pig fat on the floor. Then I waited for a cockroach to come and start eating. Sometimes I would wait for hours with no result. Other nights, I might get three or four bites and even catch one or two. As the roach began to eat, I would try to raise the string with the roach hanging on until it was over my open crap bucket, and then shake the string and drop the roach into it. I had to raise the string ever so carefully or the roach would drop off too soon. One roach climbed eight or ten inches up the inside of my five-gallon crap bucket.

If there was a gecko on the ceiling or the wall, and I had some extra water in my cup, I would throw the water on the gecko and watch it lose suction and fall off. I know these were not nice things to do. But worse, I saw a gecko on the wall and tried to make it fall off by spitting on it. After watching a cockroach die from lack of water, I watched the other cockroaches eat it. I talked to the geckos. They made a tsk-tsk sound, and I came close to duplicating it. I thought they understood me, because when I stopped, they sometimes started making the sound themselves.

29 July 1965. The cast had been on for nearly a month now, and although the wound continued to drain, the color of the dressing and the plaster had turned from light green to black in the last two weeks. The doctor came to examine the wound. He cut off the cast. He and his assistants wore face masks, and the assistants averted their faces when the doctor examined the results of the operation. The wound gave off a peculiar odor that I did not recognize. It was dead and dying human meat.

A nurse brought what looked like a beer mug to the room. After the doctor uncovered the wound, she lifted from the mug a piece of bone with a two-inch piece of meat hanging from it. The doctor cut several pieces of meat about the size of my finger and placed them into the wound, then replaced the dressing and the cast. He told me this was a process intended to help rebuild tissue around the bone that had been cut away during the operation.

"What's that material?" I asked.

"Placenta," he said.

"From what?"

"Some animal, perhaps pig or cow." He shrugged and left. To whatever animal it came from, I owe a debt of thanks. Would I be part pig, cow, or horse from that day on? That was of little consequence. Survival, I was slowly learning, was another word for improvisation. Making do. In Vietnam, you took gifts where you found them.

3 August 1965. Ironically, one of the last times I saw Stoneface, he was upset with me over an incident caused by Rudolph's inefficiency. It was the only time Stoneface's face was not stony. Toilet paper, like many other commodities in North Vietnam, was not always plentiful. And in the countryside, I was told, farmers and soldiers were accustomed to using various substitutes. One day in early August, nature called, and I realized that I had run out of the industrial strength paper used in these parts. The only thing I could use was a propaganda newspaper the Rabbit had called the *Vietnam Courier*. It was six or eight pages written in English. Over the next week or so, I used some of the paper before Rudolph finally brought me the regular toilet paper. A week later, Stoneface reappeared in my room and asked for the newspaper the Rabbit had given me to read the month before. Without thinking, I reached under my bamboo mat and gave him what was left of it. He departed but returned about a half hour later, carrying the paper open to where I had ripped out some pages.

He held up the evidence and looked at me with an expression of disbelief, like a priest confronting an altar boy for desecrating a copy of the Bible. I tried to explain to him what had happened, but he didn't understand. He continued to shake his head and look at the remains of the paper. Obviously, Stoneface had been upbraided by his superiors for this, but he appeared more hurt than angry. Finally, he left with a great sigh of regret that seemed to shrink his entire body. The incident had a positive side, however: I never ran out of toilet paper again, and the Vietnamese didn't give me any propaganda material for six months.

5 August 1965. I had never smoked a cigarette before. From the first interrogation, the Eagle and the Rabbit repeatedly offered me cigarettes, but I never wanted one until solitary pushed me to the end my tether. For months, I lay on my back thinking, thinking, and thinking. There were times when a point would arrive where I felt I couldn't think of another thing. This feeling seemed to last for minutes, but as fast as I had hit a blank, my mind would be wandering again. I knew some day this nightmare would end. I thought how horrible life must be for people who had normal functioning minds but who had some limitation placed on their senses or their physical capabilities. In a way, I experienced what some handicapped people went through for their whole lives. How tough some people must be to survive that.

One day during a whiteout–a term I used for those moments when my mind went down for repairs–Rudolph came into the room with my dinner. Before leaving, he smiled and offered me three cigarettes and some matches. The heat in the room was like a blast furnace, and the last thing I wanted was a cigarette, but I lit up one anyway. It tasted like damp, bitter leaves. The smell of the smoke was not so bad, but I still didn't inhale. For the next week, I smoked the daily ration of three cigarettes without inhaling. Another crutch for getting through the boredom. Finally, a few days later, I was feeling down, and I decided to inhale my first cigarette, appropriately named Dien Bien Phu, the stronger of the two brands of Vietnamese cigarettes. It marked the beginning of a siege against my body that would last too long. At first, I felt so dizzy I thought I was going to pass out. But that feeling passed, and in its place I was left with a quiet, pleasant sensation. I was hooked. For the next seven and a half years, the Vietnamese words *tokla* and *zimm* became part of my daily vocabulary. Cigarettes? Matches? *Cam an*!

7 August 1965. The monsoon rains brought the only daily relief from the heat now. They lasted from a few minutes to a few hours, but the water came down as if someone had released a floodgate. Then, as the downpour slowed to a drizzle, you could smell the freshness in the air, scrubbed clean by the rain. The sweet scent of bougainvillea rose through the night mist and steam, giving off a false sense of well-being. Each night, a couple of hours before midnight, the downpour would start, sounding like dozens of men running across the tile roof. The clatter of the rain on the roof in Hanoi was so loud that it muffled almost all sound. One night, I was particularly agitated, on edge. I couldn't sleep. My mind was in overdrive, but the images were so speeded up, I could not hold one coherent thought. The rain this night seemed more intense than usual. Perhaps, it would bring down another piece of plaster like the one a few weeks before. Screw it. I pushed myself up to a sitting position and did something I'd never done before in my life. I started singing at the top of my lungs, trying to compete with the racket of the rain. One of the only songs I knew the words to was "One Enchanted Evening" from *South Pacific*. Mario Lanza, I wasn't, but I kept it up for nearly thirty minutes, wondering if the Vietnamese would think I'd finally gone over the edge. Incredibly, no one came. It was as if I were all alone. The monsoon rains were excellent sound cover. Finally, when my throat became sore I stopped singing. I wouldn't do it again for a thousand bucks, but at the moment, I felt enormous emotional release. Music was truly a balm for my troubled soul.

13 August 1965. In the morning after I had drifted off to sleep, the nurse and an assistant came into the room with several buckets of water. They indicated that they were going to clean my room, which must have smelled like the side streets of Bombay. They dumped ten buckets of water on the floor and then swept the water out the door. I dozed during the cleaning, and when I woke again they were gone. And so was the little milk can that I peed in. It had a deep green fungus growing on the bottom, but it was absolutely essential to me. I remembered too well what it was like trying to urinate into the bucket lying on my side. No way. I was outraged. It was as if the Vietnamese were mucking with my mind, taking from me the one thing they knew kept me sane.

I yelled for the guard. When he finally came, I asked him to send the nurse back. When she returned, I ask her where my little evaporated milk can was. She shook her head, made an ugly face and a gesture that told me she had thrown it out. Despite my attempts to explain how important that dirty little can was, she was adamant, shaking her head. She thought I was getting upset over nothing. The dialogue continued. I felt myself losing control. I was frustrated but trying not to show it. She raised her voice, shaking her finger at me. Through sign language finally, I tried to show her exactly why I needed that little can. She shook her head again. No. That was final. I was undone with anger. I could not communicate to her how physically and emotionally essential that can was. She stood there, her lips tightly sealed, her arms folded in front of her, the picture of obstinacy and indifference. This was the last straw. I cursed her at the top of my lungs. I pleaded as best I knew how. It was no use. She left the room. The time passed, and I was oblivious to its torture. I lost my desire to eat. Several times that day, I had to urinate. It was a replay of those first days when I peed all over the bed and myself.

The next morning, the nurse came in, and I tried once more, calmly, to show her why the little can was so important. She showed no sign of understanding. Later that day, she reappeared in my room, and for the first time, she was smiling. In her hand, was my half-pint evaporated-milk can, the fungus scrubbed clean. She held it out to me and nodded. I said, "*Cam an. Cam an.*"

17 August 1965. In June, when they changed the box on my leg for a full-length cast, and I could finally lie on my side, I felt immense relief. But another two months had passed with me anchored to a bed of boards. I was supposed to have had a bone graft at some point, but my leg was still sore and didn't seem much better. The heat was unbearable. No talking, walking, exercising, or reading. My daily routine had been thrown out of sync because of the heat and nothingness of my life. Days and nights are reversed now. For months now, I lay awake night after night listening to the church bells in the distance, as they tolled the hours one by one. I kept hoping that with each passing hour I would fall asleep before the church bells rang again, but I finally doze off only after hearing a rooster crow and the morning gong ring out. Sleep comes early in the morning and only for a few restless hours filled with nightmares. My life has become an insufferable existence.

20 August 1965. Suddenly, there was a gleam of light after months of darkness. They replaced my full leg cast with a half cast below the knee. And to top it off, the doctor told me I would get crutches in a few days. I was in hog heaven! I couldn't believe it. I felt like yelling to the guys over in Heartbreak, so named by the POWs because of the loneliness associated with Presley's song and being a prisoner in that cell block, or singing the entire score of Oklahoma at the top of my lungs. But they wouldn't understand. They'd think I'd really flipped out. I felt as though I'd been released from death row and made a trustee.

22 August. 1965. A medic brought me crutches. The catch was that they were built for the average Vietnamese, which meant someone about a foot shorter than I was. No sweat. For the first time in almost five months, I could get off my bed, walk around the room, and finally do a little reconnaissance about activity outside my door. When the medic left and closed the door, I grabbed the crutches and carefully tested them, moving in the direction of a thin little crack in the door that I'd been eying ever since I arrived. Even though it was only a sliver-thin vertical opening, I could see clear across the courtyard about sixty feet away, with a field of fire of about twenty degrees. From that day on, I spent most of my waking hours with my eye glued to that crack, sitting on a chair, connecting images to a meticulously constructed world of sound. I was like a blind person suddenly given sight.

One of the first things I saw was the source of the sound of running water: a faucet at the end of the courtyard. There was a sidewalk in the middle of the courtyard. Wires were strung from one side of the yard to the other to hold the thick green grapevines that provide the only shade beside the overhanging eaves from the buildings. Heartbreak was on my right. I was no longer a voice in the wilderness. That knowledge was not as consoling as I had thought it would be. To the left of Heartbreak, a gate lead to places unknown. The courtyard was dressed up with neatly planted flowers set along the sidewalk and at the sides of the buildings, giving the illusion of a simple, peaceful life.

24 August 1965. I was at my position, eye glued to the crack in the door, when I saw an American walking across the courtyard. He was about my height, but thinner and dressed in short pants and a purple T-shirt. He had another shirt draped around his arms, which both looked as if they had been places that were not pleasant. The left arm was in a cast, and the right one was in a sling. He had a heavy beard and dark hair. I only caught a glimpse of him because he was walking fast, his head down, and he was alone. My heart quickened at the sight. I wondered if or when I'd ever meet another POW.

This was an extraordinary day. I couldn't let go of the image of the POW. I saw earlier. Then, that evening, the medic came to the room. He indicated that I should take my filthy washrag and soap and go outside to wash my clothes and myself. A bath! An honest-to-God bath! What a treat! I took off my underwear, put on the blue pajama bottoms, and hobbled out the door on my crutches. It was still hot outside, but the air smelled sweet and fresh. Even in the dark, I felt as though I was being allowed out of an airless dungeon into the bright light of day. The medic pointed to the water faucet located about twenty feet away near the center of the courtyard. Sitting in a chair beside the medic was a Vietnamese woman guard who looked like Debbie Reynolds.

I sat down beside the faucet and turned it on, letting the cold water run into my clothes and splash on my arms and legs. I felt the eyes of the Vietnamese woman on me, but I didn't care. The medic finally came over and helped me get my pajama pants off. I was bare naked now and wondering what the woman's reaction was. Glancing at her, I realized she was watching me like an animal in the zoo. I didn't give a damn. I was finally in business! For the first time in nearly five months, my body felt the tingling freshness of soap and water. I could almost feel the pores in my skin begin to open and breathe. I took my time washing, slowly, letting the water drip from the dirty cloth onto my legs, my chest, my back. I went on like that for about a half an hour until the guard came over and signaled the end. It was a bath I would never forget.

25 August 1965. Around 0800, I heard the key suddenly rattle in the lock. Rudolph told me to put on my pajamas and come with him. We walked across the courtyard to Room 24, where I had seen the bearded American go. I followed the guard through a three-foot-wide waiting area and into a room a little larger than mine. The Rabbit sat behind a desk. Beside him was an older Vietnamese man whom I'd never seen before. He had squinty eyes, a round chin, and very purplish, thin lips. His greying hair was pushed up in front, and he was dressed in a white shirt and dark pants. He chain smoked and gave the impression of being a mean son of a bitch, an intuition later confirmed. He would become known as the Fox.

The Rabbit directed me to a stool in one corner of the room about ten feet away. Now I was beginning to understand why they had let me take a bath. I had no real apprehension about this meeting, because I no longer possessed any military information of timely value. The Rabbit offered me a cigarette, and I took it. We exchanged pleasantries, and he asked about my leg.

"Can't dance too well yet," I answered.

The Rabbit turned away as if he had not heard my answer and nodded toward the Fox. "This is the new camp commander. He would like to know how a senior naval officer feels about the war, and what are your views about capitalism and communism. The camp commander would like to know how you feel about Russia and China. You can speak freely."

In the strictest sense of the Code of Conduct, I should have given the rote response: name, rank, service number, and so forth. But I felt like talking to someone beside the cockroaches, the geckos, and the guards for a change. Although I was no expert on foreign policy or the various political systems, I was a true believer when it came to democracy and free enterprise. So I let it rip. The Fox listened attentively, and then gave his counter arguments, through the Rabbit's translation.

When we began to debate the war, the Fox's tone grew strident, but his eyes seemed to dance with a newfound energy. He was obviously intelligent and a fervent believer in the Vietnamese blueprint for victory. I tried to convince him that the American effort in Southeast Asia was only a drop of the total military might of the United States, and that the DRV didn't stand a chance if we started unleashing our full military capability.

The Fox lit another cigarette, shook his grey head, and laughed deeply, as if I'd just told a dirty joke. "It doesn't matter, Commander, whether you bomb our cities, our ports, or supply lines. Our strength lies in the hearts and minds of the great Vietnamese people. Remember this, Commander. Weapons influence this war, but only people will determine its outcome. The only way the United States could ever defeat the Democratic Republic of Vietnam is to bomb our dikes and rice paddies, destroy out ability to produce enough food to eat. Everything else, everyone else, is expendable. If need be our soldiers, our people, will carry the ammunition and the bombs on their backs all the way to Saigon to defeat the Americans."

He stopped talking, lit another cigarette, sat back in his chair, and stared at me. I had nothing more to say. It was clear I wasn't going to win any converts to capitalism this morning. But his words had a much deeper effect on me than any of the other propaganda I'd been exposed to thus far. For the first time, I realized this war was not going to be another stroll in the park for Uncle Sam. These people were far more committed than I thought anyone back in Washington understood. The attitude among a lot of people back at DOD was that we were dealing with some fools who were out-gunned ten to one but didn't have the sense to realize it. It could be a dangerous arrogance if taken too far. As my eyes met the Fox's, I came to another disturbing realization: I could be a POW for a lot longer than I had originally thought. The euphoria of the past week took a nosedive.

Back in my room, my leg began to throb. It was swollen because I had sat for so long without keeping it elevated. My mind replayed the arguments with the camp commander as I ate my meal. Then I heard a jeep drive quickly into the courtyard and brake to a halt. I jumped up, grabbed my crutches, and scuttled over to the door. Outside, I saw seven or eight Vietnamese standing around the jeep. Something was up. Stoneface walked toward Heartbreak to make sure no one was looking out. Then he suddenly turned and started to walk quickly toward my room. Christ! They had caught me red-handed! I quickly backed away from the door and lay down on the bed. Just as I did, I saw the dark shadow of Stoneface looking at me through another crack in the door. My heart was pounding so hard I was sure he could hear it. But he left within seconds. Despite the fear of getting caught looking out, the need to see what's going on was overpowering. Just as I sat down in front of the door again, a man, obviously American, was being helped out of the jeep. He had a Navy flight suit on, was blindfolded, and had a bloody bandage on his head. Everyone was absolutely quiet as they led the flier into Room 24, where I had met the Fox earlier that day.

After quiet hour, the guard took me back for two more hours of "political education" with the Fox and the Rabbit. This time, the Fox took a different tack. Instead of offering his own views on "the failure of capitalism" and the war, he read some articles written by Dr. Benjamin Spock and Senator Wayne Morse, one of the first members of Congress to publicly oppose U.S. participation in the Vietnam War. I remembered Dr. Spock from his baby book, but I had no idea he was an antiwar activist. Senator Morse's opposition to the war disturbed me far more. He had been one of the few politicians I truly admired when I was in college.

Back in my room later, my mind was in overdrive, cluttered with ideas, thoughts, and images of the day. I kept coming back to the POW who got out of the jeep. I wondered how he responded to the Fox's questions. Did he tell him to fuck off? Should I have given him the same response to his propaganda? I was exhausted, but my mind would not let me go. Early in the evening, I heard the keys jingle outside my door. I figured it was another quiz with the Fox. The door opened and Big Stoop, another guard, came in with two older female guards. He gestured to me to get up and get out of bed. As I stood up, the other guards started to pack up my gear. I was being moved to another room. At first, I was very surprised, but then I helped the guards pack my gear. Despite the Spartan accommodations, I had become attached to this room and felt sad leaving. Outside, Big Stoop pointed to the door of the room next to mine. The new room was very dark, but there was a door at the rear that led to another room with a light on. He motioned me to go in. When this happened, I wanted to cry out loud. I thought they must know that I had been looking out the door and were now moving me to another room without a view of the courtyard. It had been almost five months of hell and finally, after just a few good days, it was all coming to an end. Instant depression. I slowly made my way into the back room and watched the other guards dump my gear on a bed. I was so down that I had failed to notice that the room had a second door at the rear. Then one of the female guards opened that door. For a moment, I thought I must be hallucinating. Standing there outside the door was the POW whom I'd seen earlier. I still didn't comprehend what was happening until I looked at Big Stoop and the female guards. They were smiling and looking at us. The POW walked into the room, and then I noticed that there were two beds in the room and his gear was on one of them.

We looked at each other without smiling, both of us sharing the same thought: Was this a cruel trick? Big Stoop indicated that this was no trick. I wanted to walk over and give him a big hug but instead reached out slowly to touch the American's hand dangling from the sling.

"Hi. I'm Ray Vohden. How're you doing?"

"Hi. My name's Norlan Daughtry. I'm doing fine, just fine."

CHAPTER 5 - ROOMMATE

25 August 1965. When the guards left, I had a chance to check out Norlan better. One of his arms was in a cast with the elbow bent 90 degrees, and the other arm was in a sling. Even though he was excited, he was still very weak, and moving in together didn't have nearly as profound an effect on him as it did on me. He said he was shot down on August 2, a little more than three weeks ago, and he obviously hadn't adjusted to his plight. He looked like hell warmed over, with a thick beard. He had lost a lot of weight and was somewhat apathetic. After about twenty minutes, he said he was tired and wanted to go to sleep.

He was sound asleep within moments, but I was so excited that I didn't sleep one second that night. I remained awake and mulled over and over again in my mind the events of the day. I listened to the clock throughout the night. No matter how hard I tried, I could not fall asleep. Unlike the nights before, I anxiously awaited the arrival of dawn. When the early morning gongs sounded and the room filled with daylight, I felt good for a change. So I waited for Norlan to wake up

26 August 1965. When he awakened, we continued our conversation. He was from Texas, had gone to a military high school, attended Texas A&M, but joined the Air Force as a cadet prior to graduating. He won his wings, served four years, and transferred to the Air National Guard in Arizona, where he worked part time, dusted crops, and sold used cars. He also attended the University of New Mexico, majoring in engineering. When the Vietnam War broke out, he had transferred back to active duty and was in an F105 squadron when he was shot down.

He had been hit pulling off his target, a bridge. The plane became uncontrollable, and he finally managed to eject below 500 feet altitude. Unfortunately, his speed was above 500 m.p.h. When he ejected, the air blast threw his arms behind him, causing both of them to break, one at the elbow and the other just above. After three swings in his parachute, he landed in a rice paddy and just lay there, unable to move.

It wasn't long before the Vietnamese encircled him and removed his gear. His pleas to be careful with his broken arms went unheeded because they couldn't understand English, and he couldn't speak Vietnamese. They interpreted his screams as resistance. To make matters worse, after they removed his parachute and flight equipment, they bound his wrists and his ankles. They then placed a pole between his arms and legs and carried him like a pig on a barbecue spit to a dry piece of land about 100 yards away. He screamed the entire time because the pain was unbearable. Not until they removed his flight suit could they could see his broken arms dangling from his body.

We talked at great length about our families, our shoot downs, and our experiences in prison up to now. In particular, Norlan was very interested in knowing about all the guys who had been shot down. Unfortunately, I had only met Phil Butler and heard the names of two or three others when I talked to guys in Heartbreak. Norlan was especially interested in Air Force Capt. Bob (Percy) Purcell. He and Norlan had been in the same squadron and were on the same mission in late July 1965, when Percy was shot down.

The U.S. had been taking aerial photos of North Vietnam and our intelligence community had concluded that a surface-to-air missile (SAM) sight had been under construction by the side of a river and was about to become operational. In reality, the SAM site was a fake used to attract our planes and shoot them down. The Air

Force sent several squadrons to bomb it, and while Percy was flying low above the river leading to the target, his plane flew into a triple A trap, was hit, and burst into flame. No one saw Percy get out, so they considered him dead. In fact, just a few days before Norlan had been shot down, he had attended a memorial service for Percy at the base where they were stationed in Thailand.

Even though it looked as if Percy hadn't had a chance, the guys in Norlan's squadron never gave up hope. And when Norlan was shot down and saw that the name Bob Purcell had been written on a wall in one of the rooms Norlan had been in, his hope for Percy's survival was renewed. We would later learn that Percy had miraculously escaped death and was elsewhere in the prison camp.

As miserable as Norlan's experiences were up to the time I moved in, he told me a story that lightened the mood for both of us. On a mission several days before he was shot down, his target had been one of the bridges on the main North-South highway in North Vietnam. He was carrying a bullpup missile, which was about seven feet long, one foot in diameter, and carried a pay load approximately equivalent to about a 1,000-pound bomb. It was guided by a control stick in the cockpit. The pilot could steer the missile to the target by altering its flight path to the right, left, vertically, or horizontally. On that particular day, the guidance system in Norlan's missile malfunctioned, and the missile became uncontrollable, doing all kinds of gyrations on its way to the ground. Norlan's wingman saw it heading for a small group of peasants in a rice paddy, and as the peasants ran for their lives, the missile uncontrollably followed after them. Fortunately for the peasants, the missile veered away from them at the last second, and none appeared to be hurt. We laughed at length as he related the story and imagined how some peasant must have felt so important that one expensive bullpup chased him all over the countryside and was reserved just for him!

Norlan said he had talked to the Vietnamese as I had done, but he felt bad because he had admitted having taken off from Thailand. Officially, the U.S. and Thailand were on record as saying that the U.S. was not using Thai airfields to launch strikes against North Vietnam, even though the whole world knew we were. Because this information was classified, the pilots were not supposed to divulge it. A number of them, however, were tortured into admitting they had taken off from Thailand. Norlan said he gave the Vietnamese that information only after they refused to give him medical attention.

At about 0930, Mr. Tuc, our medic came into the room and carried out the *bo*, as the crap bucket was called. The Vietnamese (and especially Mr. Tuc) did not like having to empty our crap buckets and understandably so. Having the hell bombed out of you by an American pilot was bad enough but to have to empty the pilot's *bo*–well, that was just too much for the medic. He did not like to touch the bucket with his hands, so he would use a large door key to pick up the bucket by its thin handle. He did the chore as seldom as possible, and sometimes the bucket was so full we couldn't use it, which made us uncomfortable. I believed he forgot intentionally from time to time.

In any event, as Mr. Tuc was carrying out the *bo* this time, he opened the back door of the room and indicated to us that we should go ahead and wash. Then he left. The weather had been hot and humid, and getting outside in the early morning fresh air felt good. There were two steps to the ground level, where there was a sidewalk that ran behind the building. The area around the back of our room was enclosed by a wall about five feet high and made a courtyard about twenty-five feet long and ten feet wide. Inside the courtyard was a broken-down wooden shed with a roof and three sides. Alongside was a water pipe about 3 feet up from the ground with a faucet on the end of it. It had been about a week since my last bath. I undressed, found a way to prop up my leg so the cast wouldn't get wet, and sat down with my bare ass on the concrete, and began washing my body. Although it was not as sensational as my first bath, it was a pleasure.

Not long after I had started to wash, I noticed that Norlan had to bend over to get his washrag wet and was able to wash only his hands. I told him that I would help him as soon as I finished. I dried myself off with the washrag and proceeded to dress. Without a chair to sit on, I found it difficult to put on my shorts, but I made it. Unfortunately, I was still weak and barely able to take care of myself, but I mustered enough energy to soap up Noland's washcloth and clean his head and face, his upper body, and his legs. He hadn't had a bath in 24 days and was as dirty as I had been after going five months without a bath. After about 5 minutes of scrubbing, he didn't look or smell so bad.

Because Norlan had two broken arms, he was unable to use his hands very well. So the Vietnamese had given him a short pair of pants and cut the crotch out, leaving him with a sort of modified skirt. Otherwise, he would have been unable to open the zipper to pee or to remove the pants to crap. But with the crotch cut out, any time Norlan had to go to the toilet he would lift the lid off the crap bucket by placing his big toe in the handle and then raising his foot. Having only known Norlan for a few hours and even though he had said he was married with three children, I wasn't sure whether I should offer to wash his private parts. When I finished washing everything else, I looked at Norlan, and he looked at me, and I said, "Well, what do you think?"

He said, "I don't know."

I said, "Do you want me to?"

He said, "Do you mind?"

I said, "Oh, what the hell." I took off his skirt. I lathered the washrag as well as possible, bunched it up, and washed him better than his mother did when he was a baby. I didn't look straight at him as I washed. Thereafter, I washed him every time we went out to bathe. Since both of us were heterosexuals it was no big deal, but it still was a rather uncomfortable and unusual situation to be in.

After we finished bathing, the medic came back with the empty *bo* and directed us into the room again. He gave each of us our three cigarettes for the day. Fortunately, he gave us a box of matches that we were allowed to keep. I put a cigarette in Norlan's mouth and gave him a light, and I smoked mine. I offered to take the cigarette from Norlan's mouth from time to time, but because he had been a died-in-the-wool, hooked smoker, he finished it without that being necessary. When there was nothing more than a butt left, he dropped it from his mouth onto the table and put it out with his cast.

Despite his arms having been broken, he could still use his fingers. By leaning over the table, he could take the butt in his fingers, remove the paper, and put the tobacco on a piece of paper with some more tobacco that he had saved from other butts. Then he tore a piece of toilet paper into the size of a cigarette wrapper, placed the tobacco from the butts inside, and with his fingers rolled another cigarette. He held the cigarette in such a position that when he bent his head forward he could spit on it and use the spit as glue to keep the paper together. Then he asked for another light. I was amazed as I watched. I offered to do it for him next time but he said no. I guess he wanted to do whatever he could for himself. He did, however, ask if he could have my old butts. Having just started smoking and not being very addicted, I said, "Sure."

Around 1030, Mr. Tuc brought two rations of food. He had been feeding Norlan for the first month, but now that responsibility fell to me. At first, it wasn't a problem because we were new to each other, although after a few days, things became a little strained. I didn't know how fast he should be fed–whether I should be shoving it down his throat or waiting and letting him ask for each bite. When I asked he always said it was O.K., but I just didn't feel right. Maybe it was just me, and I was imagining that there was a problem. When a baby doesn't want anymore, the baby spits the food out and turns his head. That doesn't work with civilized adults. But eventually we worked out the right rhythm by trial and error.

During quiet hour Norlan took a nap, but I still wasn't tired enough to sleep. That night, Norlan gave me an update on how the war was going and filled me in on other news. I had been here for nearly five months, and it seemed like a lifetime. I naturally assumed that the many things that had gone on in the outside world would take Norlan about a week to relate. Unfortunately, Norlan had been in Thailand for about three and a half months before he was shot down, had been very busy flying, and had not received very much news from back home. The only non-war news he told me was that Adlai Stevenson had died in June or July from a heart attack. Boy, was I disappointed not to be able to learn more about the outside world. So far as the war was concerned, I think I knew more than he did because I had read four or five *Vietnamese Couriers* over the past several months. The *Courier* was a mix of propaganda and stories about the war, and although the stories were distorted and slanted, they contained some valuable information, such as Johnson's proposals, troop build-ups, battles, and so forth. But the Vietnamese interpretation of these events was incredibly subjective.

That second night I finally fell asleep at about 2200. It was the first good night's sleep I had in North Vietnam. No wonder–I had gone without sleep for 38 straight hours.

27 August 1965. The next morning the subject of chess arose, and we both knew how to play. When we went out to wash, we found an old piece of cardboard about a foot square. Later that morning, I took a piece of cotton that had been used on Norlan's arm and still had some mercurochrome in it. I mixed water with the cotton ball, and it made some red ink with which I made squares for the chess board. I colored half of the squares red and left the other half of the squares untouched. I took some of our hard, coarse brown toilet paper and together we agreed on what the shapes of the chess pieces would be. The pawns were small circles, the rooks were square, the queen a pentagon, the king an oval, the knights triangles, and the bishops rectangles–each less than half an inch in size. I colored half of the chess pieces red.

We sat down and proceeded to play. Norlan couldn't touch the pieces, so I moved them for him. The first game lasted about an hour, and it was one of the most enjoyable chess games I ever played. Not only did it break the monotony, but also I won. Unfortunately, however, my success was short lived because other than the occasions when he fell asleep, Norlan beat me every time. But I loved to play anyway.

When I moved in with Norlan, they had not yet provided him with a toothbrush or shoes. On the third morning, the medic came into the room with a big smile on his face and some money in his hand. He disappeared for nearly an hour, then returned and presented Norlan with a toothbrush and a pair of shower shoes just like mine. Norlan was ecstatic. I helped him brush his teeth at first, but after several days he became a little more dexterous with his left hand. He held the toothbrush in his fingers, then bent his head forward and moved it up and down, brushing his teeth.

That same afternoon, I had a call from mother nature. I proudly described to Norlan how I relieved myself. I sat on the bed with my ass hanging over the side, carefully placed the bucket in the firing line, then let loose with a blast. Unfortunately, I had misplaced the bucket by about six inches, so the blast splattered on the floor. Boy, was I embarrassed. After using almost all of the small quantity of toilet paper we had, I finally got the mess cleaned up.

29 August 1965. Five days after we moved in together, Norlan came down with a cold. Fortunately, we were being taken care of by a medic, so after a day or two he brought in a shot for Norlan's cold. The syringe was about eight inches long and a half inch in diameter, no exaggeration. It was filled with a clear liquid. The needle appeared to be about three inches long and fairly thick. The medic gave Norlan the shot in the upper part of the arm that was in the sling. I had never seen a shot that size in my life. It looked more appropriate for an elephant—and maybe that's what it had been used for before. Frankly, after the medic placed the needle near Norlan's arm, I had to look away because I was so scared for Norlan. Later that day, Norlan said he had debated whether he should allow the medic to give him the shot but finally decided it wasn't worth making an issue over.

Another result of Norlan's cold was that his nose ran all the time. Because of his broken arms, he couldn't blow his nose. We didn't have any tissues, and the toilet paper was very limited. The only thing we had was his washrag. I had helped my children blow their noses, so at first it was no big deal helping Norlan blow his nose, but after several hours, the washrag became filled with snot. Even if

I had been holding it for myself, I would have had difficulty. Also I found it hard to clean certain parts of the inside of his nose, given the nature and shape of noses in general. I could tell sometimes that I wasn't getting the job done. He wasn't complaining, but in an effort to improve his situation, I thought about the bed poles that held up the mosquito nets. When Norlan couldn't be satisfied with the way I held his washrag, I hung it over the top of one of the poles, which was just the right size to allow him to push his nostril down over it and allow him to clean the parts he couldn't get at by blowing it. Of course, we had to wash the rag each day, and with limited time and soap that also became a problem.

Naturally, we constantly asked the Vietnamese for extra paper and other things to make our lives more civilized, but the normal response was *unh,* or I'll see. But we got only what they deigned to give us, and there wasn't anything we could do about it. We were forced to innovate, adjust, or just be miserable.

1 September 1965. In the back of our minds, we recognized that by asking for something and getting it, we might be asked for something in return. So there was a delicate balance in how long we would endure something bad before asking for relief. If we protested too much, we might end up worse off than before. A week after I moved in with Norlan, the Butcher came to our room. He asked me how I was, and I said O.K. Because my leg was in a cast now, I didn't need any medical treatment from him. But Norlan was still in considerable discomfort.

The Butcher took the sling off Norlan's right arm and removed the bandage. Norlan was thin to start with, about 135 pounds, but in the month he had not used his arm, it had atrophied considerably and was very thin. I could see a fairly large opening in the back of his arm just above the elbow. It was obvious that he had no control over its use, because the Butcher had to hold it to move it. Finally, he just let it hang down on Norlan's side. Then the butcher took out a jar from his tool bag and opened it. He took out a piece of bone with meat hanging off it and cut a piece about an inch square. Then holding the meat with the tweezers in one hand, he spread the wound in Norlan's arm open with his other hand and stuffed the piece of meat into the hole in his arm. Next he put red medicine on some cotton, placed the cotton over the hole, and wrapped the wound with some gauze. Then he put the arm back into the sling. He nodded good-bye and left. We had no idea what this procedure was. We took whatever they gave us.

That night, we heard the sound of keys jingling outside our door. It opened and in came Stoneface. He indicated that we were going to move. He packed our gear into our bedmats and rolled them up. We just stood there and watched, neither of us capable of helping him. He motioned us to leave, and he followed us. We went through the room in front of ours and into the main courtyard between my old room and Heartbreak. It was very dark outside. Stoneface gestured toward the far end of the opposite side of the courtyard. As we walked across, we passed a jeep about 20 feet away in front of Heartbreak. The back windows of the jeep were covered the way they are when a prisoner is in the back. When we got to our new room, we speculated that a prisoner had been in the jeep, and they were moving us so that the new prisoner could have our room.

When we got to the other side of the courtyard, we walked about 60 feet through an open passageway between two buildings two stories high. At the end of the passageway was a door. We went through it into a smaller courtyard. Directly to the right was a room with an open door. Stoneface motioned us in. He placed our gear on the beds and left. I straightened the gear out and put up the mosquito nets. We got into bed and talked about the significance of the move, the man who might have been in the jeep, and what tomorrow might bring.

CHAPTER 6 - NEW GUY VILLAGE

HANOI HILTON

Actual photo of New Guy Village

Shu's old room

September–October 1965. The new room was much larger than the one we had previously lived in. It had a wooden table about five feet by three feet, several wooden chairs, three beds similar to the ones we had been sleeping on, and a very high ceiling. An acoustic material lined the walls and ceilings. We speculated that the room might have been used as a recording studio. At the front of the room was a large metal door, which had an eight- by ten-inch access hatch in the top half. Numerous cracks and small holes in the door would allow us good viewing of the courtyard outside our room. The front wall and one side wall each had two eight- by twelve-inch vents about a foot from the floor.

The next morning, we looked through the cracks in the door but saw nothing. Later, Stoneface let us out to wash. He pointed to a building at the other end of the courtyard, about a hundred feet away. On the right side of the courtyard, from the side of our room to the side of the building, ran a wall at least thirty-five feet high with jagged pieces of glass imbedded in the top. Just outside our room sat a large concrete tub five feet by four feet by four feet deep. A faucet was near the tank, which was filled with water. On the left side of the courtyard were four or five rooms with French-style wooden doors. In the center of the courtyard stood a tall tree.

When we reached the building, Stoneface led us up the five or six steps to the doorway, and we entered what must at one time have been a fancy bathhouse. Now, the remnants of what had been three or four showers were inoperable. A faucet emptied into a sunken tiled area fifteen feet long by seven feet wide by three and a half feet deep. From the looks of it, it hadn't been used much for many years. There were also four squatters. The entire area was filthy, and large piles of trash lay in different areas of the room.

Stoneface locked the door and left, giving us a chance to recon-noiter. In the wall behind the squatters was a window with bars on it. About five feet beyond the window, we could see another prison wall of concrete and stone with jagged pieces of glass on the top. Short metal poles with what looked like electrical wire strung along them sat at ten-foot intervals on the wall. There was a room off the bath area separated by a door with cracks in it. We looked through the cracks and saw a man who, although dressed in civilian clothes, looked like a prisoner. He was always by himself and never acknowledged our presence, even though we called to him. We were disappointed, but we found it interesting to see another kind of animal in a cage, just as we were.

By the next day we had already settled into our new environment, which would become known as New Guy Village. Norlan's idea of saving cigarette butts for his roll-your-own cigarettes began to seem like a pretty good plan for me, too. Because I probably wouldn't have thought of it on my own, I felt somewhat guilty telling him that I wanted to hang onto my own butts, but he didn't object. So I made my first one, and it was great.

At first, Stoneface or the medic emptied our *bo* every morning. After a few days, however, Stoneface had a new idea. Trusting soul that he was, he opened the door to our room and indicated that we were to sit on chairs with our backs to the door and not talk. Unknown to us, POW Phil Butler had been waiting outside to fetch our *bo* and empty it. As soon as Phil came in, he said, "Hi, Norlan. Hi, Ray," and we both turned around in our seats and greeted him. We passed a few more words before Stoneface became upset and put a stop to it. We won that small battle, but the next day Stoneface came into the room and put the *bo* outside the door. Later on, another POW came by and emptied it.

A week after we moved into this room, Stoneface came by early one afternoon and indicated to Norlan to put his shirt on and they left. Several hours later, Norlan came back clean-shaven. When

Norlan had left the room, he had not shaved since the day he had been shot down, and he had a fairly heavy growth of beard after six weeks. Stoneface had used a safety razor to shave Norlan without any lather or water whatsoever. Since the average Vietnamese man does not have a heavy beard growth, Stoneface probably didn't realize how bad it would feel to have a heavy beard shaved with just a dry razor. Norlan said it hurt like hell but he survived that ordeal somehow. When he returned, he said that he had met with four American professors. They had asked some innocuous questions like how was he doing, how were his arms, etc. Later on, he felt somewhat bad that he had talked with them, because maybe technically it was a violation of the Code of Conduct. But in my opinion, if it was a violation, it wasn't a serious one.

The Eagle came to our room a few days later and asked us if we knew a man named Collins. We didn't. The Eagle said he had been wounded like us and that he would be our roommate soon. That night, they brought in an American on a stretcher. He was bald, moaning with pain and appeared to have gone through hell. The Vietnamese placed him on the other bed and left. His name was Quincy. He was an Air Force captain flying an F105 when he was shot down. He had forgotten the day and circumstances of his shoot down. As best he could recall, he had been in the hospital for the last ten days to two weeks. His treatment had not been bad. The bone in his upper leg had been broken when he ejected or landed. He didn't remember. He said the Vietnamese had put a pin in the bone to keep it in place and to help it mend. He had a nice long scar down the side of his leg that had already healed fairly well.

The next morning, the medic came to get our *bo* and placed it outside the door. As was customary, another POW picked it up and emptied it. When the POW brought the empty bucket back, he leaned over and flipped a note under the door. Unfortunately, the medic spotted the note, immediately opened the door, and took the note before we had a chance to get it.

Quincy was laid out flat on his back, Norlan with his two broken arms couldn't have picked up the note if he had to, and I wasn't a streak of lightening on my mini crutches. We thought we were in deep trouble and worried especially about the guy who had tossed the note. About half an hour later, our door opened again, and another POW bounced in with his bedroll. He was the guy who had tossed the note under the door. His name was Bob Peel, and he was an Air Force first lieutenant. The Vietnamese must have figured that we three wounded guys needed at least one well person to look after us. Bob could take care of the *bo*, and the Vietnamese would never have to touch it. He could bring our food into the room, wash our dishes, and do all things the Vietnamese had had to do before. Why they hadn't done it sooner was beyond me, but their policy of keeping us in isolation must have overridden the inconvenience of having to care for us.

Bob had been shot down on 31 May 1965. In those days, the U.S. Government was generous in that you had to fly only six combat missions before you earned $65 for combat pay. Bob had been attached to the wing command post and, therefore, did not fly as regularly as he would have if he had been in a squadron. He had flown five missions and was trying to fly his sixth so he could qualify for combat pay for the month. Unfortunately, he earned his combat pay the hard way. He got bagged and ended up as a prisoner for more than seven and a half years.

Bob had been stationed in Turkey before he came to Thailand, and we found him quite entertaining. He had lived with three other men in an area where communication was easy, and he was up to date on what was going on. I was surprised that perfectly healthy men had lived together, while I'd had to gut it out by myself for nearly five months. That could have been because I was the senior prisoner at that time. The room we were in now had been occupied for some time by Lt. Cdr. Robert Shumaker and was called Shu's old room.

We settled into a routine again. Quincy was still bedridden and had to keep his leg straight until the bone healed, even though it wasn't in a cast, and Bob Peel did all the dirty work. There were some great advantages in having four of us together. We played chess every day. Several times a week, we had a chess tournament and drew straws to see who played whom. We bet cigarettes and the winner took all. I beat Bob Peel almost every time we played, except when we played in a tournament for a cigarette, and then Bob would always win.

The Vietnamese gave us our ration of cigarettes on Monday mornings. Three per day for four guys for seven days came to four packs and four cigarettes. They also gave us a supply of matches. At first, we tried to ration them each day but we ran out of cigarettes a day and a half before the end of the week, even with non-smoker Quincy donating his ration for our use. Because the number of matches was limited, the three of us more or less had to agree when we would smoke. The early morning cigarette and the one after each meal were obvious times, but our problems began in the evening, when one of us would say, "What the hell. Let's light one before we go to bed. Maybe we can bum a few more from the Vietnamese before the week is out." Then we would discuss at some length the ramifications of such an act, and finally we would all agree to smoke.

Disagreement rose over our views on the war. Quincy always took a hard line and believed that the U.S. could do no wrong, and that the war was black and white. Maybe because Norlan, Bob, and I had been there longer than Quincy and had heard the

Vietnamese side of the story, we had concluded that this was not the most perfect war the U.S. ever fought, and that the U.S. would run into difficulty before it ended. Maybe we were a little brainwashed already. I didn't think so, but the situation between the U.S. and Vietnam was extremely complex. Although we might have privately acknowledged that the North Vietnamese views had some merit, we all believed that the reason we were there was legitimate. I believed that the way the war was being fought was all screwed up, but I never wavered in my support of the U.S. position on the war in my dealings with the Vietnamese.

We had other disagreements too, nothing serious, no fist fights, but all of us would get annoyed with another at one time or another. Arguing about everything became irritating. These were just things one had to put up with from roommates. One guy would give an opinion about something, and another guy would disagree, instead of keeping quiet, and sometimes an argument would ensue.

Quincy was one of the more entertaining persons I had ever met. He could tell jokes as well as any comedian. He had one interesting story after another to tell, and on top of all that, he could sing. In fact, he had moonlighted as a professional singer and comedian at times while he was on active duty in the Air Force. He was always singing. His favorite song was "Old Man River." Another hit was "Did You Ever See Sally Make Water." He sang this song at least three times a day. It went something like this: "Did you every see Sally make water; she can pee such a beautiful stream; she can pee on your foot as you day dream; oh, she runs the water machine."

As time went on, we learned that there was an interrogation room off of the passageway that joined our courtyard and the main courtyard. It was called the green room because there was a dark green tablecloth on the table. Sometimes the Vietnamese would take a break from the interrogation and leave the POW in the green room alone. One time we heard talking, not well enough to understand what was said, but we knew a new guy was there.

When the talking stopped for a while, Quincy started to sing the tune "Old Man River," but instead of the actual words he substituted words like "We are prisoners. How are you today? Please cough once for yes and twice for no." And he would pass word on to the prisoner, and we would get information from him by his coughs. Sometimes all four of us would send messages to the tune of "Row, Row, Row Your Boat." We made contact with a number of prisoners that way. Sometimes we sang for ten or fifteen minutes before a guard banged on our door.

In late September, the Butcher came to visit us again. By that time the bone in Norlan's left arm had healed and the cast was removed. The arm had atrophied considerably, but within another month, he gained back much of the use of it. Norlan's right arm was still in a sling, and his bandage had turned black from the drainage, so the Butcher put a new bandage on his arm and that was it for Norlan. Quincy started walking about two or three weeks after he moved in with us. We advised him not to overdo it, but he insisted on walking a lot and consequently hurt his back and leg. Of course, we chided him continuously. The Butcher cut the cast off my leg because it had a bad odor, and the color had changed from white to black. He put some brown yellowish stuff on the wound and showed me several pieces of bone chips that he took from it. The Butcher still wouldn't let me look at the wound, but I really didn't mind because the other guys told me it was still pretty messy. I had been hopeful that the leg was better, but it was not, probably because I had been walking around more than I should have. First the Butcher bandaged my leg, then instead of replacing the cast, he put the leg in a wire splint and wrapped the splint for my leg with some cotton gauze.

It felt a lot better with the new bandage and new splint because the leg had been getting sore as a result of the wetness of the bandage, which rubbed against my leg inside the cast. It was also easier to get around without the heavy cast on the leg.

Now that Norlan's left arm was out of the cast, he was able to use his hand to lift the lid of the *bo* and take his pants down by himself whenever he had to go to the toilet. It was a blessing for him.

In late September, we were allowed outside in the courtyard for fresh air and sunshine for a few minutes two or three times a week, but there were always a couple of guards standing watch. One day, Norlan had on his crotchless shorts and was joking and talking to them in sign language and inadvertently exposed his genitals to the guards. All of a sudden, the guards became upset and sent us back to our room. Later that day, Norlan went to quiz. One of the senior camp officers chewed him out for exposing himself to the Vietnamese. Norlan found the whole thing funny and still wore the pants without the crotch from time to time, but he was more careful about lifting the skirt.

Although we played chess and talked about the war, our families, and everything else imaginable, life was boring. We wondered and speculated about our pay—whether we would receive combat and flight pay as POWs. The three cigarettes we got each day were the only good thing we had in an otherwise drab existence. When Bob Peel moved into our room, he brought some *Vietnam Couriers* that the Vietnamese had given him. This newspaper was made of very thin paper, almost as thin as real cigarette paper. And now that three of us were saving our butts, the thin paper from the *Courier* was great for roll-your-owns and far surpassed the coarse toilet board paper we had used before.

We became so addicted to cigarettes that one day when we ran out of them, we gathered some dried leaves that had fallen from the tree in the courtyard, crushed them, and wrapped them with paper from the *Courier*. Whew, was that ever a strong cigarette! We ran out of matches one night, and no matter how hard we begged, the guard wouldn't bring us a light. One of the guys remembered when he was in the Boy Scouts that fire could be made by rubbing wood against wood very rapidly. So that night we broke off a leg of a chair. I got my crutch and tied some string from my pants to each end of the crutch, making a sort of bow. Then I wrapped the string once around the chair leg. I placed the end of the chair leg on the wooden bed and started moving the crutch back and forth, causing the end of the leg to rub against the bed. We worked for at least a half an hour rubbing the wooden leg on the wooden bed. We were able to get the wood smoking pretty good and made a heavy black burn mark on the bed, but it never became hot enough to make a fire or a give us a light.

To pass the time, we watched the rats that infested the court-yard. When darkness fell, Bob would unhook our access hatch, and we would watch the rats run around. Sometimes we would have leftover food and instead of throwing it away, we'd save it and toss it to the rats piece by piece and watch them fight over it. We called one rat "Head Rat" because it would carry the pieces of bread to the shower room. It must have carried at least a loaf of bread in pieces to the shower during the time we lived in Shu's old room. No other rat worked so hard. "Head Rat" would run like hell every time we threw a piece. It was also identifiable because it was missing most of the hair on its back, as if it had the mange. The rats came into our room, no matter how hard we tried to keep them out. We didn't like the idea of them jumping up on us while we were sleeping. Although the rats ran around the room night after night, only one time was I paralyzed by them. Fortunately, I was able to break the spell before they were able to attack me.

At first, our communications with other POWs were unsophisticated. Singing was the only way. But in early October, some new guys had moved into the row of cells across the way, and when Bob and Norlan went out to get the food, they had to go across the courtyard to a large bucket of drinking water. While they filled our water jugs, they pretended they were talking to each other, but they were really passing information to the other prisoners who were in hearing distance.

The guards raised hell when they did this, but they told the guard that they were talking to each other, so they got away with it from time to time, even though the guard suspected what was going on. They passed information to Cdr. Jeremiah Denton and others this way. We also started to write notes with medicine or anything that would write, and we set up note drops in the bath area. That seemed to work fairly well for a while, but then the Vietnamese found out where our note drops were. We persisted, and some of the notes got through.

In late October, we got word that Lt. Col. Robinson Risner had been captured. Although I had never heard of him, Bob, Quincy, and Norlan couldn't believe it. Risner had been the recipient of the Air Force Cross on a bombing mission in Vietnam several months before and had had his picture on the cover of *Time*. With his capture, the Vietnamese really had a prize on their hands. Risner was in New Guy Village, and we learned that he was under the gun. He was in leg irons and receiving reduced rations. Several times, Norlan and Bob were able to talk to him while getting water, and they told him that we would try to leave notes and some food in the bath area, so he could pick them up if and when he took a bath. We didn't know how much food he was getting, but we left him what little we could. We never found out if he received anything we sent, because we moved soon thereafter.

Life had not been too bad for us the last month and a half. We sang some, talked when picking up the water, passed notes like crazy, and made escape kits. We had found razor blades, saved matches, found a knife, and hoarded pieces of wire and other items that would help us escape. Not that most of us seriously considered it, but if Bob ever had the opportunity to escape, he wanted to be ready.

On 7 November 1965, a new guard showed up at our door. After the four of us returned from the bath, we noticed that our gear had been gone through. Each and every last piece of contraband had been found and taken by the Vietnamese. They had even swiped a few of our cigarettes.

The rest of the day was business as usual. That night, three guards came to the door and indicated that we were going to move. We had apparently pushed them to their limit, and they were getting tired of it. Times were changing.

CHAPTER 7 - RULES AT THE ZOO

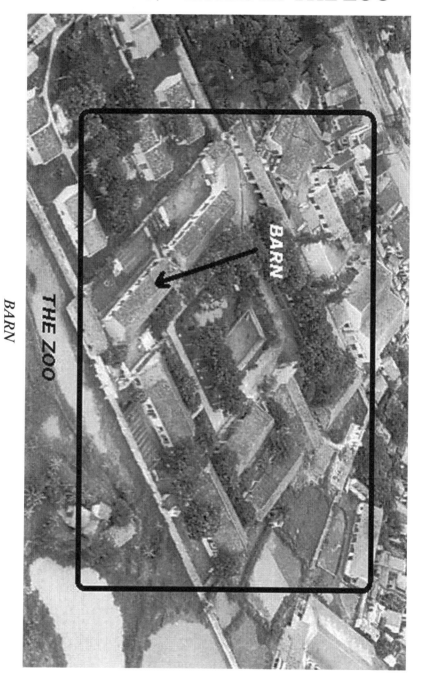

November 1965. After I rolled my gear up in my bed mat, a guard blindfolded me and led me out the door by myself. Fortunately, my blindfold was loose, so I was able to see about two steps ahead of me as I walked. When I wasn't sure what was in front of me, I would feel ahead with my crutches, particularly if there were steps, which were treacherous in my condition. I walked through the open passageway into the main courtyard, and then the guard pulled my shirt to indicate which direction to go. After a few steps, I was beside a jeep. I got into the jeep, and the guard put handcuffs on me. A minute later, I heard another person approach the jeep and get into the other side. It was Quincy.

Two Vietnamese climbed in and away we went. We drove about fifteen or twenty minutes and made at least a dozen turns. I heard horns honking and the bustle of city streets. Finally, we made one last turn and proceeded slowly down a dark alley. The jeep stopped, and the driver talked to someone outside. We drove again slowly, made a right turn, and the jeep's engine stopped. There was no sound. The guards got out, and Quincy and I just waited. Five minutes later, we heard another jeep pull up behind ours, and the motor was turned off. We could hear a number of Vietnamese talking now.

After several minutes, a guard opened my door, took off my handcuffs and blindfold, and motioned me to get out. In the darkness, I could make out a one-story building with a long porch. Norlan and Bob emerged from the second jeep, and the guard opened the large French doors to the room. With difficulty, I mounted the three steps up to the porch. The guard held a flashlight to help us see as we entered the room, but there was no light in the room itself. And no beds. So we had to put our mats down on the floor and put the mosquito nets right on top of us instead of having the net three feet above us. Even though the weather had turned quite chilly recently, that night was very warm, and we spent a miserable night under the closeness of the mosquito nets.

The next morning, the gong sounded as usual. The room was still dark, but we were able to make out things now that we hadn't been able to make out the night before. Bob, Norlan, and Quincy checked the room over carefully. Larger than our last room, it measured about thirty feet by ten feet. It had two windows in front, but they were covered with green shutters. The room also had four six- by nine-inch air vents in the upper part of the walls and two French doors. Although we couldn't see straight ahead through the shutters, by standing close to them we could see two or three feet from the building on the floor of the porch. There were numerous cracks in the doors and shutters so that we had a fairly good view outside. Our room was at the end of the building and occupied about a third of its length.

Norlan, Bob, and Quincy were delighted with the room because they had some new things to see, and they spent the early hours of the morning with their eyes glued to the cracks in the doors and windows. Unfortunately, not much was going on other than an occasional Vietnamese walking by. My leg was still bothering me, and it didn't take very long standing on crutches before the viewing outside wasn't worth it.

Around 0830 we heard some scratching and tapping on the wall from the next room. Norlan and Bob immediately ran to the wall, put their ears on it and listened. They could hear a series of taps on the wall but couldn't figure out their meaning. I suggested Morse code, but we soon concluded that wasn't what it was. Bob tapped back on the wall with random taps. Suddenly, both Norlan and Bob remembered that they had been taught a tap code when they went through escape, evasion, resistance, and survival school several years before. Each one remembered something that helped the other remember something, so that in about a half hour they had constructed what they believed was the tap code. Bob went over to the wall and gave the old shave-and-a-haircut tap, and the other guy acknowledged it. Then Bob started to tap, but unfortunately we still weren't getting anywhere. On the wall that separated us from the next room there had been a door that was now bricked up. Finally, in frustration Bob cupped his hands around his mouth and started to talk to the bricks, and the other guy could hear him.

It was Ron Storz, an Air Force captain shot down in late August or September 1965. He told us that there were three other rooms in the building in addition to the one we were in. Cdr. Denton was in the room beyond his, and the last room was vacant. Ron told us about the tap code. Bob and Norlan had had the general idea but had made a slight error when they set it up. Now we had it right. We memorized the code at once in case we ever had a need for it again.

Ron told us that during an inspection, the Vietnamese had found a note hidden in his pants, in the hole where the string ran through as a belt. It was a good hiding place, but the Vietnamese were getting smarter by the day. The note was written in code, and its purpose had something to do with using the camp electrical system to send dots and dashes, flashing the light bulbs on and off at different times of day. Unfortunately for Ron, the Vietnamese either had found out or suspected that Risner wrote the note when he was in this camp. Now we knew the reason Risner was under pressure.

In an effort to force Ron to talk, the Vietnamese had reduced his food rations. Ron was becoming weak, having gone several days without more than a little bread. This news concerned, disheartened, and frightened us. We knew that Maj. Lawrence Guarino had been in leg irons, but now in addition to putting the screws to Risner, the Vietnamese were working on low-ranking Air Force captains.

Around 0930 a new turnkey came to the door. He was pleasant looking but appeared rather lazy, indifferent, and nonchalant about his chores. Someone named him Johnny Cool. He brought us one day's ration of cigarettes and a light. This was different from before when we got a whole week's ration at one time. Johnny Cool was so disorganized that sometimes we would get our cigarettes in the morning and sometimes not. Also, he was irregular with the cigarette light. Norlan, Bob, and I were frustrated when he didn't bring the cigarettes and light on time, because we all were addicted.

At some point, a group of guards brought in two wooden sawhorses for each of our beds. They placed a bed board on top of each set of sawhorses. Since these makeshift beds didn't have mosquito net poles we placed our beds side by side, about three feet apart, and used some string the Vietnamese gave us to jury rig a system to hold our mosquito nets up.

On the fifth night, the guard opened the door, and in came the Rabbit and the Fox, both wearing military uniforms. The Rabbit had one bar, and the Fox had a couple of bars and stars. This was the first time any of us had ever seen them in uniform. With the Rabbit translating, the Fox informed us that there were camp regulations now and that we would have to obey them. The Rabbit left a copy of the regulations with us. We also learned that they had given us Vietnamese names, when the Rabbit pointed to us using these names. My Vietnamese name was pronounced "Vah," and this was what they called me the rest of the time I was there. The Fox told us that we were war criminals but were being treated in accordance with their lenient and humane policy. If we needed help or had a serious problem, we were to call out the words *bao cao*. We were to talk quietly in our rooms, and we were not to communicate with any other American prisoners under any circumstances. If we did so, it would be very bad for us. He told us that from now on we would have to stand when the Vietnamese came into the room.

After they left, we discussed the new regulations and decided that we would still communicate whenever possible, but one guy would always be looking out the window, clearing, to insure our safety. None of us liked the idea of standing at attention when the guard came in, because we felt they were making us do it as an act of subservience. But we finally agreed that we would go ahead and stand and not rock the boat at this time.

We had been communicating with Ron Storz every day, and he appeared to be growing steadily weaker. Someone came up with the idea of attaching a piece of bread to the end of a string, sticking the bread and string outside the vent in the back wall and trying to swing it to Ron's window so he could grab it. Bob leaned one of the bed boards against the wall by a vent and climbed up on it. He was able to get the bread tied to the string through the vent but couldn't swing it far and high enough for Ron to grab it through his vent. Within a week of our arrival, Ron was moved from our building. We lost track of him but later found out that he had been in other camps elsewhere and years later had died in captivity.

After about a week of complaining about not getting to bathe, we were all allowed to go wash one evening. It was the first time I was allowed out of the room since I had arrived in this camp. Norlan and Bob had been out of the room each day to bring in the plates of food, and Bob also emptied the *bo* every morning in a hole behind our building, so they had a fairly good idea of the camp layout.

Others may have called it something else, but we knew this camp as the Zoo. The same goes for the buildings. We called our building the Barn. The names of the camps, buildings, and areas in a particular camp and the names of Vietnamese guards and officers were suggested sometimes by a guy you knew or by some unidentified nameless prisoner, and for one reason or another the names stuck. Sometimes they didn't stick, and a particular guard or officer might have been known by as many five different names. But the Zoo is what I would call home for the next four years.

We were allowed to go to the bath in the Pig Sty. It had a faucet and a shower that ran sometimes. Because the weather was cold at night in the middle of November, no one took a shower, but we all washed as well as we could. The guard didn't come back for nearly an hour, so after having to stand on crutches for that long I was exhausted when we returned to our room. The next time we were allowed to wash a week later, I didn't go.

We were cold all the time now. We estimated that the temperatures were in the low fifties at night. With only one small thin blanket apiece and just a few clothes, we were particularly uncomfortable at night. We kept asking the guard every day for more clothes and blankets with no success. Finally, in the third week of November, the guard brought in a new set of khaki green clothes for each of us. The shirts had buttons, and the pants had string belts. They were the first decent clothes we had had. They had a big black TU 344 stamped on the back of the shirts, and they were all the same except for the sizes. Up to that time, we had worn whatever the guards found somewhere. The clothes that the four of us had were just about the wildest assortment of attire one would ever want to see. Bob had a pair of pants with blue stripes and a purple shirt. Norlan had a purple shirt and black pants. I had a pair of blue pajamas four sizes too small. Quincy had Norlan's pants with the crotch cut out and a blue shirt and black pants.

In late November our old medic, Mr. Tuc, came to our room and changed the bandage on Norlan's right arm. Norlan's left arm had already healed, and it worked pretty well now. Quincy was walking without much problem, except that he limped and had trouble with his back once in a while. My leg was still wrapped in the wire splint, just they way they had left it when they took the cast off two months before. Unfortunately, the leg didn't seem to be getting any better. The medic took the splint off and removed the bandage from the leg. He had a small vial that looked like it contained distilled water and another bottle with white powder in it and letters on the side that looked something like sulfa. I expected him to mix the white powder with the distilled water for a shot, but he took the whole bottle of white powder and sprinkled it directly on the wound.

At that time, I was still quite depressed over my leg, because Quincy's leg had already been healed for a month, and he was shot down five months after me, and one of Norlan's arms had mended, and his other arm seemed to be getting better. My leg was still sore, it was still draining, a bone graft seemed like a long time away, and I was tired of being saddled with my tiny crutches. In retrospect, however, I believe that Mr. Tuc's putting the sulfa powder directly on the wound is what finally led to the healing of my leg. Within several days, the leg felt better, and within a week or two it had definitely improved.

Although time passed slowly, it did not pass without its mysteries. When Johnny Cool came around to pick up our dishes after each meal we heard what sounded like a swishing noise or like a heavy sled being dragged across the ground. We pondered and argued the whole time we were in the room over what might cause this sound. A month later, when I moved into the Garage, I found out that the noise came from the Garage building's French doors sliding along the porch when they were opened and shut.

In the last week of November, some Vietnamese workers came to our room and installed a speaker. The next day they played some typical French music that was very encouraging. After eight months of confinement, the music not only boosted our morale, but it was nice to hear. The western music also raised our hopes that the war might be ending. At the same time, however, we suspected that they were only trying out the speakers.

Quincy was still as entertaining as ever. He had a comedy routine about Sam Spade that lasted for about a half an hour. Norlan, Bob, and I were quite impressed by his performance and enjoyed it very much. He was a real ham. We laughed so hard and loud that the guard got upset and brought a camp officer to our room. He threatened us with serious punishment if we didn't stop.

The next night, the guard came to our room and gave us signal to get ready to move. Five minutes later, he came back with another guard, and we left our room in the Barn.

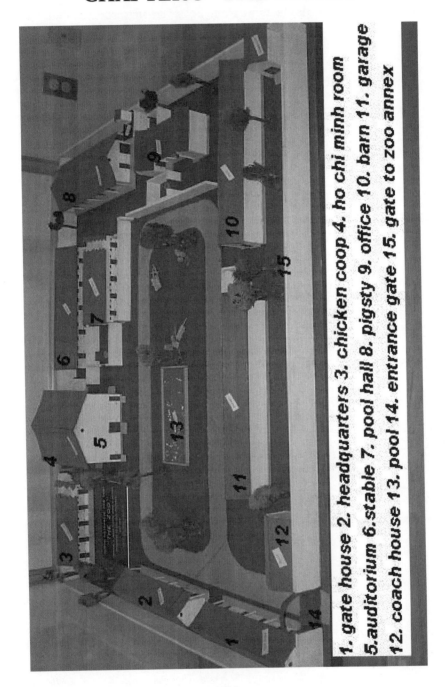

1. gate house 2. headquarters 3. chicken coop 4. ho chi minh room 5.auditorium 6.stable 7. pool hall 8. pigsty 9. office 10. barn 11. garage 12. coach house 13. pool 14. entrance gate 15. gate to zoo annex

December 1965. Quincy and I went first. After I walked down the porch steps, a guard blindfolded me and tugged me in the direction he wanted me to go. We ended up in the middle room of the Office, which was fewer than twenty-five yards from the Barn. A few minutes later, Norlan and Bob came in. Our new room was smaller than the last one and had four large windows with shutters, two in the front and two in the back. There were four sets of sawhorses with bed boards, and Bob hung strings across the room so we could attach our mosquito nets. Although it was colder now, a few mosquitoes survived to torment us if we didn't use the nets.

The next morning, we found cracks in the doors and shutters, and Quincy, Norlan, and Bob spent their spare time looking through them. We never knew when we might see someone we knew, and seeing strangers was also worthwhile because if we ever communicated with someone and got his name, we could match the face and the name. One day, Bob spotted Maj. Fred Cherry, an F-105 pilot that he, Norlan, and Quincy knew well. Fred came up onto our porch and then turned to go to one of the rooms on the side, but because the rooms beside us were separated from ours by small passageways, we were unable to communicate with the men in them.

Norlan and Bob climbed up on a bed board to look out the vent in the back wall. Beyond the camp, they saw a large open area that was mostly farmland and had a swampy lake in the middle of it. Dirt roads also crisscrossed the area. Many army trucks, some with antiaircraft guns, drove around there. One of us was watching through the cracks almost continually during the daylight hours, except when we were eating, and if the looker saw something, he told the rest of us, and we would rush to the door to see what it was. I couldn't move fast enough most of the time, so I missed a lot of the good sights, but the others filled me in with what they saw.

Soon after we moved into the Office, the Vietnamese began using the radio speakers every day. At first, one of the interrogators would read propaganda about the war for a half hour in the morning and a half hour in the afternoon. The reader generally didn't speak English very well, so we missed quite a bit of what he said, but no one really minded. They also played traditional Vietnamese music. Although I had been delighted when they put the speakers in the room, my morale plummeted when the propaganda began. At some point, they started playing an American song once in a while, which helped lift my spirits. After hearing Ella Fitzgerald sing "Don't Fence Me In" for the hundredth time, however, the song lost quite a bit of its appeal.

Our two daily meals were highlights we looked forward to, even though they might comprise only a piece of bread, some cabbage soup, and two pieces of pig fat. The louvered shutters on the windows allowed us to see the table where the food boy was dishing up the plates from his big buckets. Ordinarily, we enjoyed watching him, but one afternoon in late November, the room had become so cold it was almost unbearable. The wind had swept through the room with gale force all day long. We were sitting on our beds facing the door with all of our clothes on and our thin blankets around us, waiting to eat and wrap up for the long night. Someone mentioned that we looked like we were riding on a bus. This tickled our collective funny bone, and we laughed so loud and for so long that the guard waited an extra ten minutes to let our food cool off before he opened the door to let us go out and get it.

We had been accustomed to talking as loud as we wanted to in Shu's old room in the New Guy Village. The guards had mostly left us alone because we were fairly isolated. But now, whenever we talked too loud, the guard would bang on the door and yell, *"Eeep!"* We suspected this meant shut up. We resented this new discipline because we felt it was unfair. Bob Peel, who was a big talker, resented it more than the rest of us, so he deliberately talked loud whenever he could.

In the early part of December, one of the camp officers told us that we would have to bow whenever a Vietnamese officer or guard came into the room or we met a Vietnamese anywhere. They made numerous threats about what would happen if we didn't. We debated among ourselves at great length about whether we should bow or not. On the one hand, we suffered no physical harm whatever in bowing. It didn't violate our Code of Conduct or do any great harm to the U.S. government or our country. On the other hand, it was degrading. Although the Vietnamese told us that it was just a form of greeting, it was not our custom, and we felt that the purpose was to place us in a subservient position. Standing when the Vietnamese came in was repugnant, but we had agreed to do it. The order to bow, however, created a real dilemma. They threatened us in a general way with punishment if we didn't bow.

Obviously, the Vietnamese were becoming more organized in their treatment of the prisoners. This might have been a matter of necessity because between early 1965 and November 1965, the number of prisoners had gone from one to almost sixty. They could afford to be lax and disorganized with just a few prisoners, but now it was a different story. They learned that even as their prisoners, we were still plotting against them, and they were beginning to react in kind toward us.

As the senior man in the room, I decided that despite my personal dislike of bowing, we should bow because it wasn't worth making an issue over. Bob and Norlan were undecided but went along with me. Quincy disagreed with us, and he refused to bow. For several days, the three of us bowed, but Quincy didn't. Our guard at that time was a guy named Smiley. He had a stocky build and looked like a pretty tough individual in comparison with the other Vietnamese. On the third day, Smiley opened the door to the room to let Norlan and Bob pick up the food for the evening meal. As usual, the three of us bowed, and Quincy didn't. Smiley had been yelling at Quincy to bow every day, but Quincy had refused. Smiley seemed more adamant this night. Finally, he told Bob and Norlan to pick up the food, but he indicated that Quincy could not have his until he bowed. Quincy still refused. Smiley growled at him a few times and then left and closed the door. So there we sat, Bob, Norlan, and I with our food and Quincy with none. The question was whether we should share our food with him or he should be responsible for the consequences of his acts. Begrudgingly, we gave him some of our food.

A half hour later, Smiley opened the door again to pick up our dishes. We again bowed, and Quincy didn't. This time, Smiley had one of the sentries responsible for guarding our building with him. The camp organization had one turnkey per building to take us to bathe, give out food, and so forth, and other guards who carried guns, worked shifts, and stood watch over one or two buildings around the clock. The sentry on duty this particular night was a little bitty guy. He walked up to Quincy and indicated that he should bow. Quincy didn't. Finally, the little guy reached up and grabbed Quincy's ear and started to pull on it. He pulled and pulled for about five minutes, but Quincy wouldn't budge. The three of us almost burst out laughing at the site of the tiny sentry taking on Quincy, who was over six feet tall and could easily have knocked the sentry flat. Quincy didn't think it was funny. Finally, the little guy gave up, and Smiley cussed Quincy a few more times, but then brought in Quincy's food for him. They left Quincy alone after that and did not do anything to force him to bow. Quincy had won the battle for now. There were a few other guys who refused to bow, and they ended up being beaten. But eventually most everyone I knew bowed.

We knew this divided behavior was not good, and we had argued at great length about the pros and cons of our action, but we were individuals and wanted to do what we wanted to do, and as long as there was no serious violation of the Code of Conduct I said okay.

CHAPTER 9 - THE GARAGE

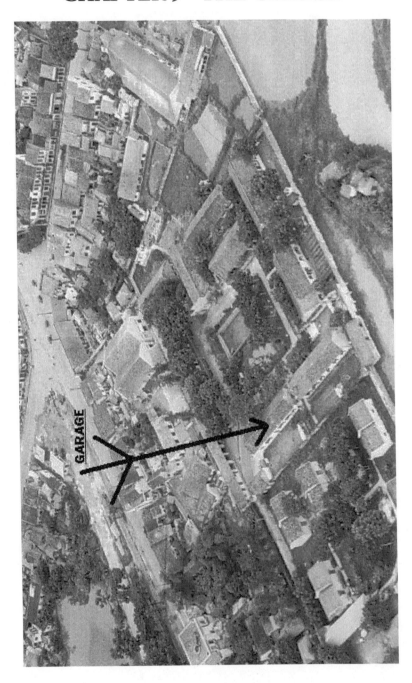

15 December 1965 – 23 December 1965. Several nights after Quincy won his victory, the guard came to our room and gave us the sign to roll up our gear and get ready to move. I was blindfolded for the short walk to room 2 of the Garage building. When, they took my blindfold off, I could see Quincy standing alongside me, and I could tell from the size of the room and the permanent installation of two beds that Norlan and Bob were going elsewhere. We found out later that they had moved into one of the back rooms in the Office building. Although Bob stayed at the Zoo for several years, and we lived in the same building from time to time, I would not see him again until the day we were released more than 7 years later.

We had been one of the first groups of four guys to live together. Most everyone else was in solitary confinement. To some degree, we might have received special treatment, but probably the Vietnamese figured it was easier for them to put the injured prisoners together to take care of each other. Perhaps if we had been less unruly, we might not have been separated at this time, and maybe that would have laid the path for others to be removed from isolation into larger groups. Unfortunately, the average American pilot would not be content with his situation and he would always try to better it, whatever the consequences. Our competitiveness and egos were so strong that sometimes that was what did us in.

The room we were in now was far worse than any I had been in before. It appeared to have been renovated with the specific intention of putting prisoners in it. It had no windows and only one small vent on top of the back wall. The walls were painted a dark color, and the room was gloomy. It had just enough space for two beds three feet wide on each side of the room, with three feet in between, and about four feet from the foot of the bed to the front wall. A dim light bulb hung from the ceiling and was lit all night long. Our daily routine continued, two meager meals each day, the radio with propaganda twice a day, and an occasional opportunity to go outside to the bath. I seldom took advantage of the chance to bathe, because the weather was so cold, and I found it hard to wash myself because of the broken leg. By this time, we had each received another blanket but with temperatures in the low forties all day and thirties at night, we were forced to wear all of our clothes and stay on our beds under our blankets almost all the time.

The day after we moved in we were ready to play with the tap code that Ron Storz had introduced us to. By putting our ears to the wall, we could hear that someone was in the room on either side of us. Quincy tried hard to contact the guy in the room next to him by tapping on the wall, but he never got a response. We were disappointed because we wanted to be in contact with everyone possible. Months later, we found out that the guy in that room was a Marine warrant officer, John Frederick, who had been the back seat radar controller on an F4-B aircraft. When he was shot down, he had burned his hands, and therefore he was unable to tap. Although he stayed in the Zoo for another year, he eventually moved to other camps. In the later part of the war, he contracted typhoid fever, and the Vietnamese reported that he had died.

In the room next to my bed was a Navy man, Lt., j.g., Dave Wheat. He knew the tap code but was as new with it as we were. At first the tapping went slowly. We made many mistakes and had to repeat simple messages over and over again, but after about a week of tapping, we were able to communicate reasonably well. Tapping was the primary means of communicating I would use with the men in the rooms beside mine for the next three years, by which time I was faster than a Teletype machine. I also developed some pretty thick calluses on my knuckles. We got all the personal background information on Wheat. He had been in an F4 that was shot down on 17 October 1965. Wheat had been caught leaning his bed board up against the wall so he could climb up on it and look out of a small vent hole. As punishment, they took the bed board from him, and now he had to sleep on the dirty, cold floor.

Our room still had an old French door that fortunately had a few cracks in it. Quincy spent a large part of the day sitting on the floor looking outside. When we looked out of a tiny crack, we could see that they were doing some masonry work in a building called the Pool Hall. We couldn't see exactly what they were doing, but it was obvious that a major project was under way.

Our boring existence of doing little or nothing continued. Sometimes we got along just fine, other times we got on each other's nerves. I knew all about his family, his career, and even the intimate details of his sex life. So when we ate there wasn't much conversation, because even though it was slop, it was all we had and slop can taste pretty good sometimes. But because it was so quiet, I could hear him loudly masticating his food, even with his mouth closed. This annoyed the hell out of me, but I survived. I never said a word to him about it. I know he heard me the same way, and it probably annoyed him too, but he never said a word either. Life in prison was hard not only because of the enemy: Living with another guy in such close quarters made life unbearable sometimes.

Although Quincy had been a bad boy from time to time with the Vietnamese, he could also be friendly and charming with them if he wanted to. He had been friendly with the camp commander on several occasions. Personally, I wouldn't ever talk to them if I didn't have to. I wanted to stay in the background and go unnoticed forever. Just to be left alone. One day the camp commander was near our room when we were returning from the bath, and Quincy asked him if he could get together with some of the other guys and form a choral group, so they could sing Christmas carols for the other prisoners on Christmas Eve. I thought the idea was ridiculous. I couldn't believe the Vietnamese would even consider the idea, because they had kept us so isolated. And even if they allowed Quincy to form a choir they would be sure to get the maximum amount of propaganda out of it. Quincy, however, believed that getting a group of people together to sing was not in and of itself a violation of the Code of Conduct. And it might get some guy out of solitary and ultimately break down the isolation of the prisoners that existed. He also thought the other prisoners who listened might enjoy it. The camp commander did not approve his request.

I had thought of my wife and children for a substantial part of my waking hours every day since being shot down. I dreamed of them at night and daydreamed of them when I was awake. These dreams had given some substance to whatever life I had since I became a prisoner. Memories of what our life had been together and daydreams of what our life would be when I came home were what gave me the strength to survive. And now it was three days before Christmas. Quincy and I had scarcely talked about Christmas because there was nothing to be gained by talking about it. Nevertheless, as Christmas approached, our lives became more and more filled with despair and sadness.

On 23 December, I went to "quiz"–the word commonly used by the POWs when they had an interrogation, a political indoctrination, or other meeting with the camp commander or one of the other Vietnamese officers. This day the quiz was with the Dog. I had never met him before, but I knew right away it was the Dog by the way Norlan had described him. He was the right age, size, and his use of the English language was outstanding. After the preliminary amenities, he told me that he had a letter for me from my wife, and he handed me my first letter from home. Then he gave me a five-minute lecture on the lenient and humane policy of the Democratic Republic of Vietnam. The letter was in an envelope that had been opened, and it was written on a plain white sheet of lined paper. It was a short note, and it revealed that my wife did not know whether I was alive or not. I was upset over this, but I clung to the last line, which said, "Just remember how much you are loved."

The Dog asked me if I wanted to write back. I said, "Yes," but then he said that he would have to tell me what I could write, and that his superiors would make the final decision whether my letter would be sent. I didn't like the idea of the Dog telling me what to say. He told me to write that the food and treatment were good. I told him that I didn't think they were very good. I knew that the food was barely sufficient to sustain life, that the medical treatment was bad, and that my first five months of prison had been one long nightmare. But the Dog caught me in a moment of weakness. It was Christmas. I wanted my wife to know I was alive. I wrote in the letter that the food was adequate and life was tolerable here. That apparently satisfied him, because my wife eventually got the letter. I should have refused but there were other highly decorated men who received far worse treatment that wrote letters praising the Vietnamese without batting an eyelash.

Several days before I went to quiz, Quincy had seen some guys with blue sweatshirts. Here were a bunch of new guys running around with nice warm clothes, and Quincy and I, both injured and having difficulty moving around, didn't have any. So I asked the Dog if we could have sweatshirts. He said he would see. The Dog allowed me to keep the letter from my wife. When I got back to our room, I told Quincy that I had received a letter from home, and that I had written a response. He was happy for me. For the next few days, I felt bad because I had written some things in the letter that weren't exactly true.

POOL HALL

23 December 1965 – 3 March 1966. A couple of nights before Christmas, we moved to the Pool Hall, the building they had been renovating across the courtyard. The front of the building had five doors. The door to the center room was open, and we went in. This was the smallest room I had been assigned to so far. The beds were permanently in place on top of mortar and bricks, with no sawhorses or moveable bed boards to climb on. The beds were the standard size of three feet by six and a half feet, and the distance between the beds was little more than two feet. The space from the foot of the bed to the front wall was about two and a half feet. There were two six- by six-inch vents high on the front wall. The dilapidated French doors had been replaced with thick wooden doors with no cracks. Instead of the simple locks we were used to, we now had a sturdy lock and a heavy bolt. In the middle of the top half of the door was a little access hatch that could be locked from the outside. This allowed the Vietnamese to sneak up on us and catch us tapping on the wall or just look in on us anytime of the day or night. The building probably had previously been composed of three large rooms, but it had been partitioned into ten rooms of equal size, five in the front and five in the back.

The mortar used to brick up the partitions and the plaster on the walls was still wet, which made the room cold and damp. For the next hour, we heard doors opening and closing, and then finally the last door slammed shut. The Voice of Vietnam, which was aimed at the American GIs in South Vietnam, came on the speakers. When that was over, the camp gong sounded, and we turned in for the night.

The next morning after the gong sounded, I became aware of some faint tapping. Within five minutes, tapping was happening all around us. It sounded like a dozen typewriters all clacking at the same time. Because we were in one of the middle rooms, we

had three rooms we could tap to now. Finally, we had good communications, although it was slow going at first because most guys
were still learning the code. As time went on, we found out that
each of the ten rooms had two guys in it. Facing the front of the
building from left to right, Bob Lilly and Art Cormier were in room
1; Fred Cherry and Porter Halyburton in room 2, Quincy and I in
room 3, Pop Keirn and Al Brudno in room 4, Norlan and Bob in
room 5, and in the back rooms from left to right were Robert Jeffery
and John Reynolds in room 6, Everett Alvarez and Tom Barrett in
room 7, Larry Guarino and Ronald Byrne in room 8, Red Burg
and William Robinson in room 9, and Smitty Harris and Robert
Shumaker in room 10. When the Voice of Vietnam came on the
radio that morning, the tapping stopped, but as soon as it finished,
the walls started vibrating again.

Suddenly there was a loud bang on one of the walls. Someone
had hit the wall with his fist. It didn't take a genius to figure out what
that meant. All tapping stopped. A Vietnamese was approaching
the building or maybe the turnkey was ready to open the door. After
the morning meal, DumDum, a camp officer who had one Bar and
a Star and a poor command of English, announced over the speaker
that there would be a big dinner on Christmas day. He added that
there would be a program on the speaker tonight to commemorate
the birth of the "Bee Bee" Jesus.

The Christmas Eve broadcast was professional, unlike the usual
garbage produced by the camp authorities or the Voice of Vietnam.
The speaker spoke good English, with a Canadian or Australian accent.
Songs like "Ave Maria" and Christmas carols were interspersed with
Vietnamese propaganda and music. When I heard the American
music, I felt homesick. On the same program, they played the song
"Mack the Knife," which was popular back home, but they were im-
plying that Secretary of Defense Robert McNamara was Mack the

Knife and a bloodthirsty warmonger. They also talked about Tiny Tim and Scrooge and tried to make parallels between Scrooge and President Lyndon Johnson, which were absurdly amusing. Later they brought a bottle of beer for each room and four or five little pieces of sugar coated carrots or watermelon rind that were supposed to pass for candy. The big treat was an extra cigarette that night. It was not a lowly Truong Son cigarette but rather a Dien Bien Phu, which was what the camp officers smoked from time to time. The Christmas broadcast lasted about an hour, and then the Voice of Vietnam came on, and there was more Christmas music and a sort of church service. A Vietnamese minister, a priest, and a translator talked about the Bee Bee Jesus and how if Jesus were alive today, he would be against the U.S. war of aggression. The tape recording was so bad that we couldn't understand very much anyway.

I am sure that no one enjoyed the programs. Later that night, the Dog opened the access hatch and jovially asked how we liked the entertainment that the Vietnamese had prepared for us on Christmas Eve. We gave him some bull. Then he lectured us about how humane and lenient the Vietnamese people were to us. For the next seven years the Christmas Eve program was basically the same.

They had brought six turkeys into the camp in the early part of December and allowed them to roam throughout the compound. They were the scrawniest turkeys I ever saw in my life. Most of them were missing half of their feathers, and their bare skin was visible. They crapped all over the place. We wondered if we would get to taste a piece of them. Compared to what we normally ate, we had a good Christmas morning meal, including some green vegetable similar to spinach, a few small pieces of lettuce with a bit of oil dressing, some bread, about two ounces of turkey apiece, and a deep-fried Vietnamese egg roll. Its contents were unknown to any of us, but it was eaten with relish by all because anything fried in deep fat had to be tasty. We also received a bottle of Vietnamese beer, which was O.K., and a few pieces of candy. The highlight of the meal for smokers was two extra cigarettes and a cup of hot, black, heavily sugared coffee.

The Vietnamese took pictures of the food table and then took pictures of the guys in two rooms getting out together to pick up their food. Even though these guys had not met each other face to face before, the Vietnamese let them out together for propaganda purposes. Also their plates of food were probably much better than what the rest of us received. The guys who were singled out had no idea how much everyone else got, however, so they couldn't be considered as having taken special favors. The Vietnamese really made a big deal over the Christmas meal. We kept hearing all day long about how lenient and humane their treatment was. For the next four days, however, they gave us the worst food possible.

The weather was very cold now, and the sky remained overcast for most of the next three weeks. Because Quincy and I still didn't have much in the way of warm clothes, I stayed in my bed, on my back or on my side under the blankets for twenty-three hours a day. But even if I had possessed warm clothing, I wouldn't have done anything differently, because there was nothing for me to do. I got up only to eat, use the toilet, and go to wash once a week. We just froze our butts off most of the time. We finally received some blue sweatshirts in late January, and that made us a little warmer.

Part of Larry Guarino's guidance was that everyone should try to exercise every day. Some of the older guys who had never gone in for athletics resented being told to exercise and refused to participate. They could have just not exercised, and no one would have known, but because someone told them to do something, they made it public that they didn't like that kind of order. Most guys, however, exercised because they knew it was good for them. As the senior ranking officer, Larry didn't do very much, and at that time I had the impression that he didn't give a damn. Of course, there wasn't much he could do, and we had no great need for leadership.

As time went on, communications improved. Although we did not have continuous camp-wide communication, we were able to maintain a list of prisoners. In fact, by the end of January 1966, I had an accurate list of all but one man who had been shot down in 1965, and he had been shot down in mid-December. But we made lots of mistakes. For example, when we tried to contact the two guys in one of the rooms next to us, the names we got were Brudno and Ceirn, and because we had never heard of the name Ceirn in the POW system, we were really baffled. It took a week before Quincy and I figured out what had happened: We had forgotten that the letters C and K were the same in the tap code, and when Pop Keirn tapped a K, we thought it was a C. They were the only two letters in the alphabet that had the same tap sequence. This was not the last time that we were confused over the C and K. To avoid the problem, later on we just devised a new signal for a K, like six slow taps or some other unused sequence of taps.

A more serious mistake happened when Shumaker and Harris communicated with Capt. John Pitchford in a room in the Pig Sty after they washed the dishes. If the guard didn't come to get them as soon as the dishes were clean, they tapped to guys in that building. John had been shot in the elbow during his capture because one of the Vietnamese thought he was going for his gun, when he was only trying to raise his hands over his head to surrender. John had heard other gunshots in the area and suspected that his backseat man might have been killed. At any rate, this man, Capt. Trier, never showed up in the prison system. When Pitchford tapped Capt. Trier, Shumaker and Harris thought Pitchford had tapped Capt. Tried. And when the word was passed around the Pool Hall, it caused quite a stir because the Vietnamese had from time to time raised the possibility that, because we were war criminals, we might be tried some day.

When Norlan, Bob, Quincy, and I had lived together, we had played a game called famous personalities. We used to give biographical information about a person, and the others would try to guess who it was. Sometimes we would repeat a person's name for the fun of it, and two names that we often joked about were Alfred E. Neuman and Myron Kosnofski, who were characters in *MAD Magazine* of years gone by. One day, for the fun of it, we tapped to Al Brudno in the next room that Captains Neuman and Kosnofski were new POWs. When Al passed the word to Bob and Norlan, they got a big kick out of it, but poor Al Brudno and Pop Keirn became so confused, it took us two days to straighten it out for them.

Several weeks later, we passed on the news that Air Force Capt. Frank N. Stein and Joe Twofp had moved into the room next to us. We made up a story that Capt. Stein was about seven feet tall and that when the guards had caught him tapping on the wall and tried to punish him by making him kneel on the floor, he got so mad that he threw all three guards out of the room and was now pacing around the room like a monster. Every fighter jock had heard of Joe Twofp, an acronym for The World's Oldest Fighter Pilot. A famous picture of him looking like Popeye without teeth and an over-sized hard hat was posted in pilots' ready rooms throughout the world. We also passed on names such as Clark Kent, Capt. Marvel, and others. It was juvenile, but we had no end of fun using our imagination and making these fictitious characters do all kinds of strange things. The only danger was that someone, not knowing that this was a hoax, might get these names and include them in his list of POWs. Actually, some of the true stories and names that we got were almost as far out as the stories and names that we made up. For example, there really was a Capt. Marvel who was a prisoner–Marine Capt. Jerry Marvel.

One night, I was taken to the hospital, blindfolded as usual, and put in a medical room. My leg seemed to be better but was far from healed. There were many Vietnamese in the room, and the doctor removed my bandage. It hadn't been changed since November. They made me lie down when they changed the bandage and still wouldn't let me see the wound. The doctor had a green jar with white cream in it. He spread some of the cream all over my wound with a stick. Whatever it was it seemed to precipitate a tremendous leap forward in the improvement of my leg. When the medic from the Hanoi Hilton came by several weeks later and checked my leg, he indicated that I might go to the hospital and have a bone graft soon. My leg was feeling much better, but I didn't know if the skin was strong enough for a bone graft operation yet.

Quincy had not lost his sense of humor yet and still liked to have fun. He seemed quite gutsy at times, but I suspected that he was that way because the Vietnamese had never given him a hard time. But then, maybe he was a tough cookie. At one point, Quincy had severe stomach problems. The cabbage and green soup and pig fat gave him lots of gas, which caused him considerable discomfort. It was not unusual for him to fill up an entire five-gallon bucket at one sitting when he had a bowel movement. To relieve the gas pains, he would lie on his back, bend his knees upward, and break wind with gusto. He would do this as many as a hundred times on many nights. He never let the pain get him down, but the odors in such a confined space were foul.

One night, a couple of guards stood outside of our door talking. Quincy got up, walked to the door, bent over, pressed his butt tightly against the door, and expelled gas with such force that the door shook. This time, the guards just walked away, but on other nights, the guards would open the flap and chew both of us out, because they didn't know who the culprit was. Quincy took great delight doing this and I enjoyed watching him put on the show despite the stench I had to endure. The entertainment came to an end after Quincy stumbled over some stones and hurt his back on the way to wash. His back improved over time, but it never quite got back to normal, and the pain prevented him from breaking wind at the door anymore.

The camp regulations said that if there was a need for medical assistance or a legitimate need for a guard, we were supposed to call out *"bao cao."* One time, Al Brudno had a fainting spell, and when Pop Keirn called, *"bao cao,"* the guards came running so fast I couldn't believe it. He had medical treatment within a few minutes. As time went on, we may have abused the call, because if we didn't get our cigarette on time or we needed a light, we would call, *"bao cao."* They soon caught on to us. One Sunday, which was a slow day because we did not get to wash, the guard had brought us our meal but forgot to bring a light for the cigarette after the meal. I yelled, *"bao cao,"* at the top of my lungs every two minutes until the guard finally came and gave us a light. It was probably a marginally legitimate use of the call, but the guard was really burned up.

Norlan and Bob Peel were starting to feel their oats again, so on one dull Sunday afternoon, they decided to play a game they called "run rabbit run." They both yelled, *"bao cao,"* at the top of their lungs as fast as they could five or six times, and then as the guards ran like mad in the direction of the yell, trying to find out who needed help, they would not say a word. When the guards couldn't find the source of the *bao cao,* they realized they had been tricked. Luckily, Norlan and Bob never got caught when they played this game.

In late February, we received guidance from another commander to go ahead and bow and not make an issue over it, because the Vietnamese were pushing it again. Quincy and some of the other guys were still resisting it by refusing to bow sometimes but then bowing if the guard pushed real hard. Norlan and Bob decided not to bow for a while, but then the Vietnamese separated them and harrassed them by withholding their cigarettes and bath. Eventually they bowed again.

One day Bob Peel was picked to dump all the *bo*s in the building, and when he returned, he said to Norlan, "I have just seen the biggest turd in my life." It was about two feet long and seven inches in diameter. He wanted to know who it belonged to and immediately started tracking down the perpetrator. It turned out to have been Mike Wanko, who had not had a movement for more than ten days. It became a standing joke that the famous turd must have been the remains of weeks of bread, cabbage soup, and many side dishes of cabbage and pig fat.

The water for our water jugs was always boiled in the kitchen near the headquarters building and then carried in ten- or twelve-gallon cans to the building where the prisoners lived. For the most part, 17- to 20-year-old girls carried two large water cans on the ends of a stick carried on their shoulders. When the girls started out from the kitchen, they could barely lift the cans of water, but once the stick was on their shoulders, they would just bounce along. A water girl apparently wasn't considered to be in the highest strata of Vietnamese society. Their clothes were just about one step above rags. Occasionally, though, a water girl was quite attractive underneath her dirty clothes and dirty face. The water girl would stop in front and back of each building and fill up the water jugs from each room. Even though we had new solid wooden doors without cracks, it was impossible to seal off the bottom of the door, so some guys looked out under the door, even though the viewing wasn't great. One day, a guy in the back was looking under his door when suddenly the water girl stopped about three feet away, pulled down her black pants, squatted, and peed. When the news of this, in complete and minute detail, got around the building that day, we realized that this was the closest thing to sex we had had since entering captivity. It caused quite a furor.

Because the Vietnamese had found it worthwhile to inspect our rooms, we endured inspections almost weekly now. Four or five guards always came into the room as part of the inspecting team, and we had to face the wall with our hands over our heads. As I was on crutches, I didn't have to put my palms on the wall as the others did. The guards inspected our clothes and any other possessions we had, and frisked us from the tops of our heads to the bottoms of our feet as we stood. For the most part, Quincy and I didn't collect any contraband at this time because it really wasn't worth it. Nonetheless, Quincy had to make his displeasure known. When we heard the thump warning that the Vietnamese were coming inside the building, Quincy would take the lid off the *bo* and swish the contents around. The odor was almost enough to knock us out, but at least it was ours. Then just before the Vietnamese came into our room, he quietly replaced the cover on the *bo*. The stink however remained. The guards inspected our room so fast we couldn't believe it.

Although the trick worked for some time, one day a Junior officer and interrogator named Spot, because he had a white spot on his face, happened to hear Quincy put the cover on the *bo* just before the inspection team came into the room. When Spot came in and smelled the room and put two and two together, he was really angry. He chewed both of us out for ten minutes. He made all kinds of threats about what would happen if we ever did that again.

Although we might have been severely punished, it would have been well worth it.

When I went through survival school, the trainers emphasized that we had to give name, rank, serial number, date of birth, and nothing more. Another sentence in the Code of Conduct, however, said, "I will evade answering further questions to the best of my ability." In survival school, the second sentence was never discussed. It was not even mentioned. All they taught was name, rank, serial number, and date of birth. We were frequently told that death was preferable by far to the dishonor of spilling your guts. In addition, the trainers made repeated references to guys from the Korean War who were court-martialed when they were released from captivity. So, we were all not only indoctrinated in the moral and ethical aspects of behaving well as prisoners but also made aware that if we violated the Code of Conduct, we could be court-martialed when we returned home.

In the middle of March, Cdr. Denton moved alone into the back end room of the Pool Hall. Several days later, Navy Lt., j.g., Skip Brunhaver was moved into the room behind us. Because other moves had occurred, there was a vacant room between Denton and Brunhaver. Denton was more isolated this way, with only one common wall to tap to. The Vietnamese, however, did not know that we were able to tap two and sometimes three rooms away. Denton told us that he had been tortured but that they had finally let up on him. He issued guidance to "resist until you no longer have the will to resist, but resist again when your will to resist returns again." This was great guidance. It clarified that part of the Code about evading further questions to the best of your ability. I could resist until my will was gone and resist again when it returned. So far as I was concerned, that was the best advice I had received since becoming a prisoner.

The notion of dying before spilling your guts or writing an anti-war statement was one thing, but now I was here and would most likely be tested before the war ended. I felt that I could have been in trouble for what I had done during my first five months, but I didn't believe they would do much to me, because what I had given the Vietnamese was a cock-and-bull-story. Now, however, they might want me to write an anti-war statement or something even worse. Denton's guidance was reasonable. I used it throughout the remainder of my time in prison and passed it on to everyone else I met. He also said if communications were lost, the senior man must take charge. All orders of the previous commander were to be followed, and changes, depending on circumstances, could be made within the rules of the Code of Conduct.

Although Denton had a common wall with the guys in the room in front of him, he preferred to do all of his tapping with Skip Brunhaver, who was two rooms away from him in the back. Although he never said why, we suspected that Skip Brunhaver was able to receive Denton's tap code better than the guys in front of him. Since we were all to memorize his policies, he wanted them to be passed out as accurately as possible. It was easy to tell how well someone received the tap code. If you asked a guy his name, and he tapped back when he was shot down, you had a fair idea how well he communicated with the tap code. Some guys took longer than others to be proficient with the tap code, but eventually we were all pros.

In addition to the policies of resistance, Denton inaugurated Sunday church services and the weekly pledge to the flag. His program started after the morning meal and cigarette every Sunday. When he thumped the wall three times, we all had to stand and recite the pledge to the flag. After four thumps we had to recite the Lord's Prayer, after five thumps everyone would pray individually.

For some time, we practiced this wherever I lived, but once a guy told me that he thought this was ridiculous, and he just lay on his bed while all the thumping resounded through the building.

CHAPTER 11 - BIOGRAPHY

THIS BUILDING IS NOT THE GARAGE BUT IS TYPICAL OF THOSE WE LIVED IN

130

Late March 1966 – June 1966. The weather had been cold and the sky overcast nearly all winter. I had washed about three times since Christmas, but my leg was getting better. The cast had turned light brown, but then the discoloration stopped. My leg didn't hurt much any more. The fact that I had rarely moved from my bed for the past four months had probably helped.

Around the last week of March 1966, Quincy and I were relocated into the middle room of the Garage. This room was larger than the one we'd had in the Pool Hall. We now had a large shuttered window in the front wall and small air vents high up in the front and back walls. The room had the old French doors with cracks to look through. We were in room 3, Pop Keirn and Al Brudno were in room 2, and Jeffery and Reynolds were in room 1. In room 4 were two new guys, Lt., j.g., Glenn Daigle and Lt., j.g., Ray Alcorn, both shot down in December 1965. The room next to theirs was still occupied by Warrant Officer John Frederick. Our new room was much more pleasant than our last one. It was a bit brighter, not only because of the window but also because springtime had come, and the clouds were gone.

We called our new turnkey Tiny because he was so small. He was an officer with one bar, so we assumed he was getting some experience working with prisoners before he started working as an interrogator. He was absent-minded. He would often walk from the headquarters building at the time he was supposed to pick up the dishes or start the daily routine for the prisoners, and he would stop in front of our building, stand there as though he was thinking, pick his nose, feel in his pocket, then walk back to the headquarters building and return two minutes later with the key jingling in his hand. He walked pigeon toed and looked pretty stupid.

I was the senior ranking officer in the building. I passed on Denton's guidance and had church services and the pledge of allegiance to the flag, as he had done. Although I wasn't that keen on the idea, I suspected others derived some benefit from it. My leg was feeling better, so Quincy and I took turns during the day looking out into the courtyard through the cracks in the door. Just to watch the Vietnamese–the water girl, the food boy, and the guards–walk around doing their chores without suspecting that they were being observed was fascinating. The highlight was to see any prisoner who came in view. The door had no peephole, so I was able to sit on the floor and look out.

Our plan was that if ever a Vietnamese approached the door while I was looking out, I would alert Quincy, and he would rush over and help me get up and away from the door. It might have taken too much time for me to get up and away from the door by myself. One time when both of us were looking out the door, the turnkey approached from the side instead of the front, thereby giving us no warning and surprising the hell out of us. We both scrambled from the door as fast as we could, but fortunately he did not come in. Had he opened the door, I probably would have been caught. After the Turnkey left, we both had a good belly laugh about how strange we must have looked scrambling away.

The Barn was under renovation now. The Vietnamese also put a small brick building with a shower between the Garage and the Barn. The number of prisoners was increasing, and they needed more rooms and facilities. The Barn and the Garage were about twenty feet apart. The new bath facility was an absolute necessity because up to that time the only thing available was the Pig Sty. The room in the barn where Quincy, Norlan, Bob, and I had lived when we first moved to the Zoo had also been renovated. In place of the one large room with French doors and a window, there were now three small, windowless rooms with solid doors and wooden beds permanently attached in the room.

As an extrovert, Quincy had a real need to communicate. There were just so many things to talk about, however, so after living together for seven months, we ran out of things to say to each other. Consequently, Quincy was tapping to the guys in the rooms along side of us almost continuously, but tapping didn't satisfy him. One day, he remembered when Bob Peel had talked to Ron Storz through a bricked-up wall where a door had been. The wall in this room was different, but Quincy still wanted to try talking through it. Even though our door did not have a peephole that would allow the guard to quickly look in our room, I objected to Quincy trying to talk through the wall, because I was afraid the loud talking would bring the guards to our room and cause us trouble. Plus, I figured that the chance of talking through a wall one foot thick filled with bricks and concrete was almost zero.

But Quincy persisted. He tapped to Brudno and Keirn to hold their ears against the wall five feet from the front of the building and five and a half feet from the floor. Then Quincy cupped his hands to his mouth and spoke in a soft voice. Miraculously they heard him. Quincy improved on the idea by rolling his blanket into a donut that fit around his face and placing the donut against the wall. This muffled the sound considerably, so we were now able to talk to the guys next door almost as if they were sitting in our room. To my knowledge, Quincy was the first to come up with the idea of talking through the wall. In time, as the men in our building were moved throughout the camp, this method of communicating spread rapidly.

Jeffery and Reynolds, who were in our building, improved on Quincy's idea at a later time by using drinking cups against the wall both to talk into and to listen. This was a big improvement over the use of the rolled up blanket, which was hot in the summer. That was about as refined a system of communications as we ever had.

Most of the old guys knew my shoot-down date because it was an early one. So I was not all that surprised when on my first anniversary, April 3, 1966, Dave Wheat, who was solo in the end room of the Barn, about seventy-five feet away yelled out from his room during quite hour, "Congratulations to Ray Vohden on his first year." Half of the camp heard him, and he did it at a great risk to himself. As the years went by, the shoot-down anniversaries were no longer a big deal. When I had one year, though, some guys had only had a month, so they thought a year was a long time. After seven years, the guy who had one year less than me was just as much an old timer as I was.

In May, we noticed the Vietnamese were carrying boxes and furniture into the middle room of the Office. This room became a library. Several days later, the guard took us there. The room had four or five chairs and three tables with magazines, newspapers, and books on them. The newspapers were current and old editions of the *Vietnamese Courier*. Quincy and I had already read most of them, but there were also magazines from Russia, Vietnam, and China that we had not seen before. They were in English and had illustrated articles about each country. The Vietnamese magazine was mostly about the war and contained the same propaganda that we heard on the radio twice each day, but there were pictures. The Russian and Chinese magazines had nothing about the war and had some interesting articles about what was going on in those countries. There were also paperback books about Ho Chi Minh and other Vietnamese leaders, the French Indo Chinese war, the history of North and South Vietnam, and other books by communist western journalists. I knew these books were loaded with propaganda, but they also contained interesting geographic and historical material. I saw no harm in reading them, because I was going to follow the

Code of Conduct come hell or high water. At least it helped pass the time.

There were some prisoners who refused to go to the library and criticized those of us who did, because they felt brainwashing might occur, and the Vietnamese might consider those who read their books and magazines as sympathetic to their cause. This attitude annoyed me, because I knew I couldn't be brainwashed. I believed in the American way of life, its government, and its institutions, and no one could ever make me change those fundamental beliefs.

Some of the books, however, riled me. One in particular was called *Upstream Mecong* by Wilfred Burchett. He was an Australian journalist and communist sympathizer. The book was for the most part non-political. It dealt with the history, geography, and life in Cambodia. In one part of the book, though, he talked about a U.S. Ambassador to Cambodia who would go to gatherings at other third world country's embassies dressed in hunting clothes that he had not had time to change and accompanied by his hunting dogs. Burchett described the Ambassador as an unbearable, condescending slob and quite offensive to the people from the third world countries. Having seen and lived in Vietnam and having heard some stories about our State Department people, and having read a book popular at that time titled *The Ugly American*, I could see how this could possibly be true. But I figured it was probably B.S.

One day, we got word that some of the senior officers were being tortured, and one of them confessed that he had given the Vietnamese so much that he was contemplating suicide. It was a frightening harbinger of what was to come, as torture filtered down through the ranks.

In late May, Jeffery and Reynolds, moved out. They were either the most optimistic or the dumbest guys I had ever met. They were also big bettors. They were so sure that the war would be over soon that they were offering a bet of ten bottles of scotch to one that we would be home before the end of June. Believe it or not, they couldn't get anyone in the building to take the bet.

That night, we heard the door to their room open and the sounds of someone moving in. The next day, Pop Keirn and Al Brudno tried all day to contact the guy by tapping, but he wouldn't answer. It was not uncommon for a new guy who didn't know the tap code to refuse to communicate at first. After several days of this, Pop and Al became so frustrated that they took a gamble after the quiet hour began and talked under the door loud enough for the new guy to hear. The gamble paid off. In no time, we found out that he was Navy Lt., j.g., Brad Smith, shot down just a few days before. After months without contact from the outside world, we had a guy shot down just several days ago. We couldn't wait to hear what he had to say, but the first thing we got from him was, "When do you guys think we will get out of here?" If he didn't know the answer to that question and expected me to know after being in prison for a year then I figured I was in deeper trouble than I thought I was.

A couple of weeks earlier, I'd had a quiz after the last meal. The Dog told me I was going to meet with a western journalist, who just happened to be visiting Hanoi. I knew that other guys had met with visiting delegations, and that Cdr. Bill Franke had given us guidance in this case: "You must go where they take you, but it is what you say that counts." I had felt good that I had never been asked to go, because it made me feel like they didn't trust me to say what they wanted. But now they were putting me on the spot. Even though I had the guidance from Cdr. Franke, visiting any delegation was not good. Also Cdr. Denton had never given us guidance for this problem. No matter what I did or said, they would make propaganda out of it. I didn't want to go.

I told the Dog that I hadn't felt well and that I didn't want to go because it would violate my Code of Conduct. He said that I had no choice and that I must go. I refused again, and then he said if I didn't go, I would be punished. I still said no. We continued for another ten minutes. I kept saying no. He raised the threats higher and higher. He told me that there were others who disobeyed the camp regulations, and they had been severely punished. I knew this was true. He told me if I didn't go, they could make me do very bad, bad things. Finally I said to myself, is this worth being tortured over? Cdr. Franke had said it was O.K., and if I could tell the truth about my confinement, would that really be so bad? In addition, my leg was still in a cast more than a year after I had been shot down. I also felt curious about getting out of the camp. Life had been a bore. And if I told the truth, what harm could come of it? I finally said, "Yes, I'll go, but I will tell the truth." The Dog said O.K., and I went back to my room.

That evening, they came to get me. I was blindfolded, put in the back of a jeep, and handcuffed, and away we went. After ten minutes of driving through the city, we arrived at our destination. They took off the handcuffs and blindfold, and I climbed up three flights of stairs on my crutches in what looked like a public building. They put me into a small room off a rather large hallway. There was a full pack of cigarettes, matches, and a beer on the table. I didn't drink the beer, but I smoked three cigarettes as fast as I could and put another four or five in my shirt. In all, I got about ten cigarettes at that time.

A few minutes later, they took me to sort of a conference room. It had some soft chairs, and a number of Vietnamese officials were standing around. I could see a camera and a camera crew at the other end of the room, as well as bright lights around the room. A chubby, Caucasian man in his mid-fifties introduced himself. He said that he was a western journalist and that his name was Graham. He told me he was visiting Hanoi, and the Vietnamese had permitted him to interview several American pilots. He asked if I minded if he asked me a few questions? I said no. There was a relatively attractive woman in a red dress who sat on the sofa next to the Dog during the entire interview. The journalist introduced me to her as his wife. Although she was somewhat plump and about five years older than I was, she was the first Caucasian woman I had seen in more than a year, and she didn't look bad.

He asked me if I objected to recording the interview and I said yes. He said that's fine. Then he asked if I had any objection to having movies taken of the interview. A microphone wasn't going to be used, so I said I didn't mind. We both sat down next to each other on straight back chairs. He had a pencil and pad of paper, and as we talked he took notes. He asked me my name, questioned me about my family, and inquired a little about my shoot down and about the medical treatment and the food. I told him that the food was sufficient to sustain life. I told him about the cabbage and pumpkin soup, the pig fat and pretty much the way it was. This didn't bother the Vietnamese, because in their eyes the food they were giving me was pretty good. I told him that I was thankful that I had received some medical treatment, even though I felt it was very primitive compared to U.S. standards. Nevertheless, it was medical treatment. I told him that I was living with another man now but also how hard my first five months had been. There was no doubt that they would get some propaganda from this, but I was telling the truth to the questions he asked about me. And although my first five months in prison had been one continuous nightmare, I am not sure the Vietnamese intended it to be. Even though I had told them at every opportunity about my problems, I don't think they ever realized how bad my life had been that first five months.

I told him about the bad medical treatment, that weeks would go by before my bandages were changed, and after a year my leg still was not healed. In my naivete, I thought this journalist would print some of the truth, but I found out years later that there was an article in a French and Arabian magazine about the interview, and he had written only the things that were favorable to the Vietnamese. He also asked me my views on the war, and I told him that I believed what the U.S. Government was doing was right, and that I supported President Johnson a hundred percent.

At the conclusion of the interview, he asked me if I thought I was a war criminal and explained to me why the Vietnamese thought I was one. I said, "No, I do not believe that I am a war criminal." After the interview was over, I left the room and they put me in a bathroom. It was the first time in Vietnam that I saw a western toilet with a flush bowl. It was nice to see something like that again. I found out later that Cdr. Denton and Major Guarino had met with the same guy around the same time, and that Cdr. Denton had blinked torture with Morse code by opening and closing his eyes during the interview. Guarino said he had been tortured before his interview.

I knew the policy was NO INTERVIEWS, but I questioned the value of that policy. Many men went to interviews and answered the questions about food and medical treatment truthfully and were even rude to the interviewers. Of course, they were called "the blackest of all criminals" and received few packages and letters from then on. If the POW said that he had been tortured, the interview might have ended right there. They might have beat the hell out of him, but they would probably never take him to another interview.

The next day, Dum Dum brought two bananas and a few pieces of candy. I offered half of them to Quincy, but he was indignant that I had gone to the interview, so he refused them. Sometime

139

later while still in prison, I happened to see a picture of "Graham," the journalist with whom I had had the interview. It was Wilfred Burchett.

In 1978, five years after I was released from Vietnam and back on full duty in the Pentagon, I read in a newspaper that Wilfred Burchett would be giving a talk open to the public at a particular location in Washington, D.C. on such and such a night. He would then be traveling throughout the country for the next month, lecturing at a number of prominent universities. After I almost threw up, I regained my composure. I decided to go to the lecture with a friend to listen to him and see if he was really the same guy I had met in Vietnam. He was the same guy. Within minutes of his beginning to speak, I could see that he was espousing the communist doctrine and way of life to the American public, right in the middle of the capital city of the country where freedom had developed into the greatest democracy in the history of mankind. It was hard to believe that our government would allow such a man to enter this country. Maj. Guarino and Cdr. Denton both said they were tortured to meet him, and his Australian passport had been revoked because he was named as K.G.B. agent in sworn testimony. Obviously, the Carter Administration did not agree with me. If American servicemen knew that if they ever became a prisoner of war, they could be tortured to meet with Wilfred Burchett, and that this guy could then visit their home town, I'm not sure how many guys would consider making the service a career.

And to add insult to injury, Burchett was not only a personal friend of Harrison Salisbury, but he also visited Henry Kissinger in the West Wing of the White House in mid-October 1971. Moreover, President Richard Nixon shook Burchett's hand when Chou En-lai introduced him to Mr. Nixon on one of Nixon's trips to China. Mr. Burchett got around.

Meanwhile, back at the Zoo. The food boy, or Billy the Kid, must have been no more than fourteen years old when he started carrying the food from the kitchen and dishing it out on the food table in front of each building. He was rather tall for his age, but his high-pitched voice was a dead giveaway of his youth. His loud soprano voice could be heard around the camp as he played with the water girl or just went about his business. One Sunday morning, we heard the loud yelping of a puppy. We looked out the crack and saw Billy playing with a puppy that was on a primitive leash. The leash was about five feet long. Billy would grab one end of the leash and swing the leash in a circle while the other end of the leash was tied around the puppy's neck. The puppy yelped so loud he couldn't possibly have been enjoying it. After about five minutes of swinging the puppy in a circle, Billy made one last hard swing and let go of the leash. The dog sailed through the air and landed on its back about thirty feet away. Billy went about his business, and the puppy shut up.

Billy grew up in the Zoo. One day in the late 1968 or early 1969, we saw him dressed in an army uniform, with the rank of private, and carrying a gun. He had been promoted from food boy to soldier who guarded the prison's buildings. When we congratulated him on his promotion, we could tell he felt very proud of himself.

In the early part of June 1966, we learned that the camp officials were trying to force all the POWs in the camp to write their biographies. Two men in our building were told they had to write their biographies. One of the guys had painful boils on his neck and needed medical attention. After many threats of torture and the withholding of medical treatment, they both wrote their biographies.

When the Vietnamese were after something from one side of the camp, it was only a matter of time before the other side of the

141

camp would be under the gun. Several days later, I went to quiz, and Dum Dum insisted that I had to write my biography. I refused. After some threats, he just let me sit on the stool for an hour and then sent me back to my room. I was somewhat relieved and hoped that maybe he would let me alone. But no such luck. I went back to quiz again the next day. There were more threats. I still refused. Then he said I would be punished. I had to stand in the corner of the room on my crutches for a couple of hours, but I still refused. I returned to my room just before mealtime but not before being sternly warned that if I continued my bad attitude and reactionary behavior, I was going to be in a lot of trouble. I should think very carefully about what he said when I went back to my room.

The next day I went to quiz early in the morning. Dum Dum asked me to write. I said no. There were more threats, and finally he made me stand in a corner. I stood there through the first meal, and just before the second meal he asked if I would write again. I said no. He said if I didn't write tomorrow, he couldn't be responsible for what happened.

I went back to my room. My leg had swollen up inside the cast like a balloon and was throbbing. My armpits were raw from the crutches rubbing against them, and I was totally exhausted from standing on them all day. The throbbing in my leg didn't stop until just before I got up in the morning. I'd had a bad night's sleep. My will to resist was just not that great now. I knew it was a violation of the Code of Conduct to write anything, but all things considered, I would write as little as possible and lie like a dog. The next morning I went to quiz and, after standing on my crutches for some hours, I agreed to write. I wrote about one page of B.S., and that apparently satisfied Dum Dum. I then went back to my room.

When I came back to the room and told Quincy, he was quite upset at what I had done. He thought I should not have written unless I was tortured. I did not feel that what I wrote was worth losing my leg over. There was no guarantee that the torture would screw up my leg, but there was that possibility. I told him I was not up to taking torture, and with my leg not healed, I was still weak. But Quincy made a big deal over it. He said he didn't want to live with me anymore. We did not talk for three days. He sang "God Bless America" and the "National Anthem" and acted like a super patriot. He hoped the guards would move him out of our room to get away from me. There were hard feelings between us now, and if the tension relaxed even for a minute, in no time we would be arguing over the smallest things again.

But even though Quincy and I fought like dogs, there was no question about our unity in being loyal to our country, and we were unified in our resistance against the Vietnamese. We disdained them and the treatment we received. There was, however, an unspoken competition among the prisoners about who was the toughest and who could take the most torture. Violating the Code of Conduct was serious and potentially could have not only ruined a guy's career but also landed him in jail when he was released. There were a few guys who were never tortured or forced to write a word.

Several days later Quincy went to quiz. He had three quizzes just like mine had been. On the third day while Quincy was at quiz, I went to wash alone. When I returned, all of Quincy's gear was gone, and he had moved. I was back in solitary again. But sometimes solitary confinement wasn't all that bad.

CHAPTER 12 - BOMBING OF HANOI

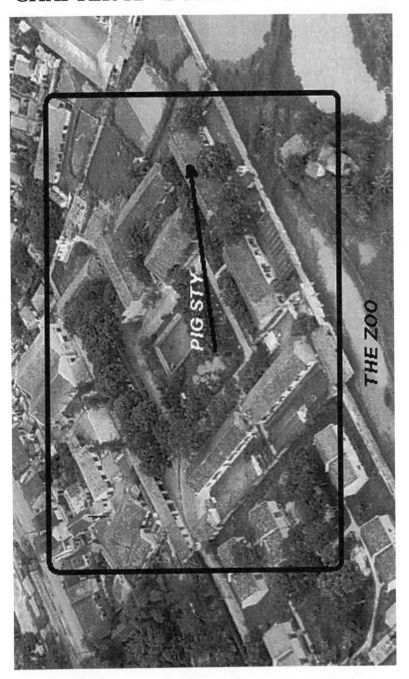

THE ZOO

PIG STY

PIG STY

Early June 1966 – Early August 1966. In early June, I moved to the middle room in the Barn. Ron Storz had lived in the same room when the four of us moved next to him in November of 1965. An open porch had been in front of the room then, but it was enclosed now. Three steps led up from the ground to the porch and three more steps to my room. The windows had been bricked up, but the back wall had two small vents. Before the day was over, I found out that I was the senior ranking officer in the building, so I passed on all the previous guidance I had received.

The next day, I learned that two rooms down from me was a man from my ship who had recently been shot down. I set up a time to tap directly with him, because I did not want to bother the men in the two rooms in between by boring them with the info passed between us. I wasn't sure that we could hear each other tap, because our rooms were fairly far apart, but because we had a common back wall, I hoped we could pull it off. Even though we traded some information, the whole operation did not work well, because we were just too far away, and the acoustics of the wall did not permit it. I found out, however, that about eighteen guys had been shot down from my air wing on the U.S.S. Hancock. Some good friends had been killed. I had mixed emotions. Although I felt sad that they had died, it made my plight seem a little less difficult, because even though my existence was horrible, I was still alive and had hope that someday life would be better.

In April, we were hearing more and more about the War Crimes Tribunal being held by the peace activist and philosopher Bertrand Russell. The purpose of the tribunal was to evaluate and investigate American foreign policy and intervention in Vietnam. The tribunal had no power to impose sanctions or anything. During this same period, the Vietnamese were probably considering trying us prisoners for war crimes. The Vietnamese in their daily camp broadcasts and at quiz unequivocally maintained that we were war criminals and told us that we might someday be tried for our crimes against the Vietnamese people. They made frequent reference to Bertrand Russell as one of the greatest philosophers in the western world and used his words and those from the tribunal to try to persuade us that we were indeed war criminals. The thought that they might try us became a reality when in June or July 1966 they started a camp-wide effort to get everyone to admit to being a war criminal.

Additionally, they read anti-war statements by Senators William Fulbright, Ernest Gruening, and Wayne Morse and other prominent American activists like Dr. Benjamin Spock. I was beginning to wonder what was going on with the war. I had read some of Bertrand Russell's work when I was in college and knew he was a prominent and internationally known philosopher. I had read about Fulbright and Morse when I was in college and had admired them. But now, how could they be so wrong? I was starting to have some doubts about the war. Our captors' threats about us being tried as war criminals always ended by their saying that if we were not tried, it was only because of the humane and lenient policy of their leader, Ho Chi Minh, and the Vietnamese people. I could see that the war was complicated. The reason we were fighting the war was to stop the advance of Communism, and the reason they were fighting the war was to unify the country and gain its independence. If both sides had realized this early on, peace might have come sooner.

In late June 1966, another reshuffling of the prisoners took place. I moved into the Pig Sty. It was an improvement over some of the other rooms I had been in. It had air vents high up on the front wall, a French door, and shutters on the window. The window had bars on it, and the side of the building I was on faced the perimeter wall of the prison. The Vietnamese weren't concerned about us looking out the crack of the door or the shutters of the window, because there was nothing to see.

Bob and Norlan were back together again in the room behind me. Capt. Pop Keirn and his new roommate, Red Berg, lived in the other room next to me. There were a total of twelve rooms in the Pig Sty. One was the washroom, and the other rooms were for prisoners. There was a Navy commander who lived solo in the building, but we never heard much from him. He did not assume command as Denton had done, but at that time we didn't have any great need for leadership.

The Vietnamese kept one of the two rooms adjacent to the washroom vacant and put me in the other one probably because they figured that my being on crutches would make it hard for me to communicate. At that time, the men in the Office and the Pool Hall were using the Pig Sty washroom throughout the day, and I would always try to communicate with them. In the hot summer, any water on the body was important, so unless there was some earthshaking news, they washed first and then, if they had time, they communicated. In addition, the guards watched carefully and checked frequently to see that they weren't communicating with me. It was no fun communicating, because I had to stand on the side of the room opposite my bed on crutches, and if the shutter was opened quickly I could easily be caught.

We also communicated with the Pool Hall when men from our building went to one of the rooms there that the Vietnamese had set up as another library. This was another example of how quixotic the Vietnamese were. Using one washroom for three buildings was a necessity, and the men were in the washroom for short periods of time, thereby limiting communications. But taking men from our building and letting them sit in the library for as long as an hour at a time was not an ideal way to stop communications.

When I communicated with the guys in the washroom, the room next to me kept watch for guards. But if I received a signal from the bath area that things really looked clear, I would move to the front of my room by the window, and the guys in the shower would stand by the their window, and we would talk very softly. One day, Marine Capt. Harley Chapman and Air Force Capt. Bruce Seeber, were trying to contact me with an urgent message. I tried to get Pop Keirn and Red Berg to clear for me, but they were out somewhere that morning. There hadn't been any news from the other buildings for several days. I went to the front of the room and looked out through the shutters, and I could tell that no one was right in front of the window. I paused for a minute while I listened carefully, and when I didn't hear anything, I moved to the side wall and gave them the clear signal. They started to tap to me. Because time was short, and they had so much news, they wanted to talk outside the window. I didn't have clearance to tap, let alone talk, but I decided to take a gamble. I was as interested in what they had as they were in passing the news to me. I gave the clear signal and they started to talk. I stood by my window and they stood by their window in the bath, and they passed the news that they had. They gave me the names of some new shoot-downs and new lineups in other buildings. Then they had some questions for me. I had been talking for about thirty seconds, when suddenly the shutter opened and I was face to face with the guard. I had been caught in the act. The guard had a look of great satisfaction. He had caught me red-handed, and I could see he was quite proud of himself. He yelled at me in Vietnamese and pointed his finger to his mouth. He yelled some more and then left.

Ten minutes later, Spot came to my room and asked me if had been talking to the people in the next room. I knew it was against command policy to admit communicating, but I had been caught outright. I asked myself what good could be accomplished in denying that I had been communicating. So I said, "Yes." I told him I was talking out the window because I was lonely living by myself. He said, "You will be punished." He told me to stand in one of the corners of the room with my face to the wall. Then he left. I had to stand on my crutches for hours and did not get any food. Standing on crutches with only one leg is not the end of the world, but after a few hours my leg became painful. I knew I could take a chance and sit down, but I also knew that the shutter was open, and I could easily be caught. No telling what the Vietnamese might do then. I could hear the guard come to the window to check on me every once in a while. I was in deep enough trouble already and knew they had tortured guys for communicating. So even though my left leg and shoulders ached beyond belief, I hung in there until several hours after the last meal of the day, when the guard finally told me I could sit down. This was not one of my better days.

Several days later, I had a quiz with the Rabbit, and he was in a nasty mood. He raised hell about my communicating and made all kinds of threats about what would happen if I did it again. He wanted to know what we talked about. I told him that it was just about our families and that the only reason I talked was because I was lonely from being solo again. He told me I had a very bad attitude and that as punishment I would never get another roommate. I went back to my room feeling very relieved. Not having a roommate was far easier than standing on crutches for hours on end.

The afternoon of 29 June 1966, the air alert sounded halfway through the quiet hour. We heard the sounds of SAMs (surface-to-air missiles) being fired, the thundering drone of aircraft approaching the city, and then the sounds of aircraft rolling in and pulling off the target. We could also hear the triple A and loud explosions of bombs falling not too far off. It was sometimes impossible to tell whether the explosion was from a bomb, triple A or a SAM. I squatted on the floor in the front of the room with my back to the wall in case debris came through the window. I heard a continuous deafening noise coming from every direction. The building was shaking so much from the concussion of the explosions that large pieces of plaster fell off of the ceiling and walls. The raid lasted for about ten minutes, and then the drone of the aircraft faded, and the SAMS and triple A stopped. It was quiet now just like any other quiet hour, but in contrast to what the noise had been just a few minutes ago, the quietness was unreal. It was so quiet I could hear the silence.

Fifteen minutes later, I heard the drone of aircraft approaching Hanoi again, then the SAMS and triple A being fired. A minute later, I heard the sound and felt the concussion of the bombs exploding. Ten minutes passed, and then silence fell again. There was a large wave of aircraft every ten minutes for about one hour. It sounded to me like the whole city was being bombed, and although I was somewhat frightened by the whole ordeal, the bombing really made me feel good. I was excited because we were finally escalating the bombing to Hanoi. I said to myself that this would fix the Rabbit and Spot. It was a just and fitting punishment for their being mean to me. The bombing had given me double satisfaction.

The next day, the same thing happened again. Another big raid. We plastered the living hell out of them. The building shook, and it was another frightening experience, but we were all happy and excited again. The camp officials told us that we had to take shelter under our beds from now on during the air raid alerts. Within the next month, they dug numerous holes around the camp, about three feet in diameter and four feet deep. They put a concrete tube inside each hole. We were told that these were air raid shelters, but the holes were nearly always filled with water, and even when they were dry, the Vietnamese never used them.

I was quite surprised to hear the Voice of Vietnam on the radio that night. The announcers ranted about the escalation of the war to Hanoi and how this would make the iron will of the Vietnamese even greater than before. They said that the U.S. had bombed hospitals and schools and that our bombs had killed many women, children, and old people. They bragged that they had shot down fifteen or twenty aircraft and captured many American pilots, one of whom was Air Force Capt. Murphy Neil Jones. They made a big deal about him on the radio, and we found out later that they had paraded him through the streets of Hanoi. In time, we heard that he had become so famous that large colored pictures of his being captured were being sold to anyone who would buy them in Hong Kong.

The next day, we were given rice instead of bread. We had had bread with our meal every day up to that time. For the next two and a half years we ate cold, warm, or hot rice with the carcasses of weevils, pebbles, sticks, stones, and even rat feces now and then. But whatever was in it, we ate it. And there were many, many times when I was so hungry that it really tasted good.

Later, we found out that the target had been the oil refinery in Hanoi. We also heard that the Air Force major who had led the attack had been bagged. He had been an ace in the Korean war and had received a great deal of publicity about his role on the mission, even getting his picture on the cover of some prominent American news magazines. Three years later, he would be sitting in a room next to me.

The camp authorities and other Vietnamese obviously were unhappy over the bombing of Hanoi, but they restrained themselves from any overt appearance of hostility toward us. We continued to get the Voice of Vietnam on the radio every day, and along with daily condemnations of the U.S. escalation of the war, we were hearing more and more about how we were war criminals and about the Bertrand Russell War Crimes Tribunal. The tribunal's conclusions seemed to be the likely foundation on which the Vietnamese would rely if and when they tried us. They were telling us every day that we were criminals and that we should see the error of our ways, confess our crimes, and ask for forgiveness from the Vietnamese people.

One late afternoon in early July, a guard came into my room and, without saying a word, took a set of my long pants and long shirt. A couple of hours later, I could hear the doors opening and closing throughout the building, and then they stopped. I knew something was up but figured it was not a good idea to get caught tapping at this time. I went to sleep as usual, but later that night I awoke when I heard the doors to the building opening and closing again. I went to sleep again. Early the next morning, Norlan tapped to me that Bob Peel and all the other well prisoners wearing their prison garb had been blindfolded and taken in trucks to downtown Hanoi. They got off the trucks, were handcuffed in pairs, ordered to look straight ahead, and about fifty guys were marched two by two about a mile through the streets of Hanoi. The streets were lined with thousands upon thousands of yelling, jeering, and frenzied Vietnamese. The cadres who were using loudspeakers were inciting the mobs, who were spitting on the prisoners and throwing sticks and stones at them. At times, the crowd got so close that they were hitting some prisoners with their fists and hands. Some prisoners ended up with black eyes, broken noses, and an assortment of other injuries. They ended up walking to a large stadium, then returned in trucks to the prisons they came from. This was one of the few times that I was glad I had a broken leg and didn't have to participate in the festivities. The only saving grace from all of this was that some of the prisoners got to see each other for the first time in months or more.

That same night, some men were taken to quiz when they returned to their camps, and the Vietnamese demanded that they write confessions for their crimes against the Vietnamese people and condemnations of the cruel and inhuman U.S. imperialist, President Johnson. When they refused, some were chained to trees and beaten with fists and sticks in their kidneys and stomachs and other parts of their bodies. Many guys were tortured and wrote their confessions that night.

For the next week, things were relatively calm for me. I had two quizzes with Spot and he tried hard to convince me to write my confession. He said many other prisoners had already seen the light and confessed their crimes against the Vietnamese people and had asked them for forgiveness for what they had done. I politely told him I couldn't do that, because I was not a criminal, and I had not committed crimes against anyone.

In the middle of July, I moved back to the Pool Hall in room 4 with Quincy. It was the same sized room as the one we had lived in before, and it had a window with bars and a shutter on it. The Vietnamese had built a ten-foot-high brick wall around the building, so we were unable to see the other buildings or any activity in the center of the camp. Only half of the rooms in our building were occupied. The room we were in wasn't too bad, and Quincy and I were getting along quite well again. He told me he had written his biography but gave no details. Even the weather for that time of the year wasn't too bad. The Vietnamese had replaced the white light in front of the building with a soft yellowish-orange light bulb, which created a relaxed and soothing atmosphere around the building and our room.

For the next three months, there were so many moves in the camp that it was impossible to keep track of where most of the men were. The bombing of Hanoi stirred the Vietnamese up as if they had stepped on a hornets' nest. In the middle of that first night in the Pool Hall, we were awakened by the sound of a truck driving into the courtyard. It stopped in front of our building, and some guys got out. We heard a door open and close in the back of the building. Then two guards came to our room and gave us the signal that we were going to move. We were blindfolded and taken to a jeep. After about a twenty-minute ride, we arrived back at the Hanoi Hilton. They let us out of the jeep in the middle of the courtyard that I had last seen when I washed under a faucet for the first time.

They took my blindfold off in the jeep, and I could see that some of the courtyard had changed quite a bit in the year since I had left. The French doors on the rooms where I had lived had been replaced by solid metal doors. It was obvious that they were designed to keep prisoners. The grapevine that used to spread over the courtyard patio in front of Heartbreak had been cut down, and the charm and quaintness was gone, replaced by a cold, austere, almost dungeon-like atmosphere. The guard told us to move straight ahead. We walked toward the Heartbreak area and then entered a passage about twenty-five feet long that went through a building and was big enough for a small vehicle to pass through. Halfway through the passage, we came to a short stairway, which led to an open hall, and the guard opened the door to our new room. We were in Heartbreak.

We did not unpack completely because of the unusual circumstances of the move. We put our straw mats on the beds and put up our mosquito nets. We talked about why we were there and wondered what was going to happen next. We suspected that it was our turn to be worked over. But my leg was still in a cast, and

Quincy's leg still wasn't well, so we were hoping they would have mercy on us and not force us to write confessions. As I lay on my mat trying to sleep, I could hear the church bells off in the distance sound out the hour, and it brought back memories of when I had lived there a year before.

Later that night we heard what sounded like a guy being brought in to one of the other Heartbreak cells. He was moaning and sounded delirious. He called weakly for help several times, and the Vietnamese came, but by daybreak he was quiet. The Vietnamese came to his room later that morning, and one guy looking under the crack of his door saw the Vietnamese carry him out on a stretcher with a blanket over him. We figured that he had probably died, but because we never found out who he was, we were never sure. We did not sleep very much that night.

Early the next morning the guard brought us our cigarettes. As soon as we finished our cigarettes, Quincy gave a super sophisticated cough that sounded like he coughed up a mouth full of phlegm from the bottom of his lungs and that any American pilot would recognize immediately as an indication that we were ready to make contact. Less than ten seconds later, we heard the same cough come from one of the other cells. As we were in the cell next to the hallway entrance, Quincy got down on his knees and looked under the door so he could see if any Vietnamese were about to enter the Heartbreak passage. When the coast was clear, he whispered softly, "This is Vohden and Collins. Who else is here?"

Even though the recent climate throughout the camp had been one of threats and gloom, neither Quincy nor I had been tortured for the specific purpose of forcing us to do something against our will. We had been there longer than most guys and pretty much knew what was going on, so we weren't afraid to gamble on communicating. Down the hall a guy whispered, "This is Jerry Coffee."

Although we had heard of him, we had never been in contact with him, but we knew that he had been in the system long enough to know what was going on. Jerry had been in Heartbreak about a week and had been under continuous pressure. They had cut his food and water ration by about a half.

It was strange the way the Vietnamese operated. They didn't use the same method of torture for everyone. With some guys, they didn't fool around, they started right off with maximum torture. With other guys, they tried starvation. With prisoners like Quincy and me, who were injured, they used a gradual escalation of pressure. In most cases, they tried to get what they wanted with the minimum amount of torture. Although withholding food had been used from time to time, it was still an uncommon means of putting pressure on a guy, and after the end of 1966, I rarely ever heard of it being used as a way to force men to do things against their will. Maybe they found this method ineffective, or it was being used only in other camps, and I had not heard about it.

Jerry said he was weak but in good spirits. He hadn't given up yet, but he suspected they would start working on him soon. He said that some of the other cells were occupied but that none of the guys would communicate with him. With Quincy clearing and the new guys hearing Quincy and Jerry talk, they all quickly identified themselves. Jerry was closer to the new guys, so he filled them in on what was going on. He did a good job, passed out the standard guidance, and gave words of encouragement to the new men. We also got the names of four or five more new guys.

We went through the day without any unusual incidents but continued to speculate about what was in store for us. That evening, the guard came to our room and gave us the roll-up signal. We left the room, got back into the jeep, and returned to the same room we had left back at the Zoo. As bad as that room had been, we were both relieved to be back again. The Vietnamese apparently had had something planned for us at the Hilton but changed their minds. After we unpacked our gear and settled down, we tapped to the back room and found out that a number of POWs had been worked over the night before at the Hilton. They had written their confessions and various other propaganda statements that the Vietnamese wanted. We were told that Cdr. Denton had been tortured again in May or June and had also written a confession.

Prior to the bombing of Hanoi on June 29, 1966, I had not heard of very many instances of torture. Communications were poor back in those days and they were not great now. However, as time went by, we got word that a few of the most junior guys had been tortured as far back as October 1965. I wondered why the Vietnamese started the torture and rough stuff with the most junior men, while holding off on the more senior men until later. But it was almost impossible to figure out why the Vietnamese did what they did.

We resumed our normal daily routine. We got our daily bath and cigarettes as usual. Quincy started to smoke again, so I no longer got to smoke his ration of cigarettes. We also began to get a new kind of a mushy food. We found out that it was made of small, unripe bananas that had been cut up in one inch pieces with the peels still on and then cooked. There was always plenty of it to eat, and it was good because it filled the hole real well.

One afternoon, Quincy heard a commotion out in the courtyard, and his curiosity got the better of him. He climbed up on the windowsill, so he could look through the vent on the front wall. Suddenly, several bricks gave way under his foot. He did not slip or fall, but the bricks and a few pieces of concrete fell on the floor, and one of the bars in the window came loose. Quincy got down as fast as he could, but now we were in deep trouble. We tried to put the bricks and fallen pieces of mortar back in place, but there was no way to keep the Vietnamese from knowing what had happened. After some thought, we agreed that the best thing to do was to tell them about the damage. We made up a story that Quincy was exercising in the room and suddenly got a bad pain in his back, and when he grabbed for the bar in window to support himself, it broke. We yelled, "*bao cao,*" and when the guard came we asked for an English-speaking officer. When we told the officer what had happened, he was quite upset, but finally he bought our story and let us off the hook. That was a close one.

Several days later, Quincy was tapping to Capt. Bob Purcell who was in the library in the next room. Quincy got caught red-handed, when the guard opened the shutter by surprise. Purcell was immediately taken back to his room. Five minutes later, the guard opened our door and accused Quincy of communicating. Then the turnkey Happy came in the room accused Quincy of tapping. Ten minutes after Happy left, the guard came back into the room again while two other guards watched outside. The guard, who was the same man who had earlier pulled on Quincy's ear to make him bow, had a gun that was almost the same height as he was. He indicated again that he knew Quincy had been communicating. We were both standing at attention in the center of the room, and the little guy walked in front of Quincy and threw a punch from the bottom of the floor that landed on Quincy's chest and knocked him clear across the room. Then the guard shook his finger at Quincy and indicated that he was to get up. Quincy got up and stood where he was before. As the little guy reeled back to hit Quincy again, Quincy held up his hands in defense. The guard shook his finger at Quincy and motioned to him to put his hands down. Quincy dropped his hands. The guard punched Quincy another four or five times. Although he caught Quincy by surprise on the first swing, the rest of the punches did not do any real damage, because the guy was so small. Nevertheless, it was no fun for Quincy. He was a hell raiser, and he paid the price.

The Vietnamese continued their push for our confessions. Quincy and I had at least four or five more quizzes with Spot, where he threatened us with all kinds of bad things if we did not confess. We were getting a full dose of propaganda for several hours in the morning and afternoon on the camp radio in addition to the Voice of Vietnam and almost every day we heard a tape recording of another prisoner confessing his crimes and condemning the U.S. Imperialist war of Aggression. We heard about Bertrand Russell and his War Crimes Tribunal daily and listened to what were alleged to be Risner's and Denton's confessions several times a week.

At the end of July, we had an outstanding second meal of the day, including a few small pieces of meat and a good-sized chunk of pineapple, which was the first pineapple I had ever had in Vietnam. It was ripe to perfection and absolutely delicious. Spot came by while we were eating and asked us how we liked the food. We told him, "O.K." Obviously the good meal had been planned, and Spot was trying to make some political hay out of it. He told us about the lenient and humane policy of the Vietnamese people and all about the good treatment we were getting. After the big pitch by Spot we figured something was up. Early the next morning, Quincy and I moved to room 5 of the Pig Sty. That night another four or five guys were moved into the Pig Sty. We got an extra heavy dose of propaganda on the radio that afternoon and night, but other than that, things were the same.

In early August, the guard came to our room at 0830 and gave me the roll-up sign. I was moved solo into the library room in the Pool Hall. It was obvious that this was only a temporary holding place, so I did not unpack my gear. I had three quizzes that day. The first was with Spot in the morning. He told me that I must write my confession and apologize for my criminal acts and that many others had seen the light and come over to the people's side. I politely said no. He sent me back to my room. After quiet hour I went back for another quiz. There was more of the same propaganda but many more threats. He said if I did not confess, I would be tried as a war criminal and when convicted, I would never be able to return home to my family even if the war ended. He explained in some detail again the basis for declaring me a war criminal in that we were fighting in an undeclared war. I still said no. He sent me back to my room. Early in the evening, I went to a third quiz. This time it was with Dum Dum. There were more threats. I said no again. He said, "We will see," and sent me back to my room.

I still hadn't unpacked my bedroll, because there were books on the beds, but as it was getting to be evening now, I figured that this was where I was going to spend the night. Just as I began to unpack the bedroll, the guard came and indicated I was to move again. It was all I could do to get my stretched right arm around the bedroll and still be able to grasp the handle of the crutch. I moved to the other side of the camp to room 3 of the Barn. Life was filled with a continuous atmosphere of fear and terror. You never knew when you would be asked to do something that was bad. You had to refuse and suffer the consequences.

CHAPTER 13 - CONFESSION

GATE HOUSE

PHOTO PROVIDED BY CAPT. JAMES F. BELL. HE WAS ALSO AN OCCUPANT OF THIS BUILDING.

GATE HOUSE

August 1966 – September 1966. As I went into my new room, I made note of how the door on the peephole opened, and I put my gear on the side of the room where it would take the guard longer to catch me tapping when he used the peephole. I did not want to be caught communicating now. I would be at risk if I sat on the empty bed on the other side of the room and communicated, because even if I knew the guard was coming, I would have a hard time moving quickly to the bed where all my gear was. If the guard caught me on the empty bed, he could easily accuse me of communicating. Of course, I had an alibi for why I was there, but there was no guarantee they would believe that I was trying to kill a cockroach.

After I arranged my gear and hung the mosquito net, I noticed that the Vietnamese had removed the light bulb. Now I was going to be in the dark at night. They weren't worried about me escaping. I had become accustomed to having the light on all night, and I would have a hard time getting to the *bo* without it. Plus, psychologically I felt the way I had when I was sent to my room with the light turned off for being a bad boy.

The next morning, I awoke at the normal time and wondered what the day would bring. Around 0800, I heard the peepholes in the other rooms being opened and closed. I knew the guard was passing out the daily ration of cigarettes. I waited and waited for my peephole to open. It didn't. I sure could have used a cigarette. I was really hooked on them. Three a day made my existence a little more bearable. Maybe he had just forgotten and would bring them later. During the morning, I heard the men from the other rooms going out to bathe. I waited for my turn so I could ask the guard what happened to my cigarettes.

Around 1030, the turnkey opened the door. I had seen him around, but he had never worked a building I lived in before. He was known as Pierre because he looked like a dapper Frenchman. I bowed and then looked at him. He just glared back at me. I made a smoking motion with my hand, as if to ask for my cigarettes. He looked at me for a few more seconds, then left and slammed the door. No bath and no cigarettes this morning. I thought maybe he would bring some cigarettes in the afternoon, and perhaps I'd get a bath later in the day. In time, I would learn that because I had not confessed, he was going to make my life miserable, and because I knew that he enjoyed it, I called him Scum.

The food was normally dished up on a table in front of the building as much as half an hour before the guard let the rooms out one by one to pick up their rations. In the winter, the food would frequently cool off by the time it was picked up, and in the summer, the soup would stay very hot. At around 1100, Scum opened my door and motioned for me to pick up my food. I walked out to the food table on crutches, picked up a side plate and a piece of bread, brought it back to the room, and then returned to pick up the bowl of soup. As I walked slowly on crutches back to my room, Scum appeared to be annoyed because it had taken me so long to get the food. He said a few words in Vietnamese as he slammed the door. This guy was going to be a pain in the ass.

During quiet hour of the first day, I found out that Art Cormier was in one of the rooms next to me. He was an Air Force sergeant and a medic on a rescue helicopter. I did not tap with him very much, because he was on the dangerous side of the room. He was also being pressed for his confession, and because he was an old timer, he did not have much news that was worth being punished for. After about fifteen minutes of tapping, we were both up to speed on current events.

When I tried tapping the other wall, I found out that Capt. A.J. Myers had moved into that room in the morning. He had been shot down on 1 June 1966 and had an injured ankle but was able to get around without crutches. Because he had been shot down so recently, he had some interesting news from the outside world for me. But he neither tapped well nor understood my tapping well, so there wasn't a whole lot of news passed. When I tried to contact him the next day during quiet hour, there was no answer. I found out later that he had moved that morning.

It didn't take very long to settle into the routine. I knew that I wouldn't get any cigarettes, but I still waited for the turnkey to bring them every morning. Even the relief turnkeys forgot my cigarettes. Scum made me sweep the floor of my room twice a week with a broom that had no handle. Standing on one leg, holding on to one crutch while bending over and sweeping with the other hand was a real back breaker, which Scum enjoyed watching. I was allowed to bathe once every two weeks now instead of every day. I had to empty the *bo* every two or three days when it was full, which required a real balancing act, negotiating the stairs on crutches while carrying the pail. The room was hot day and night. Without the daily bath, the dust and dirt clung to my sweaty body and made me feel grimy and sticky all over. At mealtime, Scum was becoming more and more annoyed because it was taking so long for me to carry my food from the table on the porch back to my room. After three or four days of waiting impatiently and yelling at me, Scum decided that either he or the food girl would pass the food to me through the peephole right after it was dished up on the porch. The soup bowl was so hot that it would burn my fingers before I could get it to the floor, let alone to my bed where it could be eaten.

Several weeks after I moved into the room, I had another quiz with Dum Dum, and he asked me to write my confession. He gave me nine yards about why I had to confess and accompanying threats of what would happen if I didn't. I refused and was sent back to my room. I had a feeling that they did not want to resort to using the more violent forms of torture on permanently injured prisoners. I had not heard of any wounded prisoners being tortured up to that time, but I suspected they might have already tortured wounded some men when they were shot down to get military information. I don't think they wanted to do it, because it would violate their policy of lenient and humane treatment. Although by our standards, the treatment wasn't even close to what would normally be considered as humane by western standards, I thought that the Vietnamese honestly believed the treatment we were receiving was lenient and humane. It was just a matter of which side of the war you were on.

One afternoon during quiet hour, another man moved into one of the rooms next to me. After the evening meal, I tried to contact him by tapping the old shave and a haircut routine, but he did not answer. The next morning, I noticed Scum gave him cigarettes and he got a bath. I figured he was a new guy and didn't know the tap code or was afraid to tap. Every day at the start of quiet hour, I sat on my bed and tapped on the wall. One tap, then two taps, then three taps, then four taps, all the way to twenty-six taps. I hoped that he would understand that I was substituting numbers for the place of the letters in the alphabet. In other words, if I wanted to tap my name, I would tap eighteen times for an R, one tap for an A, and twenty-five taps for a Y. This method of tapping was very slow, but I hoped that once we made contact I could teach him the much faster Air Force Survival School tap code. I tapped one tap, then two taps, then three taps, all the way to twenty-six over and over again. I did this for at least a half hour every day but never got a response. When I finally finished each time, I was so frustrated that I would bang on the wall with my fists as hard as I could. Here was another American pilot probably loaded with all kinds of news from the outside world and me not having had any news for months now. I said to myself that if I ever met that guy I'd kill him. Each morning as he went to bathe, I got a look at him through a crack in the door, so even though I did not know his name, I knew what he looked like. After more than two weeks of this, I moved to a new room.

This was not the first time I had observed a POW through a crack and thought poorly of him. Although I never fought the issue of bowing, whenever Norlan, Bob, Quincy, or I bowed, it was the absolute minimum bow we could get away with. Many times I only made the slightest nod of my head. One day, when Quincy and I were in the Garage, we were looking out a small crack in our door when we saw a prisoner walking down the street in front of our building. An unimportant Vietnamese worker in ragged clothes was picking up garbage in the street. He was a guy that we wouldn't bow to in a thousand years, and the Vietnamese camp authorities wouldn't make an issue of if we did not bow to him. That guy undoubtedly never expected anyone to bow. Well, this POW walking down the street spotted him and gave the guy the most obsequious bow you would ever want to see. He bowed so low his nose almost touched the ground. We had no idea who the guy was at that time, but when we met him four years later, to hear him talk, he was so tough the Vietnamese trembled in their rubber-tire shoes when he was in their presence. Quincy and I knew better. One peek through a crack in the door sometimes gave a picture quite different from the picture the POW gave of himself. Or maybe it wasn't fair of me to judge someone from just one incident.

In any case, the food was worse now than it had ever been. Several days a week the vegetable side dish did not have pig fat. Almost every day we were getting a vegetable that I had never seen or tasted before. One of the guys in the building guessed that it was bamboo. The bamboo we were getting was not like the soft tender bamboo shoots available in Chinese restaurants in the U.S. This bamboo had gone far beyond being classified as a shoot. What we were eating now not only tasted like wood, but it was wood. It was bitter, foul tasting, oily, stringy, and hard to chew. My stomach was getting clobbered, but my spirits were high because we thought the Vietnamese had to hurt before the war ever ended. And if this was an indication of them hurting, then it made us happy.

It was customary for most of the turnkeys to pass out the three cigarettes and first light early in the morning and then pass out a light after the two meals. But Scum carried the cigarettes spread out loosely on a tray and he delivered the cigarettes one at a time three times a day. He always left the tray of cigarettes where I could see it, and frequently he was smoking when he picked up my dishes.

The Vietnamese did not want me to forget how good a cigarette tasted, because then the absence of cigarettes would not serve as a punishment for me. So each Friday night Scum offered the tray of cigarettes to me, and I was allowed to have one. It would have been wise of me to refuse, but then the Vietnamese might try to do something else to make life more unpleasant for me. Or maybe I should have just taken it and then thrown it away, but I took it and enjoyed the hell out of it. I looked forward to it every Friday, and when it arrived I got a light, rushed to my bed, sat down, and enjoyed every puff. Luckily, I was able to mentally adjust to the fact that it would be another week before my next one.

During periods of maximum isolation, when very little was going on, time passed far more rapidly for me than it normally did. Thus, by putting me solo, the Vietnamese didn't make me suffer as much as they meant to.

During August, the weather had been super hot, but for a period of three or four days towards the end of the month, we had heavy rain. The water flooded the whole camp. They even had buses standing by to take us elsewhere if the water got higher. It was a blessing for me, because the room cooled off nicely, the heat rash I had begun suffering disappeared, and there were no quizzes. Forty years later, I'm still happy when it rains. That feeling of relief has never left me.

On one of the last days of August, I moved to the end room of the building. My new room was worse than the one I was in before, because I would have only one guy to communicate with, and it would be much more dangerous. The door to the room was on the side of the building, so now I would never get any advance warning of a guard approaching. In the other room, the guard had had to walk past two doors before he got to mine, so even if the guys in those rooms were not officially clearing for me, they would respond to a shadow or the noise of a guard near the building by automatically thumping the wall lightly to warn anyone who might be communicating.

The next day I made contact with the man in the room beside me. He responded immediately but he didn't know the tap code. After about fifteen minutes we were communicating with the long alphabet code. At first it was slow going, but within several days he had learned the Air Force tap code, and we were in business. He was Air Force Capt. John Britton, a relatively new shoot down. Most of the time we tapped only during quiet hour. I was as careful as possible about tapping softly, keeping my ear to the wall when the other guy tapped, so he did not have to tap loudly, and I watched the peephole continuously so at the instant it started to open, I could move my hand or my ear from the wall. It was always risky to communicate, but as I was under pressure for my confession, it was even riskier. It would give them an excuse to punish me, and while I was being punished, they would insist that I write the confession. This meant that I would have written the confession as a result of my breaking a camp regulation rather than as a result of the Vietnamese initiating the action to force me to write it.

One of the first questions John asked after we started to communicate was whether I had a chain and iron ball attached to my leg. He was hearing the noise that came from my walking on crutches. He was relieved after I told him what the noise was. The entire time I lived next to Capt. Britton, I never saw him. But it was no problem remembering his name. Several years later, when we finally met face to face and he introduced himself as John Britton, I realized that he was the guy who had lived next to me in the other room in the Barn and had refused to respond to my tapping. I did not try to beat the hell out of him as I had sworn I would. In fact, I never even mentioned the incident to him. Eventually we ended up living together in a big room, and he was as fine an officer as I had ever met. He had obviously had his reasons for not communicating at that time, so I let the matter drop.

On 2 September 1966, we had a nice meal in celebration of North Vietnam's Independence Day. It had a few small pieces of some pretty good meat for a change. It tasted like beef but was probably ox or water buffalo. I even got three cigarettes that day. The next day, the routine was back to normal. No cigarettes, no light, no bath, carrying out the *bo*, guard handing me hot bowls. About a week later, I was taken to quiz with Lump, the deputy camp commander, who had a large lump on his forehead. We talked about the war for about half an hour, and then he began talking to me about writing a confession. He acknowledged that my treatment was not the lenient and humane treatment that others were getting, and he said that my treatment would improve only after I confessed my crimes against the Vietnamese people and asked their forgiveness. He said that my treatment would get far worse than it was now if I did not repent soon. He made a few more threats and asked me if

I wanted to write the confession today. I politely told him no. He said, "Go back to your room."

Early the next morning, Scum came to my room and gave me the roll-up signal. As I walked down the steps from the room, the bedroll slipped from my arm and everything fell all over the steps and the ground. Scum shouted at me in Vietnamese, then he walked over and slapped my face as hard as he could. I felt like clubbing him with my crutch, but I sat down on the porch instead and gathered my things together.

I walked past the Garage building and headed toward the Gate House, which was immediately to the left of the main headquarters building. It might have been used for storage at one time. Until the confession thing started a few months ago, the only prisoner I had heard of who lived there was Navy Lt. J.J. Connell. I heard that he had pretended that his hands were broken, so he wouldn't have to write anything. He got away with not writing, but he paid a heavy price for it by living in real solitary confinement. The Gate House was a building with three rooms. I moved into the room on the far left. The room was about three times the size of the room I came from, but the floor was filthy. There were no windows, vents, or lights. As I entered the room, I could barely see anything. After a few seconds my eyes adjusted enough so I could see that the bed board was on the floor and that there was a *bo* in one corner of the room. Scum scowled at me as he slammed the door, locked it, and left. The Vietnamese had sealed off almost all of the light from outside. After the door was closed, I was in complete darkness. I had difficulty putting up the mosquito net in the dark. I soon realized that mosquitoes liked dark places, and they were swarming all over the place.

The lack of a bed to sit on made my dependency on crutches a major predicament. Each time I sat down on the bed board or got up from the floor, I had to do it with only one leg. At mealtime, Scum left the food on the sidewalk outside the door. On crutches I bent over, picked up the hot soup, and put it just inside the door, and then did the same with the side plate and bread.

Using the *bo* to defecate was almost impossible. With a normal bed board about two feet off the floor, I could sit with the cheek of my butt on the side of my broken leg on the bed and use the other leg as a support and then put the bucket under my behind so I could defecate. But now, defecating in any sort of sanitary fashion was impossible. I could not sit on the bucket because it was too small, and even if I could have done so, I wouldn't have been able to get there on one leg. And to squat over the bucket with only one leg was impossible. So in order to defecate, I had to lean my back against the wall and then little by little edge my left foot forward until my body was at about a 30 degree angle from the wall and my behind about eighteen inches above the bucket. And in this position I had to have a bowel movement.

As luck would have it, the first night in the new room, I came down with diarrhea, and I had to use the *bo* at least four times. Needless to say, the mosquitoes ate me alive as I leaned against the wall with my pants down around my ankles. Staying clean was impossible, and my bed and clothes smelled far worse now than ever before. Living in that room would have been unpleasant if I had been in fair physical condition, but it would have been tolerable. Living there with only one functional leg really made my life miserable.

The Vietnamese had gone to great lengths to cover up every crack in the door to the room that they could see from the outside, but they apparently never went inside the room where it was dark to see if any light was coming in through the door. As it happened, the door had a small crack close to the floor. It didn't let in very much light, but it was big enough for me to get a great view of a large part of the inside of the camp. I spent most of the day now sitting on the dirty floor watching all the activity outside. Because there was no peephole, the guard couldn't sneak up and catch me looking out. I could see the guards coming and going all day, and occasionally a prisoner going here and there, and a multitude of other activities associated with running a prison camp.

The Fox was the camp commander at this time, and during the week he always wore his uniform, but on Sunday he and the other Vietnamese walked around in front of the headquarters building with only their underwear on. I watched them take their meals outside. They took turns cutting each other's hair, sat around on the grass just relaxing, and even went fishing in a scum-covered pool for what looked like two- and three-inch fish. They probably cooked the fish themselves for dinner. Compared to my first five months lying on a bed twenty-four hours a day and staring at four walls and the ceiling, looking out that crack was more entertaining than a three-ring circus. Even though the mosquitoes were a problem, wearing long clothes was making it twice as hot as before, and getting around on crutches was miserable, looking out that door made life worth living again.

Air Force Maj. Al Brunstrom, who was under pressure just like me, was in the middle room of the building. In the next room was Lt., j.g., Larry Spencer, who had been in leg irons and had his hands cuffed behind him for about a week. He had been able to open his handcuffs with a piece of bamboo, so whenever he didn't expect the Vietnamese to open the door, he took the handcuffs off and rested comfortably.

Although looking out of the door was entertaining at first, I soon tired of it and of my existence. One morning in late September, I had a quiz with Lump. In addition to spouting the same propaganda and the same old threats as before, he showed me the confessions Cdr. Denton, Lt. Col. Risner, and my ex-roommates had written. Denton was the senior Navy prisoner at that time and Risner was the senior Air Force prisoner. Lump explained that they had all seen the foolishness of their ways and now were happily enjoying the lenient and humane treatment of the Vietnamese people. I knew they had all been forced to confess but acted as if I believed they had confessed voluntarily, as Lump said they had done.

I told him that it didn't make any difference to me what the other prisoners believed or had done, because it was a violation of our Code of Conduct, and I could be severely punished by my government for writing such a statement if the war ever ended and I was released. I said that so far as I was concerned, I was not a war criminal nor was the U.S. waging an illegal and immoral war of aggression, but rather we were fighting to help the South Vietnamese defend themselves from the North Vietnamese Communist aggressors. In addition, I told him very politely that I honestly believed in our economic and political systems and free way of life and that I supported President Johnson one hundred percent. I told him these things in the most polite and respectful tone of voice that I could, because I was trying to get him off my back without having to write. Lump said that he understood, but that I had no choice, and that I would have to write my confession even if I did not see the error of my ways. I said that I was very sorry but I couldn't write what he wanted. He replied that he could not be responsible for the consequence of my acts and told me to go back to my room.

Scum took me back. No sooner had I taken off my long clothes than the door opened again. Scum came into the room and dropped some leg irons and a piece of rope on the floor by my bed. Then he tied an iron bar to which the leg irons were attached to the bed. I was not sure what was to come but figured that if I wore long pants,

I would be better protected from the mosquitoes, even though it would be much hotter that way. I showed him my pants as if to ask whether I could put them on. He nodded yes. The look on Scum's face said he was in his glory. After I put on the long pants, he motioned for me to put my left ankle in one shackle of the leg iron. He couldn't put my right leg into the other shackle, because I had a cast on it. So he took some rope and tied one end around the cast at the ankle and then tied the other end to a hole in the bottom of the bed board, so that the leg in the cast was as restrained as the other one.

Then he went just outside the door and brought in a pair of handcuffs that had been sitting in the direct sunlight on the hot sidewalk and were sizzling hot. He told me to put my arms behind my back, and he put the handcuffs around my wrists as tight as he could. I realized that he had wanted them to be as hot as possible when he first put them on so they would burn my wrists. Then, as they cooled off, they would tighten on the wrists. He scowled at me and left.

This was an extremely uncomfortable position to be in. In an hour, the door opened, and one of the Thai prisoners brought in my meal and put it next to the bed. Scum came in and unlocked my hands from behind but then cuffed them in front. I had no idea how long this ordeal was going to last, so I decided that I would not eat. I did not want to feel the need to have a bowel movement or urinate in addition to being in the leg irons and handcuffs. Scum came back about a half hour later, cuffed my hands tightly behind me again, scowled, and then left with the dishes.

As time went on during quiet hour, I became more and more uncomfortable. I could feel my injured leg twisting inside the cast whenever I moved and the overall effect of withholding the free movement of my limbs was beginning to take its toll. My back was getting sore. I was feeling more and more uncomfortable as time went by. I realized that now the Vietnamese had me where they wanted me, and it was only a matter of time before I would write the confession that they desired. When quiet hour ended, I had survived about four hours of misery. Obviously, no matter how long I resisted, it made no difference to the Vietnamese. They could patiently wait as long as it took me to give up. I decided that I had had enough and would go ahead and write what they wanted. As far as I was concerned, I had done the best I could.

I hoped that Scum would come to the room to fill my water jug or just to see how I was doing, so I could tell him that I would write. Unfortunately, he didn't come until two hours later, when it was time for the last meal of the day. The Thai brought the food into my room again and put it next to the bed on the floor. If I had had any doubt that I was ready to write after four hours, there was no question at all about it now. Scum came in and unlocked the cuffs from behind me. As soon as my hands were free, I nodded my head as if to say yes and told Scum, rather sorrowfully, that I would write. I made a writing motion with my hand. He shook his head from side to side and said no. I said, *"bao cao,"* and pointed out toward the door and indicated that I wanted to talk to one of the officers. He didn't pay any attention and left. I said to myself, "What if that rotten son of a bitch just to get even with me doesn't tell one of the officers that I gave up and was ready to write my confession?"

I ate next to nothing and did not drink a drop. I had to urinate now. When Scum came back for the dishes, I told him so. He brought the five-gallon shit bucket next to my bed board and un-locked one of my hands. Then he left. It was a great feeling to have my hands free again, but there was no way I could urinate into the *bo,* so I emptied the water from my drinking cup into the *bo.* Then

175

I urinated into the cup and threw the urine into the waste bucket. Not very sanitary, but better then sleeping in wet pants all night.

Scum returned five minutes later. I told him again that I would write and also indicated I wanted to talk to the camp officer. He placed the cuffs on my hands behind me as tight as he could and left. I was really in deep shit. I had been in leg irons with my hands cuffed behind for more than six hours, and being restrained like this was far more than uncomfortable now. Not only were my legs and hands restrained, but the cast was cutting into the backside of my leg whenever I bent the leg slightly. Discomfort was rapidly changing to pain. I was hurting all over. My wrists were sore, and the slightest body movement seemed to pull the area apart where the piece of bone was missing in my leg.

The door opened early in the evening. I breathed a sigh of relief. They were going to let me write my confession. Dum Dum came in and asked me what I wanted. I told him that I was sorry to have caused him trouble and that I would write my confession now. Dum Dum looked at me and said, "We don't want your confession now." He turned around, walked out of the room, and locked the door.

Soon after Dum Dum left the room, I realized that I had forgotten to pull down the mosquito net for the night. Apparently preoccupation with my predicament had made me forget about the mosquitoes. Also, I just didn't believe they would leave me like this all night long, when I had already told them I would write my confession. I had always been very polite and courteous to them. I couldn't believe they were going to do this out of spite. After about an hour, the mosquitoes were really driving me crazy. I yelled, *"bao cao,"* until Scum finally came and opened the door. I used the movement of my head to ask if he would unlock the handcuffs to let me put down the mosquito net. He said no loudly and then came over and slapped me in the face and left again.

I could not believe that I was experiencing this. I couldn't find any position that was even halfway comfortable. My whole body was filled with one big ache and pain. I could not scream, and I did not cry, but I was unbearably miserable. Swarms of mosquitoes buzzed all around me. I prayed that I could get through this night somehow. There was no way I could sleep. In the middle of the night, I heard some noise outside the building. My wrists had become very sore, so I yelled, *"bao cao."* Life couldn't be any worse than this. Scum opened the door, and somehow I managed to tell him about my sore wrists. To my utter surprise, he opened them a notch. I told him again that I would write. Then he left. I counted the seconds and minutes to help pass the time, but it dragged slowly by. Somehow, I managed to get through the night, and when I heard the first gongs off in the distance that morning I thanked God that He had given me the strength to survive.

Scum came into the room around 0700. I told him again that I would write. He said O.K. He opened the handcuffs on both wrists, untied my cast from the bed and took the leg iron off my left leg. I rubbed my wrists gently because they were sore. I put on my long black pajamas, got up on my crutches, and followed Scum to the middle room of the Office building where I had lived with Quincy, Norlan, and Bob ten months before. There were two small tables with chairs, and pens and paper on them. As soon as I sat down at one of the tables, Dum Dum came into the room. I asked him what I should write. He said, "Write your true feeling." It took me about five minutes to write one paragraph of bullshit. Half an hour later, he returned, and I gave him what I had written. He took it and left. Dum Dum came back ten minutes later and handed me Cdr. Denton's confession and said, "Write it like that." So I copied it word for word. I laughed to myself as I wrote–if it was good enough for Denton it was good enough for me.

When I came back from the Office building early in the morning, the air was already hot. It was going to be a scorcher before the day was over. Fox was standing on the porch of the Headquarters building with only his pants and a T-shirt on, yawning and stretching his arms over his head. He looked as if he had just gotten up. As I passed by where he was standing, I bowed, and he said something to Scum, and they both laughed. I continued to walk back to my room. I hoped with the confession out of the way, life would improve. Although I did not go back into handcuffs and leg irons, everything else remained the same. I didn't care. Living without the leg irons and handcuffs seemed like heaven.

Sometime during then night after I wrote my confession I heard two or three *bao cao*'s coming from what I thought was the Headquarters building. I later learned that one of the guys calling out was my old roommate Norlan Daughtrey, who was being tortured. He had already written his confession, but now they wanted him to write me a letter telling me that he had already confessed and to try to persuade me to confess as well. Strangely, they did this after I had already confessed. Apparently, they had started on Norlan before I confessed, and they could not stop what they had already started, because they would have lost face.

My treatment continued as it had been before. Still no cigarettes, in a dark room twenty-four hours a day, bed on the floor, no radio, problems going to the bathroom, and looking out the crack in the door much of the day. Several days later, Al Brunstrom wrote his confession and moved out of the building, and Air Force Capt. Bob Purcell moved in. Percy was a character if there ever was one. During quiet hour of the day he moved in, I was lying under my net resting, when suddenly I heard a voice call, "Hey, Ray! Hey, Ray!"

The voice was coming from the trap door in the ceiling of my room. I looked up and, lo and behold, there was Percy. We chatted for a few minutes, and then he left. He had a trap door in the ceiling of his room and somehow had been able to get up into the small attic space above our rooms. A number of other buildings also had trap doors to the attic in certain rooms, which would have made escape easy. But just getting out of the building wouldn't do you much good.

I heard that Percy wrote his confession several days later, after he had what he called the ten-minute special, which entailed tying the ropes or straps around your arms above the elbow and pulling the elbows together. For many guys, the pain was excruciating, and they gave up right away. Then they wrote what the Vietnamese wanted, and it was all over with. Other guys, however, were able to stay in the straps for hours on end without giving up and then when released from them again refused to write. Some guys were able to stay in leg irons with their hands cuffed behind them for months on end. I really admired those guys who were able to withstand amounts of torture far more than I had endured. I don't know how they did it. But I tried the best I could. I wished that I could have lasted longer.

September 1966 – May 1967. I went to quiz about one week after I had confessed to being a war criminal. A new camp officer whom I had never seen before sat behind a table. Two stools were in front of the table, and Norlan Daughtrey was sitting on one of them. In time, this new officer became known as the Elf, because he was very small and had an elfish appearance. For the next half hour, he proclaimed his views about the war. It wasn't that bad, however, because his English was atrocious, and many of the things he said didn't make any sense. Finally, he told us that because we had shown a good attitude by confessing our crimes against the Vietnamese people and asking for their forgiveness, we would be allowed to live with each other again. We both said fine. Elf said we had to obey all the camp regulations and do what the guard told us at all times. We both agreed to his demands, but we knew that we would live exactly as we had before, and that we would continue to break the camp regulations whenever it was safe and it suited us to do so.

We walked to the back of the Pool Hall building, and I moved into room 9 with Norlan. That night after the evening meal, I got a cigarette, and from then on it was the lenient and humane treatment of one roommate, three cigarettes, and a ten-minute wash a day. And of course twenty-four hours a day of captivity to contemplate our crimes against the Vietnamese people. Norlan brought me up to speed on all the news that he had, which was not much, and I did the same for him. The building was fully occupied, with either one or two men in each room. Most, if not all, had written their confessions. We had a new turnkey whom someone had named Happy. He was a saint compared to Scum. He did everything on schedule, gave us our full time at bath, and never was late with the cigarettes or the lights. He smiled from time to time and even hummed a tune as he went about his chores.

During the summer, while the Vietnamese were getting everyone to confess, they had erected high brick walls around some buildings to cut off communications. Brick walls some nine or ten feet high surrounded the Pool Hall about twelve feet from the building. For all practical purposes, there was little communications going on from building to building at this time.

Alongside our building, the Vietnamese had fenced off an area for us to wash. They built a tub of concrete and bricks that was about six feet long, four feet wide, and four feet high, then ran a hose from another building and filled the tub whenever it got low. We washed our clothes in a smaller tub of bricks and concrete about ten inches by eighteen inches by one foot deep. We filled an old worn out porcelain enamel soup bowl with water and threw it on our bodies to get wet. Then we soaped down and rinsed off by throwing water from the soup dish on our bodies. My first bath in almost a month felt pretty damn good. It was also a great feeling to wash my clothes again.

Communications within our own building had become quite sophisticated now. We were all pretty good at tapping, because everyone had been practicing the tap code for at least six months. But for the most part, tapping was used just for short messages during the day and at night. The bulk of our communication was done every quiet hour. Air Force Captains Jeffery and Reynolds had refined the art of talking through the wall. Now we were using our drinking cups instead of a blanket to muffle the sound. The man talking put the bottom of the cup on the wall and talked into the open end. He put his hands around his mouth and the rim of the cup to muffle the sound. The guy in the other room put his ear on the bottom of the cup to listen.

As soon as the guys in the end rooms were on the floor looking below the doors and watching out for guards, they would send back two C's, indicating it was clear to start communication. For the most part, guys did not enjoy clearing, but they did it because we couldn't survive without it. Once in a while, a guy would gripe about clearing when other guys were just shooting the shit, but most guys would clear for hours on end without a complaint. It was just the luck of the draw as to which room you got in a building, and everyone would get his turn clearing sooner or later. Sometimes if a guy was lucky, he could watch the shadows under the door just by lying on his bed, but this was risky because the shadows could be misleading. At times, the guards were restless and moved around the building rapidly, making it almost impossible to communicate. About the only good thing I got out of having a bad leg was that I rarely ever had to clear.

My old roommate Quincy Collins moved into the room in front of us about a week after I moved in with Norlan. His roommate was Capt. A.J. Myers. Quincy's roommate had lived in a room next to me in the Barn for one day. He had broken his ankle when he was shot down. When they put his ankle in a cast, they did not set it properly. After the broken bones had grown together and the cast was taken off his foot, instead of the bottom of the foot being flat on the floor, it was at approximately a thirty-degree angle with the ankle, and consequently he walked on the inside of his ankle instead of on the foot.

A.J. had an interesting biography. When he was thirteen years old and still in grammar school, he was more than six feet tall and weighed more than two hundred pounds. When his parents divorced, the judge let him pick which parent he wanted to live with. He said if he had really had to choose, he would have picked his mother, but he didn't want to hurt his father's feelings, so he decided it would be better just to leave home. He hitchhiked to California and got a job driving a bus. When he was sixteen, he met a woman ten years older than he was, and they got married. They had a baby girl when he was seventeen. The marriage didn't work out, so a year later they got divorced. He decided that he wanted to go to college, even though he had never attended high school. He passed an entry examination for a small junior college in Minnesota, and with some fast talking, he was finally admitted on a trial basis. He completed two years of work with high grades, applied to the University of Washington, and was accepted. He also applied for the Air Force ROTC and was accepted. Several years later he graduated, and became a Second Lieutenant in the Air Force.

Although he maintained contact with his daughter over the years, he did not see her very often. But when he left the U.S. for Vietnam, she came to visit him at the base where he was stationed. According to A.J., she was seventeen years old and pretty husky, just like him. The first thing she said when she got off the bus was, "Hi, Dad. Where can we get a drink?" Between the time he left her and was shot down, his daughter got married and had a baby. A.J. proudly announced to one and all that he was probably the youngest grandfather among the prisoners at age thirty-seven.

Because the Vietnamese had pretty much cut off all camp-wide communications with their wall-construction program, the Senior Ranking Officer (SRO) of each building had the responsibility of command for the men and their problems in his building. The senior man in our building was Cdr. Jim Mulligan, who moved into room 3 of the Pool Hall in October. Cdr. Mulligan was one of the most optimistic men I ever had contact with in prison. He interpreted almost everything as a sign that the war would be over soon. From the time we first heard the camp radio and the Voice of Vietnam in late 1965, we had listened to Ella Fitzgerald singing "Don't Fence Me In," Peter, Paul, and Mary singing "Where Have All the flowers Gone," Vietnamese war songs, and Asian music over and over again. After a while, the music really became boring if not downright depressing. One night, we heard a song on the Voice of Vietnam radio program called "Down Town," by Petula Clark. We had never heard the singer's name before. The song was just about the peppiest, heart-lifting tune we had ever heard anywhere. Before the song ended, everyone in the building was so elated and moved that they were uncontrollably banging on the walls with their fists. It was probably the most exciting thing that had happened since I was shot down. Jim Mulligan went through the roof. I think we all did. The next day, he was passing out extensive guidance and policy on how we should act and behave when we were released. He said his bedroll was already packed and we should all listen for the trucks arriving in camp to take us to the plane at the airport.

One morning in mid-November, the guard came to each room and gathered up our blankets. The men whose blankets were torn or old were happy because they thought the Vietnamese were going to issue new blankets. The men who had just been given new blankets did not know what to make of it. About an hour later, we heard the doors to the building opening and closing. Then ours was opened. Happy told us to put on our long clothes. We left the room and headed for the auditorium building. This building was about forty-five feet long and thirty feet wide. Although a few of the other prisoners had been in the building and had described it as a small auditorium, neither Norlan nor I had ever been there before. The room was dark when we entered, but we could make out that the floor sloped gently to the front. The room had been divided by stretching four pieces of heavy cord from one side of the room to the other about six feet apart and also running cord the same way from the front of the room to the back. Then our blankets were hung over the cords making nine separate cubicles in such a manner that we could see the screen but could not see each other. At least

185

a dozen guards were sitting on stools in the cubicles or standing around the room watching to keep us from seeing each other or communicating. We watched a movie about the war. Although the dialogue was in Vietnamese, it wasn't too hard to understand what the movie was all about. There were numerous pictures of U.S. Aircraft being shot down, a POW being captured, and pictures of the war in South Vietnam. The movie portrayed the Americans as the bad guys, much as the American press had portrayed the Germans and Japanese in World War II.

As the years passed by, we saw one or two movies each year. In addition to their typical propaganda films, they occasionally included scenes from the U.S. of anti-war demonstrations and other news items that portrayed the U.S. in a negative light. One of the highlights of all the movies we saw was a movie that showed an anti-war demonstration in Berkeley, California. It showed a dozen or more Hells Angels on motorcycles supporting the police in containing a large crowd of demonstrators. The Vietnamese clearly wanted us to think that if such so-called disreputable people as the Hells Angels were for the war, then we were wrong in supporting it. It backfired for the Vietnamese, however, because when we saw the Hells Angels in the movie opposing the anti-war demonstrators, we all spontaneously clapped and cheered until the guards came rushing to our cubicles to quiet us down.

Air Force Capt. Bob Purcell lived in the room next to us. He and Norlan had been in the same squadron and had been good friends. Percy had an excellent reputation as a prisoner, but he was a real character, as well. He frequently ended up in a room with a trap door to the attic, and he spent a lot of time roaming around up there. I had already met him peering down from the attic when we were both in the Gate House building. After I had left the Pool Hall in March 1966, Air Force Captains Jeffery and Reynolds were both on reduced rations, because they had been caught communicating. Percy was in a room with a trap door to the attic, and every day during quiet hour he would climb up into the attic and drop bread through their attic door. It was a godsend for them. Percy had really put himself out on the limb by doing this, because if the Vietnamese had ever caught him up there, they would have beaten the hell out of him.

Shortly before I moved in with Norlan, one day during quiet hour Percy had been up in the attic over Norlan's room, and although there was not a trap door in his room, there was a small hole where the wire for the light came through the ceiling. Percy and Norlan were having a conversation, when a guard who had been patrolling the building apparently heard talking coming from Norlan's room. When he quickly opened the peephole, expecting to catch two guys talking to each other, the guard looked perplexed and just shook his head several times, closed the peephole, and left.

Percy also liked to tease the water girls. If we forgot to put our water jugs in front of our doors in the morning, it was customary that when the water girl came to get the jug to fill it and opened the peephole to the room, we were supposed to bow to her and hand her the water pitcher. She would then fill it up and leave it outside until we picked up our meal. Percy teased her by giving her what he called his super-sophisticated bow now and then. He would keep his neck straight and, with his hands at his sides, bend his body from the waist as far down as he could, as slowly as possible. This infuriated the water girl, and about twice a week we could hear her chewing out Percy in Vietnamese. Sometimes she would call the turnkey, but when he came to Percy's room, he would bow normally. He missed a pitcher of water from time to time, but he said it was worth it watching the water girl get upset.

The Elf was the Vietnamese officer in charge of our building. The day that Norlan and I moved into the building was the first time that either of us had seen or met him. The Vietnamese rarely forgot about anyone for very long. They were continually trying to extract whatever they could get from us that might be of value. So once every five or six weeks, we were taken to quiz for what we called an attitude check. Some of the Vietnamese officers were real bastards. They preached the party line to the nth degree, and if a POW didn't agree with them, he was sent back to his room after some threats and a good scolding.

Although we had no doubt about where the Elf's allegiance lay, he was one of the better officers to have a quiz with. He always gave you at least a few minutes of the party line, but he enjoyed changing the subject if a prisoner wanted to. He was a chain smoker and was generous with his cigarettes. So whenever we had a quiz with him, we would get some extra cigarettes. He told us about his family and said that he had been a physics teacher before he came into the army. He also told us that dog meat was a delicacy.

One day, Norlan and I went to a quiz together with the Elf. After a few minutes of propaganda bullshit, we started talking about things other than the war. The conversation somehow got on the subject of other prisoners. Quincy Collins lived in the room behind us, and we talked to him every day through the wall. We knew that Quincy had had a quiz with Elf several days before, because Quincy had passed that information on to us. For the fun of it, Norlan told the Elf that we had both lived with Quincy Collins many months ago. He asked the Elf if he knew Quincy. The Elf thought for a while and then told us that he knew Quincy, but that he had moved to another camp. Norlan asked how Quincy was doing, and the Elf said he was just fine. We knew that the Elf was lying, and as he talked, he appeared to be very uncomfortable and kept looking away from us. The Elf could not admit where Quincy was because of their isolation policy, and although he probably suspected we knew Quincy lived behind us, he couldn't tell us, because maybe we really didn't know.

In early December 1966, the Vietnamese made a room in the Auditorium into a library. One morning we were taken to the library and in addition to their homemade propaganda material, there was a full-page advertisement from the *New York Times*. We could not believe our eyes. They must have made a mistake. I rushed to pick it up. A short letter in opposition to the war on the top part of the page was addressed to President Johnson. The rest of the page was filled with approximately five thousand names of educators, congressmen, and other prominent Americans. We both looked at the list. I had seen letters in newspapers similar to this in years past, but they were always on a subject other than the war. We had nothing to do, so we went over the list of names, one by one. We had heard of many of the signers because they were famous, and one was a person whom I knew. He had been the chaplain at my college. I had been to his house on occasions for social functions. We would gather around in his living room and have discussions on a wide range of political and social issues. His views had never been unusual, and he had always appeared to be a decent and honorable man. But now here was a man I admired and respected, and he was advocating a position on the war with which I strongly disagreed. It bothered me to see so many supposedly highly educated, influential, and well-respected individuals from all cross sections of our society agreeing with the North Vietnamese about the bull that our captors were trying to sell us.

When we went back to our room, we had a lengthy discussion of what we had just read. We concurred that the newspaper was not a fake. Norlan asked the question, "What would we do if our fathers' names had appeared on the list?" We both agreed that if our fathers opposed the war, it would not affect how we felt about it. However, we disagreed on what our feelings toward our fathers would be as a result of their taking, in our opinion, such a stupid and uninformed view of the war. I was of the view that even though my father might disagree with the war, it would not alter my feelings toward him. Norlan was not so sure. He felt that given the overall circumstances of the situation, he might not be forgiving of his father.

Mr. Tuc, the medic who took care of Norlan and me when we were first shot down, came to our room in the last week of November and asked about my leg. Although there was an assigned medic for our camp, Mr. Tuc apparently was still responsible for the treatment of my leg. He indicated that he was going to remove the cast. The cast had been on continuously since early February, and there had been times when my foot and leg inside the cast had itched so badly that I would have given anything to have that cast off so I could scratch the leg. A coat hanger would have been a blessing; even a thin stick would have helped. But I had nothing that would work. At times, I would say to myself that there was nothing I could do about it, so I'd just have to forget that it itched. And it would stop itching, or at least my mind was distracted so the itching wasn't a bother.

The cast was filthy now and somewhat tattered around the edges. As was customary, Mr. Tuc used a dull knife with a small rust spot here and there and cut the cast from the front of my knee down to the top of my toes. My leg wasn't really bothering me much any more, and whatever soreness had developed when I was in leg irons and handcuffs had gone away weeks ago. As he jerked and pressed the knife hard against the cast and cut it little by little and pulled the cast apart, I hoped he would not do more harm than good. Finally, the hard plaster came off. The leg had been wrapped with cotton under the cast. In the area around the wound, the cotton was a blackish brown, but the cotton still covered the leg. Mr. Tuc started to take the cotton off the leg. I indicated that I wanted to do it. He let me. I managed to get most of the cotton off the entire lower leg after a few minutes.

An extremely thick layer of dead skin was on the area that the cast had covered. The wound had healed, and there was a large brownish scar where there had been a two-inch piece of the shinbone. The smaller broken bone in the back of the leg had healed and grown together so that I could at least sit on the bed and raise the leg without the foot flopping around. After giving me some water to clean the leg off, the medic left. I continued to peel the dead skin off the leg for the next two weeks. Some of it came off in big one- and two-inch pieces right away, but some of the skin was still attached to the leg. I had to wait until those pieces were completely dead before I pulled them off.

I realized immediately that the ankle did not move. When I tried to force it, the only movement was in the area where the shinbone was missing. I had seen the x-ray of the leg and knew that the ends of the bone had not been cut smoothly, and that they were somewhat jagged. I feared any movement there might cause the bone to cut the flesh and open the wound again. After trying to force the ankle at least a half a dozen times, I figured it was probably frozen for good.

I knew I was lucky to be alive and have my leg. I guessed the main reason for this was that I had just lain on my bed and done nothing for almost two years. The rooms were small, the crutches were short and splintery, and I had no energy for anything. Most of the early shoot-downs never went to a hospital, and they suffered because of that, but as time passed, the Vietnamese decided that if they were to keep a man as a POW, they might as well take care of him in the beginning. This did not mean that men who went to the hospital got care equivalent to what they would have received at the Mayo Clinic, but the later shoot-downs' initial medical care was much better than that received by men shot down early in the war.

In the middle of December 1966, it was cold as usual, but at least we had our two blankets and a full set of clothes. By putting on all of our clothing and then folding the blankets into sort of a sleeping bag, we managed to survive at night. I took the string that acted as a belt from a pair of one of my long pants and tied the blankets together at the end by my feet. This kept the blankets from coming undone during the night and kept all of the body heat in.

Around this time, the Vietnamese were asking POWs if they wanted to tape short Christmas messages to their loved ones at home. The tapes would then be played on the Voice of Vietnam radio program for their loved ones to hear. I never met anyone who wanted to make such a tape. Even if it was just "Hi Mom, I love you," "I'm O.K.," or "Merry Christmas, Mom," we knew the Vietnamese would get propaganda value from it. Everyone hoped that he would not be asked to make a tape, no matter how innocuous it might be. I was not asked to tape a Christmas message, thank goodness. If very many POWs refused, then the Vietnamese would start threatening and escalating the pressure until they got enough messages. In my opinion, in the overall order of importance of what one should or should not do in a prison camp, making a Christmas tape was not something one volunteered to do, but taking torture before making a Christmas tape was going too far. Some agreed with me. Others didn't. They considered it a serious violation of the Code of Conduct, and I understood their point of view. At any rate, even if a guy was selected and pressured into making a tape, he still did the best he could to screw it up.

The Vietnamese played a tape from a different guy each night, beginning about a week before Christmas and ending about a week after. Most of the tapes were innocuous, with simple messages to loved ones. But once in a while, a guy would try to put one over on the Vietnamese. One night, we heard a tape by Air Force Lt. Al Brudno. He said hi to his wife and parents and wished them the standard Christmas greetings. He added, "We all had a big fine dinner. It was a real BFD." Capt. Murphy Jones sent the standard Christmas message and then concluded by saying, "I want you to know, Mom, that we had my favorite meal that you always cooked on Christmas day, cabbage soup. Goodbye, Mom." It was true that we had cabbage soup, but Jones's mother not only did not serve cabbage soup for Christmas, she had never heard of it. The jokes might not have been hilarious, but in the environment we were in, the laughter and banging on the walls could be heard in downtown Hanoi.

On Christmas Eve, they brought around a cup of heavily sugared black coffee, some extra cigarettes, and several heaping hands full of unshelled peanuts for each guy. Cdr. Jim Mulligan was the SRO in our building, and for his Christmas greeting to the men in our building he announced that he would not eat nineteen of the peanuts he was given in honor of the nineteen guys in the building, and that when he was released, he would eat nineteen peanuts every Christmas Eve thereafter in honor of the holiday he had spent with us.

On the special Christmas Eve radio program, a young boy sang "Jesus loves me." After a sermon by Protestant and Catholic clergymen that was filled with propaganda about the war, they played some songs by Frank Sinatra and Perry Como and then White Christmas by Bing Crosby. I think all of us were homesick when we listened to the music, but we did not dare talk about it. At least, Norlan and I didn't.

That night, a guard came to the door, opened it, and indicated to Norlan that he was going to quiz. Norlan got dressed and left the room. About fifteen minutes later, he came back. He had a letter and some pictures in his hand. He told me that the letter was from his wife, and the pictures were of his children. Hoping he would say no, I asked him if they took a picture of him receiving the letters and pictures, he said, "Yes." Then he passed me the pictures, so I could look at them. As he handed me the pictures, he broke down and cried. I felt so sorry for him. And almost cried, too. But his eyes were so filled with tears that he never noticed how moved I was.

The emotional shell that I had before I was shot down was getting thinner by the year. I suppose he cried because of the joy of seeing his wife and three children for the first time in nearly a year and a half, but also because he had boasted that he would not accept pictures if he had to give them any propaganda. I said, "Don't feel bad. I would have done the same thing," and I really would have. Half of our day was spent talking about our families, so it wasn't hard to pick out who was who in the pictures, because I knew so much about them already. The Vietnamese never gave anything without getting a price for it. Each prisoner had to decide whether he would pay the price or not.

Cdr. Denton moved in with Cdr. Mulligan in the early part of January 1967. Denton had been a prisoner for eighteen months, and he had been in solitary confinement the whole time except for a few days. Both he and Mulligan were excited to be together. They talked so much that the guard had to bang on the door and threaten them in the middle of the night to go to bed.

Cdrs. Denton and Mulligan moved out of the Zoo after being together only a few days in early 1967. They were the last of the senior officers to leave the camp. With all of the lieutenant colonels and commanders gone from the camp, the men upon whose shoulders fell the responsibility of SRO for the bulk of the prisoners during the three most difficult years of our imprisonment were the senior 04's and in particular Air Force major Larry Guarino.

The senior officers, although isolated now, no longer had to worry about being punished or threatened for giving guidance or orders to those junior to them, nor did they have to worry about the daily problems of the masses. These problems now fell on the senior 04's and ultimately on Larry Guarino, if there was contact with him. In my opinion, up to that time, Cdr. Denton had provided excellent guidance in addition to the Code of Conduct regarding resistance and prisoner conduct in North Vietnam. It was sound, fundamental guidance that provided a means by which we could exist as prisoners. And for the most part, the guidance remained applicable for the whole time I was there. I had never been in close contact with Lt. Col. Risner, but he had also exercised command and provided some reasonably worthwhile guidance.

When Denton and Mulligan left, I became the SRO of the building. We had a review of the Code of Conduct. Some of the younger guys who had recently completed various training schools had a better recollection of exactly what the code said. We were able to reconstruct the Code of Conduct verbatim with the whole building working together. Then we all memorized it. I had a number of reasons for doing this. It gave everyone something to do for a while, and in general it was a good idea for everyone to know the code verbatim now, because we were living the life for which the Code of Conduct was written. And admittedly for selfish reasons, I wanted to avoid having to give orders to anyone junior in rank to me who was not doing what he should have been doing.

The Vietnamese did not want any sort of command structure to exist. Their whole modus operandi was to prevent any kind of organization and command. Isolation, frequent moves, and no use of rank were examples. They did not want seniors telling juniors to do or not to do something. They wanted to be the boss of each man, for obvious reasons. Whenever the Vietnamese got wind of someone giving orders or assuming command, they tried to stop it. In my opinion, there really wasn't a need for the senior officer to have to be punished because he told someone not to do something, except under very unusual circumstances. The Code of Conduct should have been the culprit responsible for the resistance and not a particular person. Therefore, if a man was misbehaving, all that was really necessary was to remind him what the Code of Conduct said. Then if he resisted, he couldn't point the finger at me as the one who told him to resist. If he was punished really harshly, he still might finger me just to get them off his back, but in general, a guy has a propensity to tell the truth when his arms are twisted long enough.

We followed the Sunday routine that Cdr. Denton had started and Cdr. Mulligan had continued. One day, my old roommate Quincy asked if he could be appointed building chaplain. I didn't know exactly what he had in mind, but I agreed. What harm could he do? It turned out to be no big deal, just a short religious message each Sunday. Sometimes a number of verses from the Bible, and other times a short religious message that he thought up himself. It didn't take very long, however, before a few other men, just for the fun of it, decided that they would pick their own day of the week to send a special message to the building. Percy picked Monday, Norlan Tuesday, etc. Before long, all kinds of daily messages were floating around the building. Norlan's was the medical hint of the day. One of his hints was, "The best thing for chapped lips is to put some shit on them." He said, "It won't help the chapped lips, but it sure will keep you from licking them." Jerry Coffee said, "Incest is O.K., if you keep it in the family." This became quite entertaining as time went by.

When January came, the temperatures felt like they were below freezing. This was particularly hard on POWs undergoing punishment. Two Air Force Captains, Bill Means and Larry Barbay, who lived in one of the rooms in our building, were caught looking out of the air vent in their room. Means was standing on Barbay's shoulders, when one of the guards just by chance happened to see Means's face in the air vent. Their punishment was one week in leg irons with their hands cuffed behind them. It was impossible for Means and Barbay to keep their blankets on and stay warm. The irons and hands cuffed behind were torture enough, but coupled with the icy temperatures I didn't know how they survived. Maybe it was because they had everyone in the building praying for them.

One of the main holidays for the Vietnamese is called *Tet*. The holiday lasts for four days. It is the Vietnamese name for the lunar New Year, which is based on the moon revolving around the earth as compared to our New Year, which is based on the rotation of the earth around the sun. During the early part of February 1967 and just before *Tet,* we heard on the Voice of Vietnam radio program that North and South Vietnam had agreed to a cease-fire for the *Tet* holiday. We were all encouraged by this news, because we knew there had to be a cease-fire before the war would end. We were extremely hopeful that the four-day cease-fire would somehow turn into a longer cease-fire and eventually result in an end to the war.

We knew that the main purpose of the Voice of Vietnam radio program was to broadcast propaganda to the GIs in South Vietnam in hopes of demoralizing them. We received it because it wasn't much of a problem for them to broadcast it to us through inexpensive speakers in each room. From time to time, we had radio blackouts because things were broadcast on the radio solely for the men in South Vietnam, and the Vietnamese didn't want the prisoners to hear them. Many reasons probably existed for withholding certain kinds of news or information from us that they wanted the men in the South to hear, but there were probably just as many reasons unrelated to the content of the news for not turning the radio on for several days at a time.

In addition, over the years numerous cease-fires or pauses in the war occurred. Sometimes the news would be very encouraging about a proposed bombing halt or cessation of hostilities. We would hear about it on the radio for several days, but then all news about it would stop. Early on, whenever the radio was turned off for any period, or there was news of some break in the war, I was very optimistic. When this happened, we were climbing the walls, packing our bags, and getting ready to go home. But after living through radio blackouts, pauses, cease-fires, and bombing-halts so many times, I finally became totally unaffected by them. The optimists, however, would still get on their soapboxes and start talking. To a degree they were justified, because we knew the last thing the North Vietnamese wanted to do was make us feel good.

The Vietnamese always gave us a special meal for the *Tet* holiday. This celebration was even bigger than for Christmas. On *Tet* Eve quite frequently there were quizzes with the camp officers. They were always pleasant, sometimes giving a cup of tea, an extra cigarette, and a few pieces of Vietnamese style candy. We always had an outstanding meal on the morning of the first day of *Tet*. The meal consisted of a few small pieces of meat, a Vietnamese style sausage egg roll, a few leaves of lettuce, a beer, two extra cigarettes, and maybe a cup of coffee. But the real highlight of the occasion was a rice cake. It came in different forms, but the most common was in the shape and size of a small brick. It was sticky rice with a few nuts or a spoonful of some shredded meat in the middle, and it was wrapped with banana leaves. I'm sure that today I would have some difficulty eating it, but in those days it was considered a real treat. Some men ate the whole thing the day they got it, and others liked it so much that they ate a small piece each day for several weeks until it was gone. It was called *ban jong*. As with the Christmas dinner, the Vietnamese made up for what they spent on that meal by making the meals for the next three days absolutely horrible. The Vietnamese normally left us alone during the holiday period.

Quincy and A.J. Myers moved to another room in the building in early March 1967, and their room was left vacant. Several weeks later, two other men moved into the vacant room. We tapped on the wall at the first opportunity in an effort to contact them, but they would not answer. We figured they were really scared of the Vietnamese or had just been shot down. We hoped they were new men, because we had not had much news from the outside world for six or seven months. We tapped to the new guys at the beginning of every quiet hour, but they still would not answer. After five minutes of trying to contact them, we gave up and did our normal communicating. At the end of quiet hour, which was signified by the sounding of the camp gong, all the men in the building would bang the wall in synchronization with the gong as hard as we could. We hoped that this would lessen any fear they had of communicating with us. When the gong ended, Norlan and I just beat their wall as hard as we could. He guessed they were FNG's (Fucking New Guys) and as it turned out, they were.

We finally got a response during quiet hour of the fourth day. Our patience would be rewarded now. Norlan made contact with them. We learned that the men Air Force Capitan Ken Cordier and Lieutnant Mike Lane his GIB (Guy in the Black Seat) had been a crew on an F4C and had been shot down on 3 December 1966.

Cordier explained that Mike Lane was a pilot with flight controls in the back seat whereas in the Navy the F4B had no flight controls in the back seat and had a NFO (Non Flight Officer) there. The Vietnamese didn't usually keep crew members from the same plane together, but it happened every now and again. They had lived in one or two different buildings since that time but had never communicated with anyone. We were amazed that guys could have been in the system for three months and never have been in contact with anyone. But then, Norlan and I were early shoot downs and not only knew the ropes but were part of the men making the ropes. So by this time, we were old pros and were able to make the best of a bad situation.

Life was tough for a man who was shot down now. First he was beaten, then he was threatened with death if he didn't obey the camp regulations, and finally he was put into a building with other new men who had no idea what was going on either. Some guys took a long time to get into the swing of things and know what was going on. And these were the men the Vietnamese loved, because they were much easier to exploit than the old timers.

We got all the news Cordier and Lane had in one long session. They were both quite witty and got up to speed in no time at all. Someone in the building was taking a poll about sex, and one of the questions asked was, "What percent of adults French kiss?" Everyone gave an honest guess, but Lane's answer was 95 percent and the other 5 percent don't have tongues. Somehow they each got hold of a fantastic cup. Each cup had six buttons on it. One button was for beer, one for milk shakes, one for coke, one for orange juice, one for gin, and one for scotch. They had just about anything they wanted to drink anytime they wanted it. They offered to lend us their cups, but we never took them up on it. They also mentioned one day that they couldn't communicate, because they were both completely exhausted from lying awake trying to catch each other masturbating.

Since I became a prisoner, I had shaved anywhere from once a week to once every two or three months. We were shaving about once every week now. Our Turnkey, Happy, would start out in the morning with room 1 of the building and give them a safety razor with a new blade. To carry water for shaving, Happy was using a one-gallon white pot. One morning, when the men in the building were shaving, Happy had everyone put their *bo* outside the door, so that he could get one room to empty all of them. During the morning, Happy handed Cordier and Lane the small white pot without any water in it. Nor did he pass them the safety razor at that time. Maybe he just wanted to stash it somewhere for a while and give them the razor and water later on. Because Cordier and Lane were new in the building, they did not know the white pot was for shaving. And as Happy had taken their *bo* that morning, they guessed that the white pot was for their toilet needs. So one of them took a good healthy bowel movement in the white pot.

Shortly thereafter, Happy came by and asked them for the white pot, so he could put some water in it for them to shave. When they handed the pot to him, they realized they had made a mistake, but they didn't know what to do about it. When Happy saw the contents a strange look came over his face, and then he just walked away shaking his head but not saying anything. Cordier and Lane didn't shave that day, but the incident provided quite a bit of laughter throughout the building for the rest of the day.

Life was by no means all play and no work. Other than the quiet hour for communicating, two meals, three cigarettes, ten minutes to wash, the Voice of Vietnam half-hour radio program twice each day, a half-hour visit to the library once each two weeks, and a half-hour quiz every month or so, we just sat in our rooms with not a whole lot to do. We played chess now and then with a set made from pieces of paper, but just as soon as we made it, the Vietnamese would take it during a room inspection. We still talked, but after living with Norlan for nearly ten months, there wasn't much he didn't know about me and I didn't know about him.

To pass the time, Norlan would walk in circles in the room to relieve whatever excess energy he might have. He walked so much that he had started to wear a path on the floor. I just lay on my bed all day long because the crutches were so hard on my armpits. As Norlan walked hour after hour, his rubber tire shoes made a sound like flop, flop, flop, flop, over and over and over again. This noise really started to get on my nerves sometimes. It had nothing to do with Norlan, because we were getting along fine. I couldn't ask Norlan to stop, because he needed to walk. But the noise was getting to me. So sometimes I would take my shoe and slap it on the floor with each flop flop that Norlan made. I never told Norlan why I did it, and he never asked. He must have thought I was crazy. Maybe I was.

One day, Norlan and I had a quiz with the Elf. It was nothing more than an attitude check. After we told him that we supported President Johnson and the U.S. position on the war, he gave us nine yards on the iron will determination of the Vietnamese people, and said that it was only a matter of time before the imperialists would fail. In a short time, we got to smoking cigarettes and shooting the bull. The question of the accuracy of the lost plane count arose. The Vietnamese on average claimed about twice as many planes shot down as there actually were. We knew for a fact that the count by the U.S. was relatively accurate. The Elf hemmed and hawed about their count, but he wouldn't buy our side, nor we his.

Out of this conversation, the subject of truth came up. Norlan and I had been taught that truth was fact or reality, so we were surprised to hear the Elf say that "truth is what helps the state." Apparently, that was the definition of truth he had been taught. Given that definition, it made sense that the lost plane count could be any number they wanted, or that they could distort reality in any shape or form they desired. If they really knew the actual count and were inflating the numbers for propaganda, that would be one thing. But if they believed the inflated numbers, that would be quite another. It seemed to me that in that case Communism might collapse on its own because of the inability to know what was really going on. At the very least, it would cause the system to be inefficient. At least we had the press to monitor the lies of our government. But in time, I learned that democracies also lie. We camouflage the truth whenever it suits our purpose.

Norlan was a very congenial person, easy to talk to and was always more than willing to discuss ways to find solutions to problems that we had. Our diet consisted of cabbage, greens, pig fat and numerous other gas-producing foods. Frequently our soup was mixed with grease when it was cooked. Consequently, breaking wind was a fact of life in North Vietnam, and the resultant odors ranged from bad to absolutely rotten. We discussed two alternatives to the problem. (1) Alert the other man of the existence of the gas, so he could take evasive actions by putting his head under the cover or walking as far away from the other guy as possible. In this case, we agreed that it would be a polite thing to do. (2) Break wind and let the other man take his chances, because sometimes the odor might dissipate partially or completely because of a draft in the room. The disadvantage was that it was unpleasant to suddenly find yourself in the middle of some foul odor. We concluded that both alternatives were bad, but the best thing to do was not to alert the other guy and hope for the best. Now it would not be considered an impolite act to fail to warn your roommate of the impending doom.

On April 3, 1967, I had been a prisoner for two years. Only Alvarez, Shumaker, and Lockhart had more time than I had. On that day at the beginning of quiet hour, the celebration of the anniversary of my shoot down began. It was a complete surprise to me. Navy Lt. Jerry Coffee and Lt., j.g., Larry Spencer were the coordinators for the celebration, and they had assigned each room the responsibility for an event or a gift. The celebration began in the late morning. Happy came around and opened all of the doors in the building and let everyone out into the courtyard. The guys in room 1 had arranged to have a smorgasbord on a long table in front of the headquarters building. When I saw the food on the table, I salivated. Everything I could imagine was there. On the other side of the courtyard, a platform had been erected, and the London Philharmonic Orchestra was playing Beethoven's Fifth Symphony. The Mercedes sports car that they had bought for me was by the main gate, and it had a $45,000 price tag on it. Alongside the car was an expensive and elegant stereo set with one hundred of my favorite long-playing records. After the London Philharmonic finished Beethoven's Fifth, the entire cast of the stage show from the Sands Hotel in Las Vegas came into camp and put on a full performance. We hadn't seen such lovely girls for so long. After the show, several jazz bands alternated playing, and an open bar was set up. In the evening, five chefs from the Waldorf Astoria Hotel in New York City prepared the most sumptuous dinner I had ever had: Filet mignon, prime rib, baked potatoes with gobs of butter and sour cream, a wide assortment of exquisitely cooked vegetables and breads, and fantastic wine. We had baked Alaska for dessert.

After dinner, the Vietnamese told us we had to go back to our rooms, but just then the two junior guys in the building rolled out a cake on a small trailer. The cake was about six feet in diameter and about five feet high. It had four layers covered with four different,

204

delicious icings. Then, just as I was about to cut the cake, a charming and lovely young lady stepped out of the middle of it. At first, I was not sure who she was, but at second glance I could see it was our water girl. The two junior officers in the building had been assigned to clean her up and make her presentable. They assured me that she was as clean as they could get her after scrubbing her for nearly twenty-four hours, but they admitted she was not perfect, because it was impossible to get all the dirt off when she hadn't had a bath in five years. We all went back to our rooms and had our cake and coffee there. Norlan moved in with Percy for the night, and the water girl spent the night in my room with me. Without a doubt, it was the best party I ever had, and I know the guys who threw the party for me enjoyed it as much as I did.

We had counted about forty-five days of continuous overcast by the end of April 1967. This kind of weather was not conducive to bombing, so there had not been any bombing near our camp for months now. The *Tet* cease-fire had long since ended, and the war had resumed. So we figured that if we were ever going to get out of there, the U.S. had better get on with the bombing. I and some others had already concluded that sweet talk, negotiations, bombing halts, cease-fires, the carrot-and-stick policy, and all the other ploys used by President Johnson were not going to succeed. Just as the Vietnamese knew that threats alone could not make us write our confession, we believed that the only way to defeat North Vietnam was with bullets and bombs of iron and steel. That was the only thing the Vietnamese understood. That was how World War II ended: with the nearly total destruction of Germany and nuclear weapons in Japan. And that was probably the only way this war was going to end. The Vietnamese people were going to have to suffer, and people were going to have to die. Lots of women, children, and old people would have to die before we ever left Vietnam. I was convinced that these people were as determined to win the war as they said they were. In late April, the air alert sounded from time to time, and we could hear either the triple A or the bombing or both off in the distance. Even though the bombing wasn't very close to Hanoi, we were encouraged that it had started again.

Lt. Cdr. Doug Burns and Lt., j.g., Fred Purrington lived in room 1 of our building now. They had been doing some clean-up work for the Vietnamese around the kitchen on three or four occasions over the past several days. This kind of work was not commonly done by POWs, but many times the Vietnamese would let men out to do various kinds of work. Prisoners swept the sidewalks, street, and even the dirt walkways with the hand brooms that were provided to us for sweeping our own rooms. The men would sweep in code so anyone within hearing distance could copy. Sometimes guys dug up the garden, dug a hole for the sewage, or did many other kinds of odd jobs. Most guys enjoyed this kind of work, because they got out of their room, got some fresh air, exercise, and the opportunity to pass on information. Sometimes each room in the building would get a turn. But Norlan and I never got out, because of his broken arm and my broken leg. We complained to the officers that we never got out, but they only laughed at us. Some POWs considered this kind of work beneath the status of an officer, and they objected to doing any kind of work. They were technically correct in refusing, because under the Geneva Convention on Treatment of Prisoners of War, officers could not be required to do manual work. But given the pros and cons, I preferred to work.

Burns and Purrington had finished their work and probably had done a good job. Because it was work in the kitchen, it was beneficial to the prisoners. That day, everyone in the building got their normal ration of food at the last meal. Burns and Purrington were the last to pick up their food, and they noticed that the guard had put some extra pieces of meat on their plates. They took their plates inside their room. Then they debated whether they should eat the extra food or not. They thought that it could be considered a special favor, because others were not getting the same amount, but they also knew it would be no big thing to eat it. So they tapped to the room next to them to check with me for guidance. Before the question got to me, the guard had come to their door to pick up the dishes and, believing that it was better to be safe than sorry, they had decided not to eat it. The guard noticed that they had not eaten the extra portion of meat. The issue was moot now, because the guard had picked up their dishes. The question never got to me that night.

The next day, we learned that in the evening one of the camp officers had come to Burns and Purrington's room, opened the peephole, and said to them, "I have caught you communicating," and then he left. Ten minutes later, he came back with a guard who had leg irons and handcuffs. The officer told them they were being punished for communicating. They had not been communicating when the officer opened their peephole, but he obviously wanted to teach them a lesson for refusing the extra food. He did not want to let them know the real reason so he used the trumped-up charge of communicating. When word of what happened came to me, I couldn't do anything about it. If I had known before, I would have told them to go ahead and eat it and forget it. It was an isolated case. In my opinion, it would have been okay to eat a few extra pieces of meat.

The issue did not end there. It became controversial in our building. There were good arguments pro and con. The issue was debated for more than a week while Burns and Purrington remained in leg irons. Heated arguments broke out, and some guys stopped talking to each other. Some arguments became so fierce that a fist fight or two took place. The twenty guys in the building split 50-50 whether the men should have taken the meat or not. The older guys said, "Take it," and the younger guys said, "refuse it."

During the same time frame, another problem arose. What should be done with leftover food? In general, the younger men were bigger eaters than the older guys. For the most part, the rations of food were the same. But for a multitude of reasons, sometimes a man would not finish his meal. And at the same time, a guy two rooms down might still be hungry. So while some guys were throwing food away, others were begging for more. Some of the POWs thought that if a guy left food on his plate, the Vietnamese would think we did not need as much food as they were giving us, and they might cut the rations across the board. This would cause the guys who were hungry to be even hungrier. The chow hounds wanted all the extra food dumped into the *bo,* so the Vietnamese would think that because no food was being returned, the portions should be increased. In all probability, the Vietnamese couldn't have cared less about whatever we did. There was also the possibility that if they caught us throwing the food into the *bo,* that they might be mad, because they always had a dog, pig, or chickens around to eat the garbage. The argument raged for several days. I didn't think it would make any difference one way or the other, but to appease the chow hounds, I passed out the guidance to throw left over food into the *bo.*

Air Force Lt. Bernie Talley moved into the building in early May. He was a new shoot down and provided us with a lot of up-to-date news. Several days after he moved into the building, he told us that when he went out for the first time to wash, the guard escorted him to the bath area and locked him in, as he did with everyone else. Bernie said he looked around and was not sure how to wash, but finally took off all of his clothes, climbed into the large water storage tub, and washed himself with his soap. When Happy returned and saw him in the big tub, he almost went through the sky. Bernie did not know why Happy got so mad until he told a guy in the next room what had happened, and he learned what the proper procedures for bathing were. New guys certainly did some strange things. Even though we all washed with soapy water for the next few weeks, we had a good belly laugh over what he had done.

We got the word one day that Bernie had a quiz with the Elf. He said it was the best quiz he ever had because he smoked more than twenty cigarettes in an hour. Bernie figured if the Elf didn't say anything, it was O.K. to take them. We all knew that the Elf was generous with his cigarettes at quiz, but not that generous. We knew now where the coughing came from the day Bernie went to quiz.

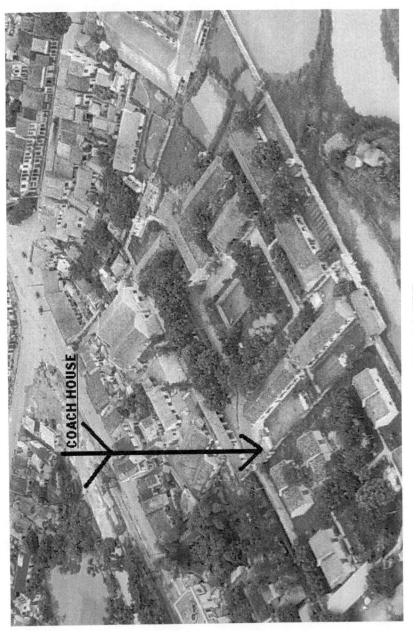

COACH HOUSE

May 1967. Norlan and I went out to wash early in the morning of 1 May 1967. It was a lovely day. The sky was clear blue, and it was going to be hot again. Shortly after we began to wash, we could hear explosions far off in the distance. We figured that the U.S. had started bombing again on the outskirts of Hanoi. Whether to protect us, prevent us from seeing anything, or just to get us out of the way, whenever any sign or sound of bombing occurred, the guard made us go to our rooms immediately. But on this day, he must have forgotten we were out in the yard. So we finished our washing as quickly as possible and then just enjoyed listening to the rumbling of the bombs and triple A off in the distance, while our eyes scanned the sky for a glimpse of one of our aircraft zooming by.

After ten minutes or so, Happy came and took us back to our room. Whenever bombing took place, the Vietnamese always seemed upset, and immediately the relations between us became more strained. Today was no different, as Happy snapped at me for walking too slowly back to my room. Perhaps in honor of International Workers Day, May Day, the Vietnamese gave us bread instead of rice with our meals that day. It was a real treat after a steady diet of rice for almost a year.

The bombing raids became more frequent over the next few weeks, and although they remained off in the distance most of the time, occasionally a raid came closer to the camp. Each day, we listened very carefully to the Voice of Vietnam to hear how many planes they claimed were shot down. We knew that they exaggerated, but generally if they said they had captured any pilots, they had probably bagged at least one.

As Norlan and I were talking to each other one night a couple of weeks after May Day, Billy the Kid–formerly food boy and now a sentry–suddenly opened the peephole and accused us of communicating. We had not been communicating, but it made no difference. He slapped me on the face four or five times, then slapped Norlan and left.

We went to quiz with the Elf the next afternoon. He accused us of having communicated the night before, and we told him that we were only talking to each other. It apparently made no difference, because he scolded us for the next five minutes. He left the room and about five minutes later returned with Quincy Collins and A.J. Myers. They moved all four of us into the Coach House, which was alongside the main gate directly across from the Gate House. The Coach House had not been renovated to accommodate prisoners. It was a one-room building about twenty feet square, with two large French doors in the front, four bed boards on sawhorses, and no vents. We realized that the air circulation was going to be bad. To my knowledge, this was the first time the Coach House had been used for prisoners.

All of the rooms in the Pool Hall that had only one man or had been vacant had been completely filled just before we left. Our move together may have taken place because so many air crewmen were captured in late April and early May, and the Vietnamese were in a temporary bind for space. Also, because Quincy, Norlan, and I had already lived together, and all four of us were injured, they could free up two high-security rooms temporarily without risk of four men escaping.

The weather the next four days was perfect for bombing. The sky was clear blue, and the air was still. The French doors had many holes and cracks in them, so we were all able to get a pretty good view of what was going on in camp. In addition to watching the normal camp activities, we could see an occasional white fleecy cloud pass overhead. The sun shone clear and bright all day. The heat was severe and didn't dissipate at night. We were so dehydrated, that after one day the *bo* was still only about a quarter full. Four guys would normally fill the bucket in one day easily.

The U.S. took advantage of the good weather, and the bombing around Hanoi on 18, 19, 20, and 21 May was more intense than it had ever been. On the eighteenth, raids came in at a rate of at least one every hour all day long. The noise and concussions from the triple A and SAMS were just as powerful as the noise and concussions from the exploding bombs, and the sounds were almost indistinguishable. The raids stopped around sunset, but the Vietnamese did not. Throughout the entire night, we could hear tractors, trucks, and other vehicles moving. We surmised that they were probably repositioning their triple A and SAM sites or repairing damage from the bombs.

On the nineteenth of May, Ho Chi Min's birthday, the raids grew more intense than before. Maybe the heavy raids on that day were supposed to have some negative psychological impact on the Vietnamese. The time between air raids was so short that they did not even sound the air raid alert and clear siren any more. As wave after wave of aircraft approached the city, the noise from the SAMS, triple A, and bombs was deafening. We knew that gun emplacements were not far from our camp, and we hoped that a bomb, unexploded shell from the triple A, or debris from the sky would not fall on us. We needed no urging to abide by the camp regulation requiring prisoners to be under their beds during air alerts. The Coach House did not have a peephole, so we didn't have to worry about being caught out from under the beds. Nevertheless, we scrambled under the beds whenever the explosions came close.

The room we were in did not have a speaker, so we could not hear the camp radio or Voice of Vietnam radio program. We knew when the radio was on, however, because we could hear the speakers in the building closest to ours. We strained our ears to hear what they were broadcasting. Even though the propaganda was atrocious, we could get some reasonably accurate information by assuming that the reverse of what they said was true, or by cutting in half the figures favorable to the Vietnamese and doubling the figures unfavorable to them. Sometimes they actually announced the names of men who had been captured. We were able to hear long lists of the pilots who were supposedly captured, but we could not make out their names. That day was one of the worst of the air war. We actually lost eight planes and twelve crewmen, but the Vietnamese claimed that they had shot down thirty planes and killed or captured forty men. They always inflated the numbers. Whether they knew the actual count or not is debatable.

The intensity of the bombing continued throughout the third day. Without explanation, the Vietnamese served us a fantastic meal. We each got a whole plate of melted butter and delicious hot bread. It was the first time I'd had butter there. We noticed that the Vietnamese often gave us special meals when they were having hard times. Some of us felt that instead of trying to take out revenge on us, they tried to show their strength by giving us a treat.

The triple A and SAMS had been fierce the first two and a half days, as the planes approached and bombed targets around Hanoi. But toward the end of the third day, the defenses seemed to weaken. After the first few raids on the fourth day, wave after wave of our planes came in, and at most there would be an isolated shot here and there. It must have been a blessing for the pilots, who had spent three days facing intense anti-aircraft opposition. The Vietnamese must have run out of supplies and were now sitting there like ducks in a pond.

The next day, the bombing stopped. In fact, a long time would pass before Hanoi was bombed again with the intensity of the past four days. There would be more than enough time for the Vietnamese to stock up on ammunition for their triple A and SAMS. I'll never know why we stopped bombing at that time. Many pilots who flew missions over Hanoi were killed because of the intense air defense. It made me sick to know that when we were finally able to drop bombs in complete safety and with minimum risk, we stopped the bombing. One of the guys killed during that period had been a friend of mine. Military men might be expendable, but to sacrifice lives and then not take advantage of their sacrifice just didn't seem right to me. I wondered whether the admirals, generals, and high-ranking Defense Department officials really knew what was going on and what explanation there could possibly be for discontinuing the bombing.

The night the bombing ended, Scum came to the door right after dark and gave us all the roll-up sign. He came back five minutes later after we got our things together. Scum motioned me to go ahead. I expected Norlan to follow, but instead Scum locked the door behind me. It was very dark out. I passed the garage, and he directed me to the end room of the Barn, where I had lived back in August 1966. He unlocked the door and motioned me in. The room was dark when I went in, but I could make out that another man was there. I was absolutely certain that Scum had made a mistake and had put me in with the wrong guy. There was no reason to separate me from my old roommates. It was not the nature of the Vietnamese to give me another roommate. I said to the other prisoner, "Talk softly. I'm sure the guard made a mistake, and as soon as he finds out, I'll be leaving." The door slammed loudly behind me.

I waited and waited for Scum to come back. I didn't even unpack my bedroll, but I realized after half an hour that I indeed had a new roommate. Moving the four of us together the day before the intensive bombing started and then separating us after the bombing had stopped made me wonder if the Vietnamese knew when the bombing would start and stop. How did they know? It had been fun living with A.J., Quincy, and Norlan, and even though I had a new roommate, it wasn't going to be as good as it had been in the Coach House.

CHAPTER 16 - THE BARN

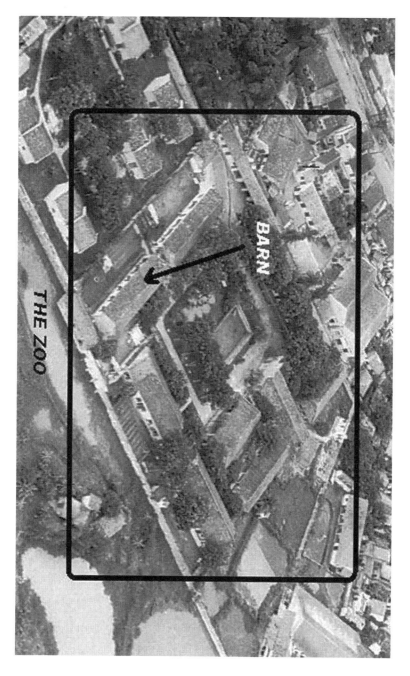

June 1967 – Early September 1967. My new roommate was Maj. Will Gideon. He had been flying an F105D when he was shot down on 6 August 1966. He was a real fighter jock. We sat and talked for a few minutes, but because of the darkness, the mosquitoes were quite bad. Will helped me put up my mosquito net. He told me that the light was not out as a punishment, but apparently the light switch had a problem. After exchanging some more chitchat, we decided to call it a night, because it was already quite late. We said goodnight to each other. For the next five minutes or so, I lay on my bed going over the day's events in my mind, and just as I was about to doze off, I heard the loudest snore I had ever heard in my life. But after half an hour of listening to Will snore and thinking about how I was going to cope with this new disaster, I finally fell asleep, too.

The next morning, I told him what had happened. He said that it was nothing new, and that he had snored loudly ever since he was a youngster. He and his wife had agreed many years ago to use separate bedrooms. If ever a woman was justified in not sleeping in the same room as her husband, it had to be Will Gideon's wife. He expressed sympathy with my plight and told me that I should shake him, and that would make him stop for a while. Thank God, I was a pretty good sleeper and fell asleep first most of the time. Otherwise, I just shook him until he stopped snoring, and then I would usually fall asleep before he started snoring again.

Will had two children, a boy and a girl. He called them a gentleman's pair. He was from Arlington, Virginia. He talked about sitting alongside the Potomac River when he was a kid and watching the used condoms and Moon Pie wrappers floating down the river. Then we talked about his shoot down. He had been hit by ground fire and ejected, but he didn't remember anything else until ten days later. Although he had broken his leg, it was healed now.

He had been a stick and rudder guy most of his career, and even though he was an American, he had been a member of the British Air Force acrobatic team, which was their counterpart to the USAF Thunderbirds and USN Blue Angels. He had an excellent career going for him. And he was just about the easiest guy to get along with that I ever met.

I tried to figure out why the Vietnamese had moved me in with him and why I had been moved so many times in the two years I was there. Did they have a master plan or some legitimate reason for shuffling the prisoners around so often? Or were the moves merely happenstance? I never found out the reason for sure, but I suspected they probably had a good one. Ho Chi Minh, Pham Van Dong, Le Duc Tho, and General Giap, the Vietnamese leadership, had all spent considerable time in prison, so they were probably well-versed in how a prison camp should be run. We had read what the Vietnamese had written about how the French occupied Vietnam. They said the French philosophy was to divide Vietnam every way possible–territorially, politically, economically, and religiously. The more successful they were in dividing Vietnam, the easier it would be to conquer the country. The French made every effort to oppose any kind of unity by the Vietnamese. The more united the Vietnamese, the stronger they stood; the more divided, the easier to conquer. We thought that the frequent moves might have been intended to destroy any unity of purpose that might develop among the POWs. In addition, shuffling the prisoners resulted in a continuous change in leadership and command structure, keeping us off balance, as well as minimizing the opportunity to escape or engage in other forms of resistance.

Although our room was small, it had a window with bars on it high up on the front wall. The window was about three feet long by two feet high. This made living a little more pleasant because the room was not as unbearably hot as some were. We had a new turnkey I had never seen before. Will had already named him Einstein. The exact mental opposite of Einstein, our turnkey frequently forgot to let us out to wash, and he was terrible with the cigarette lights. Most of the time, he looked as if he was in a daze. He walked back and forth from time to time, as if he had forgotten something, remembered it, and then forgotten it again.

During June, the weather was very hot, and the sky stayed crystal clear blue, day after day. The weather could not have been any better for bombing than it was now. We had not one air alert, however, or even the sound of explosions from triple A or SAMS off in the distance. During this same period, there were times when the Voice of Vietnam radio program didn't come on for several days or more, so we were somewhat hopeful that the four days of intensive bombing in May might have made the North Vietnamese more tractable. Nonetheless, they appeared to be preparing for more bombing. They started using large searchlights to spot enemy planes coming in to bomb, and they also began employing huge barrage balloons. I had heard of them being used in World War II as an impediment to the flight of enemy aircraft. It was a new thing here. If an aircraft ran into one of them, it might damage the plane or even make it crash. They were anchored to the ground with rope or wire and varied in size from ten to twenty feet in diameter. We surmised that they were filled with a special gas, because they appeared to be at least two or three thousand feet high in the sky. On some days, we could see as many as twenty or thirty of them at different heights, scattered over a large area. On more than one occasion, a balloon would break loose from its anchor and sail off into the wild blue yonder. These balloons were used for several months, after which I never saw them again. We figured the balloons were located near an airfield to protect it.

Communicating wasn't nearly as much fun in this room as it had been in the Pool Hall. As we were in an end room, we only had one room to talk to, instead of the three rooms that Norlan and I had had in the Pool Hall. Will always had to be on the floor clearing, while I did the communicating. Also, this building didn't house as many guys as the Pool Hall did. Consequently, we played a lot of chess. Making a chess set was easy. We would tear up some paper in different shapes and sizes for the pieces and draw a chessboard on the floor with a stone, or line some paper by folding it and making creases. We always kept the set under our bed mat when we weren't using it.

One day, we heard a large gathering of Vietnamese outside our door, and because Einstein had made Will sweep the floor that morning we concluded that there was going to be a room inspection. Our chess set was the only thing we had against camp regulations. It was no big deal to get caught with it, but as it was easy to replace, Will took the set and threw it into the *bo*. When the inspection party came in, Spot was in charge. He pointed at the *bo*, rushed over to me, and shouted like I had never heard Spot shout before. He had heard the *bo* being closed just as the door was being opened. Spot told us never to do that again or we would be punished severely. Will was totally befuddled and had no idea what Spot was talking about. It dawned on me immediately that Spot had remembered the time he caught Quincy putting the lid on the *bo* after stirring up the contents before an inspection, and he thought we were pulling the same trick again. I told Will why Spot was so upset after the inspection. Will never opened the *bo* before an inspection again.

This reminded Will of another misunderstanding that had happened to him years before when he was stationed in England. He said he and his wife had been invited to a party at his British squadron commander's house. They drove to the house, got out of the car, and walked to the front door. After he knocked on the door, he sneezed. As he covered his mouth, a booger stuck to his hand. At the same time, the door opened, and before Will could dispose of the booger, the squadron commander extended his hand to Will. As they shook hands, the booger stuck to the commander's hand. Apparently the commander didn't notice what happened, so Will was relieved. That night as Will and his wife were leaving, however, the commander shook Will's hand and placed the same booger back on Will's hand. He said without a smile, "Sir, I believe this belongs to you."

The food was still as bad as ever. Rice or bread, a chicken foot, chicken head, pig's ear or eye, pig fat, chicken bone, dried fish bones, and of course greens, kohlrabi, carrots, and other assorted vegetables along with it. One day, we got bread, greens soup and a side plate with a cup and a half of sugar. I told Will, "It's finally happened. They are trying to kill us now." The side plate usually had a larger portion of the vegetable that was in the soup and something that was supposed to be the protein or meat portion of the dinner. That was bad enough, but now the side dish was a bowl of sugar. I finished my soup and then started to eat the sugar, spoonful by spoonful. I ate about five spoonfuls and said the heck with it. Before long we got bowls of brown sugar, too. The Vietnamese were not all that bad, however, because they started to mix the sugar with hot rice. Another specialty that substituted for the soup on Sunday from time to time was the same size soup bowl filled with hot tea and lots of sugar in it.

We continued having a quiz every three or four weeks. In general, everyone was getting the same propaganda and being asked to do such things as repair hospitals that had been bombed, work on the construction of new hospitals, repair non-war-related things damaged by bombs, and even help play with and take care of parentless Vietnamese children. Sometimes they would single out one guy for something and another guy for something else. They might really put the pressure on one guy and leave another alone if he refused. There appeared to be no rhyme or reason why they did what they did.

Spot was our building officer now, and he had a good deal for everyone in the building. We did not have to write anything, but to show our good will, he wanted us to help undo the damage the U.S. had caused. There were no takers in our building, but Spot continued to feel us out. He asked everyone in the building if we would like to receive money from home? We would be allowed to write home and ask our families for money if we wanted to. When the money came, the Vietnamese would buy things for the person to whom the money was sent. They would buy candy, beer, extra food, and other things that the person might want.

It sounded as if it might be a good deal, but unless every prisoner was able to take advantage of the offer, we had to refuse. No one in our building accepted the offer, but we heard there were a couple of guys who took the Vietnamese up on it and asked for money from their wives. Their wives sent money, and the Vietnamese bought stuff with it for them. When the POWs finally got the word that what they had done was wrong, they made a big pitch to divide all the goodies with the people in their building. When the Vietnamese said no, the men had no other choice but to refuse the items purchased from the money sent by their families. I do not know if the guys did anything for the Vietnamese for this favor, or whether they just got snookered. There was no doubt that this was a dumb move, because they were able to receive rather large amounts of things that others couldn't have.

In mid-July we were still without a light in the room. We figured that someone must have told Einstein to get the light fixed, because one night someone came to the outside of our door, and it sounded like he was working on the light switch. After about twenty minutes, it still didn't work. But now we could hear the switch being turned on and off without success. The guy tried a number of times before Will started to count, just for the fun of it. After he turned the switch on and off more than one hundred times, the light came on. Will and I could never figure out how this happened, but we both acknowledged that if this guy was a typical Vietnamese, they had a lot of determination and patience.

Einstein let us out of the room one day so that Will could sweep the sidewalk. He let me just sit and watch. At this time there were two prisoners from Thailand living in the camp with us. At first, they both lived alone, but after a year or so, they were allowed to live together. We weren't exactly sure who they were or what their status was, but they worked as sort of trustees for the Vietnamese. They were let out of their room in the early morning, worked all day, and then went back to their room at night. Maybe to maintain that trustee status, they did not bother too much with us. One Thai spoke some English, the other none at all. One day, we were out, and both of them were mixing some mortar near where we were. Einstein left the area for about ten or fifteen minutes, which enabled us to talk to them briefly. I showed them pictures of my wife and children, and they seemed to be pleased with that.

Around the middle of July, the bombing started again. Many raids took place during quiet hour, when the heat was intense. Perhaps the U.S. strategists hoped that bombing during the time that the Vietnamese normally took a siesta would disrupt their routine more and have some negative psychological effect on them, as well. From what I could observe, they couldn't have cared less. The air-raid siren would sound, and when it stopped, the silence was deathly, and we would wait. The silence would last five, ten, twenty, or even thirty minutes, and if the bombers didn't come, the all-clear would sound. The only sound to interrupt the silence now and then was Billy the Kid, who would yell out something in his high-pitched voice

Sometimes, the alert would sound, and we could hear the drone of jet engines off in the distance, but then the noise would fade. Other times, we heard the jet engines, triple A and SAMS being fired, and then the bombs exploding. The most exciting times were when the bombers came close to our camp. Then we heard the triple A, SAMS, and bombs go wild. We could hear the planes rolling in on their run and hear them pulling off the target and flying what sounded like right over our camp. These were old familiar sounds. A plane could be could be almost two or three miles away from the camp, and the wind could carry the roar of the jet engine so it might sound like the plane was overhead.

We always knew that one of our aircraft had been hit, when all the guards would shout and clap their hands. One day, the raid was off in the distance, and Will and I were looking at a small piece of the sky through our window. I had heard SAMS being launched for years now but had never seen one in flight. The Vietnamese did not have them when I was shot down, but they had plenty now. Suddenly we saw a SAM come into view. Seconds later, we could both see the SAM approaching an F-105 about 12,000-15,000 feet high in the sky. Frightened and sickened, we watched as the SAM exploded into a large orange ball of fire when it approached the aircraft, and then the aircraft came apart. We never saw a chute, but we lost view of the aircraft while it was still quite high in the sky. While all this was going on, we could hear very loud cheers and clapping from the guards.

I had several quizzes with Spot during the last few weeks of August 1967. Spot was not one of the worst officers, but he did what he was supposed to do. It appeared to me that many of the Vietnamese officers manifested feminine characteristics. I don't know whether this was a cultural thing or just typical of the men we came in contact with. Spot could often be seen strolling around the camp holding another officer's hand or walking with his arm wrapped around another man's waist. One time, word was passed around that Spot had been seen walking with one of his hands in another Vietnamese guy's pocket. At quiz, however, he never showed any feminine traits.

Spot accused me of having given orders when I was in the Pool Hall. Only three months had passed since I left the Pool Hall, so many of the old guys were probably still there. As a result of Spot's questions, I suspected that they were under pressure to write and do other things just as we were. The Vietnamese always kept the pressure on. Apparently, someone in the Pool Hall had been caught doing something and had been forced to relate the guidance I had put out when I was the SRO there. When a guy was tortured, he tried to get the Vietnamese to stop by giving as little as possible. Because I had passed out nothing more than innocuous guidance when I was the SRO, maybe the POW figured that if he told them what I had said, it would get them off his back but not get me in serious trouble. I never found out who told the Vietnamese about the guidance, but I knew someone had fingered me, because Spot accused me of four or five things that I had in fact passed out. The Vietnamese were vehemently opposed to anyone giving orders and especially orders to resist them in any way.

In late August, I had another quiz with Spot. He accused me of violating the food policy of the Democratic Republic of Vietnam by telling the prisoners to throw food that they did not eat into the *bo*. I could not explain to him why I did this, because it would entail admitting to having communicated, and that could possibly compound the problem, even though the charge of communicating is an inherent part of giving an order. I denied the accusation. I spent the next few days in the quiz room, either with him or alone standing in a corner of the room on my crutches. At first, just standing in a corner on one leg on crutches wasn't too bad, but after three or four hours it became a drag. It was not going to kill me, but it was not pleasant.

I finally wrote less than one page about how the Vietnamese considered me to be a war criminal and not a prisoner of war, and how the Vietnamese believed they were giving us lenient and humane treatment. The next day, I went to quiz again. Spot said that he did not like what I wrote and that I would not get anything to eat that day, because I had violated the food policy of the DRV. I stayed in the quiz room all day again on my crutches and missed both meals. I figured I was pretty lucky to get off as easily as I did. It could have been much worse.

On 2 September, Vietnamese Independence Day, we received one of the worst meals that we ever had. It was half-cooked fish heads. The presence of so many bones made the food inedible. They also forgot to give us our cigarettes. I had the feeling that maybe our bombing was beginning to take a toll. Such a day surprisingly raised our spirits, because we figured that things were going to get bad before we finally got to go home.

CHAPTER 17 - CUBAN PROGRAM

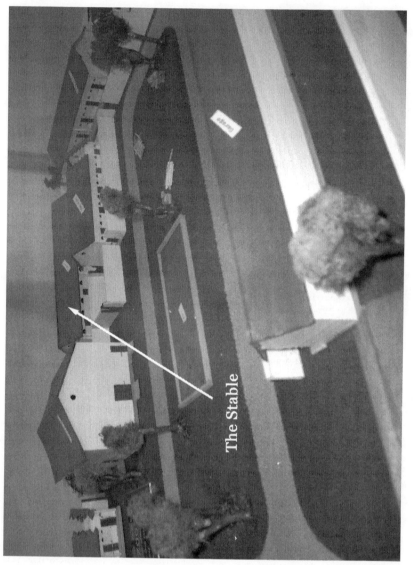

September 1967 – March 1968. The next day, we got word from the other side of the camp that a few guys had had a quiz with a Caucasian. This was really big news. Prisoners had met with Caucasians from the United States and Western European countries who were part of visiting delegations before, but always in downtown Hanoi. We couldn't believe that the Vietnamese would ever let a Caucasian into the camp, so he could see how we actually lived. I felt sure the Vietnamese suspected that some members of visiting delegations were agents, and in truth, some probably reported everything they observed to the U.S. government. Therefore, this Caucasian really had to be trusted by the Vietnamese. One of the guys who had had a quiz with him was Norlan Daughtrey.

Several nights later, just after the Voice of Vietnam Radio program had ended, the gong had sounded, and I had begun to doze off, I heard the sound of keys jingling outside our door. The lock was opened, the bolt thrown, the door opened, and a guard entered the room. I pretended I had been asleep, so I was sitting on the bed when he entered the room, and I did not get up and bow. He called me by my Vietnamese name, Vah, wrapped his arms around his shoulders indicating that I should dress. I put on my long black pants and pajama tops, tied the belt strings, got on my crutches, and left the room. After a two-minute walk to the headquarters building, I entered the quiz room, and sitting behind the table were Lump and a rather large-framed man who was just as much a Caucasian as I was.

The camp interrogators were all military officers and although they almost always wore civilian clothes, they wore their uniforms occasionally. The only exception I knew was Lump. We surmised that he was a fairly high-ranking civilian who was a staff assistant to the camp commander and the senior interrogator. Off to the side of the table was another Caucasian sitting on a chair. I bowed, and the Caucasian told me to sit down on the stool in front of the table. Although he appeared to have some Latin features, my first impression, based on the type of shirt he was wearing, was that he was from Rumania, Bulgaria, or another middle-European country. I also had a hunch that maybe he was a professor or anti-war activist from some visiting delegation whom the Vietnamese really trusted, and they were going to let him talk to a few prisoners right in camp.

I soon realized that this guy knew what he was talking about. He asked me military questions about my ship, and I gave him some bull. I found it fairly easy to lie, because everything related to the period of my shoot down was already two and a half years old, and besides Soviet trawlers had followed us twenty-four hours a day for the last month before I was shot down, so there was nothing to hide. Although he spoke with a slight accent, his English was excellent. It was far better than that of any of the Vietnamese. I was surprised and frightened. He seemed almost like an American, but an American who had gone over to the enemy side. After some military questions, he asked about my feelings on the war. I told him that I believed we were there to stop the spread of Communism and help defend South Vietnam against aggression from the North Vietnamese, and that I supported and backed President Johnson all the way. This appeared to irritate him, and for the next forty-five minutes, he lectured me about U.S. imperialism, the U.S. war of aggression, and the just and noble cause of the brave and heroic Vietnamese people.

Then he and Lump went outside and left me with the other Caucasian, who spoke fairly good English. He had a very corrugated looking face that reminded me of a friend's brother when I was a kid. He gave me some more of the same crap, but then he told me that his friend was a very important person, and that I would be wise to understand the true nature of this imperialist war of aggression by the U.S. He said, "You would be a fool not to take this deal." I didn't know what deal he was talking about. A few minutes later, Lump and the lead Caucasian came back into the room. I got a good look at him on his feet, as he walked to the table. He looked to be about 6 feet 2 inches tall, weighed about 185 pounds, had dark brown hair in a crewcut, and penetrating dark brown eyes. After another half hour's harrangue about the U.S. war of aggression, I was sent back to my room.

I told Will Gideon what had happened, and he couldn't figure it out any better than I could. It had been an unusual experience, and I lay awake wondering what my encounter with the Caucasian was all about, until late in the night when I finally fell asleep. The next day was business as usual, and after a few days I forgot all about my meeting with him.

On the following Sunday morning, the turnkey came to the room to let us empty the *bo* and put our water pitchers outside the room so that the water girl could fill them. Will emptied the *bo* and returned to the room. A little later, the water girl came by and as she was filling one of the jugs with water, she dropped it. We could hear it break as it hit the concrete steps. When mealtime came, the turnkey opened the door to let Will pick up the food and our water jugs. The turnkey did not know that the water girl had broken the jug, so he chewed out Will for it. My jug was the one that broke, but Will shared his water with me.

This was not the first time that my jug had broken. They always brought another one eventually, but because they had logistical problems and our not having enough water was not a matter of life or death, two or three weeks might pass before they brought another jug. It was no small inconvenience for us, because when it was hot, we needed every drop of water we could get.

11 September 1967. On Monday morning the routine began as usual, but just before our first meal normally would have been served, the turnkey came to the door and gave me the sign to move. I said to myself, "Oh, not again. Am I going into solitary again because the Vietnamese want something from me, or will I get some roommate that I don't get along with?" I had been with Will for more than three months, and he was a good roommate, so when I realized that he was not moving with me, I was immediately depressed. I had already moved many times since becoming a prisoner twenty-nine months ago, so I knew I would survive this move. I left the room with all my possessions minus a water pitcher. The turnkey got one of the guards to carry my bedroll, and as I walked out of the door, I said goodbye to Will.

I walked on the road to the other side of the camp, past the front of the Pool Hall building, made a right turn and walked alongside the Auditorium until I got to the Stable. I had seen the Stable building before but had never lived there. Like the Barn or Office, it was not a desirable building to live in because there were only a few rooms. The guard opened the door to room 1. This room was three times larger than my last room. As I went in, I saw another prisoner standing by his bed. We introduced ourselves. He was Air Force Maj. Jack Bomar, and he had been shot down in February 1967. He seemed like a fairly pleasant guy, and we talked about this and that, as I unpacked my gear and prepared for the noon meal.

Soon after we finished the meal, a guard opened the door again and another prisoner came in. His named was Gene Dundas and he was an Air Force captain. Both had been captured less than seven months ago. In a very short time, we learned that we all had had quizzes with the Caucasian within the proceeding week. That afternoon, someone suggested we call the tall Caucasian Fidel and the short one Chico. One of the guys thought they might be from

Cuba, given their accents, knowledge of the U.S., and the strong tie that existed between Cuba and North Vietnam. In comparing notes about our quizzes, Dundas said that Chico had told him that this was the opportunity of a lifetime. I told them that Chico had said that I would be a fool not to take this deal. After some considerable discussion, we made an educated guess that maybe this had to do with some sort of early release program.

As had always been the custom with all other prisoners with whom I had ever had contact, we told each other what our date of rank was in order to establish who was the senior man. Once again, I was the senior man. As I had been there the longest, I obviously knew a lot more about what was going on than they did. I passed on all the guidance that had been previously issued. That guidance in general was to follow the Code of Conduct, but more detailed guidance dictated that we were not to make any propaganda statements, written or oral, not to tape or read anything for the camp radio, nor do anything for the Vietnamese. We were expected to take torture to the utmost of our ability before we did any of those things.

I passed all of this on to Bomar and Dundas. Bomar took it all in stride, but it appeared that Dundas did not like what he was hearing. In no time at all, he started acting strange. He questioned my date of rank. He said maybe I was lying. "For all I know, I'm the senior man." Then he said, "Who the hell are Lt. Col. Risner and Cdr. Denton?" He said he had never heard of them. He questioned not only my authority as senior officer in the room, but the guidance from Risner and Denton, as well, and told me without batting an eyelash that he wasn't about to be tortured before he would write a propaganda statement or do other things that violated the Code of Conduct. He said, when he was captured, they had put one of his legs in a stock and tied one of his hands to the other stock for a day or so. And he had talked. I understood why. But you didn't give

Ray Vohden

up forever. I wasn't the strongest resister in the world, but at least I tried as best I could. I said to myself, "Where did this guy come from?" I had been in contact with many prisoners in the past, but I never heard a man talk like this. I continued to pass on the rest of the guidance that I had received and stated that I intended to follow it to the best of my ability. Dundas told me that he would do what he wanted to do, and that is where that conversation ended.

Maybe there was a personality conflict between Dundas and me, but the problem did not end with the Code of Conduct. I still had not been given a new water jar. Bomar said that he had a kidney problem before he was shot down and had to drink all the water he got in his pitcher, and Dundas said he would give me whatever water he had left over each time. This left me less than happy, and although the water girl filled up my small cup each time, my water intake was cut down considerably. Boy, did I miss the good old days now.

12 September 1967. The next day, each of us had a quiz with Fidel and Chico. According to what Bomar and Dundas said and what I observed, the quizzes were similar and for the most part pleasant. We could smoke all the cigarettes we wanted. Fidel gave us his view on the war and wanted to know what our views were. He said we could speak our minds freely. There were no threats or any other unpleasant things about the quiz. We figured he was giving us the soft sell by trying to be a nice guy. During the next few days, we all had one quiz a day in a similar vein. As we got to know Fidel better, we realized how well he spoke and understood English and how familiar he was with our slang, double entendres, and idioms. He frequently asked us about our wives, children, and families, and he was always talking about how nice it would be to be back home again with our families.

18 September 1967. After the same old routine, we all began to be impatient and wondered what was going on. The early release idea kept popping up. In a way, it was a nice thing to think about. Hell, who wouldn't like to get out of this dump? Based on the way the war was going, an early release might have been the only way we would ever get out of here. Early release was nothing new. The Vietnamese had talked to many guys about it before. Unfortunately, the price for an early release was just a little less than selling your soul. As pleasant as Fidel was sometimes, at other times he appeared to be trying to establish a position of authority over us.

I could see nothing but trouble down the road. I decided that I would try to be a little less polite and maybe even a little obnoxious, so that he would consider me unqualified for whatever purpose he had in mind. And then send me back to my old roommate. At the next two quizzes, I refused cigarettes, acted bored with what he was saying, and gave only yes and no answers to his questions. He soon stopped being friendly to me. At the end of the second quiz, he accused me of being a wise guy and having a bad attitude. He said that he was going to teach me a good lesson. As I left the quiz room, I thought my plan was working, and the lesson he was going to teach me was that I would be thrown out of his early release program or whatever he had going.

20 September 1967. Two days passed by, and in the evening the turnkey came to the door and gave Dundas the roll-up sign to move. Bomar and I didn't know what to make of it but went to sleep anyway.

21 September 1967. The next morning, the guard came to the door and indicated that I should get ready for quiz. I got dressed and left the room. This time, I did not go to Fidel's quiz room but to another building. When I entered the room, I saw the Elf sitting behind the desk. I felt relieved and was almost happy to see the Elf again. He was without a doubt one of the better interrogators to have a quiz with. He told me to sit on the stool in front of the table. This morning, he appeared to be somewhat nervous and uncomfortable. Without any introductory nice talk, he asked me what orders I gave when I was in the Pool Hall. I told him that I had never given any orders and that I did not communicate. He said that I was not telling the truth. In no time, he told me four or five things that I had passed out to the guys in the Pool Hall when I was the SRO there. Spot told me the same thing a month ago, so I knew someone had spilled the beans. He mentioned at least three times that I had ordered the men in the building to throw their extra food into the *bo* instead of leaving it in the plates to be picked up. He said that it was very bad to waste the people's food and that it was a crime against the Vietnamese people.

He wanted to know all the other orders that I had given. I told him that I hadn't given any. He walked to the door and said something to one of the guards. He asked me four or five more times if I gave orders, and I still said no. I began to wonder what was going on. Five minutes after Elf had talked to the guard, about six guards came into the room, and one of them was carrying some parachute straps and manacles. I couldn't believe what I was seeing. I had only given a few harmless orders, and now they were going to give me the straps. Should I just go ahead and admit it?

Before I knew what was happening, one of the guards pulled me off the stool, and I landed on my butt. Elf said something to Magoo. They made me sit up straight. One guard grabbed the right arm and pulled it behind me, and another did the same with the left arm. They manacled my wrists together. Three or four more guards came into the room. I had heard that this was always a clue that someone was about to be bent. The manacles were screwed tightly together. Then they wrapped the nylon strap around my arms above the elbows in a way that enabled them to force my elbows together by pulling one end of the strap with one or more guards. Wrestling for eight years and walking on crutches had tightened up my shoulder muscles a bit. And although I was very thin, it was impossible to get my elbows within a foot of each other when they were placed behind my back.

While Magoo and another guard were putting on the manacles and straps, the Elf kept telling me all I had to do was confess to giving orders and tell him what the orders were, and I would not be punished. I really don't know why I didn't admit to giving orders. It was no big deal. Maybe what I told Dundas and what he said to me made me do it. Perhaps I thought this would insure that I would get out of the Fidel program. I told the Elf again that I gave no orders. He just looked at me and then he nodded to Magoo to go ahead.

The straps were snug now. They rolled me over on my side and one of the guards started to tighten the straps. As they were tightened, it started to hurt at the wrists because they were twisting. The straps became tighter around the arms, and now I had a feeling in the whole arm like when the doctor took my blood pressure as he blew up the band around my arm. The shoulders and the lower part of the back of my neck began to hurt. I moaned and groaned a bit. It hurt like hell, but I could still take it. This was how it all began. Little by little, they tightened up on the straps. The pain was impossible to describe, but it hurt like hell. I said to myself, "This is a lot different from wrestling," because with two human bodies, there was always a little bit of give, but with the manacles and straps it was a mechanical thing, there was no give. I became frightened because even though it hurt, the numbness and loss of feeling became worse. What if I lost the use of my hands?

After about ten, twenty, or thirty minutes, I lost track of time. But the pain was too much for me, and I started to cry and yelled that it was hurting. The Elf told me to be quiet, or they would put stones in my mouth. I yelled out again, and one of the guards went outside and returned with a handful of dirt and stones. Then he tried to stuff my mouth with it, but I stopped yelling before they could get the dirt in. I said to myself, "Enough of this bullshit. I've had enough." I said, "O.K., I'll tell you all the orders I gave, and yes I told everyone to throw their garbage food in the *bo*. As soon as I gave up, Elf told me he would not release me now. He said I would have to wait awhile so that next time I would think twice before I gave any orders.

After some indeterminable time, they loosened the straps, and the pain started to go away, but the arms and hands were still numb. As they were unscrewing the manacles, the door suddenly burst open and in came Fidel, ranting and pointing his finger at me and telling me that I'd better have a good attitude now and do everything he said. Not about to give him a hard time, I shook my head in agreement. When they finally got the straps and manacles off, Fidel told me to sit on the stool. The guards helped me to get up. As soon as I was seated, they put the manacles on my wrists again, but this time my hands were in front of me. Then Fidel came over, shook his finger in my face, and said, "When I give you cigarettes to smoke, and you don't smoke them, I will make you eat those cigarettes until they come out of your ears, you fooker." Then he slapped me on the face with his open hand about six or seven times, while telling me again and again that I'd better be nice and do everything he told me to.

I couldn't believe all this was happening. As they had pushed me around, I could feel my leg stretching and pulling at the spot where the piece of bone was missing, and as Fidel slapped me, I thought for sure the wound would open up. Fortunately, it did not. Everybody left the room, and now I was alone. After about fifteen minutes, the feeling started to return to my hands and arms, and the pain had almost disappeared. Fidel came in again, stood behind the desk and asked me if I was going to do everything he told me to do. I said yes. He said, "If you think what you just got was bad, you haven't seen anything compared to what you will get if you ever cheat me."

With that, he called the guard to unscrew the manacles. He said, "Now prove to me that you will do anything I say." He took a piece of paper from a notebook, tore it in half, gave one piece of the paper and a pen to me, and told me to write that I surrendered to the Vietnamese people and would do everything they wanted me to do. After I wrote what he dictated, he told me, "Now eat the paper to prove you will do everything I say." I ate the paper. It was very hard to chew and did not break up very well. It tasted terrible. I finally managed to swallow it, after almost gagging and throwing up. Fidel just stood there and watched. Finally, Fidel left, a guard brought my crutches, and with God's help, I was still able to use crutches. I walked back to my room.

When I walked into the room, I could see that it was empty. Bomar had moved. I said to myself as I sat down on the bed, "Thank God that's over with." I had just finished changing into my short pants, when the door opened and Magoo came in with leg irons. My heart dropped into my stomach. He connected them to a bed board on the floor, motioned me to get on the bed and put my ankles into the irons. I was wrong. It wasn't over. As soon as my legs were in the irons, and I was sitting on the bed, Magoo said, "Commander," in terrible English, shook his finger at me, drew back his hand, and hit me on the face as hard as he could. He left. At least they didn't cuff my hands behind me, but getting up on crutches from the floor was going to be a real problem.

22 September 1967. The Elf had given me the straps so that I would admit to giving orders. But Fidel couldn't have cared less about tossing food in the crap bucket. It was a clever way to get me under his control without his being responsible for the straps. This was not good at all. The next day, I had a quiz, and Fidel told to write about my aircraft. I wasn't in any mood to get the straps again, but I still didn't want to give them anything of value. I wrote some bull about the aircraft and mentally made up reasonable explanations for any mistakes, if I was caught in a lie. Fortunately, he never asked me another thing about the plane. The next day, I had another quiz, and Fidel told me that I had to make a tape for the GIs in the South. He told me some things that I should write. I wrote as badly as I could. Fortunately, Fidel did not like what or how I wrote. He told me that for an American officer, I could not write very well, and that he could write far better than I did. He was so egotistical about his command of the English language that he decided to write the statement for me. When he finished the statement, I had to make a tape of it, so it could be broadcast over the Voice of Vietnam. I was happy that he wrote the statement, because even though he had a fairly good command of the language, it was still not written the way a native speaker would have written it.

29 September 1967. Eight days had passed since my session with the Elf and Fidel. I was still in leg irons twenty-four hours a day, except when at quiz. I was besieged by mosquitoes at night, because I could not tuck my mosquito net under the part of the bed mat that was behind me. The leg irons and mosquitoes made sleeping difficult. In addition, when Magoo came into the room three or four times a day, he would walk up in front of me, point his finger and say, "Commander," and then slap me with an open hand as hard as he could four or five times. I was beginning to feel like a punching bag.

Because I had no water pitcher, they only filled my water cup twice a day, which meant that my ration of water was cut by perhaps two thirds, compared to what I'd had when a water jug was available. Maybe because of this as well as the emotional pressure I was under, I gradually lost my appetite. I was having problems going to the bathroom, and whenever I urinated, I had to go in the lid of the five-gallon bucket, and about half the time I would spill some on myself or the bed mat or whatever.

Life was becoming meaningless for me, and I started going downhill. I became depressed after Magoo slapped me. Although it jarred my leg each time he hit me, it was not the pain from the blow that got me down, but rather the anticipation of the hit and the overall situation. I was totally demoralized and was eating less and less each day. After some time, I completely gave up eating.

2 October 1967. I hadn't eaten anything for two days Magoo came into the room, left the noon meal near my bed, hit me as usual, and left. An hour later, he returned to pick up the dishes. He took the food and left. About five minutes later, Fidel came in carrying the food. He was screaming at me that I was trying to cheat him again, and that if I did not eat, they would hold me down and stuff the food in my mouth. He said I must do everything he said, and he told me to eat the meal. I tried but gagged on it. I just could not eat it. I sat there without a word and hung my head. I didn't care whether I lived or died. Fidel was powerful enough to make me do what he wanted, but now I was at a point where, even if he started torturing me again to make me eat the food, it would have been physically impossible for me to eat it. I felt completely helpless. Fidel just stood there and looked at me. I don't know what he was thinking. In a minute or two, I looked up and told Fidel that I was not eating because I was not hungry. Fidel didn't say anything, and he did not force me to eat the food. Apparently he had not intended that I be put in the condition I was in. Without saying a word, Fidel left.

Later that afternoon, I moved to the Ho Chi Minh room. This was a small room in the rear part of the Auditorium building. The room was in an isolated and remote area of the camp. Contact with anyone was impossible. Even if I screamed at the top of my lungs, it was unlikely anyone would hear me.

I received a water jug, and although I was still in leg irons, Magoo stopped slapping me. I received one cigarette that night and a full ration of three the next day. The following day, I went to quiz, and Fidel had my meal brought into the quiz room. He had a tape recorder and started playing music like Montavani. He said I could eat my meal while listening to this beautiful music. He was becoming friendlier. I started to eat a little food, and in about a week, I was eating normally. Then one day, I went to quiz, and when I returned to the room, Magoo didn't put me in leg irons. He acted as if he had forgotten, because the next day I was back in them again. But after a week he took the irons out of the room altogether. I was getting my full ration of water and even some fruit now and then. Fidel was easing up on me. He even let me write a letter to my wife.

As was the custom since the early part of the war, there was a handwriting analysis of that letter by the Department of Defense. Whoever analyzed my writing really hit the nail right on the head. Even though I wrote the letter about two weeks after my low point, I was still in bad shape. The analysis was as follows: It is our opinion that the referenced letter was prepared by LCDR. Vohden: "In the ten months in which the subject has not written (9 Dec. 66 to 10 Oct. 67) a noticeable change has taken place. A process of mental and emotional regression seems to have taken place. His mental function is more restricted and he seems to be in a kind of a stupor, just trying to relive and remember the past. Emotionally he has become more withdrawn, somewhat dull, and almost unresponsive. Apparently he has lost his capacity for participating in events going on around him. Physically he appears to be somewhat weaker and there is some increase of physical discomfort and possible organic disorder, which he evidently tries to disregard. The entire picture seems to suggest a considerable loss of contact with reality."

5 October 1967. In the middle of the morning, I could hear voices coming from the nearby building where quizzes took place. I could tell that the voices were Fidel and Jack Bomar, although I could not hear what they were saying. Fidel turned on his tape recorder, and there was some great American music. Amidst the talking and music, I could hear some slapping and Fidel shouting louder at Bomar. Fidel didn't want me to forget what was in store if I refused him again. Five minutes later, I heard groans from Bomar. Fidel turned up the volume on the tape recorder to drown out Bomar's yells, but I could still hear them. I had just gone through this days before, and I could picture what he was going through. I was saying to myself, "Jack, give him anything he wants, it isn't worth it," but I was proud of Bomar.

10 October 1967. Fidel let me out of my room in the afternoon to sit in the sun for more than half an hour. He was more pleasant every day. I still had a daily quiz, and he continued to give me the North Vietnamese version of the war and other propaganda. Although he was nice to me now, he still asked me if I would do everything he told me to do and warned me that I better not return to the reactionary attitude that I'd had before. Once in a while at quiz, after he asked me if I would do everything he wanted me, and I said yes, he would ask me to describe my true feelings about the war. He'd say that he wanted to know my honest opinion of the war and that I could say anything I wanted, without fear of being punished.

243

Then I would tell him that I still supported the U.S. in the war one hundred percent.

16 October 1967. Magoo opened the door to my room and indicated that I was moving again. I packed my gear, and Magoo offered to carry it for me, but I said no because I figured the less I took from the Vietnamese the better off I'd be. I moved back with Jack Bomar and Gene Dundas in the same room again.

For the next two weeks, the quizzes with Fidel continued for the three of us. In the course of one of the quizzes, Fidel found out that we were playing chess in our room with a board and pieces that were made from toilet paper. The next morning, Fidel walked into our room with a real chessboard and real chess pieces. We said, "Thank you very much, but we really don't want it. We already have a good chess set made out of paper." He said in a stern voice, "You take it and use it." So we took it.

At another quiz, the question of smoking cigars came up, and Fidel learned that I was a cigar smoker before I was shot down. He learned that the three of us had had a chess tournament and that I had won. Two days later, he dropped by the room and gave me a cigar. He said it was a prize for winning the tournament. I said no thanks, and in an authoritative voice he said, "Smoke it." I had not had a cigar in more than two and a half years, and although I had smoked them, I never inhaled. But now I inhaled cigarette smoke, which I had never done before I was shot down. I tried the cigar, but after taking a few drags, I really did not enjoy it at all. He said he was going to bring me more cigars, but he never did. He also upped our ration of cigarettes from three to four, and Magoo brought in a water jug filled with warm tea each morning. Every afternoon, the three of us got outside for some sunshine, and from time to time, I would sit on a stool in front of the auditorium, while Bomar and Dundas jogged around the prison camp.

Our quizzes with Fidel continued, and we still got the nice-guy treatment. Tea and extra cigarettes at quiz, always accompanied by a lecture on the party line of the North Vietnamese. If Fidel was not there, Chico would run the quiz. At quiz, they sometimes played good American music and had U.S. magazines including *Newsweek* and *Time*. Fidel showed us pictures of new cars, women dressed in the latest fashions, and any article that showed the U.S. in a bad light. For example, he showed us an article about Bishop Sheen preaching a sermon against the bombing of Vietnam. But he would not let us look at the other things in the magazines.

He told us that we only had to admit that we had made a mistake against the Vietnamese people, and then he described how nice it would be when we were home with our families. At quizzes, we discussed everything from how chickens had intercourse to whether the music and the pictures of fashion models reminded me of my wife and made me homesick. We were allowed to read books written in English about the exploitation of workers in the U.S., the exploitation of the Central American people by the United Fruit Company, and *Lady MacBird*, a supposed best-seller, which detailed how President Johnson had planned the assassination of President Kennedy. Others included short stories depicting the hard times of U.S. working people like steelworkers and migrant farm workers.

To us, the interesting thing about all of this is that he seemed to really believe all this garbage. Not a day went by that the war was not discussed and that he did not lecture us about the U.S. imperialistic war of aggression. Although he warned us every day about being reactionary and what would happen if we were, to test us he asked if we would still do anything that he wanted us to do. We always said yes, but whenever given the opportunity, we were allowed to express our support for the war.

We followed this routine for more than three weeks. Every day, we discussed and debated how to deal with the situation. From the very beginning, we suspected that many of the things that were being done pointed to some sort of an early release program. So we had a number of problems to deal with. We did not want the extra Vietnamese cigarettes, the American cigarettes, the chessboard, the tea, the music, the magazines, the extra time outside in the sun, and the opportunity to exercise and run around the prison camp grounds. Without a doubt, these things were special favors, because we were the only prisoners getting this kind of treatment. We did not want them, but we had been through hell with Fidel a short time ago, and although our health had improved, the question of where, when, and how to start resisting again was always present.

From past experience, I knew that if I assumed the active role of SRO, took command, and openly gave orders, whether necessary or not, I would eventually be caught. This was a difficult time for me, because as the SRO, I was responsible for the conduct of the group, although this did not mean that each man was not individually responsible for his conduct. Because I had been tortured for giving orders in addition to making me surrender my will, I did not want to get bent for giving orders again. I knew that if I told these guys to resist in any way, the way Fidel leaned on people, I would be fingered quickly. The guidance I gave to them was to follow the Code of Conduct, and I set the tone that early release was unacceptable.

Fortunately, we were never asked to write propaganda statements or seriously violate the Code of Conduct after we initially surrendered. But the special favor problem lingered on. We told Fidel whenever it was possible that we did not want the extra things we were getting, but we were always threatened with punishment if we refused. Our fear was repeatedly reinforced by daily warnings that any reactionary behavior on the part of anyone would result in drastic repercussions for all of us. And that if we did not go along with Fidel, he would force us to do things far worse than we were doing now. Although the acceptance of the favors was recognized as wrong, they were being forced on us against our will and they were not favors of any great magnitude. After taking into consideration the guidance to resist again when your will to resist returns, the things that we were doing to violate the code–i.e., receiving extra things–and the certainty of what would result if we resisted again, I adopted a policy of making no waves at this time. Others might have decided differently, but I did not think there was any way to beat Fidel, and I was only trying to minimize my losses.

One day late in October, the subject of woodcarving came up during a quiz with Fidel. The next day we had a carving knife and several blocks of wood. To pass the time, Bomar made a number of things, including a wooden spoon and a pair of wooden shoes. He also made little wooden trucks, cars, and things like that. Fidel even gave us paint with which to decorate them. Without doubt, these things would be used for propaganda purposes, but they were made as sloppily and shabbily as possible and under threat of punishment if we refused. Although we never knew what he did with the items, we suspected that if we were ever released early that they would have been seen, as our captors were wont to say, as "concrete acts of goodwill and peacefulness toward the Vietnamese people."

November 1967. During the first week of November, Navy Lt. Al Carpenter joined us. He said he had submitted without being tortured, because he had been caught up in a communications purge just before the start of the Fidel program. Several days later, Air Force Lt. Tom Barrett joined us. There were five of us now, and the treatment remained the same as before. Within several days, Fidel told us that our room was too crowded, and that he was going to move us to a much larger room in the same building. Fidel wanted to be sure that the room was escape-proof, however, so we had to put barbed wire on the ceiling. This was not only hard work but also a violation of the Code of Conduct. Given our predicament, we hesitatingly did the work. Bomar used his ingenuity to our advantage, and he made sure that if a man wanted to get through the barbed wire in the ceiling, there were a number of places where he would have no problem pulling the wire down. After about a week of working three or four hours each day, the large room was ready.

Near the end of November, the five of us moved into the big room, and several days later, four more men joined us, for a total of nine. The four new men were Capt. Norlan Daughtrey, Lt. Ed Hubbard, Capt. Glen Perkins, and Navy Lt., j.g., Larry Spencer.

In the room where Bomar, Dundas, and I had lived, we had been unable to communicate with any other POWs. Our new roommates had been almost as isolated as we were, and had been waiting in the wings to join the main group. But now that we were all together, we were able to share our experiences. Each in turn had been made to submit and, in most cases, then punished for several more weeks. Most POWs did not submit until actual beating and torture forced them to do it.

Now all nine of us received four cigarettes a day instead of the normal ration of three, we received tea every morning, and we were allowed outside for sunshine, which included jogging around the camp several times a week. I sat on a stool and watched as they ran.

As time went by, Fidel involved us in other projects. We dug a hole about seven feet long, five feet deep, and about five feet wide in front of our building. We filled the hole with water, and Fidel put some fish in the pond. One day, he mentioned that he knew of fish that could swim underground through mud to get to cadavers in graveyards and eat them, but he said we didn't have that kind of fish in our pond. Norlan thought there might be fish like that in Cuba.

There was a large pool in the center of the camp. Given the condition it was in, it obviously hadn't been used for swimming for years. The pool must have been at least thirty feet wide, sixty feet long, and seven feet deep. On the bottom of the pool were rolls and rolls of old movie film that had been partially unrolled now and were all tangled up. Our next job was to retrieve the tangled rolls of film, untangle them, and then roll them back on the spools. This job took weeks, and we never actually finished it, but whenever things got slow, that work was always available. Fidel told us the reason he had us doing these things was to improve our treatment, because we had submitted and surrendered to the Vietnamese people and were no longer reactionary.

Fidel or Chico was always present to supervise us, as well as engage us in conversation individually or collectively when we worked outside. When they were together, they were always careful to speak English in front of us. While we worked outside, we could see that Fidel and Chico ate like kings. We washed their dishes from time to time, and they left some good pieces of meat on the plates now and then. Some of the younger guys with big appetites ate the leftovers with relish.

Fidel could be quite charming, friendly, and likable. He liked to talk and talked about everything, including how hard it was to be a Communist. Although he wore the largest clothes made in Vietnam, they fit so tightly that he looked like Lil Abner. He was very friendly with the Vietnamese and walked alongside the short guards with his arm drooped over their shoulder, perhaps as a symbol of Communist solidarity. The Vietnamese called him Vet. They treated Fidel and Chico very well, driving them to and from work every day in a fancy car. In a way, I could not help liking Fidel because he was an interesting and pleasant person. But as I learned what cruelty he was capable of, I decided that I could kill him and not feel an iota of guilt, if I could get away with it.

We played chess and bridge or other games with cards made from Vietnamese cigarette package wrappers and talked about almost everything under the sun. Now, instead of hearing the jokes of just another guy or two, there were jokes and stories from nine guys. So for the most part, the living conditions had improved, and life was more bearable. Despite the obvious advantages of living with many men, however, almost as many disadvantages presented themselves. Although we were being forced to live as we were, our self-esteem was diminished by the fact that we were all more or less continually violating the Code of Conduct by living in a large group while others were more isolated, and by getting the extra cigarettes, tea, and outside time. We weren't proud of ourselves. I suppose we could be compared to those who lived through the revolution in Russia. Once forced to submit to a new regime and finding no way to escape that existence, one accepts his plight and gets on with his life.

There were only two crap buckets, and they got filled up much faster than before. Instead of taking a dump in privacy or in front of only one or two people, it was now a gala extravaganza for an audience. The diet of greens, cabbage, and pig fat always gave at least one or two guys diarrhea. The odors from that and the accompanying gas were enough to make us gag sometimes. There was one guy who ate everything in sight, a small guy about 5 feet 6 inches and 110 pounds, but when he wasn't eating he was on the *bo* with diarrhea.

There was another guy who got up early in the morning and exercised so strenuously that when he began to perspire, the guys down at his end of the room put their heads under their blankets because he smelled so bad. Sometimes, everyone in the room had their heads under the blankets. This man was a hell of a nice guy, but he just smelled really bad when he perspired. Disagreements, arguments, and bad feelings occurred over silly things, such as how fast Jesse Owen ran the hundred-meter race in the 1936 Olympics. Some guys became irritated if they lost at chess or cards. In one case, two guys became so angry at each other over a chess game that they not only stopped playing chess with each other, but they also would not talk to each other for a month. Then there was the problem with the Voice of Vietnam radio program. Some wanted to listen and enjoy the music and try to glean some bit of news from between the lines of the Vietnamese version of what was happening, and others completely ignored the radio and continued to talk.

Another problem was that the Vietnamese did not accept our chain of command, which was based on the seniority of the prisoners. Although Fidel knew I was the senior man and I talked to him in that capacity, he would never do anything I asked. Instead, he told us that Jack Bomar was to be in charge, and Norlan Daughtrey was to be second in command. Whenever Fidel wanted the group to do something, he would call either Bomar or Norlan to quiz and have them pass on what he wanted. On two or three occasions, when we were making too much noise, he called out Bomar and Daughtrey, made them kneel on their knees, and slapped them five or six times on the face. Since I was in fact the senior man, I should have been the one slapped instead of them, but under the circumstance, I could do nothing about it.

The only humor that came out of this period was about bowing. As was the custom when the guard came into the room or to the door, we all had to bow. We had long since given up fighting the bow, because everyone did it now. One night, the guard Floyd opened the peephole and looked in. He insisted that we get into two lines close together and then bow at the same time. He was trying to exert his authority over us. We formed two rows in an incredibly bad line not necessarily on purpose, and when we were all together, we bowed. The Keystone Cops couldn't have done worse. As soon as we did it, we realized how funny it must have looked, and we all burst out laughing. It must have looked funny to Floyd, too, because he burst out in a big belly laugh. Laughing in the presence of prisoners just wasn't done, but he apparently couldn't help it. As he laughed, he shook his finger at us and then slammed the peephole. When we finished laughing, we could still hear Floyd chuckling outside our room. He left and never came back to bother us again.

Christmas 1967. As with all the previous Christmases, we figured we would go to quiz this year for sure. The guard came to get us well after dark. When we got to the quiz, Fidel was on the porch to greet us. He was dressed as well as I had ever seen him. He had on a full-dress Vietnamese army uniform, which would have done wonders for the average Vietnamese officer, but on Fidel the pants legs were about six inches too short, and the arms on the coat the same. The collar was supposed to be buttoned, but because his neck was so big he had to leave at least two buttons on the shirt and collar of the coat open. We almost burst out laughing when we saw him. For the next few minutes, he took some pictures of us and even some pictures of himself with some of the POWs. Fidel acted like dad taking pictures at a family reunion. Chico was there and also participated in the activities. Then we went inside, and some sat down while others stood, and we got another five or ten minutes of bull about the war. We received the usual three or four pieces of candy, a cup of hot tea, and letters and pictures from home for some of the guys. We also got some of the "wouldn't it be nice to go home with your family" bullshit.

January 1968. During the first week of January, I had a very long quiz with Fidel. He was very pleasant, gave me some more of the Vietnamese side of the story of the war, told me how nice I had it, and told me how even though I had bombed and killed Vietnamese people, they had treated me very humanely. Bomar and several others had similar quizzes.

Several days later, I had another quiz with the Rabbit and a former camp commander who had been at the Zoo for a short time and spoke English exceptionally well. I had not seen the Rabbit for nearly a year and a half, and he had not changed. Although he appeared to be arrogant at times, today he was very polite. They started out with the usual amenities such as how are you? How is your leg? How do you like living with eight other men, etc.? Then he came right out and said, "How would you like to go home?" I thought for a while and said, "What do you mean?" Then he said, "What would you say if we released you?" I told him that I supported President Johnson and the U.S. Government in the war in Vietnam, and I would tell the truth about the treatment I had received. I knew this was tantamount to saying no but it was an easy way of refusing their offer. It was the offer of a life time but I had had time to weigh the pros and cons of making such a decision. I had been there long enough to know the price was far more than I was willing to pay and it was just wrong to go home early. The Rabbit and the camp commander continued to be pleasant. The quiz lasted no more than ten minutes, and then they told me to go back to my room. I believe that I had been a contender for early release, but that they removed me from the list after that quiz. Only the Vietnamese know for sure. Several other guys in our room had similar quizzes that same day, and so far as I know gave the same answers that I did.

Although the daily routine in the room did not change much, we rarely had a quiz any more, and it appeared to me that Fidel had lost a little wind out of his sails. Little by little, the group was getting larger, and the purpose for which Fidel had come to Vietnam seemed to be changing.

Though nine men were in the big room, a tenth guy, Air Force Capt. Don Waltman, had been in the Fidel program from the beginning. Waltman lived in a small room next to us. He still had not been forced to surrender. Fidel was giving him the long-term lousy treatment. This guy loved his cigarettes, and Fidel knew it. So three or four times a week, the guard would open the peephole, take a cigarette out of the pack, and as he passed it to Waltman, would tear the cigarette in half and pass in the short half. Waltman was so hooked on cigarettes that he took the half cigarette whenever they gave it to him. He should have quit. But I would have done the same as he did.

In mid-January, we got the word that three new men had come under Fidel's control. They lived together in a room in another building. They were Lts., j.g., Charlie Rice and Earl Lewis and Air Force Capt Earl Cobeil. Earl apparently had been badly beaten and tortured at Heartbreak Hotel before coming to the Zoo. The men who lived with Cobeil suspected that something was wrong with him, because sometimes he did not appear to be completely rational, and he appeared to be somewhat withdrawn and uncommunicative. Some guys speculated that he had suffered a head wound when he was shot down.

Also during the month of January, seven more men gradually joined with us when we worked outside. Lt. Cdr. Rivers was senior to me, so it took some pressure off me for the conduct of the group, but after I told him what had gone on, he had nothing new to offer. This was really a big deal now. We had around fifteen or sixteen guys working outside now, and Fidel had to find new work for us. This time, we dug a pool about twenty-five feet long, twelve feet wide, and five feet deep behind the Pig Sty. We also made an elaborate fireplace out of mud bricks for the Vietnamese to bake bread or whatever. They never used it. Fidel stocked the new pond with even bigger fish than the other pond. But most of the fish died, and after Fidel left, the pools turned into stagnant water holes, where mosquitoes bred and green slime grew. Whatever Fidel's purpose was in Vietnam, the Vietnamese surely will always remember him for the useless things that we made for him. They were probably glad to see him leave, because they did not need more holes in North Vietnam. The bombs had already taken care of that.

Mid-February 1968. Just before the camp radio came on one morning, the Elf came to the outside of our room and disconnected the wires to our speaker. This gave rise to all kinds of speculation. Later that day, we heard from the Pool Hall that three U.S. pilots had been released. We felt good that none of our group was included.

During the next week, the men from our room and five or six more new men continued digging the pool in back of the Pig Sty for three or four hours a day. In the last week of February, I moved into the Pig Sty. As it turned out, I was the only man ever to be removed from the Fidel program. I was so happy to leave because being involved with Fidel was hell. To get out from under the daily direct control of Fidel was a blessing. My new roommate was Lt. Cdr. Paul Schulz. He was a recent shoot down and a fringe member of the Fidel group. He had never been asked to surrender or had many quizzes with Fidel, but he had participated in the pool digging with the group for several weeks. Although I lived with Schulz now, we still worked outside with the big group.

We heard that Fidel had Earl Cobeil under pressure to submit, and that Earl had been moved into the Coach House by the main gate. No one had contact with him, but some guys saw him enter and leave the building on occasion. Several nights later, he was moved into a small shed in back of the Pig Sty building, about twenty feet from our room. The shed was right next to the area where we were digging the pool. One end of the pool was about four feet from the end of the shed. The next morning the fifteen of us were out digging again in the pool. We tried to make contact with Earl when the guard wasn't looking, but Earl did not respond. We suspected that he had been worked over by Fidel but did not surrender. Perhaps, Fidel figured that if he was faking, we would advise him to surrender, maybe he wanted Cobeil to know that he could be in a large group with us if he surrendered, or maybe he was checking to see if he would respond to us and thus show that he was faking. Only Fidel knew why he put Cobeil in the shed.

Several days later, Cobeil was moved into the room next to mine with Don Waltman. That night Waltman tapped and said that Earl was all mixed up. He said that Earl accused him of being a Russian spy and would not eat the food or drink the water, because they were poisoned. He said that Earl had obviously had the straps, because his wrists were swollen.

The following day, late in the morning, Fidel came to my room with the turnkey for the Pig Sty, and he gave me the word to move. I gathered up my gear and left the room. Fidel took me aside and told me that Cobeil was trying to cheat him and was faking. Fidel ordered me to get him squared away or I would get twice as much as Cobeil got. The turnkey opened the door to Waltman and Cobeil's room. They were both standing. Waltman bowed, but Cobeil just stood there with a vacant stare. He was barefooted and had on his long clothes, which were covered with dirt and grime. Fidel yelled at him a few times to get squared away, but Cobeil just stood there motionless.

I suggested to Fidel that the best thing to do at this time would be to get Cobeil a bath. In the bath area, there would be an opportunity for me to evaluate him and try to decide what action to take. A bath was so important in those days, because it was so hot and when we missed washing for a day or more the sweat and dust combined to form a thin layer of sticky, grimy dust all over the body. One day without washing was bad enough, but three days without a bath was unbearable. I hoped that some cold water might bring Cobeil to his senses.

Fidel said okay, so Waltman, Cobeil, and I went to bath at the end of the building. As was customary, as soon as the door was closed behind us, Waltman and I took off our clothes and prepared to wash. Right away I noticed that Cobeil just stood there and stared. I could not believe my eyes! Was it possible that a guy as filthy as he was did not want to take a bath? There wasn't much water that morning so Waltman and I just put water on our washrag and rinsed our bodies off. I told Cobeil to go ahead and wash and that it would make him feel a lot better. All of a sudden, he walked over to the spigot and started to drink from it. Everyone knew the water from the spigot was dirty and would make you sick. We told him to stop, but he continued to drink for fifteen or twenty seconds. Then he just stood there.

Grimsey the guard came to the shower room a few minutes later and took us back to our room. Fidel was standing at the door. All three of us lined up, and Waltman and I bowed, but Cobeil just stood there again. I said, "Hey, Cobeil, bow." Nothing happened. Suddenly, Grimsey raised his leg and pushed his foot against Cobeil's chest, and he tumbled ass over tea kettle toward the back of the room. Fidel yelled loudly at Cobeil to stop cheating him, or he would teach him a lesson he would never forget.

We got our meal, and then the door closed. Waltman and I started to eat, but Cobeil sat on his bed, silently staring at the floor. I tried to talk to him and encourage him to eat, but he would not. After eating, I talked to him some more and told him that if he was trying one of those tricks they used in the Korean War, like the story we had all heard about the POW who started barking every time the Koreans came, that that kind of stuff wasn't going to work with Fidel. Cobeil had been worked over badly, his wrists were three times the normal size, and they had the telltale marks of the manacles.

After having seen Fidel almost every day for six months, I knew that he was going to get his way. He was the most egotistical man I had ever met. He was tall, dark, good-looking, confident, and above all, he was not going to let the Vietnamese see him fail in any endeavor. I was certain that he would take a man to any limit to get what he wanted. In addition, the difference between the Vietnamese and Fidel was that once the Vietnamese got what they wanted, they let up, at least for a while, but Fidel wouldn't do that. He didn't let a day pass without threats and warnings. After seeing Cobeil in his present condition, I knew that he had had more then his share of punishment, and that if he was really tough and faking and of sound mind, eventually Fidel would get to him. Although we were almost certain that Cobeil was off his rocker, we were not absolutely positive. I showed him my crippled leg and told him who I was. I showed him pictures of my family, trying to convince him that I was an American prisoner and that I was trying to help him. After a few minutes of talking with him, I felt as though I might have made a little progress.

I told Cobeil that it was necessary to resist efforts by the Vietnamese to gain propaganda, but that it was not necessary to go to the point that Cobeil was at now. I told him to knock off his play-acting or faking, if that was what he was doing, and go ahead and write whatever Fidel wanted. I told him his life was not worth the surrender statement or propaganda statement that Fidel wanted. The Code of Conduct just did not apply here. It was my personal belief that the writers of the Code of Conduct never expected a man to resist to the death, just so he wouldn't have to write a propaganda statement. If such a statement could affect the outcome of any war, then we should seriously question whether we should be in that war. For the rest of the quiet hour, Waltman and I tried everything we could think of to get Cobeil to come down to earth, but we were unsuccessful.

Shortly after the gong sounded ending the quiet hour, Waltman went to quiz. At the same time, Fidel came to the door and told me to come outside. He asked me if Cobeil was squared away? I told him that in my honest opinion Cobeil was not cheating, that he was not all there. Although Fidel had the upper hand and was without a doubt a Communist, was filled with hatred for us, and was probably one of the most diabolical men in Vietnam, I hoped he would realize that Cobeil was really mentally ill and would let up on him. He listened carefully as I talked, and I thought I might have convinced him that what I was saying was true, but after several more minutes, he accused me of trying to help Cobeil cheat him. I insisted that I wasn't and that there was nothing I could do to help Cobeil. Fidel continued with more threats of torture against me unless Cobeil behaved. Then he put me back in the room again with Cobeil. The door was closed, locked, and bolted. I started to talk to Cobeil again.

I had been talking for less than a few minutes, when suddenly Fidel jumped up in the window holding the bars and screamed out in his loud fierce voice, "I caught you, I caught you cheating me." I was totally surprised because Cobeil had not said a word. Seconds later the door slammed open, and Fidel said, "Aha, I caught you both lying." He screamed at me, "Get out, get out." As soon as I got outside of the room, Fidel told me to go stand at the end of the building. Four guards were standing outside the room where Cobeil was, so he left the door to the room open, and he and Cedric the guard went somewhere.

A few minutes later, Fidel returned with what looked like a fan belt from a car, but the belt was cut like a whip. When I saw the fan belt, I was surprised because up to that time I had never heard of anyone getting hit with it. As Fidel passed by, he looked at me with the glazed eyes of a madman. He was breathing heavily, and he told me that if I made one sound or moved one inch of my body, I would get twice as much as Cobeil was going to get. Shaking, Fidel said, "He's trying to cheat me. He's trying to cheat me. I'll show you. I'll show him. I'll make him so happy to surrender and bow, when I finish with him, he'll come crying to me on his knees begging me to let him surrender."

By now, about seven or eight guards were standing in front of the door of Cobeil's room. Fidel went in with Grimsey and Cedric at his side. I could hear the thud of the belt falling on Cobeil's body again and again, as Fidel screamed, "You son of a beech, you fooker. You are cheating me. I will show you. I will show you." Fidel hit Cobeil about twenty or thirty times. I could just imagine Fidel, almost twice the size of Cobeil, in good health and strong as an ox, beating on a frail, weakened Cobeil. I almost threw up each time I heard the fan belt hit Earl's body. Enduring the straps had been far easier than going through this.

I was terrified while all this was happening, because as angry as Fidel had been with me when I surrendered, I had never seen the blood-curdling look in his eyes or the emotion that engulfed him at this time. To hear what was going on and know there was not anything I could do about it was sickening. I said to myself, "Give up, Earl. Do what the bastard wants." I thought briefly that I should go to Earl's room and try to help him, but I realized that if I did, he would have been subjected to twice as much as he was getting now, and I would have received ten times as much for interfering.

Fidel was in the room for about five minutes, still shouting at Cobeil. A guard approached me with a big smile on his face. I knew why he was happy. The bastards always enjoyed seeing an American get worked over. The guard motioned me to go into the washroom and locked me in. I never saw Cobeil again. He eventually moved into the big room with the other men in the Fidel program and was beaten unmercifully for months, before he left camp and disappeared.

Contrary to the prevailing opinion of some men in the Cuban Program, I believe that the operation was an early release program. In summary, the reasons for my opinion are as follows:

1) Early on, Fidel and Chico stated that this was "a good deal" and recommended that we "don't turn it down."

2) The composition of the group selected to participate suggested that early release was the goal. Nolan Daughtrey and I were good candidates for release because we were wounded, and releasing injured personnel would have looked good for the Vietnamese. One of the recent shoot-downs had written a song about the Red River Valley for the *Pilots in Pajamas* TV documentary and had visited a delegation. Two of the men were main characters in that documentary, which was a major propaganda coup for the Vietnamese. Some of the men may have seemed to be weak resisters, including a man who had questioned my seniority and authority, as well as the guidance coming from our leadership, and had stated that they would never have to torture him for a statement. Another man had submitted without a fight because he still suffered from

261

the aftermath of a previous torture. Another played the organ for a Christmas service.

This was not a random group of men. The Vietnamese would have had to go a long way to randomly select seven of nine men with similar backgrounds. Some of the men had been tortured previously, but I did not know that much about some of the others. Even though each man considered himself a strong resister, I suspected that each of us had given the Vietnamese some indication that we were potential candidates for release.

3) The sequence in which the Cuban Program progressed is also suggestive.

A) September through October 1967: Bomar, Dudas, and I moved in together. All of us submitted. We were forced to have tea every morning, received extra cigarettes, outside exercise time, access to American magazines and music at quiz, and improved mail privileges. We were forced to carve wood and make toys.

B) Early November: Carpenter and Barrett joined the main group. This five-man group put up barbed wire in the ceiling of a larger room to prevent escape. The privileges continued.

C) End of November: Daughtrey, Hubbard, Perkins, and Spencer moved into the large room with the other men. Good treatment continued. We dug fishponds, wound old movie film back onto spools, and made a rustic outdoor oven. Acts of good-will.

D) Early January 1968: Daughtrey and I refused early release.

E) Mid-January: Cobeil, Charlie Rice, and Earl Lewis were added to the program. *Honor Bound* states the "possibility that their entry into program was to groom more recent captives for repatriation." Cobeil was alleged to have had a head injury when he was shot down. It was unusual for Rice and Lewis, as healthy new POWs, to join our group. They were probably the only two POWs to be given tea and extra cigarettes two months after being shot down.

F) Late January: Rivers, Schoeffel, Schulz, Bliss, Flescher, and Kerr joined the main Fidel group working outside. They had some quizzes with Fidel, but they were much less intense than those endured by the original group. None of them was forced to submit. These men were never really part of the main Cuban Program, and most of them returned to the prison population within weeks of joining the group. They were probably there so that any man released could say he worked with a large group of men.

G) Mid-February: The Vietnamese officer known as the Elf disconnected the speakers in our room so that we couldn't hear about the release of three American POWs.

H) A few days after the release of the three POWs, I was moved out of the Cuban Program and put in with Paul Schulz. The full group worked no more than one or two more days digging a fishpond, and then that activity ceased entirely. I never again had contact with the original group. The main thing they did from then on was to take care of Cobeil and make coal balls.

In the months to follow, Fidel's brutality toward Cobeil and Kasler (a POW who was tortured in April-May 1969) was so shocking that this brutality eventually drowned out the original purpose of the Fidel program. Although Fidel almost killed Kasler and beat Cobeil into a stupor from which he eventually died, this brutality was separate from the events that had transpired in the previous months.

In retrospect, if Fidel's plan was to coax some of our group to accept early release, it failed. Everyone took more than their share of punishment before submitting, and in the end, we defeated his plan. Although Fidel might have thought the Stockholm syndrome would work on us, we proved him wrong. As a result of the Code of Conduct, those who had been tortured before took their turn again, and those who had done dumb things before raised their resistance standards and became an integral part of the POW population.

Offers of early release were nothing new. This war was as much one of propaganda as one on the battlefield. For propaganda purposes, many men had already been released in the South. At the end of 1967, the North Vietnamese decided to release some prisoners, too. It was not uncommon for the Vietnamese to propose early release to a POW, some were serious offers others not so serious but they were looking for anyone who would pay the price to go home early. Fred Cherry, John Pitchford, Quincy Collins, A.J. Myers, and Lt. Col. Risner, to name a few. Dale Osborne said he could have been home before his ship got there. Turning down early release was in line with the Code of Conduct, which also required the senior officer to take command. Refusing early release was easy: All you had to do was say no. It was a violation of the most important provision of the Code of Conduct and disobedience of a lawful order to go home early, and it was disgraceful to leave your friends behind. I was disappointed that twelve airmen accepted early release by the North Vietnamese and that others even considered it. It was probably their greatest propaganda coup of the war, and it was a terrible blight on the POW record. How much prouder we would have been to be part of a group where all the men waited to come home together.

CHAPTER 18 - RESPITE

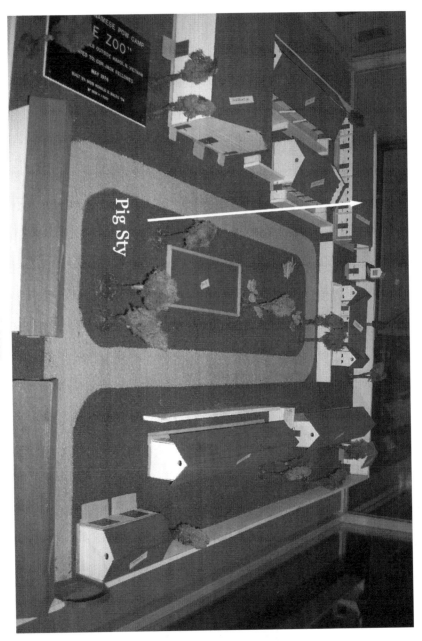

Pig Sty

February 1968 – July 1969. After they beat Cobeil, they moved him elsewhere, and I moved back with Paul Schulz. I told him what had happened, and we got on with life. Living with Paul was a double treat. I was out of the Fidel program, and I had a new guy to talk to. He had been shot down on 4 November 1967. Even though my old roommates were less than thirty-five feet from our building, the intervening brick wall made communications impossible. Working outside in a large group ended, and we lost track of what was happening to Cobeil. Don Waltman moved in with us about a week later, and although the room was more crowded, it was better with more company.

I had lived in the room next door in May and June 1966, but the windows had been bricked up about three-fourths of the way since then. The room still wasn't bad. If we looked out the windows, we could see an occasional army truck, artillery, or Vietnamese peasants in the large open field on the other side of the prison camp wall. From time to time over the next year, the guys in the rooms on either side of us would clear, and I could look out the window by sitting on Paul's shoulders.

The Pig Sty had six rooms in the front and five rooms in the back. As the SRO, I asked for a volunteer to handle the Sunday service. I waited for three or four days, but no one volunteered. The main part of this job was to see that a service was held. Cdr. Denton had started the custom. On the first thump of the wall, everyone would stand in his own room, facing the front; and on two thumps, we would pledge allegiance to the flag. On three thumps, we would say the Lord's Prayer; and on four thumps, we would all pray silently for one or two minutes. Five thumps would end the service. The service was not mandatory, but we hoped it would not only give us religious strength but also be a unifying action.

Finally, after waiting four days, I asked again for a volunteer. The next day, the name of one of the guys several rooms down from us was given to me as a volunteer for the job. The following Sunday morning, the service never came. I thought that the guy had probably just forgotten. The next Sunday, there was still no service. The following day, I asked through another communications path what was wrong, and I learned that the guy whose name was given to me had not volunteered for the job and had no idea he was supposed to have initiated the service. Someone in the other communication link had turned his name in to me as a joke. I never found out who the culprit was. I was as much amused as they were. After asking for a volunteer one more time and not getting any, I finally decided to appoint Capt. Pop Keirn. He lived in the room behind me. Although I had never met him face to face, I had lived next to him for a long time and knew he would accept the responsibility if assigned. He did a fine job.

Our turnkey was named Slug, because the name suited both his appearance and his behavior. Kingfish, one of the guards for our building, was the spitting image of Kingfish on the *Amos and Andy* show, and he was just as much a character. Kingfish often walked around the building carrying his gun and singing loudly to himself. He would sit on the steps in front of our room at all hours of the day and night singing or talking to himself. When this happened, invariably the next morning, we would find an unwrapped banana leaf with what looked like burned tobacco, on the floor of the porch or inside the washroom. We suspected he was high on something.

We got three cigarettes a day now. Three for Don, three for Paul, and three for me, but as Paul didn't smoke, Don and I each had four and a half per day. Don was the guy whom Fidel used to give half a cigarette twice each week when he was in solitary. We were both really hooked. Paul was very generous in accepting the cigarettes for us, because there were a number of POWs who didn't accept them for their roommates. I don't know why they wouldn't take them for the other guys. We only got three lights each day, so we had a problem. At first, we smoked two cigarettes after each meal. Then Don would smoke a cigarette after the meal, and just before his cigarette went out, I would light mine, and he would light his as mine was finishing, and then I would get the last light. Staggering the lights helped, but we would have preferred the other two cigarettes spaced through the evening.

Finally, Don came up with an idea to take some of our toilet paper and roll it into a string like punk. We found out that by doing so, we could keep a very small smoldering fire for several hours with just a small amount of paper. We couldn't use too much, because then the Vietnamese might suspect something. So now when we finished the cigarettes after our last meal, we lit the punk. Although Paul wasn't happy with Don and me filling our small room three times a day with cigarette smoke, he tolerated it. Now with the punk spilling smoke in the room for several hours each night, he put his foot down. To accommodate him, we hung the punk near the window, so the smoke would go outside the room. If the punk was in the right place, only a fine column of smoke would be coming from it and going out the window.

One Sunday, late in the afternoon, we had the punk burning. Suddenly, we could see Kingfish's face in the window outside of the bars. He must have seen the smoke trailing out of the window and climbed up to see where it was coming from. He was totally dumbfounded. As he pursued the matter further, we showed him what we were doing. Ten minutes later, officer Sweet Pea came to our room. Kingfish had squealed. We explained to Sweet Pea what had happened. He chewed us out and told us never to waste the people's toilet paper like that again, or we would be in deep trouble. We all said O.K. The next day, we had the punk burning again.

Paul had an enormous appetite. He ate everything he could get his hands on. From time to time, extra bowls of soup were left over. Don and I might eat some, but Paul wouldn't stop until it was all gone. Unfortunately, sometimes the food wouldn't stay down, and he would puke up the soup, plus his full meal. Although an extra bowl of soup might show up once every few months, most of the time, the food was not in abundance. So with Paul's huge appetite, neither Don nor I was surprised to hear Paul crunching on something from his soup one day. We asked him what it was, and he said it was a cockroach that he had found in his soup. We said we didn't believe it. He turned his head away from us, spit into his spoon, showed us the partially chewed cockroach. We watched in disbelief as he put it back in his mouth and ate it. At times, I was pretty hungry in Vietnam, but it never got so bad for me that I would eat a cockroach.

Don and Paul would walk in the room to pass the time. As the room was small and had even less space than some of the other rooms, because it had three beds, if the two of them walked at the same time, which they always did, they had to be careful not to collide. So they made a pattern that would enable them to walk the most varied route possible without colliding every few minutes. They would walk for hours sometimes, each absorbed in his thoughts, and miss colliding with each other by fractions of a second. They were not even aware that they were so close, because their pace was perfectly timed to the pattern. I was well entertained by their coordinated walking.   Paul had very blond hair and was as typical a German as could be, including being as stubborn as a mule. Just imagine Schulz, Vohden, and Waltman in one room. All of us were of German descent and stubborn, as well. Sparks flew at times. For the most part, Paul and I rubbed each other the wrong way, but Waltman was easy going and got along well with both of us. One time, however, they almost came to blows in an argument over the difference between a wiener and a frankfurter. The bottom line was that Don was using the definition he had learned as a boy in Idaho, and Paul the one he had learned in Pennsylvania. The argument went on for several days. Finally Schulz accused Waltman of being chicken. Apparently in Pennsylvania it was not the end of the world if someone called you chicken, but you had to watch out if you called someone a chicken in Idaho. I had to stand in front of Waltman on my crutches so he wouldn't attack Schulz. Even though Schulz was forty pounds heavier and three inches taller, Don was ready to go at it. But they got over it the same day, and both of them were having great delight in passing me the queen of spades in a game of Hearts that night.

In the spring of 1968, the Vietnamese didn't bother our building very much with quizzes, but they still provided us with their propaganda books and the Voice of Vietnam program twice each evening. They would give a book or magazine to a room for three or four days and then pass it on to another room for three or four days. They did the same thing with the *Vietnam Courier*. Along the way, someone wrote "Fuck Ho" on one of the *Vietnam Courier* newspapers. No one in our building ever admitted to having written it. When Air Force Captains Wendel and Blevins were given the paper, they didn't notice that anything was written on it. Nor had the guard noticed anything amiss.

When the guard came to pick up the paper, he noticed the writing on it and showed it to an officer. The camp authorities blew their stacks. Of course Wendel and Blevins were accused, but as they hadn't written anything, they didn't know what to do. They decided to deny writing it. The Vietnamese separated them right

270

away. One stayed in the same room, and the other moved into a room in a small building behind ours. Then the guard would whip them ten times each day. They asked for my guidance or suggestions from anyone. There was no easy answer. If they had confessed right away, they might have been punished less. Finally, after two months, one of them had had enough and said he did it. Then the Vietnamese let up on both of them and put them back together. The guy who wrote "Fuck Ho" on the *Vietnam Courier* probably thought that it was a great idea and that everyone would get a kick out of it. I am sure everyone did except Wendel and Blevins.

Several months after we were moved together, the guard selected us to wash the dishes. After each meal, the guard would take the dishes through the peephole of each room and place the dirty dishes on the porch floor. After he let us out of our room, Paul and Don would collect the dishes and carry them to the wash area. In no time, we worked out a routine. Paul roughly cleaned and rinsed the dishes with water. Waltman soaped them down, and I rinsed them off. I shook the water off because we didn't have a towel. Normally, washing dishes wasn't that good a deal. Paul, however, was in his glory because he had an unlimited amount of garbage to sift through. Some of the twenty-five or thirty guys in the building would not finish their meal every day. Don and I would get pissed at Paul sometimes because he would spend too much time pawing through the garbage looking for the best leftover food.

It wasn't long before Don and I had passed the word to the rest of the building that we would use their cigarette butts if they didn't want them. With the extra butts, we were smoking four and a half regular cigarettes and one or two roll-your-owns each day, which made both of us happy.

Sometimes, we didn't have enough soap to wash the dishes. The Vietnamese would give the dishwashers in each building an extra bar of soap each month whether there were fifteen or thirty guys in the building. Because there were so many guys in our building, soap was always a problem. We had to use some of our own, and therefore our bodies and clothes were not as clean as we would have liked. In addition, whether from the bombing or the summertime scarcity, sometimes the water flow would be almost non-existent. At times, we had less than several quarts of water to wash thirty bowls, thirty plates, and thirty spoons. We would complain, but we learned that there were limits to what you could gain by complaining. Once, there was so little water that we refused to wash the dishes. The Vietnamese responded to our disobedience by emptying the bowls and filling the dirty bowls with the new meal. The next time, we did the best we could. The way life was, half of the men thought we should have done the best we could, and the other half thought we should have raised more hell.

One day while we were washing the morning dishes, we heard a commotion outside. The door to the washroom had enough small cracks for all of us to look out if we spaced ourselves properly. At least twelve or fifteen Vietnamese guards were yelling and chasing a barking dog. Paul looked out and saw the guards throwing stones at the dog and the dog trying to escape from them. Each time a stone hit the dog, he would let out a loud yelp and the guards would cheer. The rock throwing lasted about five minutes, and the dog had probably been hit at least a dozen times. Finally, Paul could see that the dog had stopped running and just lay on the ground, still alive. Then about five guards who had different size sticks started to hit the dog as hard as they could all over its body. They could have killed the dog quickly by hitting it in the head, but they just beat the body. The more the dog yelled, the more the guards cheered. One time, the dog got a burst of energy and tried to get away, but the other guards hit it with stones again. Finally, the dog stopped yelling, but they continued to beat it. Sometime later, I asked the officer why they killed the dog that way. He told me that it made the dog tenderer when they ate it.

Another day, when we heard some commotion outside the washroom, Slug was holding a rat with his bare hands. After five minutes, at least ten guards had gathered in front of the washroom and were all chatting excitedly. One of the guards poured some gasoline on the rat. Slug threw the rat on the ground just hard enough to stun him. Then another guard who had a small torch burning lit the gasoline-drenched rat. The rat ran off in flames. From the cheers of the guards, they obviously really enjoyed the show.

In the spring of 1968, one of us was called to quiz and, to our amazement, received a package from home. In several weeks, most everyone in the building had a package. Of course, we had to listen to a lengthy talk about the lenient and humane policy of the North Vietnamese, and the packages had obviously been picked over. They contained soap, candies, maybe toothpaste, and items like that. One guy got an Almond Rocca bar. After three years, I couldn't believe what was happening. We were all optimistic. Each time we got a package, however, the Vietnamese had always mixed up something. For example, Dean Woods might get package addressed to Don Woods, and we wouldn't have ever heard of Don Woods. So we thought he might be a new shoot down. In some cases, the guy showed up as a prisoner, and in other cases, he just never showed.

The summer of 1968 was one of the hottest. We didn't have much rain, so the dust was more plentiful than usual. Don and I both came down with bad cases of heat rash and a form of jock itch. Don used to sleep in the nude under his mosquito net at night, but if the guard saw him, he would bang on the door, wake all of us up, and make Don put on his short pants. They gave us some iodine for the jock itch, but because there was so little of it, and the jock itch was in the most inaccessible place to reach, Don and I doctored each other's jock itch in the most private of places on our bodies.

One time, my heat rash was so bad, I had trouble sleeping for several days. I was desperate to do anything. In my package, I had received a bar of Camay soap, and it said on the label that the soap had some kind of cream in it. I decided it might help if I lathered up the soap and rubbed it on my body, which I did about one hour before our scheduled bath. By the time we were ready for the bath, I suspected that my act of desperation was not turning out as I had hoped. The itching had gone from bad to impossible. And on top of this, when we went to bath, there was no water. When I returned to my room, I used my drinking water to wash the soap off as best I could. For the next week or so, until we had a rainy spell, I was in constant misery. To lighten my burden, Paul told us that he had mixed luck as a teenager because he had zits on his ass instead of his face. His ass sure hurt when he sat down. We laughed.

My leg had not been a problem for some time, and although I walked on crutches, there was no pain in the leg anymore. In September 1968, however, the leg started to drain again. At first the drainage was slow, and the spot just remained moist all the time. I told the Vietnamese about it but got no response. Then the drainage got worse. Soon the drainage was heavy. One morning, I woke up and when I looked at my leg, the area around the wound had ants crawling all over it, and the lower part of my bed was covered with ants. It was a bizarre and sickening sight. I took some of my drinking water and washed the ants off my leg. Because the nerves were all shot in the area of the wound, I couldn't feel the ants on my leg. I asked to see an officer. For several days, I got no response, and the ants continued to find my leg each night. But finally I had a quiz with Sweet Pea. I told him my problem, and perhaps because

I shamed him into it, he told the medic to give me some bandages to cover the drainage.

Also during this time frame I received a pleasant surprise. One of the guys who lived in the building let me in on a big secret. He told me that somehow he got some information from the outside. He gave no details about who or where he got the information. Only that it was legitimate and worthwhile. I couldn't believe what I heard. He told me that he had recently heard about it and it was something like we should keep faith in God and our country, and their best estimate was that the end of the war was in sight. We were jubilant. Because the message was a morale booster, we discussed whether it should be passed out to the whole camp. The problem was that I could not reveal where or how I got it, but if I could not lend some credibility to the message, it would be accepted as nothing more than bull. We debated whether I should pass the message for more than a month. For nearly a year, the Vietnamese had pretty much left me alone. I'd had an occasional quiz now and then, but they had not asked me to do anything. It was pretty much the same for the whole building. Life was still for the birds, but at least we weren't being tortured or pressured every day. Now all we had to do was wait for the war to end.

We finally decided to take the gamble, because I thought it would be a great morale builder, and I didn't think there was much risk of this information being divulged to the Vietnamese. When I finally told Paul and Don what I had decided to do, they thought it was not a bad idea. Also, the guy who got the message thought it was a good idea, and he was the one who pushed me into spreading the word. I finally passed the message out to the whole camp. To lend credibility, I told them the only information I could give about the source was that it came from the outside and that, on my honor, it wasn't bull. I shortened the message to "Keep faith in God and country, the end is in sight," so it could be passed easier from building to building and through the walls by tapping. In general, the feedback I got from the message was good. Any morale builder was more than welcome.

In October 1968, I received personal messages from two guys who shared a room. The messages were passed via the senior man in the room between us. The problem was that they were not getting along with each other and had actually engaged in fisticuffs. Each told me what he thought of the other, and one ended his description by saying that his roommate was the centerpiece of a bouquet of assholes. They wanted my advice as to whether they should ask the Vietnamese if they could have new roommates or whether I had any other suggestions.

I had experienced similar problems, as many others had at one time or another, and told them so. I told them about a guy who disliked one of his roommates so much that it took four guards to forcibly return him to his room with the guy he didn't like. Being caged day after day, week after week, month after month in the same room, under barely minimum living conditions, and having to endure a totally deprived life created tremendous frustrations for each man, and it was inevitable that frictions between men would arise. There was no easy solution. I suggested that they both try to not bother each other and to talk to each other about what bothered them and then try to avoid doing the thing that pissed off the other guy. I recommended that only in the most extreme circumstances should they let the Vietnamese know that they were having problems getting along. They somehow managed to survive and were separated some months later.

In one of the end rooms of the building, two Navy lieutenants and one ensign lived together. They appeared to be filled with more than a normal amount of juice and vinegar. They appeared to be having their own internal problems. Because they were at least four rooms away from mine, they never passed any details of their personal problems. The ensign decided he was going to give the Vietnamese a hard time, either because he wanted to be moved from his roommates or just for the fun of it. He began to act strange, hiding under the bed when the Vietnamese opened the door and pretending he was sleeping when the Vietnamese found him. He would also bark like a dog in their presence. At first, the Vietnamese didn't make a big deal about it, probably because of his youth and very junior rank, but eventually they became perturbed. They tried to get him to cooperate but to no avail.

One day, the Vietnamese opened up the door of their room and told them that someone would tap to them from the back room. Maj. Kasler and Lt. Cdr. Pete Schoeffel lived in the room behind them. The Vietnamese opened Kasler's door and told him about the dumb things that the ensign was doing and told Kasler to tap to him on the wall and tell him to knock off his antics. It was no secret to the Vietnamese that we tapped, so for the fun of it, Kasler started to tap to the ensign's room. Kasler sent some info like, "go ahead and do anything you want," while three or four Vietnamese guards watched him tap on the wall and three or four guards watched the ensign in his room. This scene was probably one of the most surreal that I had ever heard about over there. It was not only the Vietnamese watching them tap, but also the entire episode demonstrated the lengths they would go to keep one American from seeing another. If they had really wanted the ensign to stop his nonsense, they could have just as easily brought him and Kasler together at quiz and achieved a solution to the problem. Eventually, the ensign gave up his nonsense, and some sanity was restored to their room. The ordeal was comical, but the significance was that we knew for sure that the Vietnamese knew we communicated. Guidance had been to deny communications at all cost, but this was no longer good advice.

We hoped we would have a big dinner for Christmas, because in the middle of November, the Vietnamese brought about twenty turkeys into the camp. The turkeys had free reign to travel anywhere they cared to. We were always annoyed when the turkeys jumped up on the food table between the time the food boy dished up the food and the guard opened our door to let us pick it up. When they were walking on the food table and through the food, we hoped they wouldn't defecate on it. But from time to time there was an accident.

We had a big dinner, some beer, and the usual Christmas Eve program. On the Voice of Vietnam, we heard the traditional messages from the prisoners. One Air Force guy who had just recently been shot down said all the right things like, "I am fine, Ma, and miss all the kids," etc., and then closed by saying, "and please be sure and keep all of my insurance premiums paid up." This comment amused us no end.

In the first month of 1969, everyone had a mug shot taken in the auditorium, and they gave us each a number to hold when they took our picture. The Vietnamese told us that this was our criminal number. Pop Keirn realized that his criminal number was the same as the date he entered the service. When everyone checked, they realized their criminal number was also the same as the date they entered the service. We assumed that they got this from some U.S. official document. In the Navy, it would have been easy to get the numbers out of the register of officers, because the book was published each year, with a considerable amount of information in it about each officer. Probably some American anti-war activist had given the book to the Vietnamese.

One Sunday morning in May1969, we got word that someone had escaped the night before. The message was very sketchy at first, and we had no details. This explained why the guard and officer had come around in the middle of the previous night checking on us. For the rest of the day, we knew that something was up, because the guards continued to check on us. The guards became very cool toward us. After several days, we learned that Air Force Captains John Dramesi and Edwin Atterberry had escaped. They had been living in an eight- or ten-men room in an area that was called the Zoo Annex. It was an area outside the wall of the main camp and had been opened only in the last few months. About seventy or eighty of the guys were junior officers, mid-grade officers, or recent shoot downs. In the main compound, we were all elated that the Vietnamese had at least improved the treatment for them and hoped that the advent of larger groups would be a forerunner for us. Despite our initial exuberance, the result of the escape was bad. Both men were captured the next day. Atterbury died either from torture or punishment. Many men were worked over mercilessly, communications were disrupted, and our treatment was set back years.

During the next three months, the guards and camp office remained very aloof and official in their relations with us. Even the guards who had been friendly previously were all business now. One unpleasant Vietnamese, whom we called Lenny or Gold Tooth, was about twenty-two years old. His status was unclear: He was not a guard or an officer. In any case, he had dark stains between his teeth and a large gold front tooth. We never knew why he had such an ugly disposition, but from his attitude toward the prisoners, American bombs must have killed his entire family. If there was ever a guy who hated us, it was Lenny Gold Tooth. You could see the pleasure in his eyes, when a prisoner was being punished.

One night he stopped by our room, opened the peephole, just stood there and looked in. I had had several run-ins with him before, nothing serious, but just enough for him to remember me. He made us stand after we bowed, and he cussed us out in Vietnamese and finished by saying, "Fuck you," about five times, then slammed the door. His eyes had been very glossy, and I suspected for the first time that drugs were probably being used quite extensively in North Vietnam. After Lenny slammed the peephole to our room, he went to the next room and did the same thing there.

After the escape, Pop Keirn moved into the Coach House for three or four days. We learned that someone had mentioned his name during the escape purge. When he returned, we learned that they hadn't done anything to him, but he laid a bombshell on me: He said the Vietnamese had asked him where Ray Vohden got the information that he passed through the camp about "Keep faith in God and country, the end is in sight." It appeared that during the torture of the prisoners, this information had been divulged. Pop Kern confirmed to the Vietnamese what the other guys had said, because there was no use denying something that numerous guys had probably admitted to. I was shocked. I knew the Vietnamese were not fooling around and apparently tracking down every piece of information they got from the tortured prisoners. I wasn't sure what to do. To have to divulge the source of my information would be a disaster for my informant, and it could eliminate the only means of contact we had with the outside world.

Several days later, two guards gave us a thorough room inspection. When they left, I realized that they had taken all of my letters and pictures. I had two or three letters saved at that time, and I was disappointed that they were gone. My immediate concern was that they would find out that I had uncensored some things that they had censored in my letters. In the first few years, the letters were two and three pages long. Later, all letters were on a standardized letter form and had room for only six or eight lines. But in the first two years, if the Vietnamese didn't want us to read something, they would censor it with dark ink. Of course, when I got the letter, the part I was most interested in was the censored part. I found out through experimentation that, by rubbing my fingernail lightly over the censored part, I could scrape off enough of the censoring ink so that I could read what was inked out. I had done this with all of my letters. To my disappointment, none of the censored information had amounted to anything.

I knew it was just a matter of time before I would be confronted with the "Keep faith" problem at quiz. I racked my brain for days, trying to find a way out of my predicament. The atmosphere was calming down now, and by the latter part of July, the Vietnamese were slacking off on the torture. They apparently had all the information they wanted. They had really shaken up and cleaned out all the cobwebs in the closets of the Annex and the Zoo.

One night after dark, on one of the last days in July 1969, the guard came to the door and gave us the sign to get our gear together to move. We were getting signals from everyone in the building that there was to be a big reshuffle. We heard the doors open and close and then the guys walking past our door. In time, the guard came and opened our door again. A guard handed me my bedroll. I knew then that I was leaving Don and Paul.

I had the same old bitch of a problem carrying the bedroll with my crutches. Blindfolded, I walked down the steps in the back of the Pig Sty, then went around a wall, and finally ended up in room 3 of the Pool Hall. I was sure Don and Paul were not with me. I had experienced camp-wide moves before. They weren't always bad. I always liked to get a new roommate. The room, however, was not new. I had lived there before. The door was closed and the bolt locked. I could hear many doors opening and closing in the Pool Hall and throughout the camp. I got my things in order after about thirty minutes. Far fewer doors were opening and closing. I knew I was going to get a roommate when I left Don and Paul. The only question was who. After about an hour, no more doors were opening and closing. A guard opened the peephole. I asked him when my roommate was coming. He just slammed the peephole shut as hard as he could. It finally dawned on me that I wasn't going to have a roommate.

The loneliness I had experienced having moved into solitary after living with roommates on a number of previous occasions crept over me again. Living with the right guy or guys is far better than being solo. But I could only feel sorry for myself for so long. I got into my bed, under the mosquito net, and tapped on the back wall. I got an answer right away. It was Lt. Cdr. Jim Bell. I had heard his name but had never lived in the same building with him. The reason he came up so fast was because he was also solo. We tapped for a few minutes and then I tapped GNGB (Good Night God Bless) and that was it for the night. I went to sleep very late that night pondering the events of the past few months and what the future would bring. In the Pool Hall were the seven or eight most senior 04's in the entire prison camp system.

I knew what real solitary confinement was during my first five months, when I had had no contact with anyone but the prison staff. I was solo now, but I would have someone to tap to, and that made living alone duck soup. To call living solo while in contact with other POWs solitary confinement would be stretching the truth.

CHAPTER 19 - RETRIBUTION

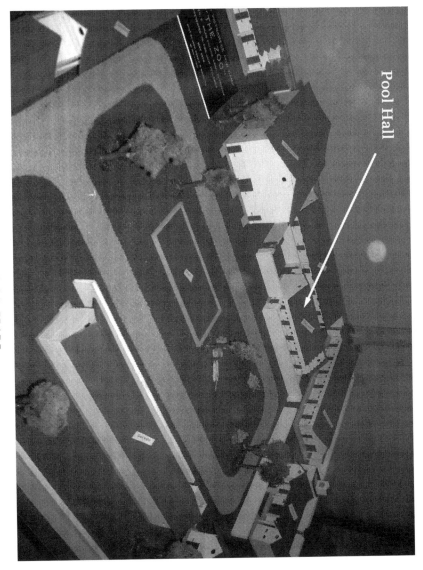

July 1969 – September 1970. The next day, we realized that the Vietnamese had not finished cracking down. The turnkey's attitude towards us was very cool. The Rabbit was our building officer. One of the men in the back of the building, all of whom were solo, was Maj. Guarino, who had been tortured so much that he not only refused to take command, he even refused to communicate. Another was Cdr. Wendell Rivers, who assumed the command functions. The others in the back were Maj. Bud Day and Lt. Cdr. Jim Bell. Major Kaslar and I were solo in the front of the building, and three other rooms had three men each. Bud was a new guy who had been shot down in late August 1967 and wasn't good at tapping, so it took several weeks before we got him up to speed. Communications were at a minimum because of the aftermath of the escape and threats by the Rabbit.

A few days after we moved in, we heard a tape by two POWs on the camp radio about the Code of Conduct. I asked Jim to ask Bud if he knew who had made the tape, because Bud had lived in the Plantation, where most of the propaganda came from. Bud knew how to tap, but he was not good at it, and he had a broken ear drum. He had trouble hearing, so Jim had to really tap loudly on the wall. Jim tapped, "Who makes tape we hear on camp radio about Code of Conduct?" Bud's reply was "Eisenhower 1956." Jim knew that Bud had misunderstood because the correct response would have been the names of the men who made the tape and not the president under whom the Code of Conduct was made. All that exchange, the question and answer, took about forty-five minutes. That was enough risk-taking for one day. The next day, Jim tapped again, "Who makes tape we hear on camp radio about Code of Conduct?" Bud tapped back, "Ike Eisenhower in 1957." Jim passed Bud's response to me, and because it was customary to ask for a shoot-down dates on new men, I said, "Get a shoot-down date on Eisenhower." That was enough confusion and joking for a week.

Shortly after I moved into the Pool Hall, I had a quiz with the Rabbit. I had not seen him for well over a year. At first, he was friendly and asked how I was and how my leg was. Then he accused me of ordering the ensign to do all the crazy things he had been doing when we were in the Pig Sty. I replied that I had never ordered him to do anything, and on the contrary, had told him to knock it off. He also accused me of ordering two other POWs to stop making tapes for the camp radio. He further accused me of conspiring by teaching Spanish to those in the building. This came about as a result of my being caught one day with Spanish words written on the floor. I had studied Spanish in college and was just practicing. He intimated that I was using Spanish for some evil purpose. The Rabbit was apparently shooting in the dark, accusing me of everything I might have been remotely connected with, and hoping I would be frightened by his threats. I told the Rabbit that I had not given any such orders. He made more threats and said that he could not be responsible for the consequence of my acts if I was not telling the truth. He made no mention of the message that I had passed throughout the camp.

A few days after we moved into the Pool Hall, the Rabbit started to put pressure on everyone not to communicate anymore. Because the Vietnamese had tortured so many guys mercilessly, everyone in the building had no desire to get the same again. Rabbit's threats of punishment became more severe as time went on. When men had a quiz with Rabbit, they readily admitted we were communicating, because punishment for the lie would be far worse than punishment for the act. But finally Rabbit accused Bomar of communicating and put him on his knees for ten hours one day. On 8 August, we all agreed that we would stop communicating as of 11 August, so that if two guys were pulled out separately, they would be telling the same story. But the Rabbit did not believe it and said he would continue the pressure and torture people if we started to communicate again.

Someone broke the communication silence, so we had to have a new starting time for our self-imposed communications silence, in order to be in agreement as to when it stopped. Some guys were really irritated when I told them the clock had started to run again. Rabbit had all of us in such a bind at this time, because of the torture that had taken place, that we had no other choice but to actually stop all communication. And to cover our asses, we had to agree to stop at the same time. Communicating was just not that important anymore. After a month and a half, all communication between the rooms had stopped. The Rabbit had won. The threat of torture and its likelihood had virtually all of the sixteen most senior 04's in the prison system silenced. This was a manifestation of the atmosphere of terror that existed in the camp.

Several days after we stopped communicating, I had another quiz with the Rabbit. It was about the fourth one since I had moved back into the Pool Hall. He asked me when I communicated last, and I truthfully told him when, as we had all agreed. He seemed to be satisfied with my answer, and he was becoming confident that we had actually stopped communicating. He accused me again of giving orders to the crazy ensign and other POWs, and he started to pressure me into writing an article about their humane treatment for the camp magazine, *The Runway*. He wanted me to write an article about my shoot down and the good medical treatment I had received.

Several prisoners had previously suggested to the camp authorities that the prisoners publish a camp magazine with articles written by the prisoners for the prisoners. The camp authorities bought the idea. I never understood why the POW's did this. The prisoners named it *The Runway*. Although their intentions were probably honorable, so far as I was concerned, the whole idea stunk, and it backfired. The magazine contained articles about hiking or fishing, but they only lent credibility for other articles of obvious propaganda value for the Vietnamese. And now the Rabbit had a selling point in trying to get me to write. At first, I refused. He told me to go stand in the corner and think it over. He left the room.

The atmosphere was very somber in the camp now, and the Rabbit was not in a joking mood. I worried that if I refused to write the article and they tortured me for it, they might confront me with the secret message I had sent. The message had unquestionably been compromised. I had a cover story for it, but I was not sure they would buy it, and I knew what torture could make people do and say. I finally decided that I would go ahead and write the article, because the consequences of compromising my source far outweighed any benefit the Vietnamese might get from my contribution to the magazine. When the Rabbit returned, I wrote an article about my medical care. They had saved my leg, so to some extent that was good. The problem was that it was only half the truth.

I went to quiz with Rabbit several weeks later. They had my article for the camp magazine. What else could he want that wouldn't cause me problems? I went in and sat down. He seemed somewhat more relaxed than before. He asked me how I was and how my leg was doing. He was making small talk, when out of the clear blue sky, he asked me, "Where did you get the information in the message that you sent through the camp?" I acted dumb and said, "I don't understand." He said, "The message about 'Keep the faith in God and country, and the end is in sight.'" He stated the message almost word-for-word exactly as I had sent it. As I had practiced in my room at least a thousand times since the Vietnamese took my letters from me, I said, "Oh, you mean that message." I said, "Oh, that's nothing. It was something about what the Chief of Naval Operations wrote to the ships in the Tonkin Gulf that my roommate Paul Schulz saw in a message on his ship before he was shot down." I told him that the message was mostly about how optimistic the CNO was, and that I added the "keep faith" stuff to make it sound better. The Rabbit paused and looked at me. I tried to look as nonchalant and innocent as possible, even though my heart was pounding away. The Rabbit appeared to buy my story. He warned me never to communicate again and sent me back to my room. I deserved an Oscar for my acting that day. As relieved as I was that this episode was over, however, I still practiced my lines every day until I moved to a new camp almost a year later. I had become the consummate liar. In Hanoi, you had to learn to lie with a straight face or else. Lying and pretending had been part of my life for years now.

The guards and turnkey continued the harassment and bad treatment. This building, like all the others I had been in before, was developing its own personality. Each room with its occupant or occupants, the guards, the officer in charge, and the prevailing prison environment created an unfriendly and unhappy personality for all. One time, the turnkey came into my room and wanted me to do something. I did not understand what he wanted. I was standing in the middle of the room. He came over to me and suddenly pushed hard against my chest. It was so unexpected that I lost my balance and fell on the floor, crutches and all. If I'd had two good legs, I probably would have killed the little bastard. But I thought twice and held my breath. I knew that losing my temper in a prison camp, especially in the current atmosphere, was not the thing to do. I couldn't count how many times I'd had to hold my breath when my heart was filled with hatred and disgust for them. The fear of what my life would be with just one leg and without the use of an arm or hand lost from torture made me hold my breath far more than I wanted. The turnkey's knocking me over was just about the last straw that I could take. My morale was so low that, as the Vietnamese used to say, I would need a forty-foot ladder to climb up to the belly of a snake.

Later that day, an English-speaking kiddy (a young Vietnamese officer trainee) named Joe Louis opened the peephole. I had had it with the turnkey, and I figured that life could not be much worse than it was now. I knew that sometimes a guard or turnkey would make life miserable for a particular prisoner or several prisoners on his own, without orders from the camp officers. So it might be worth a gamble to raise the issue with an English speaker. There was always the possibility that the turnkey was doing what the officer told him to do, however, and the treatment would get worse. Or the turnkey might become more belligerent because you squealed on him. In any case, I told Joe Louis about my problems and said that I was really upset from this continuous harassment. Luckily, the turnkey slacked up on the bad treatment somewhat.

Life became quite boring now, because we were not communicating. So to occupy my time, I played with the ants in my room. I slept on one bed, and as I was solo, the bed on the other side of the room by the door was unoccupied. We would get sugar for a meal from time to time, and I would take some of it and put it on the empty bed and allow the ants to eat it. They loved it. I used to talk to the ants and tell them that they could eat all the sugar they wanted on the other bed, and I would take good care of them. But if they came on my bed, it was going to be war. Every once in a while, they would come on my bed, and there was war. I would wipe out hundreds of them. I figured that the ants lived and bred in the small hole in the floor by the door. After I gave them a good bit of sugar, a week to ten days later, hundreds of ants would always show up in the room in that area. I had a feeling that the sugar contributed to their reproduction. Or maybe the word just got out about the free sugar. The ants also lived in a place behind the unoccupied bed.

Several times late in the afternoon, when the rays from the hot sun fell on my wooden door, the door got very hot. Thousands of ants would come out from their nest near the door and march about fifty abreast across the floor, then up on the wall about one foot, and finally under the unoccupied bed. I found it fascinating to watch this huge migration of ants. Once in a while, however, when I was mad at the ants, I took my shoe and crushed hundreds of them. They would end up in a large black smudge spot of dead ants on the wall. And then sometimes just for fun, I wiped out thousands of them. I was the kind of person who couldn't be trusted.

One time late in the afternoon, when the area near where they lived became very hot, they gathered on the floor for about two feet behind the door across its width, which was a good four feet. The mass was solid with thousands of good-sized ants swarming all over. I became nervous, because I had never seen so many ants in one place. I felt like I was watching a science-fiction movie. I did not have a great fear of them, but I wondered what I would do if suddenly they came and crawled over my bed and me. So I went over to them, took off my shoe, and started killing them by the hundreds. I just did not want so many of them in my room. They began scattering in a thousand different directions. They climbed all over my feet and legs. It took me about ten minutes of swatting and squashing to keep them off me and from coming up on my bed.

I had watched them for hours on end, day after day. I observed that there was apparently a queen ant, much like a queen bee, and she seemed to lay the eggs. One night, I observed four or five ants running around on the floor and up and down the wall near my bed in a very frenzied manner. I watched them for about five minutes. Suddenly, a much larger ant appeared on the scene. I surmised that it was the queen, and the other ants were looking for a place for her to lay her eggs. I watched until finally they all disappeared under my bed. Several weeks later, there was a new colony of ants under my bed. I did not like the idea of ants under or near my bed, so I declared war again. I spent hours one day waiting for the ants to come out of their hole in the floor. As they came out one by one, I killed them. I killed hundreds that day. Apparently, one queen ant lays quite a few eggs. I felt bad about making the black smudges on the floor and wall, because it made the room dirty. But I really had no choice. It was either play with the ants or go stir crazy, and besides the Vietnamese whitewashed the room every few years.

On another occasion, I made an obstacle course for some ants to see how smart they were. I took a piece of thread from my blanket, ran the thread through three pieces of paper two inches apart and then tied the thread to one end of my crutch. I put some sugar and water on the bottom piece of paper and laid the paper near some ants. As soon as three or four ants started to eat the sugar I lifted my crutch and hung it off my bed, with the other end of the crutch touching the wall. For the ants to leave, they had to go to the wall. If they came to my bed, they died. At first, the ants ate. Then they would start running around looking for a way out. In time, one would find how to get to the wall, and the others would follow. Then their buddies would return with them, up the wall, over the crutch, down the thread and over the paper, to the sugar. All of this was time consuming. It took as long as an hour or more sometimes for the ants to escape, and sometimes they never escaped. It was interesting to observe, because I never knew what the end result would be. Sometimes I would let them go. Other times, I would cut the piece of thread and drop the paper in some water.

For several days in September, the camp became unusually quiet. Quizzes had stopped, and little activity was going on. The guards and turnkeys were serious and went about their work in a business-like manner. Finally, after two days of this, the guards and turnkeys showed up wearing black armbands. On the camp radio, we learned about the death of Ho Chi Minh. The announcers told us the story of Ho Chi Minh's life, and they provided us with a detailed report of his funeral. We heard about Communist and neutral countries that were sending delegations to the funeral. At each broadcast, they read the names of the countries that sent flowers or wreaths for the funeral. I remember the citation on the wreath from Red China was, "Our grief is boundless." We got his life story and information about the funeral at least twice a day until he was finally buried.

I suspected that the camp authorities debated whether to tell us about his death, but finally decided that they should and planned how they would do it. We heard quite a bit of funereal music on the radio. Although normal camp activity was quiet during this time, some workers were making the brick wall surrounding our building higher. On the day of the funeral, we could hear the twenty-one-gun salute off in the distance and then the planes flying over the city in tribute to their fallen leader. Surprisingly, some of the workers continued to work and bang away with their tools and bricks during this time. I didn't know the significance of this, but I inferred that at least some of the North Vietnamese felt indifference, or even dis-respect, toward Uncle Ho.

Little by little, the pressure subsided, and by mid-October, we were communicating again. Not a whole lot, as in years gone by, but at least everyone was in touch again. Sometime after Ho Chi Minh died, the Vietnamese announced on the camp radio the results of their elections. They proudly announced how each man running unopposed received one hundred percent of the vote and was unanimously elected. Ten minutes passed before the roar of laughter died down in our building. Also within several weeks after Ho's death, our treatment improved considerably. Baths were regular, the food was a little better, the attitude of the guards was friendlier, and we got four daily cigarettes instead of three. One day around this time, the Fox came to each room and personally told all of us that we no longer had to bow. Instead, all we had to do was stand up. One night, an officer came to our rooms and asked us our names and wrote them down. This event, which happened about once every year or two, resurrected our eternal hope that negotiations were going well, and perhaps we would be released soon. Everyone had his own opinion as to why the treatment improved, but only the man who made the decision really knew why. One thing for sure was that within a month after Ho Chi Minh's death, things improved a lot.

To my knowledge, only on rare occasions did any hard torture occur after his death. Atterbury's death might have had some effect on our treatment. It was my opinion that the Vietnamese never intended to kill a prisoner when torturing him. They merely wanted to get what they wanted at the minimum sacrifice to the prisoner. This is not to say that they wouldn't hurt a guy if he pissed them off. They punished people for infractions of their rules. Atterbury's death might have been the result of an accident and might have frightened them. I talked to camp officers, not in a threatening way, but reminded them of the Nuremberg War Crimes Trial where the German torturers were hanged. They called us criminals, but we let them know what we thought of their so-called humane policy on the treatment of prisoners. Although they scoffed at our warnings, they seemed to give thought to what we said. Although their policy might not have been to kill, their torture was rough enough so that at least fifteen or twenty guys probably died as a result of it. Therefore, the threat of torture was always a life or death matter for us.

Although I was solo again, and communication was still at a minimum, every night I would get under my mosquito net and tap to Jim Bell, who was in the room behind me, for about an hour and a half. We got to know a lot about each other, and as time went by, we became good friends. We tapped for more than four months like this. The days went fairly fast, and the communication at night was just enough to take the boredom out of the day for us. During the day, the guys in the next room talked to me on the wall. Then I passed whatever news they had on to Kasler. The guys in the other side room, Cole Black or Paul Schulz, would clear for both rooms when I talked to Kasler. About three months after I moved in, Jim Bell tapped to me that he wanted me to talk to him. He was getting lonely, because no one had talked to him, as he could not get clearance out back. So one day, he said the hell with clearing, and I talked to him for a while. He was elated. This was another example of how such a simple thing could make a man happy.

In the middle of November, some workers from outside the camp came to our building and took measurements of the rooms. We suspected a renovation, and several weeks later, the Rabbit told someone at quiz that they were going to knock the walls down, and that we would all live together. Another officer told someone else a different story. A number of other rumors about what would happen floated around. We had been told over the years that things would improve, and that we would live together. We had been lied to so much by the Vietnamese that we never put much stock in what they told us, but we were always optimistic that the isolation would end.

In late November, workers came in and knocked down the wall between the front and back end rooms. While the work was going on in those rooms, the men who had lived there were moved in with men in the other rooms. There were rooms with four or five guys living together for a day or two. When the Vietnamese got the brick walls knocked out, they moved four men into each of the large rooms. At first, everyone was excited. They played bridge and chess and were having a ball. In no time, however, some guys were not getting along. They had personality problems, and the sparks began to fly. Years later, Larry Guarino told me that he had asked one of the officers if he could move out, because of problems in his room.

About the same time, the workers also knocked the bricks out of the window in Jim Kasler's and my rooms. The Vietnamese still kept the shutters closed, so we couldn't see the other men as they passed by our rooms. Within a week, however, they were allowing whole rooms of three and four guys out for some fresh air, sunshine, and exercise in front of our rooms, and they started to leave the shutters open. Kasler and I were allowed to stand at the windows in our respective rooms and watch the men outside, and they could see us, but we couldn't talk to each other, even though we had communicated with each other every day, and in many cases had met and even lived with each other. We felt stupid just standing there like dummies. Word was passed down from one of the other rooms that Kasler and I looked like monkey see, monkey do, as we stood at the window watching the other men walking back and forth. The Vietnamese were probably working up to moving all of us into bigger rooms, and they were testing us along the way. If we had not done what they told us to do, we might not have been allowed to move in with each other.

In any case, several weeks later, Jim Kasler and Jim Bell moved into my room. I loved having companionship again. Then before the day was out, we moved into another room, and Jim Bell ended up sleeping on the floor, because there were only two beds. Kasler moved out in less then a week, and Jim Bell and I stayed together. He was an outstanding roommate, and we got along just fine. His sense of humor is best described by how he used to pile all of his blankets on top of his bed, about two feet up, then stand on them and urinate into the *bo*. Because he was so far from the bucket, the whole building could hear the urine falling into the water. It almost sounded like Niagara Falls. We always had a good laugh when he did that. He also had a weekly nightmare that scared the daylights out of me, because his yells were so loud.

Jim was shot down 16 October 1965, while piloting the RA-5C Vigilante. He ejected over the sea at a high rate of speed, which resulted in a broken shoulder and his Mae West flotation device being torn away. A few minutes later, he was picked up by local fisherman and tied to the boat's mast. He had seen the movie *Two Years Before the Mast* the night before in the ship's wardroom, and he laughed aloud at the irony of the situation. With that, the Vietnamese fishermen decided he might be a decent guy, and they brought him a cold beer to drink. It was his last beer for some time.

Jim's shoulder injury was quite painful, but the Vietnamese did nothing for him. Eventually, it healed crookedly, and he got some limited use from it. He bragged about being the 39th POW captured in the North, but this didn't carry much weight with me, as I'd been number four. He told me about the Hanoi March and about how he had the hell beaten out of him because he was with Ralph Gaither as the last twosome in the march. When he was at another camp early in the war, he was caught communicating and put in a four-foot deep hole, with his wrists cuffed behind for sixty days. Ralph Gaither managed to give him a handcuff pick, which he used to unlock the cuffs at night. It made his difficult position much more bearable. Jim was one of the silent majority POW's. You will not hear much about them because they were good POWs and made few waves. They were tortured, lived years in isolation, never went out of their way to annoy the camp authorities, he even avoided writing a confession. He took his lickings, blended into the background and the Vietnamese forgot about him. He was the epitome of how a POW should be.

As a result of the renovation in the building and men moving together, some rooms were vacant. Soon, the Vietnamese moved in some new guys. Capt. Lou Makowski and Maj. Dave Burroughs moved in behind us. One day, Jim was standing up at the window, and he got a look at two new men who were moving into the room next to us. One was Lcdr. Ned Shuman, who had been a classmate and friend of Jim's at the Naval Academy. The other man with was his back-seater Lcdr. Dale Doss. They had been shot down in March 1968, so when they got settled in, we received a lot of news from them. They gave us many new names and news from the other camp. Jim had never written or received a letter, so having Shuman move in was a godsend, because he had a lot of news for Jim. Shuman did not know anything about Jim's wife, but he had other items to report.

My leg had still drained off and on for the past year. Although I did not know the significance of the draining, I found it depressing, because I knew it was not good for my leg or my body. Jim got a package with high-potency vitamin and mineral tablets for Christmas. He asked me if I wanted to share them with him. At first I refused, but he insisted. I tried them. Miraculously, the leg stopped draining after three days. So as a test, I stopped taking them. The leg started to drain again. I took the tablets again, and it stopped draining. I figured why not take them after that. Jim was extremely generous in sharing his tablets with me for the remainder of the time I lived with him. After that, in every letter I wrote to my wife, I asked her to send that same tablet, but either she failed to send them, or the Vietnamese kept them for themselves.

Although the Vietnamese had relaxed the pressure, they never let up completely. They were always springing something else on us. This time, the good deal was that anyone who wanted to paint pictures or draw could do so. They provided watercolor paints, crayons, chalk, and paper for anyone who wanted them. In fact, a number of new guys and one or two old hands had already decided on their own, in the absence of any guidance on the subject of painting, to go ahead and paint. A quiz room had been set aside to exhibit a number of paintings made by the prisoners. Some of them were quite good. The Vietnamese allowed other prisoners to view the exhibit once or twice.

As usual, a controversy arose whether one should paint or not. The Vietnamese would likely make propaganda out of anything we painted, but the recreational value and enjoyment for those who painted was significant. As with most problems confronting the SRO, about half of the guys said go ahead and paint, and the other half said it violated the Code of Conduct. Whichever way the SRO went, he was sure to make fifty percent of the men unhappy. Larry Guarino, the SRO, said, "Go ahead and paint if you want to. If the Vietnamee get some propaganda value, so be it." Some guys started to paint and were enjoying it, but there was still some bitterness toward them from some of the other men. On one occasion, Ned Schuman and Dale Doss were going out to empty their *bo*, and as they passed the window of one of the rooms where some guys were painting, Doss accused them of violating the Code of Conduct. One of the guys who was painting tried to tear the bars out of the window. If he could have gotten out of his cage, he would have attacked Doss. Another day, a POW had had it and refused to stay in the room with one of his roommates. Three or four guards tried to put him back in the room but failed. They finally put him in solo.

With the significant change in our treatment, the escape a thing of the past, and the situation somewhat under control, the Rabbit was no longer our officer in charge. Now we had one of the kiddies. I don't think he was an officer, but he spoke some English and was probably a potential officer candidate. We named him Boris. He was young, about twenty at most, fairly pleasant, and easy to get along with. He came around at night and stood at the door and just shot the bull with the guys about this and that. He appeared to be very efficient, and he would have made a perfect butler back in the U.S., or he would have been an excellent administrative assistant, but like all the rest he was always trying to get us to paint or write something, and he would undoubtedly have tortured us if his superiors told him to do so.

One time I went to quiz with Jim Bell, and Boris was in charge. He tried the usual soft sell to get us to paint or write something, but when we refused he gave up. Then to get us talking and liven up the quiz, he asked some questions about birth control and sex. It was a gimmick they used to get the prisoners to talk, and I had seen it before. Somehow the subject of the penis came up, and Boris seemed to be rather embarrassed about the subject. In addition, he couldn't pronounce the word *penis* correctly and kept calling it a peanut. Jim and I were quite amused by the whole affair, and when we got back to the room, we passed on how Boris pronounced penis, so that no one would ever correct him.

Sometime in the spring of 1970, the Vietnamese allowed each of the rooms in our building to have a deck of playing cards. I had played duplicate bridge for around five years before I was shot down and had enjoyed it immensely. It takes four to play bridge, and as Jim and I didn't have roommates, we appeared to be out of luck.

Dave Burroughs and Lou Makowski were in the room behind us, however, and they also wanted to play bridge. We put our collective heads together and came up with a plan that allowed us to play. How we arrived at this plan was complicated, but the result was worth it. By tapping, we arranged partners. Each room had a deck of cards, and they were arranged in order from ace through the two of spades, then ace through the two of hearts, ace through the two of diamonds, and ace through the two of clubs. We dealt the cards out into eleven stacks, as one would deal in solitaire. When all the cards were dealt, we had eleven stacks of cards in each room that were the same. Now the dealer would tap a number between one and eleven. Each room would take that numbered stack and place it down in front of the dealer. Then the dealer would tap a number between one and ten, and that numbered stack would be removed and placed on top of the first removed stack. Then the dealer would tap a number between one and nine, and that stack would be removed and placed on top of the other two. And so on, until all of the stacks were on top of each other, in the same order in each room. Then the cards were dealt. We would bid by tapping on the wall. As each card was played, we kept them in the same order in each room. If the order of cards got mixed up, we would start over again. Mathematically, the combinations of hands that existed for picking up twelve or fifteen stacks at random were quite high, actually in the millions. Nonetheless, the distribution of the cards dealt that way seemed somewhat more unusual than when the cards were shuffled normally. We played three or four hands almost every night after the last meal, and on Sundays playing bridge was a godsend.

In the spring of 1970, we were allowed out in the sun sometimes for as much as fifteen minutes a day when we went to bath. During the hottest time of the day, we would occasionally see fairly large lizards sunbathing on the top of the brick wall around the bath area. They were at least a foot long and ominous looking. I was glad that they never came into our rooms, because they wouldn't have made good bed partners. That spring, the Vietnamese planted a garden of red hot peppers in the bath area. They were free for the picking, but they were hot beyond belief. If you cut one with your fingernail, the mere touch would burn your skin. One piece, half the size of the eye of a small needle made a whole bowl of soup good and hot. Some of us really enjoyed them. They added flavor to the rather tasteless soup. When I was released from prison, I didn't have any worms. The doctor did not understand why. I knew. There was no way a worm could survive in a stomach with peppers that hot.

Jim made a little ball out of an old piece of cloth, and when we got outside for a few minutes now and then, we played catch. I would sit on a low wall and Jim would stand about fifteen feet away. We had a turnkey named Piggy. He looked like Porky the pig. Piggy would sit between us on a chair and watch the ball like a spectator at a tennis match. Our throwing and catching the ball fascinated him. Then one day when we were throwing to each other, Piggy came and stood behind me. Once in a while, I missed the ball, and if it was near him, he would pick it up and hand it to me. We suspected that Piggy wanted to get in there and play catch too. So one day Jim threw the ball to Piggy. He had one of the biggest smiles on his face that we ever saw, when he caught the ball. Jim played catch with him for a few minutes. He tried to be very nonchalant and appear very confident as he played, but he obviously had played catch very little, if at all. But he really seemed to enjoy it.

After Ho Chi Minh's death, the relaxation of tension, and improvement in our treatment, two differences of opinion on how we should conduct ourselves emerged in the building. Some took the improved conditions in stride. Others, however, went out of their

301

way to give the Vietnamese a hard time. Some guys gave the guards fits all the time. Bud Day and Jack Fellowes did not smoke, but they took their ration of cigarettes, so they could give them to someone else. Instead of hiding them in the bath area for the pickup, however, they would take a gamble by leaving the enclosed bath area, running to one of the rooms in the back of the building, opening the peep-hole, saying, "Hi," to the occupants, and throwing in the cigarettes. They probably had a ball doing this, because it worked for a while, but they finally got caught, and the guard raised hell.

There was a bamboo screen that surrounded a small part of the bath area, so we could not see out. When Day and Fellowes went for a bath, they would get as close as they could to the screen, so they could look out. One time, they saw the turnkey on the outside of the bamboo screen apparently spying on them, so Day went over to where the guard was looking in and put his eyeball on the bamboo screen right opposite the guard's eyeball. The guard went ballistic. When we heard about this, it was worth a good laugh. Sometimes, they refused to stand when the guard or turnkey came to their room. As a consequence of their shenanigans, they frequently missed baths and seldom got outside for fresh air, but they had a lot of fun stirring up the pot. Soon thereafter, they were moved out of the Zoo.

Two other guys were having problems living together. On more than one occasion, we heard them wrestling around the room, and the guys in the rooms next to them could hear them having fistfights once in a while. In addition, they were also giving the guard and turnkey a hard time every day. They would not stand up when the guard or turnkey came at bath time. So the guard would not take them to bathe. Everyone in the building was concerned about their not getting along.

I went to quiz one time with the Fox. I'd had a lengthy quiz with him in 1965. He never forgot how I bragged that the U.S.

would kick the living daylights out of Vietnam in no time at all. He had told me how they would win. Almost every May Day, I had a quiz with him, and he would rub it in by reminding me what I had said and how wrong I had been, because the U.S, was being defeated. This day was no different from those other quizzes. After he was satisfied that he had chivied me enough, he asked me about the treatment. I told him that it was inhumane to keep some guys together for so long, and that we should be given new roommates now and then. But the two guys who were at odds with each other continued to have a good fistfight every once in a while.

In the late part of spring 1970, a new man moved into one of the rooms in our building. The men in the next room tried to contact him, but he would not answer. One day they got a look at him from under the door and recognized him as an Asian whom they had known from another camp. One of the guys said he had tried to contact this man, when they were both solo in adjacent rooms in the other prison camp, but the Asian would not answer. The guy said that a couple of days later, he went to quiz and was confronted with the fact that he had tried to contact this Asian. He concluded the Asian had ratted on him and was a traitor. He might even have been a spy, so we named him Brutus.

All of us had had some contact with other Asian prisoners and never heard of them giving any Americans trouble, and two of them had been outright friendly to me, when I was living with Will Gideon in 1967. So some of us took what this POW said with a grain of salt, and besides branding a man as a traitor is a pretty serious thing. So we debated at some length whether he was a spy and perhaps in the building to listen to our communication, or whether he was just another prisoner. The general agreement was that he was a prisoner, because he ate the same food as we did and had the same daily routine as the rest of us. Many of us doubted this POW's opinion, because at one point the Vietnamese accused us of communicating almost every time we had a quiz. We always said no. I did not want to conclude that this Asian was a traitor. I suspected he did not tap to us because he did not know how, and it was not fair to consider him a traitor on such flimsy evidence. At this point, however, it really didn't make a hill of beans whether he was a spy or not, because we continued to communicate as we had always done.

To add more fuel to the fire, Paul Schulz once had a couple of seconds when he was picking up the dishes, and the guard wasn't around, so he opened up Brutus's flap, poked his head in, and said, "Do you speak English?" Brutus said, "No." Paul said, "I am an American," and then Paul asked him what he was. Brutus just shook his head, which indicated that he did not understand or he did not want to communicate. About a week later, Schulz was called to quiz and was accused of talking to Brutus. So this was considered evidence that Brutus had betrayed us. As far as I was concerned, this was still no guarantee that he was a traitor, because the Vietnamese could have been watching Paul open the flap and talk to him, or the Asian may have told Boris not knowing that Paul wasn't suppose to talk to him. Years later, we found out when we were in camp Unity, that he was a Thai, and from those who had personal contact with him, he obviously was not a traitor and could be trusted just like the rest of us.

Almost a year and a half had passed since I moved into the Pool Hall building. When we moved in, the camp was living under a siege of terror. The torture had been rampant, and the treatment had been as bad as it ever was. But now, relatively speaking, we were living high on the hog. The torture had ended, the pressure for statements and to violate the Code of Conduct had ended, we were getting more sunshine and cigarettes. There was even a lessening of the isolation. But we were not out of the woods yet. Our day still consisted of two poor meals, and many of us still spent ninety-nine percent of each day alone in our rooms. We had come a long way, but the battle wasn't over yet.

CHAPTER 20 - R & R

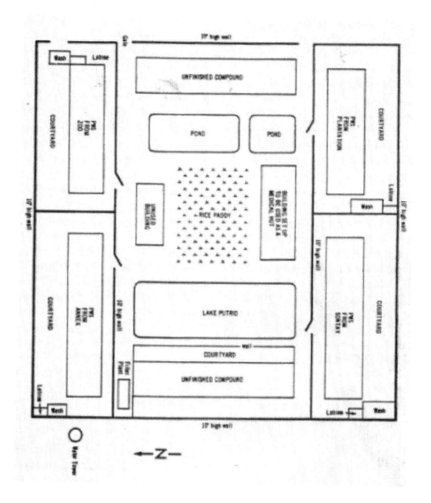

CAMP FAITH

September 1970 – November 1970. One night in late September, we had finished communicating and were getting ready to play bridge, when we heard buses in the camp. The guard came to our room and gave us the roll-up sign. I left the room alone and got into a bus in front of our building.

After the bus was loaded, several guards got on and handcuffed each man to a seat. Then we were blindfolded. Some men expressed concern about being handcuffed to the bus, because if there was an accident, we would be trapped. Our complaints went for naught. We drove for about forty-five minutes. Finally, we arrived at our destination, about nine miles west of Hanoi. Although it was dark, we could see a number of buildings, which looked like an army camp of some kind. As a special treat, the Vietnamese gave us each a huge glazed donut, and they even gave us hot water for instant coffee that one of the guys had. The donut was not the kind you buy at the local pastry store but something that weighed half a pound, was greasy, and had some sweet stuff on it. Although it was September and the weather still warm, I thought how pleasant it would have been to live in this place in the heat of the summer.

The next morning, we learned that fifty-seven men were in our compound in five rooms. Our room had twenty men, who were generally the most senior of the group. The beds looked as if they had just recently been installed, and the room had big windows with shutters in the front and back. We also had a table and some chairs. Other than at quiz, this was the first time in five years that I could sit on a chair at a table. It felt good. Off the main room was a small room that could be used for a bathroom.

The other rooms had twelve, ten, eight, and seven men in them. A large courtyard, probably forty yards long, was in back of our building, and a clothesline ran the length of the courtyard. They had even planted flowers in certain areas, and a brick path ran the length of the yard down to the washroom, which had a water tank three times the size of the one at the Pool Hall. Adjacent to the washroom was a bathroom with squatter toilets. It was the first time that we had such elaborate toilet facilities, and we put them to good use. About forty yards beyond the compound was a water tower at least fifty feet high. About a hundred yards beyond the water tower were a number of antennas and towers. Some of the electronic experts among us concluded that it was probably a shortwave radio-transmission station. On our side of the camp was another building about fifty feet away. It had a large red star with gold trim on the front of it. We guessed it was some sort of a Vietnamese Army Headquarters building.

The main camp had a wall around it and was divided by high walls into four sections, each with a building in it. Atop the wall at each corner of the camp was a small tower, which was manned twenty-four hours a day. They kept the lights on in the courtyard and in our rooms all night long. In time, we would learn that about 220 men were in the four compounds, but we had no contact with the compounds on the other side of the camp, which had opened in July 1970.

We organized the room. I was the SRO. Al Runyan was second in command and an able assistant. We agreed on most issues. I never made a decision without consulting him. We had a cigarette-control officer to ensure the cigarettes were divided evenly each day. Ray Merritt volunteered to be the education officer. Red McDaniel was the chaplain and conducted church services every Sunday morning. Jack Van Loan organized duplicate-bridge tournaments. He was also the recreation officer. Doug Burns was the communications officer. His responsibility was to establish communications with other prisoners in the camp as soon as possible.

The weather was great and at first each room got out separately twice a day for half an hour. Even though all the windows were open in the building, the guys who were in the yard were not allowed to talk to guys in the rooms. All we could do was look at each other. Later, they let two and three rooms out together for about three hours each day and in a month they let the whole compound out twice a day. Besides just talking and taking in the sunshine, guys had contests throwing a big rock like a shot put. Red McDaniel was probably the best, followed by Bill Metzger and Charlie Rice, who were both pretty hefty guys. Some guys would race the length of the compound. The guards never liked it when we did this, but they didn't say we couldn't. We also made balls out of old ragged clothes, and many of us had fun playing catch with the balls.

When we were locked in our rooms during the day, a chess game was going on all the time. It was just as much fun to sit and watch sometimes as it was to play. The Vietnamese also had set aside a reading room that had the *Vietnam Courier* and other propaganda magazines and books. Nobody ever went there. Some men got up early and exercised, some would sleep, and some would walk. All of my past roommates had walked to pass the time. Waltman and Schulz had devised the most intricate pattern to avoid running into each other, if they both walked at the same time. Now with a larger room but many more guys to walk in it, I was amused to watch as many as ten guys walking around the table and between the beds at one time, without bumping into each other. Kay Russell and Charlie Zuhowski were mathematics majors in college, so we had math lessons galore. I continued with a review of the calculus that I had learned from Dean Woods, and before long, I was deriving the equations used in calculus and had mastered the fundamentals fairly well.

The nights were generally reserved for group participation. Although some of the guys had never played bridge before, we made an effort to teach everyone how to play. Two or three nights each week, we played about fifteen hands of duplicate, with at least four tables and once in a while with five. To balance out the good and bad players, the pair who came in first was always partners the next night with the guys who came in last. After we got our game underway, several of the other rooms tried it, and soon a game was going on in each room every night. The education officer arranged for a series of lectures by experts on such topics as hi-fi equipment, electronics, music, art, and other subjects. The lecture series might last anywhere from one to six nights.

At first, we were not sure that other POWs were living in the camp with us, because the walls were fairly high around our compound. But within a week, we saw a guy's head looking at us from the other side of the wall. It was Bob Purcell. Apparently, the guards in their compound had left them unattended for a minute or two. Doug Burns, our communications officer, greeted him, and they quickly established a daily communications link. They picked a particular point on the wall where notes would be left. The note would be placed on top of the wall at a time when the guard was not looking. It might take two days of watching for a safe time, but that was the communication team's responsibility.

We didn't receive any startling revelations from the other compound. They had about the same number of guys as we did, and their treatment was the same. Even though living conditions were greatly improved over what they had been, life was not without its difficulties. One major problem was that the bread was brought to the camp twice each week from Hanoi. After the first day, the bread became old. It turned moldy, sour, and stale, and after three days was almost inedible. We ate it because we were hungry, but the upset stomachs that resulted barely made it worthwhile.

One morning, Charlie Southwick woke early and went into the so-called bathroom. Everyone was awake or half-awake. Charlie proceeded to piddle in the *bo,* and while he was doing this, he broke wind. It was perhaps the longest fart that any of us had ever heard. It was absolutely fantastic. It was loud, melodious, and the noise continued for at least twenty seconds. By the time he had finished, the whole room was awake, and we gave him a hearty round of applause. When Charlie came back into the room, he had a big grin on his face, and he bowed to show his appreciation for our applause. Charlie wasn't the only man skilled at breaking wind in Vietnam. The diet of pig fat, cabbage, and other gas-producing foods guaranteed that many guys had prominence in this area.

Our packages were another problem. When there was only a little more than nothing, that little more could be a problem. This was the first time that any of us had been together in such a large room, and we had to come up with a solution. Some people wanted to keep the packages for themselves, others wanted the entire room to share, and others wanted to divide up into groups. A survey said the room was divided about what to do. We knew we were going to get packages again, and we had to decide beforehand how to handle them. Probably a third of the men got a package at any one time, and that third varied, with different guys each time. Although some got packages every time, others never got a package. I suspected that the Vietnamese did this on purpose to sow dissension among us.

We decided to let each man do with his package whatever he wanted to do. Some decided not to divide their packages, and others went into groups. I went into a group with six guys, and everything was fine. But some hurt feelings were generated when a guy who didn't go into a group did not get a package. Even though other guys wanted to share with him, that guy refused. We always had controversies over packages, and how to handle them while living together peacefully turned a trivial matter into a major problem.

After we were there for a short while, I had a quiz with Bushy, the new camp commander. It was the first time I had met him. He was pleasant and appeared to be just doing his job and not inclined to go out of his way to make things difficult for us. Sweet Pea was our officer in charge, and for the first time he recognized the SRO. He knew that I was the senior man. He came to me with his problems, and we worked together nicely. He did that with the rest of the rooms, too. So far as I was concerned, this was a major breakthrough and something we had worked for over a long time.

The Vietnamese were not pressuring us for anything, although they still asked us to do this or that. Mike Christian had at one time told them that he could play a guitar. They offered him one but he refused to take it. My old roommate Quincy was still trying to set up a choir of men in all the compounds, so we could be in contact with the other men. The question of the propaganda benefit to the Vietnamese versus the good we derived by being in contact with other compounds arose. Most guys didn't like the idea, and only two men volunteered, so that problem solved itself.

The normal procedure for letters was to get them at quiz and, with the officer watching, read the letter there. But several times they brought letters to our room, gave them to the men, and allowed us to keep them for a half hour. Getting a letter once a year in a prison camp was a big event. Although each letter was five lines long, we would read it over and over again because we weren't allowed to keep it. Most of the time there wasn't much in the letter, but I would read mine repeatedly so that when I no longer had it, I could digest what had been written. Most of the time, the Vietnamese were always rushing us when we read our letters.

In late October, we heard some news on the radio indicating that North Vietnam and the U.S. might be close to negotiating an end to the war. During this period, we had some good Russian canned fish. Each man would get a can, half the size of small tuna fish can, almost once a week. It was probably the best food I had ever had since I became a prisoner. The treatment and living conditions were better than ever. I thought there was a good chance the war was ending. The camp we were in was a model camp. When the war ended, and we were repatriated, there was no better place than here for the release to take place. Compared to how I had lived, this was a real show place. After being treated like an animal for more than five years, life was looking up.

On November 21, 1970, when we went to sleep, everything was normal. In the middle of the night, we heard a lot of gunfire, triple A, and SAMS being fired. It lasted for maybe fifteen minutes. We had no idea what was happening. With twenty guys in the room, we had at least ten opinions as to what had happened. Most, however, thought that negotiations had broken down, and the air war started again. We all went back to sleep. The next day, the routine was normal. We saw signs during the second day that we might be moving. In the evening, they told us to prepare to move. In less than one minute, by tapping to the room next to us, we found out that the whole compound was going to move. We waited until midnight before we got into the bus and left the camp. The Vietnamese remained fairly pleasant to us and even brought us each another glazed donut – not a Dunkin Donut but one that was half the size and weighed five times as much and was greasy, too. We were still puzzled, because if the air war had started again, we felt that they would be acting like bees whose nest had just been stirred up. Maybe what we heard had just been an exercise. We rode in the bus blindfolded again for about a hour. When I got out of the bus, I

313

knew we were not at the Zoo. The bus had parked about a third of a block from the entrance, and though I was blindfolded, I recognized many small signs that told me we were going to the Hanoi Hilton.

CHAPTER 21 - LEADERSHIP

ROOM 1, HANOI HILTON

November 1970 – December 1970. We straggled along the sidewalk to the main gate. We walked through the gate and then through a short tunnel in the prison wall into an open courtyard. By the noise, I could tell that a large group of us were going in the same direction. Although I was blindfolded, I knew the area well enough to know where I was and where we were heading. Finally, we got to the end of the courtyard and went through another open tunnel alongside Heartbreak. When we passed through this tunnel, I was in an area that I had never been in before. We made one or two more turns and walked about fifty yards in a wide-open area before we got to our room.

At some sixty feet long and twenty-five feet wide, it was huge compared to any room I had been in before. Instead of beds, there was a concrete sleeping platform about two and a half feet off the floor. It started at one end of the room and ran to about ten feet from the other end of the room. The platform slanted up at a slight angle toward the middle of the room for about seven feet and then sloped down and away for another seven feet. Near the ceiling on the sidewalls, running the length of the room, were large windows with bars on them. Eventually this would be known as room 1.

Although the room was large compared to anything I'd seen before, by the time everyone had entered, it was so overcrowded that we were stepping on each other. I couldn't believe what I was seeing. The fifty-seven men who had been in my compound at Camp Faith were all together now in one room. Within a few minutes, a number of men were complaining vehemently about the crowded conditions. We had complained for years about isolation, and finally so many of us were together. I thought the overcrowding would be nothing more than an inconvenience, but as soon as I saw a Vietnamese officer, I reluctantly pointed it out to him. He said it would be temporary, and nothing could be done at this time. He said they would take care of the overcrowding as soon as possible.

When we had put as many bed mats on the platform as we could, about twenty men still did not have space for their mats. So we squeezed the mats together as close as possible. This allowed just enough room for a man to be on his back and touch the next man's shoulders with his own. But fourteen men still had no alternative but to spread their mats on the floor by the side of the wall. Not only was it dirtier and colder on the floor, but six-inch-square drains at the bottoms of the wall were like open doorways for rats to come into the room. The crowded conditions were not nearly so bad as they would have been in the summertime.

This was the first time I knew of that such a large group of men had been put together. We were delighted to be with old friends and new ones, and many talked into the late hours of the night, but some of the men remained unhappy because of the cramped conditions. Nonetheless, we all managed to survive the first night. The next morning, I decided that we had better get organized as soon as possible. I called a meeting with the five next senior men in the room: Shuman, Mullen, Bell, Runyan, and Makowski. We divided the room into sections and kept the men together who had been together previously as much as possible, because some guys still had their packages and had been sharing with the guys they had been living with at Camp Faith. Within an hour, we had a temporary organization set up.

Each section in turn would have the duty for an entire day. Their responsibilities included bringing the food in the room, dishing it up, washing the dishes, sweeping the room, emptying the *bo*s, and bringing the water into the room. If the Vietnamese wanted some men to pluck feathers from ducks or do some other similar work from time to time, the duty section would do it. We discussed

317

the problem of our crowding at great length, but we were unable to come up with any good solution. That morning, Camp Faith's Commander Bushy came into our room with another former camp commander, and I complained to them about our overcrowding. The Vietnamese gave us bed boards for the men on the floor. They were long heavy planks, about one inch thick, two feet wide, and six and a half feet long. They helped keep out the cold and dirt from the floor. Although this was not a perfect solution, it helped.

The room had a small, enclosed bathroom with two squatter toilets in the floor and a long urinal drain along side of the wall. The Vietnamese took all but one of the five-gallon crap buckets we had and put them outside of our room. Lou Makowski, my second in command, did not like the idea of losing the *bos*. The toilet area had a bad odor because it was like an outhouse instead of flush-toilets connected to a sewer. Under each hole was a fifty-gallon drum, which when filled would be carried away by the Vietnamese and used as fertilizer. The *bos* all had covers, and by using them, we could have contained the odors in the room much better. I agreed with Lou and tried to have the guard bring the crap buckets back into the room, but the Vietnamese would not let us have them. I explained to the room officer why we wanted them in the room. He said "NO, use the bathroom area in the room." Lou kept after me, complaining and arguing that I had not done enough to get the *bos* back. I felt I had done as much as I reasonably could have.

After the first meal and before quiet hour, I had the section leaders decide within their section who would sleep on the floor, and who would sleep on the ramp, because some guys who were on the floor didn't think it was fair for them to be there. Some of the boards were on the floor in the back of the room, some in the front, and others on the side. I noticed during quiet hour that Doug Jones did not have enough room to put his bed board down on the floor, and he appeared to be quite restless and put out about it. I couldn't understand why he hadn't gone to his section leader, but seeing him in distress bothered me, because as the senior man, I hated to see people unhappy or disgruntled. Lou Makowski noticed the problem about the same time I did, so about halfway through quiet hour, he got up and woke three or four other men, and they rearranged the bed boards on the floor. It was interesting how grown men could have problems over such simple things, and although some may have disliked what Lou did, this was an example of the need for leadership.

When a problem arose, action needed taking, or a decision needed making, somebody had to be in charge, because among themselves the men could not settle their differences. They just needed someone in authority to say, "Do this or do that," and the problem was solved. It was that simple. I always had mixed emotions about being the SRO. By military tradition and law, the senior man had to assume the responsibility of command in a prisoner of war camp, and I had some satisfaction and fun being the boss. Nonetheless, the job came with some big disadvantages. The Vietnamese would tear one apart for giving orders to resist or oppose them in any way, and you could not be an effective SRO without being part of the opposition or resistance. So by just being the SRO, you were always under pressure, even if you did not aggressively fulfill your role. Also, resolving problems between the prisoners themselves was sometimes more difficult than dealing with the Vietnamese.

At Al Runyan's recommendation, I appointed Earl Lewis first lieutenant for the room. He was one of the most junior men in the room, and I made him responsible for its cleanliness. His first task was to clean the toilet area and prepare it for a white-glove inspection. I reckoned that the toilet area had not been cleaned since the prison was built more than sixty years ago. Earl selected the two men in the room who were junior to him to help. They scrubbed the living daylights out of the bathroom area for well over three hours, and although it did not pass the white-glove inspection, it was cleaner now than it had been since the prison was built.

The day after we moved in, we were in contact with three other large rooms in the camp. They confirmed that Camp Faith had had three other compounds like ours, and that each compound had been moved into a big room like ours here at the Hilton. Seven large rooms surrounded about two-thirds of a courtyard that contained several small buildings. The other third of the courtyard had a large fence in front of some other buildings. At least one of the other big rooms contained Vietnamese prisoners. I had the opportunity to go by one of their rooms one morning, and from the amount of noise I heard, it sounded as if there were at least a hundred men inside. Vietnamese writing was etched and carved into our concrete platform, the walls, and the bed boards. We couldn't understand the writing, but from the way the writing was worn, the room apparently had been used for years. The fact that Vietnamese prisoners were in proximity gave us some food for thought. If we were the enemy of the North Vietnamese, and the Vietnamese in prison were against the North Vietnamese, then maybe we could be friends with the prisoners, and who knows what we might accomplish. I hoped we could establish contact with them.

In spite of allowing fifty to sixty men to live in large rooms, the Vietnamese still didn't let the rooms out together. They erected a bamboo fence about seven feet high around the inside of the courtyard and fenced off the area between the rooms into seven individual courtyards. Each courtyard had a large concrete tub about seven feet long by four feet wide and four feet deep, with one spigot. The tub did not hold enough water for the whole room to wash themselves and their clothes at one time, however, so we had one group wash in the morning and then let the tub fill up again so the other half could wash in the afternoon.

In addition, perhaps the Vietnamese thought that a female might mistakenly enter our courtyard while we were bathing, or maybe the guards did not want so many private parts of Americans exposed to them at one time, so they insisted that we wear our short pants when we washed. This went over like a ton of bricks with the POWs. The complaints and yells I got were unbelievable. The men expected me as the SRO to resolve this problem as soon as possible. As if I should march into the camp commander's room and demand our rights. I tried as best I could to plead our case with the guards and room officer but to no avail. The complaints from the men didn't abate, however. One enterprising man, God bless him, came up with the idea to use any extra bed mats we had as a shield around the bath area. Even that took a lot of fast talk on my part before the Vietnamese agreed to it.

Shortly after they brought the bed boards, some guys were becoming infested with mites in their clothes and on their bodies. We guessed that the mites had come from the bed boards. After I complained to the camp commander about this, he had the guards build a large fire in our yard to boil some water. Then we carried out the boards and poured the boiling water on them. Some of the guys were unconvinced that this would eliminate the mites, so after polling the men who were sleeping on the floor, I had a meeting with the room leaders, and we decided that we did not want the boards in the room any longer. When we refused to bring them back, the guards became angry but did not force us to bring the boards in.

Before the week ended, I was meeting daily with the section leaders. We discussed our problems each time we met. The section leaders got suggestions from their men, and we kicked a lot of ideas around. By now, we had appointed a bridge director, education

director, and communications officer. Jack Van Loan was the bridge
director, and within a week after we moved into the big room, we
had a duplicate bridge game with twelve tables one night. The game
was such an attraction that, even though some guys barely knew
how to play, we had forty-eight guys playing that first time. We
continued with the policy of having the winners and losers as partners the next game, so most everyone had a lot of fun. We played
bridge on many nights after that first game, but the number of men
who played dropped off some. Capt. A.J. Meyers was the director
of the education program. He had lectures three nights each week.
He continued with his lecture on word derivations that he had
taught on the wall while in the Pig Sty building in the Zoo. Maj.
Dave Burroughs, who had his doctorate in English and had taught
at the Air Force Academy, taught an English course, and Capt. Bob
Lilly, who had won a number of honors as a public speaker with
Toastmaster International, organized a Toastmasters program for
the room. Initially, more than thirty-five men joined his program,
so he had to divide them into two groups. Each group met once or
twice a week. Conditions in the room were pretty good, compared
to years before. Nonetheless, some in the room always objected to
whatever was decided upon, and the six senior guys in the room had
considerable disagreements among ourselves.

My bed mat was next to the wall directly in front of the door.
This location was convenient for me, because it was less likely that
someone would step on my crippled leg, and I could direct the room
when the guards entered and departed. Sometime during the first
few weeks after we moved into the big room, the Vietnamese wanted
us to make a formation outside the room, so they could count us
there before we came into the room. At first, we did not object, and
I would stand out in front of the men like a platoon leader. But
the Vietnamese did not like that at all. So after a lot of bitching

and complaining on our part, they dropped the outside formation muster and just had us stand for an informal count inside our room. When the guard came into the room in the morning, and before he closed the door after the men went outside in the morning and afternoon, the guard wanted all of us to stand up wherever we were, so he could count us.

To get some of the men to agree to do this was like pulling teeth, even though all they had to do was to stand wherever they were. We were not required to make a formation. Some guys considered this demand as nothing more than an act of subservience to the Vietnamese, similar to the bowing of years gone by. I agreed with that somewhat, but the Vietnamese explained to me that the reason they did this was to have a count on the number of men in the room. I did not think the request to stand for muster to be unreasonable. Although I was not certain, I thought that according to the Geneva Convention on Prisoners of War, they were within their rights to have us stand for muster in the room. I decided that I would not fight it, but a number of guys in the room felt I gave in too easily. In any case, when the guard came in, I would stand in front of the door and say, "Stand for muster." The guard would count the men in the room, and I would say, "Carry on." I was lucky, because the Vietnamese were acknowledging my seniority by allowing me to give orders in this manner and letting me represent the room on other occasions.

When we lived at Camp Faith, some of the smaller rooms had been given pencils and paper, and one prisoner had even received about ten pencils in a package. So now we had pencils and paper for the whole room, but I knew the pencils would not last forever. We got word that one of the other rooms had received some pencils and paper from the Vietnamese. I kept asking the guard day after day for more pencils and paper, without success. This did not satisfy

Ned Shuman. He felt I should have been pushing harder. I acknowledged that how hard one tries is relative, but in my judgment
I was doing everything possible, because sometimes if one pushed
too hard, what one is trying to accomplish can backfire. Ned continued to push me on the pencil and paper request, even though I
asked for them whenever I had a chance. Many others in the room
were also being quite pushy.

The good treatment at Camp Faith, the fact that so many men
were allowed in one room together, and other signs of relaxation
on the part of the Vietnamese were being interpreted by many as
a good omen, possibly associated with an imminent release. I was
also affected by this optimism and bravado to a slight degree, but
nowhere close to some of the other guys. I was getting fed up with
Ned's constant nagging, so I decided that I would not order the men
to stand when the guard came to the door one morning. Lenny the
Gold Tooth opened the door, and we all continued going about our
business. Lenny came to me and told me to tell the men to stand
up. I told him I would tell them to stand after I met with the camp
commander. Lenny threatened me several times but then left the
room.

Later that morning, I was called out for a quiz with Sweet Pea,
who was our room officer. I told him that we would like to have
some pencils and paper, that we had asked numerous times on previous occasions for them but had not received any, and that I wanted
to speak to the camp commander about this. I was really making
some demands now, because of the frustration of being continually
bombarded by the requests of the men in the room to get this or do
that. Sweet Pea said, "NO," and sent me back to the room. This
was pretty much what I had expected. I couldn't imagine any prison
authority conceding to the demands that I was making, let alone the
Vietnamese Communists. For several days, we refused to stand. We

did not get out of the room, and no one got to take a bath during this period. Now some of the men were demanding that I get them a bath.

Two days later I had another quiz with Sweet Pea. He told me that the camp commander would never accede to my demands, and that I could not demand something from the camp commander and expect him to fulfill my wishes. He said I would not be allowed to see the camp commander, and that I would have to be punished for ordering the men not to stand. For the next two days, they made me sit by myself out in the cold in the middle of our small courtyard on a stool for several hours in the morning. On the second day, Sweet Pea told me that if the men did not start standing that I would be punished far worse than what I was getting now. On the third day, as I was sitting by myself in the middle of the courtyard Camp Commander Bushy just happened to pass through the courtyard. He asked me what I was doing sitting in the yard. I told him I was being punished and explained my problem about the paper and pencils to him. I did not tell him that I had demanded to see him. I had made some great strides in getting recognition as the SRO, and I did not want to go overboard with him. It appeared as though he was not looking for a confrontation. He told me my request for pencils and paper was not unreasonable, but that they had run out of them. Now they had some, and we would get the pencils and paper in a few days. Then he lectured me for about five minutes on obeying the camp regulations. When I came back to the room and told everyone what had transpired, everyone was very happy. So we started to stand again. The next day, they gave us paper, pencils, ink, and even a small dictionary. So I had to admit that Ned was right.

Several nights after we got the pencils, I went to the hospital for an x-ray of my leg. They put me in a regular hospital room that had a mattress on the bed, although the room and sheets were dirty. The doctor examined my leg and asked how it was. They did not take an x-ray. I thought maybe they were considering a bone graft. I asked for medical treatment for some other guys in the room, in particular Red McDaniel, who had a battered ear as a result of his torture two years before. Several days later, they gave him some medicine for his ear. Things were looking up.

After the victory over the pencils and paper, Ned was feeling his oats even more. I decided that to more fully use his talents, he could develop a more elaborate room organization. I also assigned Dave Burroughs to work with him on the project. Dave was an extremely able individual, and I knew they would come up with something reasonable. In several days, they came up with an elaborate plan. In addition to the first lieutenant (janitor), education officer, recreation officer, and communications officer, they recommended we establish positions for a cigarette-control officer, toilet-paper-control officer, punk-control officer, and food-control officer. The cigarette-control officer would have to get the full packs from the guard in the morning, open the packs, distribute the cigarettes evenly to all smokers, and return the empty packs to the guard. The toilet-paper-control officer would distribute the toilet paper among the men and also assure that the punk-control officer had enough paper to make a punk for our cigarette lights.

The punk-control officer was the junior smoker in the room, and he was assigned the job for two weeks. Then the next junior smoker had the job. His job was to take the toilet paper and roll it into a thin strand of paper that would smolder very slowly, thereby enabling us to have a cigarette light whenever needed. The punk was kept lit whenever the door was locked. When the guard gave the cigarette-control officer a light, the cigarette-control officer would give two other guys lights with his cigarette, and the two guys would each give two other guys a light, etc., until everyone had a light. The last guy to finish his first smoke of the day would light the punk. Then whenever a guy wanted his cigarette light, he got it from the punk. When we went to bathe, the punk was put out. After bathing, we got another light from the guard. At night, we let the punk burn until about an hour after everyone turned in, in case someone wanted a light. If anyone ever put the punk out while lighting his cigarette and did not get to light his own cigarette, the least painful thing to do would be to commit suicide.

Paul Schulz and I had had conflicts when we lived together, and I hoped that the problems between us were caused by Paul, but in all honesty, it might have been just as much my fault, or perhaps the problem resulted from the frustration of being in prison. We had organized the room so that the guys in the flights were more or less sleeping in the same area, but Paul was so stubborn and independent that he would not sleep with his guys. Ned Shuman, not one to let a simple solution to a difficult problem escape him, recommended that we appoint Paul as food-control officer. As Paul was probably one of the biggest chowhounds in Hanoi, it was a natural job for him. He was responsible for dishing up the food and cleaning the dishes. Paul could not have been happier. He had fifty-seven bowls to pick through and could eat as much of the leftovers as he wanted.

After three or four weeks, another problem surfaced. Some guys awoke before dawn each morning and exercised for an hour or more, and others just got up early. Other men preferred to sit up and play bridge until midnight every night and sleep until ten in the morning. When the guys stayed up late and talked or played cards, some of the early risers could not sleep. I received complaints from both sides. Even the senior guys lived differently. Ned Shuman was probably one of the worst offenders. He had a bunch of young guys in his section who didn't sleep much, and Ned was a guy who was a gabber, a real charger, and just thoroughly enjoyed every minute of life. So it was not unusual for him to still be talking and joking as the gong sounded each night. We tried at first to get voluntary cooperation from everyone, but that worked for only about one night.

I finally bit the bullet and decided that at the first night gong everyone would get ready for bed and by half an hour later, when a distant gong sounded, everyone would be quiet. I personally couldn't have cared less. Some guys in the room interpreted this decision as giving in to the Vietnamese, because they also wanted quiet in the room after the gong. Almost every night, someone violated the curfew, but somehow we all managed to survive. I had Lou Makowski, who was second in command, do the dirty work. Whenever someone violated the curfew, he would call him out by name and tell him to shut up.

The platform on which we slept was about fourteen feet wide and thirty-five feet long. One end of the platform was against the wall, and the other three sides had about six feet of floor between the platform and the wall. That's where we walked. If a guy was at the end of the platform by the wall and wanted to get to the other side by the opposite wall, he had to walk all around the platform to get there. Of course, there was a short cut. Walk straight across the platform. But to do this, the guy had to walk on someone else's bed mat, and some guys treated their bed mats as very private property and did not like anyone walking on them, especially with dirty shoes. The overwhelming majority of guys were very considerate of others, but a few were not. So we had to encourage them to stay the hell off of other guys' bed mats.

Between three and four weeks after we moved back to the Hilton, the men in one of the other large rooms made contact with Vietnamese prisoners in the room next to them. There were some

328

Vietnamese prisoners who knew a few words of French, so with the French that the Americans prisoners knew and some handwritten signs on notes, we got information that apparently an unsuccessful attempt had been made to rescue some prisoners at Son Tay. Because communications between the Vietnamese and our men was very rudimentary, some doubted the information. Time, however, proved them to be correct. Some guys were quite excited over the news. If nothing else, it might have been the impetus to move fifty-seven of us into one room together. We had all been able to get together in the courtyard at Camp Faith even though we had been in five separate rooms. And there was some advantage to the privacy of the smaller room. Also, some guys were disappointed when they heard about the raid, because if that was the only way we were ever going to get out of here, then we were really in deep trouble.

Now that we had won a few battles with the Vietnamese, some of the men were really showing how tough they were. They were coming out of the woodwork and acting macho. When the guard would open the door in the morning, and while we were being counted, someone would always make a wise remark about the guard or the Vietnamese. But this guy was always undetected in the back of the room somewhere. Even our cigarette-control officer became overwhelmed with bravery one morning. The normal procedure was that the guard gave the full packs of cigarettes to the cigarette-control officer, who would take the cigarettes out of the packs and distribute them to the guys, and when the guard came back, he returned the empty packs to him. One morning when Lenny Gold Tooth came back to pick up the empty packs, the cigarette-control officer just threw the empty packs on the ground outside the room door. Maybe the guy had a reason for doing it, but I never asked. I did not like Lenny Gold Tooth either. Lenny was a sadistic and miserable little bastard. I had griped to our room officer about him and even given him a long list of complaints about Lenny. I didn't know for sure, but I suspected that our room officer had talked to him. Despite the kind of person Lenny was, in my opinion throwing the empty cigarette packs to show contempt was senseless resistance and nothing but showing off. Guys like that made it hard on the rest of us. Maj. Al Runyan, who was a section leader and a good friend of the cigarette-control officer told him to "Knock off the bullshit and pick up the cigarette wrappers." He picked them up. I had no doubt that Lenny sure as hell wasn't going to pick them up. If it had not been for Al, that incident could have escalated into a real problem.

With so many men and so much talent to draw from, our church service was quite elaborate each Sunday. Red McDaniel preached an outstanding sermon every Sunday. The attendance was quite high, although, a number of men attended while staying under their warm blankets. Others who had no interest in the service stayed at the other end of the room and talked quietly or just slept through the service. Finally, my old roommate Quincy Collins was in his glory. He had organized a choir, and they sang every Sunday for church service, and they were really quite good. Christmas was approaching, and the recreation chairman was planning an elaborate Christmas Eve celebration. The program included Quincy and his group singing Christmas carols.

The choir couldn't sing at Christmas if it hadn't practiced, so for three weeks before Christmas, the choir practiced five times every day, and each time the guards would come to the door, bang on it, and tell us we were singing too loud. The Vietnamese had their rules and regulations, so I tried to get Quincy to sing more softly, to no avail. After a while, the guards told us not to sing at all. Only then would the choir lower their voices. The problem was that we never knew how far we could push the Vietnamese, and if we pushed too far we might lose everything we had gained. So if we just kept it down a little, they didn't complain too much. But Quincy loved to sing so that people could hear him a mile away, and when he did, the guard banged on the door again. Then Quincy would sing softer. It was a continuous battle.

About a week before Christmas, we heard that one of the rooms had had an inspection. Everyone in that room had to go outside and wait while the Vietnamese inspected the room. The guys went back into their room when the inspection was completed, and everything had been torn apart. This was nothing new: The Vietnamese had been doing this for the past six years, but as everyone was really feeling gutsy, because of the improved living conditions, several guys gave the guards a hard time. This really aggravated the Vietnamese, and they made everyone go outside again. Now they really tore the room apart and found some secret messages in one of the prisoner's packages that had been sent by our government. This spurred them on to an even more thorough inspection, and before it was over, they found some parts of a radio that some guys in the room were trying to put together. The Vietnamese went wild. Three guys were pulled out of the room and sent to cells in Heartbreak.

Several days before their room inspection, we had received our Christmas packages from home. The next room to be inspected was ours. They tore it apart with a fine-tooth comb and took out everything except the bare necessities. The cards, pencils, paper, dictionary, and all of our packages were gone. Our morale fell to a new low. I had seen this happen many times before, and I knew there was little I could do about it. When the Vietnamese inspected the rooms, they took whatever they wanted. But again I had to face the hard chargers. "DEMAND OUR THINGS BACK. WE HAVE TO RESIST. WE CAN'T ALLOW THIS. DO SOMETHING. YOU ARE THE SRO." I tried, but all I got for an answer from the Vietnamese was, "Yes, we will see." All of the goodies from our packages were gone, and we were told that our packages would be inspected from now on. Despite having lost so much, we continued our education program and plans for the Christmas party.

Things were far worse than they had been two weeks before. But although we were down, we were not out. We still had our talent and imagination. So on Christmas Eve, we had an elaborate program. Each section had a skit, and we had Christmas carols off and on throughout the entire evening. We weren't exceptionally loud, so the guards didn't bother us. We made a Christmas tree out of branches from trees in the yard. The tree had some ornaments made from toilet paper, and we had a sign on the wall that said MERRY CHRISTMAS. That night, the Vietnamese also put on their traditional low-class, third-rate dog-and-pony show, and we got a cup of heavily sugared black coffee, two extra cigarettes, and three pieces of candy each.

We also made a big to-do out of our Christmas dinner. The custom of the Vietnamese had been to provide a relatively good meal and a beer for the Christmas and Tet holidays, and we hoped that custom would continue this year, because we had planned to have a Dining-In. The Dining-In is one of the most formal social functions for military officers. They wear their most formal uniforms, and the rules for how the affair is conducted are laid out in service regulations in minute detail.

On Christmas day, we conned the Vietnamese into letting us bring a table and several benches into our room, and with some improvisations of our own, we ended up with a table long enough for all fifty seven of us to sit around it. We dressed up in our finest uniforms. Black pants and black coat. All had been pressed by us sitting on them for at least an hour. All the strings on the coats were tied together neatly. As the SRO, I sat at one end of the table and

Mr. Vice at the other end. By tradition, Mr. Vice was the junior man, and he was responsible for the orderly and proper conduct of the dinner, as well as acting as the master of ceremonies. Seated on my left, was the second senior man in the room, and across from him and on my right was the third senior man. Each man was seated at the table in accordance with his relative rank. The Vietnamese brought in the big meal, and Paul Schulz and his food crew dished it up on the plates on the table. The Vietnamese had sent a half bottle of beer per man, so after everyone sat down, they poured a little beer in their cups. Then we all stood up around the table behind our sitting place, and the dinner began.

One of the men had improvised an American flag, and as he held it in his hands, one of the other men led us in the pledge to the flag. Then Al Runyan lifted his cup of beer, as did the others, and he said, "I propose a toast to the Commander and Chief, President of the United States, Lyndon B. Johnson." In response, all said, "Here Here." Next, Maj. Ken Simonet got up and said, "I propose a toast to the chief of staff of the U.S. Army." Everyone with his cup raised said in response, "Here Here." And in order of seniority, the chiefs of the other services were toasted. Finally, we toasted our wives and families, who with great sacrifice were waiting patiently and faithfully for our return. Red McDaniel gave the blessing, and we all sat down and started to eat. Mr. Vice amused us occasionally with jokes during the meal.

After dinner, Dale Doss delivered a ten-minute speech. We were lucky that so many of us were together for the first time, and that we were able to participate in a function that had some resemblance of a life other than that in a prison camp. We were also fortunate that the guards did not bother us during the meal. It had been the most formal occasion that any of us had attended in years and was thoroughly enjoyed by all.

Christmas had come and gone. We had been in the Hilton for almost six weeks now. The organization in our room was sound, and although the room inspection had set us back some, I did not expect the crackdown to last indefinitely. Almost always they let up after they felt things were under control again. Sometimes this took only a few weeks, and other times it took months. But obviously they were much more lenient now than before, so I was hopeful the crackdown wouldn't last very long.

In addition to being senior man in the room, I was also the SRO of the more than two hundred men with whom we had contact. The basic policy I had promulgated at first was that each room SRO should try to solve his problems internally, and if he had a major problem or one that was irreconcilable, then he should call on me. Other than that piece of guidance, my policies were to follow the Code of Conduct and the guidance previously promulgated by those senior to me. The Vietnamese were not asking anyone to do anything and just leaving us alone. During the past six weeks, our treatment had improved so much that I felt it best to just sit back and relax awhile. Others felt our improvement in treatment was because we had pushed so hard, and therefore we could not sit back and relax. We had to keep pushing them harder.

The major problem we had now, as far as I was concerned, was just getting along with each other in our rooms. I told them that it was okay to push the Vietnamese, but I wanted them to avoid big confrontations. Maybe if we showed the Vietnamese we could live peacefully, they would eventually allow even the most senior men to live in a big room. I felt the major problem facing me now was to keep the gains that we had made, without giving the Vietnamese anything in return for them. If they gave us some improvement in treatment without a price, I saw no reason not to accept it. My philosophy was to appear calm, cool, and peaceful, so we could do our dirty work behind their backs. If you made yourself noticeable, you would be the first one the big bad wolf would come for. For years, we had all pushed for recognition of the senior man by the Vietnamese. We had this now with my group and with several of the other groups. We had pushed for elimination of the isolation. This was solved. It was true that the Son Tay raid was responsible for our move into large rooms and groups in the Hilton, but the barrier of isolation had already been broken when we moved to Camp Faith. And most important of all, the Vietnamese were not asking us to violate our Code of Conduct. So I was in hog heaven.

Our major problem now was that life was far too easy, compared to what it had been, and as a result some guys were trying to show how tough they were, now that the rough stuff had stopped. Many interpreted my effort to maintain order as a weakness on my part or as my siding with the Vietnamese. Standing for muster, putting bed mats in the bath areas, so we did not expose our private parts to the Vietnamese, telling the choir to sing more softly, telling the guys to go to bed, telling the cigarette-control officer to pick up the cigarette packs and hand them to the guard, telling the hecklers to knock off their wisecracks about the Vietnamese while the guard took muster, and not protesting enough when the Vietnamese took our pencils and paper from the room after the inspection were all controversial decisions on my part. Being in this position was becoming somewhat frustrating.

The SROs in the other three big rooms were all junior 04's or very senior 03's, and at least ten men in my room were senior to the most senior SRO in the other rooms. So I had a fairly good sized group of the most senior 04's in the whole prison system. There had been the problem with the inspection in room 4 and suggestions from the other rooms regarding a letter moratorium and some other passive forms of resistance. So I decided that I should devote more time to the other rooms. I turned over the responsibility of running the room to Lou Makowski, and I was using the room flight leaders and Lou as my personal staff for the command of the two-hundred men.

That organization was in place for less than three or four days, when Sweet Pea came to the door one night and told us to prepare to move. In less than half an hour, most of us had moved two rooms away into room 5, and ten or fifteen men moved into another big room with men from other overcrowded rooms. Room 5 was similar to the one we had been living in. It was the room where the Vietnamese prisoners had been living.

CHAPTER 22 - COAL BALLS

TYPICAL LAYOUT OF BIG ROOM. OTHERS HAD BED-PLATFORM IN CENTER OF ROOM

ROOM 5, HANOI HILTON

December 1970 – February 1971. The new room was slightly larger than the last one, but instead of having the sleeping platform in the middle of the room, the platform here was divided and half of it was next to each side of the wall. Instead of sleeping head to head as we had in the other room, our heads were now against the wall. This design also provided a fairly large area in the middle of the room to move around in. Because the three other large rooms in the camp had also been crowded, the Vietnamese took about twelve guys from each of the four rooms and put them into another large room. Now there was more room for all of us, although we still had a few guys who slept on the floor.

At around the same time as we moved, almost all of the 05's (that is, the commanders and lieutenant colonels), the senior 04's, and some junior officers were moved into another large room in the same general area of the camp where the rest of us were. This was a historic event, although the three colonels remained separated. Maybe my policy of making no waves had paid off, and the Vietnamese were going to give the big boys a chance for better treatment. Or maybe it was a decision totally unrelated to the POWs' behavior. Most of those men had been either in solitary or in small two- or three-man rooms as long as they had been there. This was interpreted by almost everyone as a sign of something really big going on. Perhaps the war was about to end.

The morning after we moved, we reorganized the room. It was similar to what we had before, but we put some new faces in old jobs. Maj. Ray Merritt was in charge of the recreation and education officer. Maj. Don Burns was the supply officer and in charge of the cigarette-control officer, punk-control officer, and toilet-paper-control officer. Lt. Cdr. Cole Black was the first lieutenant and in charge of appointing men for the cleanliness of the room, including the toilet and *bos*. We also had a communications officer who was in charge of the communications team. Their responsibility was to communicate by hand signal from our window to the window of the next room and tap on the wall to the room on the other side of us. Those who were assigned responsibilities carried them out in a very serious and professional manner, and no one screwed off.

We had finished our old packages, so there was no reason anymore to keep the flights by men who had roomed together at Camp Faith. We decided to make up flights by seniority. The second senior man was in charge of flight one, the sixth senior man in charge of flight six, etc. Because we had only six flights, the seventh senior man went into flight one, and the eighth senior man to flight two. Some guys did not like this idea, because they had a special buddy they wanted to be with, and they wanted to choose the men in their flights by personalities. Since each flight had to sleep in the same area, guys who were friends might be inconvenienced. I liked the way we had organized it and one of the reasons was that when we were in room 1, some of the flights had all senior guys and some flights all junior guys. So some of the junior guys were getting off from some of the dirty work, and some of the senior guys were doing the dirty work. In general, whether back home or in a prison camp, the more junior a guy is, the less desirable work he gets, and the more senior guys get the more desirable work. Of course, the more senior a man is, the more responsibility he has.

Several days after the move, many of the men in the room got packages from home. Because the Vietnamese had found the radio parts and small tapes with lists or names of the prisoners and their ranks in the chewing gum packages, the items in our packages were all cut up into little pieces. Even the freeze-dried coffee had been opened and sifted through. There was nothing in the package that had not been inspected. Because the packages had been torn apart, and we were not allowed to keep them in the room anymore, we had a problem. Some of the men were so irate, they wanted to refuse their packages.

With forty-five men in the room now, a number of decisions had to be made about the packages. Probably most families of the prisoners sent packages to them, but some may not have done so. And even though a package might have been sent to a man, there was no guarantee the Vietnamese would give it to him. They could withhold it or give to someone else if they wanted to. Some guys asked only for coffee, which they might receive, and they couldn't care less about sharing with another guy's candy. In short, some men wanted to use the package that was sent to them for themselves, some wanted everything shared, and others didn't care one way or the other. The first question was, does each man have the right to keep the package sent to him by his family? Or are the packages sent to each individual the property of the room? Interestingly, some men who had never received a package opposed sharing, and many who got large packages wanted to share. There was some heated debate in the room for a while. With the backing of the flight leaders, and despite the grumbling of some, I decided that everything would be divided evenly, and if a man did not like one thing, he could try to trade it with another guy.

As it turned out, the Vietnamese brought the contents of three to five packages to our room each day, and we would divide them up. We got Mumbles, our turnkey, to bring hot water for our coffee, tea, or hot chocolate early in the morning after the gong sounded until the drinks ran out. We were lucky to have worked out an acceptable agreement between the Vietnamese and the room on the packages.

As the room SRO, every time I had a quiz, I urged the Vietnamese to give letters to men who had never received one, but I wasn't the only one pushing for letters for the men who hadn't received them.

Every other guy who had received a letter always pushed for a letter for those who hadn't. Two men in our room had never received letters. Maj. Don Burns had not received a letter in more then five years and Lt. Cdr. Charlie Southwick had received one short letter from his sister but none from his wife. Everyone lobbied hard for those guys. Finally, one day Don Burns went to quiz, and they gave him a letter. He read the letter in the quiz room, and when he came back to the room, he was all broken up. The letter was from his mother, and there was nothing special in it, but he went over and sat down on his bed mat and cried like a baby. There was no privacy. We all saw him out of the corner of our eyes. I could barely hold back my own tears, as I looked at him. He was about as tough a guy as you will ever meet, but he had a heart of gold. The Vietnamese had at least had the sensitivity to let me cry in private, when I got my first letter on Christmas, nine months after I was shot down.

The 05's had settled in within a few days before the end of December. An endless flow of guidance came from their room every day. I suspected that the organization in my room was nothing compared to the 05's room. They had been isolated for such a long, long time, with little opportunity to exercise the daily functions of command, but now they finally had the whole kit and caboodle directly under them. So I could understand why so much was going on in their room. In addition, they were very optimistic like the rest of us. Lt. Col. Vernon Ligon, the senior 05, had been shot down in November 1967 and had been kept fairly well isolated, so his knowledge of what had gone on from the beginning was somewhat limited. As a result, he was under the influence of the old-timer 05's. I suspected that the problems I had in my room as a result of diversity of opinion were but a drop in the bucket compared to his. With more or less forty 05's and the senior 04, all in the same room, and obviously very talented or they wouldn't have been 05's

341

in the first place, they must have had a multitude of opinions on everything from A to Z. His life must have been very difficult.

Col. John Flynn, the senior prisoner of war, was in contact with the 05's room, but he apparently rubber-stamped whatever they wanted. Col. Flynn also was comparatively new to the system, because he, like Lt. Col. Ligon, had been shot down in late 1967 and had also been completely isolated from the group.

New Years Eve was never a big deal for the Vietnamese or for us, but we usually got a special meal on New Years day. Being in a large group and feeling optimistic, we had planned to have a small celebration on New Year's Eve. We had been preparing for it since before Christmas, but with twelve men having gone to another room, some of the skits had to be revised. With some extra work on the part of the men, the skits were a rousing success. One involved the flight of a passenger aircraft from some Arab country to Germany. They had guys dressed up like typical Germans and Arabs, and one guy dressed up as a buxom German girl named Katie, who was the stewardess. She was supposed to be making out with everyone on the plane, and they made a lot of jokes about it. The choir was in full swing, and the songs included "Auld Lang Syne." Later that night, the men in one of the other big rooms yelled out, "Happy New Year," and before long each room in the camp yelled, "Happy New Year," and then we yelled, "This is room number one; where the hell is two?" etc., for the next five minutes. This was the most fun we had had since I was shot down and a highlight of my eight years in prison. We were really sticking it to the Vietnamese. It was such a significant event, that years later many POW's bragged that they were the originator of the yell.

The Vietnamese were not only surprised but also somewhat upset. In no time, the guards came to our room with guns in hand and banged on the door loudly, telling us to be quiet. Finally, the camp was quiet again. The Vietnamese probably didn't know what to make of what had just happened. They could have thought we were ready to start a riot. The next day, while we were eating our special New Years meal, new restrictions were announced over the camp radio. We could no longer have people stand up in front of the room for lectures or church services, because they did not want us conspiring against them. The choir could no longer sing. Perhaps they thought that whenever a man was in front of a group, it was for a political speech or purpose, and therefore they naturally concluded the same about us.

The men in the room were not very happy about the new restrictions, and although I felt we could work around the restrictions by having the church services and classes with everyone sitting down, a good number of the men objected strongly to the new restrictions and wanted to continue as we had. They argued that this was a right we had under the Geneva Convention On Prisoners of War, and that the Vietnamese had not tortured anyone for well over a year. The pressure on me to have church services and lectures the same way as before was continual, but I refused to let them have their way.

Finally, after several days, such as stink was raised that I gave in. We decided that one night, Dave Burroughs would give a lecture by standing in front of the room. As he was standing and lecturing, one of the guards noticed what was going on. He left and soon came back with a number of gun-carrying guards and Little Caesar, our current room officer. He told us that Burroughs had violated the camp regulations, and as we all stood there and watched, he was marched out of the room at gunpoint. The next day, we learned that he was in solitary in Heartbreak Hotel.

Now the commotion was even greater. The same vocal group in the room were up in arms again, and they were insisting that I demand to see the camp commander to obtain Burroughs's release.

I felt sorry for Dave, but I believed that neither I nor anyone else could do anything about it at that time. I thought to make a fuss would only aggravate the situation. My deputy, Lou Makowski, didn't agree with my position, and he was pushing me very hard to protest to the camp commander. The pressure became intense, so the next day I yelled, "*bao cao*." Finally, an English-speaking officer came. I told him I wanted to speak to the camp commander, and he told me very loudly, "Shut up."

The next day, the camp commander came to the room. I told him that I had ordered Dave to give the lecture, because I had not heard about the rule that there could not be anyone standing, and that Dave was only giving a lecture on English. I assured him that it had nothing to do with a political conspiracy. I hoped that I made my point, but all he said was, "Wait," and he left. Various factions of the room argued over how we should proceed now. The majority felt that I had tried, but a considerable number of guys thought I should have taken some more drastic action. I decided to take their criticism and wait it out. In my opinion, the Vietnamese always had to save face, and even if they were dead wrong, the more I insisted and demanded that Burroughs be returned, the less likely it would be that he would return.

Since my old friend A.J. Meyers was the education officer, he felt somewhat responsible for what had happened, so to try to impress on the Vietnamese how wrong it was to take Burroughs out and put him in solitary, A.J. went on a hunger strike. The purpose was to get the Vietnamese to bring Burroughs back to the room. I suspected that it was also a protest against me, so that I would take some stronger action. The immediate effect of A.J.'s hunger strike was that everyone else in the room got a little extra to eat. I told our room officer that A.J. was not eating his food, because he felt that Burroughs had been moved out of the room unjustifiably. After several days, we finally talked A.J. out of his hunger strike. After about a week, Burroughs returned to the room without incident, but not before A.J. had made another strong protest to the guard. As a result of that run-in, A.J. was removed from the room and sent to Heartbreak.

We no longer had pencils, paper, or cards. One of the guys came up with the idea of writing on toilet paper with charcoal from a burned piece of wood. We made several decks of cards but the charcoal kept wearing off. We were continuously writing the numbers and suits on the cards. Even though times were tougher now, when we had a group activity, everyone still turned out. If it was a talk on bear hunting or English literature, the whole room paid attention, even though they may not have been that interested. Two guys, Capt. Harold Searles and Lt. Jack Ambrose, never joined in the group activities. They just sat in the back of the room talking softly with each other but loud enough to become a nuisance to those guys who were interested in listening to the talk. Most considered this behavior obnoxious and inconsiderate, but no one ever said anything to them.

There was still a big push to have church services and lots of talk that we must not give in to the Vietnamese. Maintaining a position of leadership was difficult, when other men were being pulled out. So to appease the dissident group, I decided that on the next Sunday, we would have a church service, and that I would stand up in front of the room, and the preacher would sit at my side and deliver the sermon. I would stand at the far end of the room from the door, so the guard wouldn't know who was talking. The choir would sing but not too loudly. My standing in front of the group and the choir's singing were both in direct violation of the authorities' recent announcements. I figured what the hell, it might just as well be me, if someone was going to be pulled out. We felt certain that this would definitely stir up the hornets' nest, even though things had relaxed somewhat. I stood in the middle of the room throughout the service. The guard saw us and banged on the door for us to stop, but we ignored him completely and continued as if we didn't hear him. Eventually, the guard left, but to everyone's surprise, he never came back.

In the middle of January, our squatter toilets became stopped up, and the feces and urine overflowed from the top of the barrels to the floor of the bathroom. I had to *bao cao* for the guards or officers, but they were always slow to react. At times, they would get us extra portable crap buckets, but they were slow to come. It was another case in which I was in the middle, trying to get a problem solved, with an intransigent group of camp authorities and the prisoners in the room demanding prompt attention. Somehow, we always satisfied our toilet needs.

About ten days before Tet, the Vietnamese Lunar New Year, the guard came to my room and asked us to make coal balls. Coal balls are made by mixing powdered coal and mud together into a ball about the size of softball. It was not the cleanest job in the world, and when it was cold outside, the mud got cold, and so did your hands. But if you were careful, you could make coal balls without any great inconvenience. One of the officers told me that we were to make the coal balls to use for cooking the meal for our Tet dinner. I guess to some extent my decision to make coal balls depended upon where I came from. The ordeal of my first five months of captivity, the confession, Fidel, the escape, and so many years in captivity with a broken leg, walking on crutches the whole time, made making coal balls look like babies' play. I asked for some volunteers and got about ten or twelve, including myself. We worked for several hours and then came back to the room. We did this two or three times prior to the Tet holiday. Each time we worked, the Vietnamese gave us a few extra cigarettes or some extra sugar that we divided among everyone in the room.

About one third of the guys in the room would not work, because they thought officers were not required to do manual labor under the Geneva Convention on POWs. Another third had no opinion one way or the other, and those in the last third either didn't mind the work or even enjoyed getting out of the room for a while or felt it was not an issue worth making a fuss over.

Those who refused to make them were very vocal in their opposition to those who did and particularly to me. It was an issue discussed every day and at times quite heatedly. Because the hard-liners perceived that we were at least making coal balls for our special Tet dinner, however, our actions were tolerated. We had a nice dinner for Tet, and it passed without any great fanfare. Several days later, the guard came to out room and asked us to make coal balls again. I had discussed this with my section leaders on numerous occasions, and even they were not in agreement on how we should proceed. My second in command strongly opposed what I was doing. I asked, "How about the other rooms?" He said, "The other rooms do other work, and our room is near the coal ball material." Because I was one of the guys who didn't mind getting out of the room to work, I asked for volunteers. After some men volunteered, we went out and worked.

The opposition was bitter when we came back to the room, and they were vocal in their displeasure with what we had done. We received some extra sugar that I did not even eat because I did not like it. As I was eating my meal, one of the junior officers in the room came over to me and asked me if the sugar he had in his plate was given to us for making coal balls. I said, "Yes." He took his plate of sugar and dumped it into an empty plate I had and said, "I don't want this sugar that you guys begged for." Another guy came up to me that night and accused me of being gutless for making the coal balls.

Some others and I had no objection at all to making coal balls. I did not consider it a violation of any code or ethics for an officer to work. In fact, I really enjoyed getting out, and I did not believe that this was issue to make a Custer's last stand over. Because I had not wanted to bother the 05's with this problem, I had not sought guidance, but now I had had it up to my ears, so finally I asked them whether we should make coal balls or not. The answer I received was that, if we wanted to make them, it was okay, and if we didn't want to, that was okay, too. It was optional. I felt that this was not a very good answer because it didn't solve my problem. I wanted a yes or no response, which would have shut up the opposition, and we all would have gone on from there. Either we all make them, or we don't make them. If I had continued to make them, the bitterness in the room would have continued. Nothing had changed.

For nearly a year, I'd had a toothache off and on. Occasionally, they would give me an aspirin for the pain. I found out if I just swallowed the aspirin I would get relief for two or three hours, but if instead I put the aspirin between my gum and mouth at a certain place, I could have relief for an entire night. I guess that the aspirin lying against the gum numbed a nerve that went to the tooth. One Monday in early February 1971, my tooth had been hurting all weekend, and they had not given me any aspirin for the past few days. I really felt lousy. I had refused to make coal balls once before by saying the men did not want to make them, and the Vietnamese had let us off.

That afternoon, they asked us to make coal balls again. Because of my toothache and the other problems, I was fed up, so I told them that the men did not want to make them anymore. My old roommate Jim Bell suggested that I should say we would make the coal balls if they gave me some medicine for my tooth. That was nice of Jim, but to have the men do some work for my benefit wasn't right. And to possibly allow the whole room to be punished for my saying that the men did not want to make coal balls was not acceptable either, for obvious reasons. So about half an hour later, Chang, the room officer, came and told us to get ready to make coal balls. I had had enough, so I told Chang that it was my decision not to make coal balls, and that I had ordered the men not to make them anymore. Chang left. Fifteen minutes later, he returned and gave me the roll-up signal to move. I left and went directly to quiz with Bushy, the camp commander.

He asked me why I would not make coal balls. I told him that the other rooms were not getting their turn, and that I did not feel it was right for us to do it any more. He said, "You must make coal balls, because they are used to cook your food." I told him politely that we were not going to make coal balls anymore. He said, "Then you must be punished." Two guards came in and motioned me to get up from my chair. As I got up from my stool, I was wondering what the punishment would be. They blindfolded me, and I left the room on crutches, feeling my way as I walked along. I walked about fifty yards straight to Heartbreak. The guards pushed and shoved me all the way. When we came to room 4 of Heartbreak, they opened the door and told me to go inside and sit on the bed. They put both of my ankles in leg irons. The bed was next to the wall between Heartbreak and the room where the 05's lived.

CHAPTER 23 - HEARTBREAK HOTEL

HEARTBREAK HOTEL CELL BLOCK

February 1971 – June 1971. I suspected that the Vietnamese had put me next to the room with all the 05's so that I could get the word out that I was in leg irons, which might act as deterrence to others. I had been in leg irons before, but compared to that time, this was duck soup.

A.J. Meyers was in the room on the other side. I tapped the news to him on the back wall. Air Force Capt. Laird Gutterson was in one of the other cells. He had wanted the Vietnamese to pull out a tooth, and when they refused, he had given them a hard time, so they put him in Heartbreak. Other cells were occupied by the three guys who had been caught in possession of radio parts and two 05's who had been caught with microfilm tapes in their packages from home.

After two days, the Vietnamese let me out of the leg irons, and I moved into the next cell with A.J. Although he was a bit cantankerous now and then, A.J. was an easy person to live with, and I liked him. The Vietnamese rarely did anything without a good reason, but I couldn't figure this move out at all. About five minutes after I moved in, before I'd unpacked my bedroll, we heard some shuffling outside. The door opened, and in came Lou Makowski. They took off his blindfold, and two guards gave him a big shove into the room. After I was pulled out of the big room, Lou had become the SRO, and he had told the Vietnamese that the room would make coal balls, if I was returned to the room. Their answer was that he could join me in Heartbreak. Our cell was not very large. It had two concrete beds about six and a half feet long by two and a half feet wide and a space between the beds of about the same width. Apparently, the Vietnamese realized that putting me in leg irons had not accomplished their objective, so they were trying to make life miserable by putting all three of us in a crowded condition, without resorting to harsher punishment.

Several days later, the room with the 05's had its own showdown with the Vietnamese. Even though the men in room 5 had resisted for legitimate reasons the room of seniors couldn't let some junior guys steal their thunder. The following Sunday, they had a church service in violation of the camp regulations. Lt. Col. Risner, Cdr. Howard Rutledge, and Lt. George Coker were pulled out and put in a room together next to us in Heartbreak. Prior to this, the senior room had promulgated numerous policies. One of these policies was that if a man was pulled out of a room, we were obligated to take action to get him back. They had also promulgated five conditions of resistance. Condition I was normal. Condition II was to stand in a military formation to irritate the Vietnamese, Condition III was to sing songs from time to time very loud, Condition IV was to refuse to stand at all when the Vietnamese came in, and Condition V was to refuse food. Some guys thought the whole plan, and in particular the fasting, was a joke. Others thought it was a great idea. The rumor was that the fasting was Cdr. Denton's idea. He had fasted before and believed that it had accomplished something. Although I never met anyone who knew what it had accomplished, I also never met anyone who thought the fasting idea was worth much. Many guys, however, probably thought it was worthwhile.

Because Risner, Rutledge, and Coker had been pulled from their room, the 05's went into resistance posture III. Before long, they were singing a wide selection of songs. Boy, was this fun. I could hear them from my room. This really upset the Vietnamese, so they began pulling out the 05's one by one and took them to another part of the camp, where there was a cellblock similar to Heartbreak. The Vietnamese had placed a ladder against the building where the 05's lived, and a guard could climb up and watch what was going on in the room through the open window. Frequently, they did not pull out the most senior man but rather the guy or guys who appeared to be doing something bad or the man whom the Vietnamese perceived as the source of trouble.

While the 05's continued singing to get their people back, they also pressured my old room to get Lou Makowski, A.J. Meyers, and me back. Still using the coal balls as a lever and occasionally a song, they were not having much success, either. Within several days, my old roommate Jim Bell, who had been third in command, was pulled out. Then the Vietnamese pulled out number four, Lt. Cdr. Moon Mullen, and also Paul Schulz, a junior 04 who had nothing to do with the room leadership, but who was just hard to get along with. Bell and Mullen were both put on the same bed in one of the rooms in Heartbreak, and each guy had one of his ankles in one of the two stocks at the end of the bed. This was not a punishment that would make you scream with pain, but it was an extremely uncomfortable situation to be in. Schulz was put in the same room but on the other bed. They were like this for three or four days before they were let out. The 05's continued their songfest for two or three more days, and one by one, the 05's were pulled out and sent to other cellblocks, where they were put into leg irons.

After three days of Condition III (sing), the order was passed to the 05's room and my old room to go into Condition V (fast). And they did. Both rooms refused to bring the food into the room for two days. They told the Vietnamese that they would not eat until everyone was returned to their rooms. As soon as the food was refused, the Vietnamese cut off the drinking water and cigarettes. Risner had told us that if a man was in a punishment status, as we were in Heartbreak that we did not have to go on the hunger strike. When the fast began for my old room, I was happy to be in Heartbreak. Although the cell was crowded with A.J. and Lou, I could have lasted there forever. Not only did we get our normal ration but also the food refused by rooms 1 and 5 was made available to us.

The fast, however, concerned the Vietnamese, because they brought in a large number of extra guards with guns and riot equipment. The courtyard was overflowing with Vietnamese military people. With all of the people who had conceived the fasting plan out of room 7 and in leg irons elsewhere, eating their normal rations, the commander who was now in charge of the situation decided to call off the hunger strike, because it had not brought the missing men back. Maj. Al Runyan was the SRO in my old room now, and he and the other men in the room were making coal balls again. The singing stopped, and slowly things quieted down. Many men probably felt that although the "sing" and "fast" did not accomplish their immediate objectives, these acts of resistance were not completely in vain, and that if nothing else, we gained a lot of esteem from our Vietnamese captors and self-respect, as well. Moreover, the plan might have worked. I never met a man who endured the hunger strike, however, who thought that the fast was worth a darn. They hated it. They were hungry, thirsty, and cranky, and those who smoked missed their cigarettes.

The next week, the Vietnamese continued to take the 05's out of their room and put them in another area in cells similar to those in Heartbreak. They also were put in small rooms with three, four, and even five guys. Some of them were put in the same set of leg irons together. During this seven- or eight-day period of turmoil, the two 05's who had been in Heartbreak for possession of microfilm and the three other guys who had radio parts were moved out. Maj. Ken Simonet, who had been the SRO of room 4, had been pulled out for giving the Vietnamese a hard time, and he was in one of the cells in Heartbreak. The resistance had become infectious, but we were knocking our heads against the wall.

Although we had been defeated in our effort to get people returned to their rooms, our spirits were not broken. The 05's room had written the rights that prisoners of war were entitled to under the Geneva Convention on Prisoners of War on a piece of paper and posted it on a wall in their room. The Vietnamese let it stay up for several days but then decided it should be taken down. When the men in the room received this order, they became incensed. Lt. Col. Frank Rica became so angry that he yelled out several times quite loudly to the Vietnamese guards in the room, "Fuck Ho Chi Minh." Several Vietnamese in the room at that time understood English and did not like what Rica had said. So he was pulled from the room and taken to a quiz room for several hours.

In the meantime, the 05's room had passed the information about the incident to us. After quiet hour that day, Rica was brought into Heartbreak and put into a cell almost directly across from ours. Before they closed the door on him, they beat him with a strap for about five minutes. As the Vietnamese were hitting him, he kept yelling and moaning, "I am sorry, I am sorry. I won't do it again." We all felt bad for him, even though we considered it dumb to yell what he did to the Vietnamese. I didn't know what our guards would have done to a Viet Cong if he yelled out the same kind of curse to President Johnson or Nixon. When the guards left his room, they dropped the strap outside the door and let it lie on the floor for about a week. Later on, he told us that the reason he yelled out was that some crippled guy in his room was giving the guard a hard time, and he had yelled that curse to direct attention away from the other man.

In late March, about thirty men were moved from all six big rooms. Most were senior 04's, and the rest were junior officers. Some of the prisoners perceived that these guys were considered to be troublemakers, and their absence would make it easier to control the big rooms and avoid trouble for the Vietnamese. These men were first moved four and five to a room in Heartbreak for several days, but then they were moved to another camp called Skid Row. In that camp, the guys lived in two-man rooms again, and they received their food, cigarettes, and bath as usual. Everyone who moved there felt quite proud that the Vietnamese considered him a tough resister–the same way the guys who were living in Heartbreak with me felt. And the same way the 05's felt. In reality, being two or three guys in a small room is not all that bad, and in some ways it was better than being in the big rooms.

The night that the thirty men went to Skid Row, Maj. Ken Fleenor, Lt. Cdr. Ted Kaufman, and Lt. Cdr. Lou Lister moved into Heartbreak. Lister had given the Vietnamese a hard time, because they had not returned his vitamins and long underwear, which they had taken during a room inspection in December 1970. Lister felt that he had anemia and needed his vitamins, so he refused to go back to his room one day. He sat outside the room and wouldn't budge. Eventually, the Vietnamese just dragged him over to Heartbreak and stuck him in a cell with Kaufman and Fleenor.

Several months passed. The excitement of singing loudly, refusing to make coal balls, hunger strikes, the 05's returning to smaller rooms, the riot squads in camp, thirty guys moving to Skid Row, a guy yelling out "Fuck Ho Chi Minh," and our being in Heartbreak had finally ended, and the camp returned to normal. The camp leadership had made a stand, and in terms of specific objectives, they had lost. We had had church services every Sunday and men standing in front of the room for toastmasters and various lectures. None of these were permitted now. We had refused to make coal balls. Now we made coal balls. We used to have playing cards, pencils, and paper. Now we had nothing. We demanded men be returned to their rooms. Not one man was ever returned because of our demands. A prisoner cursed Ho Chi Minh, and he was punished. The 05's and the more senior 04's, with few exceptions, were all in two- and three-man rooms. Prior to the time the 05's moved together into one big room and assumed direct command of the entire POW population, substantial improvements in treatment had been made over the years through the efforts of the middle-grade officers. Within two months after the 05's assumed command of the entire group, their efforts resulted in a significant setback in the treatment that we had been working for. Nevertheless, everyone couldn't have cared less. The attitude of the seniors was even if our life of ease was lost, so be it.

Lou Makowski, who had disagreed with me numerous times, and A.J. Meyers, who had gone on a hunger strike because I had not raised enough fuss when Dave Burroughs was pulled out of the room and I were all squeezed together in a small room. Lou and I slept on the concrete bunks, and A.J. slept on the floor. Walking was impossible, so we just sat on our asses most of the day, although Lou would stand in place and run. It was very crowded and unpleasant in the room. We were getting French vocabulary words from big room 1, and A.J. was teaching me French. I also learned that the completely bald A.J. once had the nickname Curly.

One thing that was not a problem was food. The other guys in Heartbreak were light eaters, as were a number of prisoners. They would not eat what they received. This was not the case with Lou, A.J., and me. Sometimes, the Vietnamese would bring in the large food pail that was left over from one of the big rooms and dish up a ration for each of us, but there would be a lot of good food left sometimes. When we saw that the pail still had food in it, we asked the guard if we could bring the pail into our room. Most of the guards did not care and said yes. Even though we were in a punishment status, the guards did not like to see food thrown out. We would spoon through the pail and find small pieces of meat. I ate better in Heartbreak than at any other time while in prison. Not by Vietnamese design, but only by luck.

We asked time and again, "Does anyone want more food? Does anyone want to take the bucket in?" We repeatedly told the other guys that we had found extra meat in the pail, and that they were more then welcome to share the extra food with us, but they declined. Lou always ate moderately whatever was left over. He would take a good share if we had some beans, bean curd, or one of the other better foods. But he rarely overstuffed himself. A.J. and I would eat until the food came out of our ears. I frequently ended up with diarrhea the next three days after I overate, but it was worth it to eat all I wanted once in a while. Although A.J. never got sick, he had tremendous gas pains. He would continuously relieve himself for a day or two by breaking wind. He enjoyed that immensely. He got double pleasure from the food.

We made a deck of cards from the toilet paper. I played solitaire during the day, and at night we played hearts. We took great delight in getting to each other from time to time. One night, A.J. and I gave Lou the queen of spades about eight times in succession. Lou lost every game and did not know what to do. He was taking it in stride, but A.J. and I really got a kick out of watching him lose. Several nights later, they gave me the queen of spades about six or seven times. Lou and A.J. were both very easy to get along with, and we really had no problems.

To further help pass the time in the evening, I would play chess with Ted Kaufman, who was in the cell across from ours. He would have his chess board, and I would have mine, and we would yell under the door across the hall our moves, like "pawn to queen's rook 4," or whatever our move was, and we would play our game this way. Before we called out our move, we always cleared under the door, and if a guard was present, we would hold off. It was a cat and mouse game. They wanted us to kowtow, but they no longer backed up their threats. If the guard was irritated at us and did not want us to play, he would just turn off the lights in all the rooms until we went to sleep, and that ended the game.

In late April, three men who had asthma quite badly were moved into Heartbreak from the big rooms. There were more than a few guys who had severe asthma attacks over the years. Each guy had his own individual problem, but at times because of the weather or whatever triggered the symptoms, almost all of them would have trouble breathing. Some guys had such trouble breathing that they sat up all night. Sometimes if a guy was really bad, the Vietnamese would give him medicine. Some of the medicine was their traditional pills, and in later years, some of it came from Russia. The medicine helped sometimes. At other times, even if a guy was extremely sick, they would ignore him. But one thing was for sure. Whenever a man had a bad attack, it disrupted his roommates and the Vietnamese. Lt. j.g., Dave Rehmann, Capt. Wes Schierman, and Capt. Bob Lilly all had bad asthma and had been moved into Heartbreak, because in the middle of one night, they were all having such a hard time breathing that their roommates called *bao cao* so loud that it gave the Vietnamese fits. Dave and Wes moved into one room together, and Bob was solo in the room that I had been in.

As time went by, the guys weren't getting any better. Because the big rooms were much better ventilated and not so damp as Heartbreak, the men who had asthma wanted to return to their old rooms. They continually asked the Vietnamese to move back, to no avail. As senior man in Heartbreak, I felt some obligation to try to get these guys back into their old rooms. Every time I had the opportunity to speak with an officer, I brought up the subject, but nothing ever happened.

A.J. moved into an empty cell with Ken Fleenor when the weather started to get hot in May. So now it was just Lou and I living together. Since A.J. and I were the only ones who wanted the leftover food, we took turns bringing the food pail to our room. Living with only one guy had its advantages and disadvantages. It was easier to get on each other's nerves with only two guys, and the topics of conversation were cut by a third. If one guy smoked and the other didn't, then the man who smoked got a double ration of cigarettes. Lou did not smoke but took his cigarettes and generously gave them to me. Now I had six cigarettes to smoke each day. Fortunately, we still had enough toilet paper to make a punk. This meant the paper had to be used sparingly at toilet time by both of us, and I also had to tell the Vietnamese that I needed more paper because I had diarrhea all the time. I never had to worry about that lie, because the guards would be caught dead before they ever looked in our *bo*.

Lou not only gave me his cigarettes, but he also had to endure the smoke from my cigarettes and the punk, which he didn't like. The room's being exceptionally small and having poor ventilation exacerbated the problem. In an effort to minimize the problem, I took some thread from my blanket and tied some bamboo sticks from the broom together, end to end, and created a thin stick about six feet long. I hung the punk on one end and leaned the stick against the wall, so the smoke went out the window high up in the room. This more or less satisfied Lou, as far as the smoke was concerned. He also had to put up with a very bad cigarette hacking cough that I had. One time, the guard left some matches in our room by mistake, and when I woke up in the middle of the night coughing my head off, Lou really got upset. Fortunately, I had a match, and after I lit up a cigarette, my coughing stopped. Sometimes I coughed so much, I thought I had asthma, too. In addition to the noise of the coughing,

Lou complained about how it sounded when I coughed up gobs of phlegm from my lungs every morning and one or two other times a day. Lou had to be a saint to put up with me.

One night, the Vietnamese were showing a movie to the guards in the courtyard. Lou and I were playing cards, and I had the punk burning nicely by the window. We finished the game, and when I looked up for the punk, it was gone. I immediately accused Lou of putting the punk out and throwing it away. Lou had made some comments about the smoke that day, so I did not think my accusation was far out. Lou denied it and said I was crazy. I was irritated with him when I went to bed that night without my before-sleep cigarette. The next morning, when Lou looked out of the crack by the window, he could see a ladder that leaned against the building by our window. We surmised that someone who was watching the movie that night had spotted the punk and decided to remove it from our room. I apologized to Lou.

The supply of toilet paper was not limitless, and occasionally we ran out, or the punk would accidentally go out. Ted Kaufman developed a system of passing a light across the hall. The distance from our room to his was about six or seven feet. He tied some bamboo sticks from his broom together, end to end, and attached the bamboo stick to a one-eighth-inch high, four-inch square tray made from a used toothpaste tube. Then he would put either a burning butt or a small punk in the tray and push it across the hall. There was a space of about half an inch under the door, which was just enough for the tray to fit under. Whenever we passed the light, we always had a guy clearing near the entrance door of the hallway to Heartbreak.

One night, Ted was passing me a light, and the tray was about two-thirds of the way over to my room. I heard two coughs from the guy who was clearing, meaning danger. I got up from the floor and sat on my bed. I could hear footsteps approaching in front of our room, and then suddenly I heard a big foot stomp on the floor. Our toothpaste tray was obviously crushed, and the butt was out. We could also hear the guard breaking the bamboo sticks into little pieces, but that was all that happened. The next day, we all had a big laugh as Ted described the imagined expression of disbelief as the guard walked in and saw the punk in the tray being pushed by a stick. I suspected even the guard got a kick out of that one.

I was surprised to learn that the "Fuck Ho" lieutenant colonel had been relieved of command, because other than the "Fuck Ho" thing, when he took his turn talking under the door at quiet hour each day, he seemed like a very pleasant and normal guy. He told us, however, that he had refused to accept soap, toothpaste, toothbrush, and letters from the Vietnamese. He said he disliked the Vietnamese so much that he could not accept these things from them. We all thought this was a strange and rather useless way to resist, because we thought that the Vietnamese didn't care whether he accepted these things or not. It irritated the men when he asked if we would give him some of our soap to wash his clothes. Soap was always scarce and particularly so in the hot summer. No one had any to spare. But we all gave him a small piece now and then. This incident was reminiscent of when the Vietnamese gave each man a tube of toothpaste for a year. Some men used it up in two weeks, others had a quarter of a tube left after a year. One learned to use things sparingly. His clothes and his room must have smelled to high heaven. Even the Vietnamese must have been sick of him, because he was eventually moved in with Col. John Flynn, Cdr. James Stockdale, and Col. Dave Winn, the senior men in camp, probably as punishment for all of them. The lieutenant colonel might have had a method to his madness in that by keeping himself so dirty and stinking, the Vietnamese would not bother him. But the Vietnamese weren't bothering anybody anyway.

While we were in Heartbreak, one round of packages from home was passed out. Most of the men received one. Bob Lilly received a one-pound jar of peanut butter. He wanted to divide it with everyone in Heartbreak, but they would not let him. So he ended up eating the whole jar in three days, because he was afraid that if he didn't, it would go bad.

The cell that we were in had a board that covered the lower part of the window facing into a large courtyard. It had a few small holes and did not fit the window perfectly, so we could see out if we strained our eyes hard. Sometimes, at the end of the day, my eyes would actually ache from the strain I put on them. We were able to see only a small segment of the yard through each hole, so it was necessary to change holes from time to time, as the object of the viewing moved around the courtyard. Much of the time spent looking out was boring, because nothing happened at all in the viewing area for long periods. The anticipation of seeing something new or interesting kept us glued to the crack. In a way, it was like fishing, but instead of catching a fish, we got to see an interesting sight now and then. We took turns standing on the bed looking out into the courtyard through the pinhead-sized holes in the board. I had to put toilet paper on the bottom of my crutches, so I would not slip. We probably spent at least six hours each day looking out the window. Now I could see many of the things going on that I had always wondered about for the first five months of my captivity, when I was in a room off the same courtyard.

It was fascinating to watch them. Several sidewalks, paths and a small street ran through the courtyard. We decided to give names to these landmarks, so that if the watcher saw something of interest, the other guys could quickly get to the right hole in the board to also see the interesting event. I named the main street Vohden Way, Lou and A.J. named pathways after themselves, and the alley in front of the building where the food girls hung out was called Pig Alley. The street near the wall was named Wall Street. Every small part of the area was well-defined. We named all of the food boys and water girls, and although many of the guards and turnkeys already had names, we gave names to the others, as well. We watched them get into the chow line to get the food from inside one of the rooms off the courtyard and several minutes later come out into the courtyard, where they would eat their rice by stuffing it in their mouth with their chopsticks very quickly. A few of the food girls were not all that bad to look at, particularly if you had not seen a real live American woman for more than five years. They seemed to be typical girls and did the same things that American girls did: played with their hair, moved their bodies the right way, and flirted with the guards. They had no makeup on and their hair was black as coal, long, but usually rolled up.

When the weather became really hot, I suspected the girls did not wear undergarments, if they ever wore them at all. One hot June evening, one of the water girls, no more then nineteen years old, was talking to several guards. She had been fanning herself, because it was hot. She had on the traditional black pants that most of the girls wore and a short white blouse. In front of the three guards, she pulled her pants away from her belly a good three or four inches and fanned her crotch for a few minutes. She did this without the guards even noticing it. We, however, were amused.

As things gradually loosened up for the prisoners, and the communications team from room 7 became tired of passing the news through the wall every day, they began looking for a shortcut. A peep door about one-foot square at the end of the hallway in Heartbreak opened into room 7. The guard used the door to check on room 7. Some men in the room found a way to unlock the door from inside. Now with the peep door open, they could clear the Heartbreak hallway completely and verbally pass the news to all of us at one time. This was much easier for all concerned. At one time, if a POW was caught tampering with that door, his life would have been in jeopardy, but now it was an altogether new ballgame.

In the third week of June, the Vietnamese hung some clotheslines and enclosed a small area around them with bamboo right behind Heartbreak. Finally, we could go outside and hang our clothes in the sunlight. Before that, we had always had to hang our wet clothes in our dark, damp rooms to dry. For five months, I had been in Heartbreak and had been out in the sunlight only two times, going from my room to quiz. So when I got out in the sunlight for the first time for more than a few minutes, I was surprised that my eyes really hurt. I also noticed that after my stay in Heartbreak, the sight in the eye I used to look out of the crack in my room for hours on end was considerably worse than the other eye. That sight never improved.

CHAPTER 24 - TENTERHOOKS

ROOM 7, HANOI HILTON

June 1971 – May 1972. The Vietnamese had been trying to get everyone in Heartbreak to write an apology for whatever reason they were there. Everyone refused. They didn't need the space we occupied. I figured for sure that they would leave us there until we wrote the apologies. Then, just as I had completely resigned myself to this fact, one night in the latter part of June, Heartbreak was emptied. Everyone, except the guys who had asthma, was moved into room 7. The guys who had asthma went back to their old rooms.

Living in Heartbreak had been unpleasant, but it was nothing compared to the first four years of captivity, when we lived in almost the same size rooms, isolated, tortured, always under pressure to write or tape some propaganda or do something we did not want to do. For those first years, the pressure had been constant and intense. You never knew what the result would be for refusing to do something. Getting caught violating one of the camp regulations was always a potential disaster. In Heartbreak, the living conditions were bad, but the pressure was off.

The night we moved, Ted Kaufman, Ken Simonet, A.J. Meyers, Lou Makowski, Duffy Hutton, Ken Fleenor, and I all moved into room 7. Only twenty guys lived in that room, so we had plenty of space. Best of all, I was the fourth senior man in the room, so I did not have to worry about SRO problems and all the crap from the troops. This was a real relief. All of the 05's had been moved out of the room, and Maj. Larry Guarino was the SRO. Lt. Cdr. Wendy Rivers and Maj. Sam Johnson, who were the second and third senior 04's in the prison system, were on his staff. Larry told me that it wouldn't have made sense to make me a section leader because of my bad leg, and as I was a senior 04, I also became part of his staff.

It was a pleasure being in a big room again. We had decks of real cards, so I could play bridge. We were getting a cup of milk every day, and I was getting six cigarettes one day and seven the next. Wendy Rivers loved cigarettes as much as I did, and he had been collecting butts for some time. He had a collection of about two hundred, which he shared with me whenever I wanted to make a roll-your-own. Wendy affectionately called the cigarettes he made from toilet paper and the tobacco butts "Sweetdads."

Larry invited me, as a new member of the staff, to eat my meals with them. Either Sam or Wendy would carry their food and mine to the area where we ate, and the staff would eat together. I was living like half a human being again, and it was fun. Before we ate, we took turns saying the blessing before each meal. We did this for at least three or four months. Then one day, we had a religious discussion, and it became evident that no one was particularly religious, and that none of us had ever prayed at mealtime before we were shot down. We realized that we were doing this as only a matter of formality, so we never said grace anymore.

The room was well-organized already, and the new men just moved into the existing organization. Larry was the SRO, Wendy was the executive officer, Sam was in charge of communications, and I was put in charge of administration, which included recreation and training. We had four sections, and the next four senior men in the room were section leaders. The sections took turns cleaning the room, bringing in the food and water from outside, dishing out the food, washing the dishes, as well as getting the cigarettes each day and distributing them.

The day started at about 0600, when the camp gong sounded. Some guys had already been up for an hour exercising or just walking around the room. At 0630, the Voice of Vietnam came on. Some men were still sleeping under their mosquito nets. At around 0830, the guard came to the door and gave us our cigarettes. At 0930, after all of our mosquito nets were put away, he came back, opened

368

the door, and let us out into the courtyard for washing. The area outside our room was enclosed with a bamboo fence about sixty feet long, eight feet high and twenty-five feet on each end. The outside area was about the same size as the room. Room 6, next to us, was the same size as ours, and it also had a similar courtyard adjacent to ours. The guards never let both rooms outside at the same time. Even with the more relaxed policy, they were afraid to let two rooms out together at the same time. We had a six-foot long by four-foot wide by four-foot high brick cement tank filled with water and some rusty bowls, which had holes in them, with which we splashed water on ourselves when we washed. If everyone washed at the same time, there wouldn't be enough water to go around, and it would be very crowded around the water tank, so Larry had two flights wash in the morning and two flights in the afternoon.

After we went back to the room, we ate. At around 1130, quiet hour started. Some guys slept. Some guys played cards or chess, some studied or just walking quietly around the room. The communications team went into action. As soon as the team received the news, they gave a special briefing to Larry and his staff. We went outside again a couple of hours after noon. The duty section washed the dishes. Late in the afternoon, the Vietnamese brought our second meal and drinking water. We were permitted to keep a good sized can of drinking water in the room, and we always had a sufficient amount now. After we finished the second meal, we took it easy for about four hours, until the Voice of Vietnam came on again. After the Voice of Vietnam ended, we got ready for bed, and half an hour later, the gong sounded.

A group of senior officers lived in small building about thirty-five yards from our courtyard. Communicating with them was impossible, but their communicator, Cdr. Howard Rutledge, devised a unique scheme to communicate with us. He tied some sticks together, end to end, and attached a small rag at one end of the sticks. A pipe in the wall of the building where he lived extended through the rooftop. He sent messages by moving the rag on the end of the stick up and down thru the rooftop. For some time, this method of communicating worked well. In turn, we threw nuts into their courtyard with messages contained inside.

One day, our room was out in the courtyard, and Rutledge was sending us a message by moving the stick up and down through the pipe in their roof. Our communications team was watching the white rag move up and down. Out of the blue, we saw a Vietnamese on the roof creeping towards the moving white rag. Rutledge had been caught! The guard observed the rag closely for a minute and suddenly he grabbed it and pulled the stick out of the pipe. The stick was at least eight feet long. Rutledge must have been shocked to have the stick yanked right out of his hand. Although a valuable communications method had been lost, almost everyone out in the yard broke out laughing because it was so funny to watch.

Although living conditions were considerably improved over what they had been, life still had its problems. Perhaps our major difficulty now was just getting along with each other. As SRO, Larry Guarino was confronted with many of the same problems I'd had. Some guys walked on another guy's bed. This bothered some people but not others. A guy's package or banana might be stepped on. Hard feelings arose sometimes. Some men wanted to stay up late at night; other wanted to rise early. Some of the early risers bothered the late sleepers, and the men who stayed up late bothered the men who retired early. Some men urinated very loudly in the water in the *bo* at all hours of the night and day, and others made loud noises when they put the lid on the *bo*. Everybody seemed to be annoyed by everyone else. We had a 35-gallon drum filled with water so that we could rinse our bodies lightly before we went to sleep at night.

Some guys would noisily splash the water on the floor way after the gong sounded. Certain guys in the room could not get along with the Vietnamese.

These were but a few of the problems that the room encountered every day, so we needed to establish some rules for our own group. After considerable discussion with the staff, the section leaders, and the men in the room, Larry Guarino issued a number of orders that would allow us to all live together more peacefully. If guys got up early in the morning, they had to exercise quietly until 0700. Everyone had to be quiet after the gong at night. Each man had a ration of three bowls of water to rinse off with before he went to bed each night. Guys were not to walk on another person's mat or possessions.

Because we did not want to have confrontations with the Vietnamese over petty things that involved personalities, only the section leaders and staff were to be in contact with the Vietnamese. In addition, we wanted the room leadership—and not just any guy in the room—to handle our problems. Another order was that when the Vietnamese told us to do something, unless it violated the Code of Conduct or was unreasonable, we were to comply, because the treatment by the Vietnamese was much better, and we had fewer problems with them. The room leadership for the most part agreed with the rules and regulations, as did most of the other men. Day after day, we preached, "Be considerate of your fellow man; we are living in close quarters." Things would improve, but then the same old problems would resurface. It was a continual battle.

John Dramesi, who although a very personable guy, could not understand the need for rules and regulations. He had made an unsuccessful escape and bragged quite openly about how tough he was, but he interpreted the leadership's rules and regulations as being made to control the room for the Vietnamese. To an extent, what he said was true, because the rules did establish order in the room, but the real purpose was to help us live together better, rather than to help the Vietnamese. The problem was that Dramesi had a totally different philosophy on how we should conduct ourselves and especially how we should conduct ourselves toward the Vietnamese. As a consequence, he continually violated the room rules and regulations.

He never went to bed on time. He and a cohort would start to rinse off after the gong at night, take more then their allotted share of water, and splash the water loudly on the concrete floor while everyone was trying to sleep. He would continue to talk for as much as an hour after the gong. He had a very loud voice, and when he laughed, it could be heard halfway around the camp. He laughed so loud that many times, the guard would bang on the door and raise a fuss with the room. Should the whole room have to suffer for one man's lack of self-control or refusal to obey reasonable rules? The idea that the whole room would be punished for his conduct never was a consideration in our dealings with him. We would have backed him even if the Vietnamese punished our entire room because of his behavior. We told him to quiet down, because he was annoying others in the room by his boisterous manner. But he interpreted this as our disciplining him to placate the Vietnamese. We tried every way to convince him to conform. We put pressure on his section leader, who was highly respected by all, to get this man to behave.

One day, when the room was outside bathing, Dramesi and a few other guys were talking. Duffy Hutton told a joke, and Dramesi laughed loudly, which was his normal behavior. The turnkey became annoyed and told him to go back inside the room. Dramesi started to go in and conform with our policy to do what the Vietnamese told you to do. Under normal circumstances, a guy would have gone into the room, and if he came out five minutes later, the guard would have most likely forgotten all about the laugh. But instead, Dramesi ambled over to the bath area, took off his clothes, and began to wash. This upset the guard, and he started to raise hell with some other guys. Dramesi took his time but eventually went back into the room.

He continued to talk loudly about the incident, even though he had violated our room policy. Not only were the Vietnamese irritated with him, but also the guys in the room were mad at him. Finally Maj. Sam Johnson told Dramesi to knock off the noise and forget what had happened. Well, Dramesi, who was a senior Air Force captain, did not like what Maj. Sam Johnson had said, so Dramesi made some disrespectful remarks to Sam, who was the third senior 04 in prison. Sam was probably one of the most respected and fair-minded prisoners in Hanoi and had been completely within his rights and quite proper in the action he had taken.

This was a last straw. Larry Guarino had had enough of Dramesi's inconsiderate and irresponsible conduct, and the staff agreed. After some considerable thought, Larry decided that some disciplinary action had to be taken against Dramesi. Lt. Cdr. Wendy Rivers, Maj. Sam Johnson, and I agreed. We decided that he should be brought to Captain's Mast. This is comparable to a civilian court for minor offenses and an appropriate manner in the military to ascertain the circumstances of an alleged offense and award punishment if deemed appropriate.

Larry, Sam, Wendy, and I sat on Larry's bed mat. One of the section leaders acted as a master at arms and brought Dramesi in front of us. We had already decided what punishment he would get, because we knew more or less exactly what had happened, but we heard his story anyway. Larry explained to Dramesi how his conduct was offending many men in the room and why this action was being taken. But Dramesi still couldn't understand it. It had been difficult for Larry to have to resort to these measures, but given Dramesi's inconsiderate behavior to his roommates and his disrespect to a senior officer, we really had no other choice. Dramesi accepted his punishment of being restricted to the room for two weeks without incident.

Cdr. Bob Schweitzer moved into the room one evening in November. Rumors had circulated that he and two other senior officers, Cdr. Gene Wilbur, and Lt. Col. Edison Miller, had been collaborating with the Vietnamese. I had never talked to anyone who had personal knowledge of their alleged misconduct, but I had heard tapes supposedly made by them that were pretty bad. I could not swear that what the three of them had said on the tape was actually said by them, nor could I be certain that they had not been coerced into making the statements. Based on past experience and intuition, however, POWs developed a feel as to whether the statements were forced or not. Sometimes just by the way a guy said things on the tape, we had a good idea whether it had been coerced. The opinion of most POWs was that Wilbur, Miller, and Schweitzer had not been forced. The three of them had lived together for several years and appeared to be getting substantially better treatment than everyone else. The rumors of their misconduct appeared to be much more than rumor. Schweitzer's camp reputation was about as bad as it could get.

It had been the camp policy that, "We do not drag a repentant sinner to his grave." In other words, regardless of how bad one's conduct had been in the past, all he had to do was say, "Hey, I screwed up, and I am sorry. I will try to do my best to follow the Code of Conduct and the policies and guidance of the senior officers, and I will support the President of the United States and its policies." It was that simple. Almost everyone had done things that they should not have done, so no effort was made by the camp leadership to seek revenge or punishment. That particular guidance had been passed on to Wilbur, Miller, and Schweitzer.

Schweitzer had finally seen the light, and he refused to cooperate with the Vietnamese any longer. His punishment was to move into a big room where most of the senior 04's were. Although the policy was to forgive one's past acts, when Bob Schweitzer came into the room, his reputation had preceded him, and several men showed him animosity and contempt. Most, however, greeted him cordially, and because he was a relatively new shoot down, about two years, we pounded him with questions about everything from the war to whether we had been promoted while in prison.

A problem concerning seniority arose. Maj. Larry Guarino had been shot down in June 1965, and at that time had been a very senior major (04) with a date of rank of 1958. He had never been passed over, but promotions in the Air Force had been slow. Because Larry was a prisoner, his rank remained major, as although we suspected we were being promoted, we were never certain, and even if we knew we were being promoted, we still wouldn't know our exact date of rank. Bob Schweitzer's date of rank as a lieutenant commander (04) was in 1963, five years after Larry's date of rank, but because Schweitzer had not been shot down until 1968, he had already been promoted to commander (05). In effect, Larry, who was ten years older than Schweitzer, a prisoner three years longer, and who had almost certainly been promoted several years before Schweitzer, was now junior to Schweitzer. The rule that we were working under was that one's rank as of the day a man was shot down determined seniority in prison. The Navy had been short of officers, and promotions were fast; the Air Force had an abundance of officers, and promotions were slow. If the war had lasted much longer, this could have been a real problem. There was no easy solution to this problem, but wisely Cdr. Schweitzer recognized the situation and paid close attention to what Larry said.

One Sunday afternoon during quiet hour in December of 1971, I was playing bridge, and we heard what sounded like a bombing raid. We heard the sound of aircraft and triple A. The whole world exploded around Hanoi. The air war had started again. We had been marking time since November 1968, when President Johnson halted the bombing of North Vietnam a few days before the election in an effort to help Hubert Humphrey be elected president. We had all hoped for a long time that the cessation of the bombing in the North would somehow lead to our release, but it hadn't. My hopes had been raised for some time after the air war ended in 1968, because our treatment had improved considerably, but as time passed for the next three years, I became impatient. I had mixed emotions when the bombing started again. I knew that the end had come to whatever had been going on in negotiations, but if attempts at peace had failed, I was happy to get things moving again.

I had not been brainwashed, but I was beginning to realize that some of the things the camp commander had told me in August 1965 weren't that far off, and that the invincibility and omnipotence of the U.S., of which I had been so convinced, was no longer a reality. I had seen the Vietnamese operate for more than six years. They were honest to goodness clods. At best, they could be considered no more than a third-world country. In my opinion, how they ever managed to survive as long as they had was not a testament to anything they did, but rather a result of the incompetence and ignorance of those responsible for the war in the U.S. government. But now the air war was on again. I believed that the only way I would ever go home again was if we clobbered them with bombs and bullets until they had nothing left. I was sad now, because negotiations had broken down, but happy the bombing had started again.

By the third week of December, the number of men in our room had grown to about thirty-seven or thirty-eight. Schweitzer was still the SRO. It had been customary over the years for the Vietnamese to have the prisoners cut string beans, clean and peel squash, sweep up certain areas of the camp, pluck feathers from the scrawniest looking chickens or ducks known to man, and do other similar kinds of work. Some men always objected to working, and others didn't mind at all. As it had never bothered me to work outside, and I had been intimately involved with the coal-ball issue and saw its consequences, I still had no objection to working outside. Compared to the old days, snapping beans was easy. But the frustrations from the daily routine were on the rise again, and lessons from the past forgotten. Some guys were beginning to feel their oats, or perhaps they were just bored with life.

This time, the issue was not that we would not work outside, but rather some men in the room believed that we were getting more than our share of the work, compared to the men in the other rooms. We asked the other rooms about it, trying to find out how much they were working, but the information we got was inconclusive. It was Maj. Sam Johnson's turn to kick up his heels. His honest belief was that our room was doing more than our share outside, and that we should refuse until the other rooms worked outside as much as we had. It was probably true that we were called out more than the other rooms, but it wasn't clear whether that occurred because our room was first in the line of rooms, or we were being picked on because we had so many senior officers and a host of reputed tough resisters.

One day around the middle of December, we were told to snap some string beans. Sam Johnson had convinced Cdr. Schweitzer that we should not to go out and work. Cdr. Schweitzer refused to send the men out, so the Vietnamese closed the door and left. As a consequence, we did not get a bath or cigarettes the next day. They called out Schweitzer and Guarino several times for quiz, but Schweitzer continued in his refusal to work. They would say to Schweitzer and Guarino, "Who gives you your food each day? Do you think it is God?" Then they would answer the question, "No, it is not God who gives you your food. It is the Vietnamese people." Then they threatened that if we did not help prepare the food, we would not eat. Schweitzer still refused. Only the duty section got out to wash the dishes. Some of the guys, including me, were annoyed at this because it would have taken no more than a half-hour to snap the beans. The first day the cigarettes were cut off, the guys in room 6, next to us, passed some cigarettes to us with a note that was read to the entire room. It said that they were all very sorry that we did not snap the beans and had been cut off from cigarettes, but the note said, "Next time snap the fucking beans." The punishment lasted a week. Another thing they did to punish us was to keep the lights off in the room until the night gong sounded. Even though one of the section leaders would *bao cao* for an hour or more, the guards would not come. If the work was for the benefit of all the POWs, really what difference did it make who snapped the beans? But others said if we did not make a stand now, there was no end to what the Vietnamese would end up asking us to do. They said it's only fair that others get their share of the work. The issue was debatable, and debated it was.

Some time had passed since we refused to snap the beans. Then one day a guard came to our door, and some of the men were told to go out and do some whitewashing on the building. The room leadership held a quick debate and decided to refuse. Schweitzer had a problem. If he told the guys to work, some of the men would accuse him of being soft, giving in to the Vietnamese too easily, and even possibly of aiding the enemy. Some men were tired of no cigarettes and the general harassment of the room, but for others, it was no problem, and they even relished it. He really had no choice but to do what he did. He refused to send them out. Only the most heroic of the 05's or 06's could have told the guys to go work, and even they would have been hard pressed to tell the men to work now. One had to maintain his image of being a resistor. The wisdom and soundness of a decision always had to be considered in conjunction with one's image and reputation. Image building was very important for everyone. No one could say knock off the bull crap to the guys and get away with it. As far as I know, Col. Risner, who was probably one of the most respected prisoners in Vietnam, was the only one I ever heard tell a junior officer to knock off petty things he was doing to irritate the guards. And when Risner did that, he was strongly criticized by a number of guys in my room.

That night, when we refused to paint outside, we had a very thorough room inspection. Those who had advocated not working said the inspection was a coincidence and had no correlation with our refusal to work. During the inspection, the guards found all of our toastmaster material. It consisted of the organization of that group, when people were scheduled to speak, what speeches they would give, and the various levels of advancement they had achieved. These papers were rather lengthy and detailed. They also found our room administrative organization sheet, which was written in great detail. Why not? We had nothing else to do. All of this material was as innocuous as could be.

The inspection came as no surprise, because in the past at least once every few months or less, according to the mood of the Vietnamese, we would have an inspection. They cleaned everything out of the room, from pencils and paper to pieces of wire, razor blades, and whatever else we had found and were hiding. Most everything that was written had been memorized, so it was just a matter of rewriting what we had lost. We had plenty of time to reorganize.

Several nights later, Cdr. Schweitzer, Maj. Guarino, Lt. Cdr. Rivers, Maj. Dunn, Lt. Cdr. Haines, and Capt. Webb were moved from the room. This was just before Christmas. Sam Johnson, who had been the strongest advocate of not working, became the SRO, and everything more or less reverted back to normal.

We'd had an elaborate plan for our Christmas Eve party, but when those guys moved out, all of our spirits were dampened. Although we had to make a few modifications, we had our Christmas program. Maj. Howie Dunn had been in charge of the choir. Some people had been surprised when they heard that he was the choir director, because he was not considered to be that type. But he spent hours arranging music. I had the feeling that he did not know very much about music before he started on this endeavor. He was conscientious, and the results were outstanding. Since Howie was no longer in the room, however, the choir did not sing on Christmas Eve. To start the program off, everyone had put his name in a hat, and names had been drawn several weeks before. Each man had to come up with an imaginary gift he would give that night and also a gift that would be given when we were released.

I picked Bob Doremus's name. Bob was one of the chowhounds in the room. He never left a scrap. He saved his bread and used it to clean the pots in which the food was brought into the room. If he didn't have enough bread he would lick the pans and pots clean. As we were both from New Jersey, I knew that he had heard of an outstanding restaurant in Scotch Plains, called Snuffy's Steak House. My gift to him was one week of work in Snuffy's kitchen, where he could clean out all the pots and pans with bread and eat it for a week. For his real gift, I gave him two pairs of cashmere socks. A.J. Myers drew my name, and he worked out some little gimmick so that I could carry my food when I walked with my crutches.

Then we had some skits. One in particular was very humorous. Ted Kaufman dressed up in rags but almost nude. He was supposed to be Ho Chi Minh's pregnant mother. He took the lid off of a *bo* and pretended to squat on it and grunted as though he was having a bowel movement. Suddenly, one of the guys said, "Oh my goodness, she just shit, what a funny looking turd." Then someone else said, "No it's not a turd," and as they pulled a baby doll with a beard on it that looked like a turd out of the *bo*, they announced to the world the birth of Ho Chi Minh. Everyone laughed and applauded furiously.

Within a week or two after Christmas, Guarino and Schweitzer came back. Schweitzer said he had been beaten a few times, which I took with a grain of salt. Guarino had been put under pressure to talk about the organization of the room. Guarino said he didn't write a word. Schweitzer said he only wrote an apology. Later that month, the rest of the men returned. They said they didn't give anything but were treated rather shabbily, although not tortured. Each man told his story. Some of the men were nasty to the guys who had not resisted satisfactorily. There were hard feelings between some of the men in the room. Larry Guarino referred to the room as a snake pit. His opinion was that we should go ahead and work and not make an issue over it. Eventually, we went to Col. Flynn to get his policy on working outside, and he said to go ahead and work and not to make an issue over it.

Chess was a very popular game in the room. Some time in March, the next room challenged us to a room chess game. All day long, guys would study the board before we made the final decision on the move. The interest was so intense in both rooms that more than thirty bottles of booze were bet on the game. We played for about fifteen days, and the game was going well for us. Then one day, about twenty men–or nearly half of the men from room 6–were moved in with us, and the other men in room 6 moved elsewhere. Now we had a full room and more guys to talk with. And there was no more chess game.

With room 6 vacant, we were cut off from the rest of the camp, because they had been our communications link. We had to find a way to establish the chain again. One morning when we were out in the yard, we could hear some other guys across the camp, and as the guard had left us alone for a few minutes, one guy yelled out very loudly and quickly, "Check the window at noon." He said it so fast that the Vietnamese probably couldn't understand what he had said, even if they were standing right there listening, but loud enough so that one of the guys from the other room could hear. Sure enough, at noon, when one of the communications team members was on another man's shoulder looking out the window through the bars he saw a guy in room 4, fifty yards away, on the other side of the camp. We had established contact again. The communications team used hand signals similar to the sign language used by deaf people, but using letters instead of words. I never failed to marvel how fast their hands moved. I couldn't even come close to reading them. They were at the window for at least an hour every day during quiet hour.

Some of the new guys liked to play poker. They had come up with the idea of making poker chips from bread. They made a paste from bread and water and molded the dough into poker chip like shapes. Then they used cigarettes ashes to blacken some, red dust from bricks out in the yard to color chips red, and the others were white when they dried. They looked and felt like the chips made for the gambling tables at Las Vegas. There was a game going on all day and every night until our taps rule was enforced. Two men were the banker and accountant and kept track of how much every one had won or lost. The game was taken seriously, because everyone who played believed that he would pay if he lost or get what he won when the war was over. A limit was set for losing no more than $500. If one lost that much, he could not play anymore. I do not know if anyone ever paid off after the war.

To add to the entertainment, some of the guys thought they would try to make some booze. They took several water jugs that some men still had from when they were in small rooms, crushed up a half dozen bananas, added some water and lots of sugar, and then let it sit, hoping that it would ferment. After three or four weeks, they poured the liquid that was on top into their cups and drank it. I never had the good fortune–or maybe the misfortune–to drink it. I never even had the opportunity to taste it. The guys who made it claimed that it had alcohol in it, but I never saw anyone feel good after drinking it.

With about fifty men in our room, we had an almost unlimited wealth of talent. We played occasional chess tournaments, individual chess games, and bridge throughout the day. Larry Friese, a young Marine captain who had recently graduated from college, had studied Russian for four years. He really juiced up his Russian language class. He gave weekly individual examinations and assigned grades. The grades were posted on one of the walls in the room after everyone completed the exam. Each student would have his grade alongside his assigned number. Numbers were used instead of names to maintain anonymity. The entire course consisted of memorizing lengthy conversations. It was hard work, time consuming, but fun.

The room also had a medical officer. Lt. Cdr. Rob Doremus was one of those guys who had as much dislike for the Vietnamese as the next, but he also had a knack of getting along with them. At mealtime, the guard opened the door, and the duty section brought in baskets of bread, a big pot of soup, and a smaller pail of the side dish. They also brought in two big cans of drinking water. The duty section dished up the food on several tables, and then the policy was to stand in line and wait for your turn to pick up your food. If Rob noticed that someone in the duty section had not washed his hands before dishing up the food, he would make a fuss about it. He complained about guys who did not take the first loaf of bread that they touched and who felt two or three loaves before picking the one they wanted. He made such a fuss over this that we made a policy that you took the first loaf you touched, and that once you took your soup and side plate, you couldn't bring it back and exchange it for another. Some guys would dip their own water cup into the large can instead of using the dipper that was there. Rob always made a fuss about this. Watching the food kept him busy.

As hard as Rob worked to keep things clean, some things that happened were beyond our control. We got the word that three or four guys in one of the other big rooms had pink eye. We were concerned but not worried too much. The next day, we heard the whole room had it. We couldn't believe that it had spread so fast. The following day, the Vietnamese came in with eye drops for all of us. Although they did not tell us why they were giving us the drops, we knew. As was customary, some but not all of the guys took the drops. Several days later, almost everyone in our room had pink eye. It didn't matter whether you had taken the drops or not. But before the week ended, almost every room in the camp had had pink eye. It had spread like wild fire. And almost just as fast, the rooms had recovered from it. Most people had it for only a few days. They gave us no medicine. Just told us not to rub our eyes.

The area where our food was prepared was behind our room. The noise from the clanking of the pots and pans didn't start until around 0700 or so, but on the days they killed a pig, the pig would start squealing at around 0400 and make a hell of a racket. They apparently were not very sophisticated at killing pigs. Once the pig realized what was about to happen, it ran all over the place with the Vietnamese following and trying to catch it. It was depressing listening to the whole thing. Finally there was a lot of loud, painful squealing for a few minutes, and then it would stop. Everyone would go back to sleep.

Only a few early risers had been in our room before some young guys from room 6 moved in, but now about a third of the men in the room got up as early as 0500 and started exercising. Some men had very elaborate exercise programs that lasted for as long as an hour or more. I did sit-ups every morning, and some arm waving and trunk twisting for about an hour. Then to finish off, I had two guys hold the ends of my crutches over their heads, and I did about twenty pull-ups hanging on my crutches. I tried to finish my exercise before they brought the milk in the morning. I was getting into pretty good shape. Some of the younger guys walked on their hands. Lt. Barry Bridger, a young Air Force officer, could walk about seventy or eighty yards on his hands with no problem, and John Dramesi was pretty good, too. Barry was able to do a one-hand handstand, and he could jump from a standing position and land on one hand and be able to stand on it. Seeing some of those guys perform was like watching a circus.

The reason we could do these relatively exceptional feats of strength was probably because we were so thin, and years had passed since we were tortured. Many other guys practiced and participated, because there was a lot of competition. Most of the men were a far cry from being circus performers. They were content to do handstands with their feet against the wall. Although it made the walls dirty, no one really cared. And then there were most of the guys who said the hell with exercise and slept late in the morning.

One problem with the exercise was that one or two guys smelled so bad after exercising that the area within twenty feet of them stank so much, it was unbearable. Lt., j.g., Tony Arnold, who lived next to me, was a hell of a nice kid, strong as an ox, and he exercised every morning. He was one of the guys who had terrible body odor, but he got up later than I did, so I was able to move to another area of the room until he finished. This was one of the blessings of being in a big room.

I had developed a bad cough over the years because of smoking, and it was getting worse as time went on. It was so bad that I had quit for three or four days several times. When I lived with Lou Makowski in Heartbreak, I had so many cigarettes that I would take a little bit of tobacco out of the end of one cigarette and then stuff the end of another cigarette into the hole. I used the cigarette with the small amount of tobacco taken out as a filter. This helped some but not a whole lot. I had always wanted a cigarette holder, because I smoked them so close that I thought perhaps the heat from the cigarette was what made me cough. Ens. Ralph Gaither was one of the guys from room 6, and he had brought some things that could be used to make a cigarette holder. I knew that he and many others were annoyed by my hacking cough, and so to help him pass the time and maybe make me cough less, he made me a nice cigarette holder out of wood. It seemed to help some.

I had some time to spare, so I decided that maybe I could make a better one. I got a piece of wood and made it into the shape I wanted by just filing it down on the cement floor. It took about an hour a day for about a week. But the hard part was making the hole. I found a three-inch piece of one-eighth-inch thick wire out in our courtyard, and I used that to bore the hole. It took more than a week of digging the wood out, but I finally got through. It turned out much better than I thought it would. I used it for almost a year. At one time, cigarette holders were so popular that probably a third of the men in the room had them. They had them not only for kicks, but because the cigarettes we smoked were incredibly acrid and foul.

CHAPTER 25 - B-52s BOMB HANOI

ROOM 1, HANOI HILTON

May 1972 – January 1973. One early evening in May 1972, several guards came to the room and told about half of the men they were going to move that night. The men selected were all fairly junior. The next day, we learned that about 150 men had moved out of the Hilton that night. Months later, we found out that a new camp had been opened for them near the Chinese border.

The following Sunday evening, the rest of us packed up and prepared to move. We suspected that we would be going to a new camp, but we moved to room 1 on the other side of the Hilton. I had lived there when we came in from Camp Faith after the Son Tay raid. Cdr. Schweitzer was still the SRO, and although we had fewer guys again, the routine did not change very much, except we did things on a smaller scale. We continued our mathematics class, Bob Shumaker started an advance course in theory of equations, and the language lessons went on.

The men seemed to be getting along better now, although occasional arguments still occurred. Some easygoing people rarely let things bother them. Two such men surprised everyone, however, when Jim Kasler accused Dale Osborne of taking his toothbrush. They almost had a fistfight. Two months later, the brush was found stuck between some broken pieces of the platform where they slept. Even John Dramesi and Larry Guarino were getting along fairly well. Somehow, we were finally adjusting to communal living. The renewed bombing raised our morale and our hope that our imprisonment would end soon. In addition, we had heard that the major North Vietnamese seaport, Haiphong, and a number of smaller ports had been mined. This boosted our spirits. We inferred that it was having an effect on them, because we no longer got milk every morning, the imported fish from Russia was not as plentiful as before, and we got Albanian and Chinese cigarettes now and then, instead of Vietnamese cigarettes. Although many of us had long ago recognized that the solution to the war would not be easy, we figured that if the mining of the harbors continued and imports decreased, our standard of living might be unfavorably affected. As in the past, when shortages occurred, most of the guys became optimistic, because it indicated that the Vietnamese were hurting.

The men who had been in Skid Row moved into Room 2 a few weeks later. Maj. Bud Day, who had been SRO at Skid Row, was the SRO of room 2. Tom Washington, an Air Force full colonel, was also in the room with Bud Day, but the colonel had been relieved of command. He must have done something pretty bad to warrant this. Moreover, the Vietnamese had put him in a room with officers relatively junior to him. I found it awkward to meet him for the first time, after both rooms were allowed outside together, but in time I got to know him, and he seemed to be a nice guy. He did not like the Vietnamese and supported the war like the rest of us. I couldn't figure out why he'd been relieved of command.

Dudley Schneider was an early shoot down and lived in room 2. He had developed an inability to hold his food down. Whether it was physical or psychological was debatable. Maj. Day became quite upset with his behavior and said that Dudley was violating the Code of Conduct by eating extra food and then throwing it up. Throughout the period after the Son Tay raid, Dudley went back and forth from the big room to Mayo several times. Mayo was a special room for the sick guys. They always got good food, and the Vietnamese apparently were doing everything they reasonably could to keep the men alive. Also guys who had asthma were being moved to Mayo, when their asthma got bad.

We did not have direct communications with the high command at first, because some of the large rooms in the camp were empty. But new methods were devised. The Incas, as we called the Thai prisoners, lived next to the 06's and were in contact with them.

They were indispensable in helping us communicate. The notes that we put in nuts and threw did not always reach the target, so we carved out the middle of a piece of a small branch and put the coded note inside that. Then we put the stick under the bamboo fence surrounding our courtyard, and when the Incas were cleaning the yard, they would pick up the stick at the prearranged location and then deliver it to the colonels. This method could not be relied upon daily, because the Incas did not clean the yard every day, so other means were devised.

We had a large barrel about the size of a 100-gallon oil drum, and this was where the feces and urine went in the bath area in our room. Each morning, the duty section had to empty the barrel in an area where the Incas observed them. When the duty section took the barrel out, depending on the questions that had been asked of us, a guy would roll up his right pants leg or left sleeve, or two of them would do it, or one guy would drop something, etc. All were prearranged signals. The Incas would be watching and report to the high command what they saw the guys doing when they emptied the barrel. It was a very elementary way to communicate, but it expedited the answer to a question, when the Incas were unable to pick up the sticks.

During the summer of 1972, men who had been shot down in late 1971 and early 1972 were moved into rooms in the same area where we were. At first, our contact with them was limited, but by October 1972, communications improved. We had been without any real news from home since late 1968, when President Johnson ended the air war in the North days before the elections. With no new prisoners coming in, our news sources had dried up. We had received only what the Vietnamese provided us with for nearly three and a half years.

The new shoot downs organized the news by rooms. One room passed on sports news and movies, another the war and recreation, and another news of a general nature and other entertainment. Each day, one room of new guys had the responsibility to provide a short briefing on their topic, and for more than a month we received daily reports. Because there were many men in each of the new guy rooms, one guy would come up with a news item that would trigger an idea in another guy's head, so the end result was a fairly complete and accurate account of many of the things that had gone on the past three years. In about one month, we became fairly up to date on what had happened in all that time. Every quiet hour, the lengthy notes were read to the entire room by the communications team, as we all listened with astonishment to what we heard. We marveled at mini skirts, X-rated movies in public theaters, the sexual revolution, and riots. What we heard was shocking. The mini skirts and sexual revolution weren't necessarily bad, but they were different from before.

Each day a new shoot down would tell one of the men in our room about a movie, and then in the evening the man to whom the movie was told would tell the whole room about it. Some of the movies, like *Pretty Maids All in a Row*, sounded fantastic. I couldn't believe what I was hearing about the realism that was being shown on the screen. The beards and long hair were a surprise to all of us. Although some of the stories were hard to believe, when we finally got a peek at some of the recent shoot downs and saw how long their hair was, we started to believe it. In 1965, many of the pilots had worn crew cuts, and the military standard for a haircut was fairly short, so to see Navy pilots with hair down the back of their necks was really quite a surprise. If the pilots had hair that long, how long must the hair of civilians be?

In late October, the Vietnamese took down the bamboo fence in the courtyard between our room and room 6, the fence in the courtyard between rooms 1 and 2, and the fence in the courtyard between rooms 3 and 4. At first, the Vietnamese painted a line where the fence had been, and although we could talk to the men from the other room when we were outside together, we were not allowed to physically cross the line. I met and talked to Scotty Morgan the first day we got out together. He had been shot down the same day that I had been in April 1965. And for more than seven and a half years, we had never been in contact with each other. Many lists of POW names that guys had were in shoot-down order, and some lists had me as number four and Scotty as number five, and other lists had the reverse. The first thing Scotty said to me was that he had wondered all those years who had been shot down first. I was shot down between 1 and 2 in the afternoon, and he was shot down about 3 in the afternoon. It was only a small thing, but it amazed us how we could be in the same prison system for so long and never have been in contact with each other. Several weeks later, when the Vietnamese realized that we were controllable with both rooms out together, we were allowed to cross the line.

Toward the end of October, we gleaned from the camp radio and the Voice of Vietnam that peace might be close at hand. We were hearing that negotiations were going well, and that they might end successfully. We only got the Vietnamese side of the news, but even that was extremely encouraging. Most people were optimistic, given our situation at that time. All things considered, it had never looked better than now. Dreams of returning to my family and starting my life again were in the forefront of my mind. Some guys suspected that the softening of the Vietnamese position on negotiations might have been a tactic on the part of the Vietnamese to favorably influence the election of George McGovern. We had heard on the radio and read in several American newspapers that McGovern's position on ending the war was to bring all the troops home as soon as possible.

They gave us a volleyball and a net, and the men were allowed to play. Eventually, all the new guys got out together for a period in the morning, and then all the old timers got out together at a later time in the morning. They brought in a Ping-Pong table. My old roommate Norlan Daughtrey, whose right elbow was disconnected from his arm bones, enjoyed playing. He didn't care about his arm. It just flapped around like a leaf in a breeze. But he was good. This improvement happened step by step. Finally, by early November, we were all outside together. Their confidence in us improved so much that they even let half of the rooms out one night in the courtyard to watch one of their war propaganda films. Those who did not want to go were allowed to stay in their rooms. We sat on the ground and watched. I remember how pleasant it was lying on my back and looking at the moon and stars in the sky on a perfectly clear night. It gave me a feeling of contentment and a sense of freedom. To see so many men out in the courtyard together when it was dark was an impressive sight.

Three other guys in the room liked to play bridge as much as I did: Jerry Marvel, Ted Kaufman, and John Pitchford. Sometimes, we played bridge seven or eight hours a day. Ted and I were partners, and Jerry and John played together. We played to 5000 points for a bottle of booze. Life went on as usual for the other men in the room. Capt. Ray Horinek lived in the room next to ours and was a real fun guy and a kibitzer. In early December, he had a birthday. Some of the men in our room who were his friends decided to give him a gift. They cut up an old piece of cloth, which some guy had donated, and made an oversized necktie out of it. They dyed the tie with blue ink and then painted a huge red penis and testicles on it. For the next week, whenever he was outside, he wore the tie. Everyone was amused. Maj. Bud Day, who was the SRO for room 6, appointed himself to the position of "Camp Masturbation Control Officer" and promptly promulgated policy on the subject. During quiet hour, it was permissible to have one hand under the blanket, but no more than one eye could be closed. It was also permissible to have two hands under the blanket, but both eyes had to be open.

During this same time frame, we received word from the camp radio that Jane Fonda, Ramsey Clark, and others were visiting the North Vietnamese in Hanoi. We knew that Jane Fonda had been anti-war, but most of us did not know much about Ramsey Clark. When we heard that he had been the Secretary of Treasury during President Johnson's administration, we were taken aback. The thought of someone having had a cabinet level position in the U.S. government and now visiting the enemy of the United States in their capitol city and giving them aid and comfort was almost impossible to believe. But there he was. We heard on the camp radio in great detail about their visit to bombed-out hospitals, dikes, dams, and other non-military targets. For most of us who had been prisoners for years, and who had seen how the Vietnamese lied, distorted the truth, and used propaganda to their advantage, we saw them as a couple of country bumpkins eating up the bullshit the Vietnamese were putting out.

One night, the camp radio came on early in the evening and played a tape supposedly of a talk or meeting that Jane Fonda had had with a large gathering of American servicemen outside an army base in New Jersey. From the sound of the noise in the background and the applause, there must have been at least several thousand men. The tape lasted for almost three-quarters of an hour, and it was all anti-war talk by Jane Fonda. She sang, talked, and made a pitch to the soldiers about the errors of their ways and how wrong the U.S. was in waging the war against the North Vietnamese. But what was unbelievable to most of us was the filthy and obscene language that she used when talking to the servicemen. She spoke words, phrases, and language as bad as I had ever heard on the back streets of New Jersey when I was growing up.

We continued our church service every Sunday. Nels Tanner was the chaplain and did a good job. He never gave a sermon, just quoted something from the bible. We sang a few hymns, said a few prayers, and that was the extent of our church services. I didn't think Tanner had any great religious leanings, but he felt someone had to do it. The atheists still remained politely away from the church group on Sunday morning. They never changed, even when times were hard. Some guys were not atheists but somewhat lazy, so they just stayed under their blankets when it was cold, or just listened to the service from their bed mats when the weather was warm.

From time to time, guys would have nightmares. Sam Johnson and Dale Osborne were the worst. When they started to yell, they woke up the whole room. Laird Gutterson was a light sleeper and was always the first to awaken. He always called the guy who was having the nightmare and tried to wake him up, but sometimes he made a mistake and woke up the wrong guy, who would promptly get irritated. The good treatment continued. We heard that Nixon had won the election, and then in November, we had a special broadcast on the camp radio. We were told that negotiations between the U.S. and the DRV had been completed, and things had been settled, except for a few minor details. Two or three high-ranking Vietnamese officers were outside our room, listening to us and awaiting our reaction, when we heard the good news. In retrospect, what we were told at that time was mostly accurate. With this news, even my hopes were raised again. After almost eight years of listening to the news, interpreting the signs and the behavior of the Vietnamese, and having my hopes of release raised and then crushed so many times, I had long since learned to ignore what was said on the radio and all other signs that might indicate the war was nearing the end. But now this news and the events of the past few months were so convincing that even I was somewhat optimistic. We all in differing degrees figured that this was it.

The perennial optimists packed their gear, stood at the door, and waited for the guard to open it and lead us to the buses. The next day, we heard essentially the same story on the radio again, but then halfway through the program, they told us that the U.S. had backed down on the whole thing. Everyone's hopes had been raised to great heights the day before, but now they were dashed again. For the next few weeks, we heard about why the agreement had broken down and the specific points of contention that still existed. One story circulated that the U.S. had instructed South Vietnam to disapprove the agreement. We heard about the problem of mutual withdrawal from South Vietnam by the U.S. and North Vietnam, and also the problem of replacing war material, as opposed to introducing new equipment. Although negotiations had broken down again, we felt that they had probably never been closer, and we were still somewhat optimistic, because the dialogue continued.

To add to the optimism, we were told that a dentist would be in camp in several days. I had had a wisdom tooth that had been bothering me for two and a half years. It ached now and then. I debated whether I should have it pulled. I remembered when I had a wisdom tooth pulled on an aircraft carrier in 1954. The tooth had been impacted, and the dentist had to chisel and split the tooth into pieces for more than an hour before he got it all out. Even with Novocain, it hurt. Could I endure the same thing here in Vietnam? Because it had been hurting so much, I decided I would take the gamble and have it pulled. When the time came, I left the room and went to the center of the courtyard, where there was a young Vietnamese man dressed in a dirty white dentist's coat, with a soiled white hat. I sat on a stool and told the interpreter which tooth hurt. The dentist–or the man posing as a dentist–signaled to me to open my mouth. He put the pliers in my mouth, took a good hold of the tooth, and then gave one hell of a yank. I felt like my jaw had come loose from my face. He showed me the tooth in his pliers. It stopped hurting immediately, only a little soreness. I returned to my room where my gum bled slightly for several hours and then stopped. Boy was I lucky!

In mid October, the North Vietnamese released three more prisoners: Maj. Edward Elias and Lt. Norris Charles, who had been shot down in 1972, and Lt. Mark Gartley, who had been there for about four years. Gartley had a reputation for being soft, but he was on the team and was supporting the U.S. government's position on the war and adhering to the policy of the camp leadership. His mother was an anti-war activist and had been invited to Hanoi to visit her son. His mother's presence in Hanoi created a difficult situation for him. He knew that the policy of the POW leadership was not to accept early release, but with his mother there, having convinced the North Vietnamese to release him, what was he to do? It couldn't have been an easy choice.

The news of the release of these men was in a newspaper they let us read with a statement by the Chairman of the Joint Chiefs of Staff, Adm. Thomas Moorer, in which he was quoted as saying, "It's great to have them home; we'll take them any way we can get them." This statement was not only evidence of his pessimism but indicated complete lack of understanding of prison-camp environment. It was a sign of great weakness, not only on the part of the whole U.S. military, but the nation as a whole, for him to agree that the enemy set the rules for release of the prisoners. The men had to swim or sink together in a prison camp. If the prisoners were allowed to accept early release on the terms of the enemy, we would have been at each other's throats fighting to be the first in line to go. The policy of the senior officer and the Code of Conduct was not to accept early release. And anyone who was senior to a man being released was obligated to disapprove it. I don't understand how any POW senior to anyone being released early could stand by and allow it.

Three or four men were going downtown to the war museum two or three nights each week, and the high command passed the word that we were to refuse to go, because of the potential propaganda that the DRV might get. Jim Kasler and I were told to dress up and get ready to leave the room one night. We suspected what it was, but we couldn't refuse to go if they said go. Our plan was that if they told us they were taking us to the war museum, we would refuse to go by just sitting down and making them lift us onto the truck.

We left the room and walked across the camp, through the tunnel next to Heartbreak and out into the courtyard in front of Heartbreak. There was a one-and-a-half-ton army truck waiting for us. I was the senior man, so I asked the officer where we were going, and he said to the war museum. I said, "I'm sorry we don't want to go." They said that we must go and told us to get into the back of the truck. We refused to get into the truck. The next thing I knew, four guys were pulling and pushing me toward the truck. The way they were tugging at me, I feared that my leg could be damaged. This was another situation where, by refusing to do something, the consequences were far worse for me than for someone who was un-injured. But I had been ordered to refuse to go, so that is what I intended to do. As the guards showed more resolve to get me on the truck, Jim Kasler, obviously realizing my predicament, said, "Fuck it let's go, it ain't worthwhile fighting." I was happy at what he said, because I was in complete agreement with him. Being the senior man, I couldn't be the guy to back down first, but Kasler took the pressure off of me. We looked around the museum for about an hour at their propaganda and then went back to the Hilton.

No bombing around Hanoi had occurred for the past three months, but on 18 December, all hell broke loose. We had finished our meal. I had played several hours of bridge and was sitting on the edge of my bed mat. It was dark outside already. Suddenly, we heard the sound of an aircraft at low altitude scream across the city, a second later, there was a bright red flash off in the distance, followed by the concussion from bombs detonating. A minute later, the air alert siren sounded, and the guards turned off the lights in the camp. The Vietnamese had been surprised again. A few minutes later, the lights in the camp came on again. Everyone was excited. No sooner had we concluded that the air war had begun again than we heard another aircraft come screaming over the city, followed by the bright red flash, the noise of the explosion, the concussion, the belated air raid siren alert, and the lights off. Now the lights did not come on, and every fifteen minutes to a half hour, another plane came screaming over the city at low altitude. We looked at this new kind of tactical bombing with some surprise. Although the U.S. had bombed the city of Hanoi at night before, it had never been so continuous as now. The low-altitude passes were something new, also. Hanoi was experiencing something that had not been done before. Despite the noise from the jet aircraft, the triple A, and the bombs, almost everyone was asleep after six or seven sorties.

In the middle of the night, we were awakened by many surface to air missiles being fired. The whole sky lit up for a few seconds. I heard the most deafening sound of my life and then a rumbling noise off in the distance. A few seconds later, the whole building shook from the concussion, and a small piece of plaster fell from the ceiling of the room. These bombs obviously were not being dropped by fighter aircraft. Because we could not hear the engines from the aircraft, we concluded that they were probably B-52's. Based on the time from the flash of the exploding bombs to the time the sound and concussion reached us, we estimated that the target was no more than several miles from the prison. At times, however, there were multiple flashes and concussion, and then it was impossible to get a good estimate. One guy would say the bombs were dropped 3,000 feet away, and another guy might say 10,000 feet away. They dropped the bombs in five or six waves over a ten- or fifteen-minute period. That night, they seemed to be bombing very close to us. The sky almost stayed red from the bombs exploding and subsequent fires on the ground. The SAMS made one hell of a racket, too.

Although I was happy that B-52's were hitting Hanoi with one hell of a wallop, I was somewhat frightened, and after the bombing stopped, I was relieved. I had dropped bombs on the wrong target one time, and a lot of other guys had done the same thing. Whether mistakes were made due to a mechanical malfunction in the aircraft or pilot error, I knew that the guys flying the 52's were human, also. Some of the guys who were prisoners now had been B-52 crewmen at one time, and they were as concerned as I was about the accuracy of the B-52's. Knowing these guys personally, I kept my fingers crossed during all the bombings. No doubt the B-52 crews had made every precaution not to hit our camp, but there was always that possibility.

About half an hour later, the same thing happened again. It was really exciting. This all happened on Monday night. The next night, the same thing happened, but this time the target was farther from us than the night before. Hearing the B-52 bombs dropping off in the distance was a pleasure. The raids this night seemed to last for about an hour. The next day, the Vietnamese brought some large planks about nine feet long, fifteen inches wide, and two and a half inches thick. They were heavy and strong. The Vietnamese had us lean them against the wall, so we could get under them for protection from the bombing. This was late December, and it was very cold, so it was unpleasant to have to get out of your warm covers and go sit on the cold floor under these boards when the B-52's came. Everyone just stayed under their blankets or stood by the door looking out into the sky. Once in a while, a guy would get caught, and the Vietnamese would raise hell. But most of the time, the guards were probably staying close to their shelter.

The B52 bombings around Hanoi continued for three more nights. I lay in bed each night waiting for the B-52's to come. Depending upon their location from Hanoi, sometimes I could hear the drone of the B-52's off in the distance, as they approached the target, but not knowing whether their target was close to our camp or far away. Sometimes the bombing started as early as midnight, but most of the time around it happened at 0300 or 0400. The reason for this was probably psychological, because if I had trouble going to sleep knowing it was unlikely the B-52's would hit us, everyone in Hanoi must have been very nervous about what was going on. The air alert sounded only once in a while now. Everyone in the city was being awakened and listening to the drone of the airplanes off in the distance and wondering where the bombs would fall tonight. The suspense in the air was thick. We could hear the bombs fall off in the distance. Then we would strain our ears, listening for the drone of the next wave to come. There were always four or five waves each night, and they were usually spread out over about an hour.

During this period, we were not allowed outside during the day. The Vietnamese said the water supply had been disrupted, and there was only enough water for cooking and drinking. We got rice now instead of bread. No one complained, however, because everyone's optimism was higher than it had ever been before. We were all ecstatic that President Nixon was finally doing what should have been done years ago. The guards seemed to maintain their cool during the day and showed no emotion toward us for what was going on. They were perhaps even indifferent to us. We suspected that they were like this because they knew they were really being plastered like they had never been hit before. They, like us, had become accustomed to the single engine jets dropping their bombs, but now one B-52 was dropping at one time what sixteen or eighteen F-105's all together could drop. When a flight of three B-52's dropped their bombs together within four or five miles, the sound was nothing like fireworks. It was more like twenty claps of the loudest thunder you have ever heard, all within several seconds.

Although the guards generally ignored the bombing, on the third night we heard a number of them clapping and cheering. Then the whole sky became bright red, and it stayed that way for well over five minutes. At first, we thought that there was going to be one hell of an explosion for something to light up the sky with such a bright color. Then we thought that perhaps the bombing had ignited a large ammo dump, but finally we realized that the bright red lighting the sky was from a B-52 that had been hit, and its burning wreckage was falling through the sky from probably above 40,000 feet. When the wreckage finally hit the ground, the light in the sky went out. I didn't envy those B52 crewmen who were flying right over the heart of the DRV and into the most heavily defended location in the world. The Vietnamese were shooting surface to air missies faster than I had ever heard them before. It was said that the B-52 crewmen were so tough that their balls hung below their knees.

The raids continued, with fighter aircraft during the day, especially during quiet hour. One day, there was an exceptionally long raid. Not continuous, but every five minutes, a plane or planes would attack. This went on for about an hour and a half. As usual, the air raid siren sounded, then we heard the triple A and SAMS being fired. We could hear the sound of the aircraft rolling in on their target and then the strain on the engine, as the aircraft pulled off. Halfway through the raid I fell asleep, because I had been up the night before for several hours during a B52 raid. I was abruptly awakened when I heard an aircraft rolling in on target especially close to where we were. It sounded like the plane was coming right at us. I had heard them come close before, but never like this.

Of course, we could not completely rely on the sound to determine the direction of the aircraft's run, because the wind could affect the sound considerably. But that day was different. A bomb landed so close that the blast shook the walls and roof of our room and knocked off large pieces of plaster from the ceiling. Smoke and dust filled the room. The explosion of the bomb was so loud that some men lost their hearing for several days. Later that day, when we were allowed out in the courtyard, one of the camp officers showed us a large piece of shrapnel, which had fallen inside the camp perimeter. It appeared to be the fin of a 500-pound bomb. The Vietnamese officer told us that the bomb had landed about seventy-five meters from our room. On another night, the sky again became a bright red but remained so for well over an hour. We later found out from the Thais that a large-tire storage area was burning.

There was no bombing by the B-52's on the nights of Christmas Eve and Christmas. We had been planning a Christmas program, as usual. The Vietnamese even offered to allow the men in our room and one of the other rooms to decorate room 7 together. This room was empty and the largest room in camp. The room leadership rejected this offer, because it was probably an attempt by them to get some propaganda from us. We had our own Christmas show already planned.

This Christmas was probably the most pleasant we ever had in North Vietnam. The Christmas goodies were outstanding. In fact, for the past three or four months, the food had been considerably better than ever before. They brought us two books for Christmas. One was the Bible, and the other was a Russian book translated into English. It was titled *The Macro/Micro World*. The Macro part was about astronomy, and the Micro world about atoms, molecules, etc. Although it was quite advanced, it was written for the layman. Both the Bible and the Russian science book were popular, and everyone wanted to read them. We were told we had to return them in a week, so guys took turns reading the books out loud, permitting a large group to listen at the same time. In addition, on Christmas night, they brought us a good Russian movie about a circus. The dialogue was in Russian, the film was in color, there was no propaganda, and the story was quite entertaining.

For the first time, most people had almost all they wanted to eat, and there was always some food left over. Not meat, but soup, vegetables, or bread. At this time, about half of the men in the room were so optimistic about release that they used a tape measure on their waists every morning. Some of us had probably never been in better shape in our entire lives.

We had been getting some Russian canned fish for one meal a week for the past several months. In reality, it was junk fish, but compared to what we had had for the past several years, it was a real treat, even though some of the guys would have no part of it. Some would prefer to have a bowl of sugar. Considerable food swapping was going on. Most everyone had a buy-sell price for any item of food he got. Several months back, Marine Lt. Larry Friese had decided he wanted to have a good time over Christmas. Every year since we became prisoners, the Vietnamese had always brought us at least a half bottle of beer per man for our Christmas dinner. Larry had traded all of his fish, sugar, and whatever else anyone would trade for their Christmas beer. And the trade was for the ration, whether it was half a beer or a full one. Some of us thought Larry was crazy. He managed to make trades with eleven guys.

Larry had a huge grin on his face when Christmas day arrived, and the ration was a full bottle of beer per man. Everyone ate their meal by their bed mat as usual, and those who had not traded their beer drank it with their dinner. Larry took the eleven bottles of beer that he had traded for and his own ration of one, went over to the most remote corner in the room, sat down on the floor, and proceeded to polish off the twelve bottles of beer. No one paid any attention to him, but two and a half hours later, when the guard came to open the door after quiet hour, to pick up the beer bottles, and to let the duty section out to wash the dishes, Larry had a bright red glow all over his face, and his mouth was just filled with smiles and giggles. He was really feeling good.

The bombing began again the day after Christmas. Although we were getting the radio regularly and hearing all about the B-52 losses, the names of the B-52 crewmen and their press conferences, we did not know precisely what had triggered the massive bombing of the North. For the next five or six days, the bombing continued. On New Year's Eve, it stopped for good. We continued to get fragments of news on the radio about Le Duc Tho, their chief negotiator going here and there and meeting with Kissinger. Then the news about negotiations stopped. Everyone was optimistic about the radio silence, as we waited impatiently for more news about what was going on.

In the early winter of 1970, when I had moved into room 5, the Vietnamese had been building a large tower outside the prison walls. It was probably 250 feet high when it was finished, and apparently it was a radio tower of some sort. We could see the red warning lights on top of the tower through our window in room 5. The lights were on every night until the air war began in late 1971, at which time they were turned off and remained so. Ned Shuman was telling everyone now that we would know we were going home when the red lights on top of the radio tower came on again.

Lt. Col. Jim Lamar moved into our room in mid-January, and Maj. Larry Guarino moved out. Jim had been an early shoot down so it was strange to have him in the room. He pretty much continued the policies that had been established before, with the addition of passing out rules and regulations about what we should say if asked questions by the media after our release. The high command had provided us with considerable guidance on how to conduct ourselves on release. Some of it was worthwhile, like we were to go home in order of shoot down, and the first guys to be released were not to talk to the press about the bad treatment we received until the last guys shot down were released. Most of the other stuff went in one ear and out the other.

One night during the last week of January, there was a big camp-wide move, and guys who had been shot down in more or less the same time frame were moved into rooms together. They even brought back all of the young guys who had been moved from the camp more than a year ago. Everyone's morale was really up in the sky now, and it was fun to meet guys who had been shot down in the same time frame as I was and who had lived in buildings with, had communicated with, but never met. I was in room 2, and Jim Lamar remained as the SRO. The other 05's and 06's still remained separated from the rest of the group. We had been getting optimistic news on the camp radio, but nothing for sure to really let us know that the war was over.

Then on Monday, several days after the camp-wide move, we were allowed out of our room with the guys in the room next to us and told to stand in a formation of three lines. The camp commander through an interpreter said that the war had ended, that an agreement had been reached, and that he would read the agreement to us. He read the agreement paragraph by paragraph in Vietnamese and Spot, one of the English-speaking officers, read it in English. It took about twenty minutes. There were no loud cheers or wild gestures. Everyone stood listening quietly and unemotional, thankful that it was finally over, but not completely believing that the end had come. We were restraining ourselves, trying not to get too excited, because we still weren't home free.

The guards passed out about twenty copies of the agreements to the men as we broke formation and returned to our rooms. Everyone had a happy face when we returned to our room, but there were no wild cheers or hoopla. We went about our business as usual. Everyone in this room had had his hopes raised dozens of times over the years, only to see them dashed. Although things had never looked better, most of us were just holding our breath until the day we would actually be released. On several occasions, a high-ranking officer came to our door and talked to us. We tried to find out exactly when we would go home, but he never gave us a specific date. For the next two days, Lt. Col. Lamar received more instructions from the high command about preparations for going home. That same night, someone looking out the window noticed that the red lights on top of the 250-foot radio antenna tower were on again. Shuman had guessed right.

CHAPTER 26 -
SICK, WOUNDED, AND INJURED

NEW GUY VILLAGE, HANOI HILTON

There were rooms on the left side of the courtyard, and this new tree replaced an older one.

January 1973 – 12 February 1973. Several days after I had moved into room 2, I moved again, this time into New Guy Village. More than seven years had passed since I lived there, but it was still basically the same, except that the rooms along the prison wall were being used for American prisoners instead of Vietnamese prisoners. About twenty other guys moved into the area with me. We were the sick, wounded, and injured, and in accordance with the Paris Peace Accords of 1973 on ending the war in Vietnam, we were to be the first group released, followed by POWs in the order they had been shot down. Three seriously injured B-52 crewmen and two healthy B-52 crewmen who were taking care of them had been moved to that area several days before we arrived. I was the senior man in the group. We moved into rooms in groups of four or five.

In the group were three men who, by our standards, could not be considered sick, wounded, or injured, and these guys knew it. After I discussed the situation with these men, they agreed to ask to be removed from the group. At the first opportunity, they asked the Vietnamese to be removed from the group, and their request was granted by the camp authorities. Also in the group were a few other guys who I did not consider sick, wounded, or injured, but they thought they were, so I made no issue about it. At the same time, at least six other men that I knew should have been included in the group had been overlooked by the Vietnamese. I told the Vietnamese about this, and later that day the six guys were all moved in. In my case, as with several others, whether I was with the sick, wounded, and injured group or was released in order of shoot down wouldn't have made any difference. I was going to be in the first plane, because I had been the fourth man shot down.

For the guys who would not have been in the first release, and who were in need of medical attention, it was important that they be included in the sick, wounded, and injured group. Except for the three B-52 crewmen who were in dire need of medical care, it was not a matter of life or death for the rest of us. If the peace process had broken down for any length of time after the first release, however, by humanitarian standards this group deserved to go first because they were all in need of various amounts of medical attention.

The three B-52 crewmen had an assortment of injuries, and after nearly a month in captivity, none of them had improved. They were in adjacent rooms with a door between them. Two guys were in beds next to each other in one room, and the third was in the other room with the two injured but not bedridden B-52 crewmen. When I entered the room the first time, I recognized an odor that had come from the open wound in my leg and from Norlan Daughtrey's open wound. The smell of the drainage from the unchanged bandage was enough to make you gag, but the guys who were wounded had long since become accustomed to it, because they lay in the stench all day.

Lt. Klomann had a broken leg and remained flat on his back twenty-four hours a day. He must have had a head injury, too, because he just lay there in a semi-conscious state and rarely ever said a word. The other men, Sgt. James Cook and Sgt. Roy Madden, had broken legs, too. Sgt. Cook remained delirious most of the time and rambled on in conversation. Both he and Klomann had huge holes at the bases of their spines. When I saw this, I couldn't believe the holes were so big: at least six inches in diameter and a half inch deep. At first, the holes seemed to be the major problems, rather than the broken legs, but they were nothing more than bedsores from lying flat on their backs all the time on the wooden bed boards. Sgt. Madden had a break in his upper leg, which was so close to the hip that they could not put a cast on it. Although he could not walk, he was able to sit up and move on his side, so he had no bedsores.

The day we moved in, the men were divided into two medical teams. I appointed my old friends A.J. Meyers and Quincy Collins as head of the teams. They rotated each day, and each team took turns standing watch over these guys twenty-four hours a day, to help them. Although the Vietnamese medics came every day to treat them, we were at their mercy, because we had little or no medical training and had no medicine. But we had one of our guys ready to help the patients with whatever we could do around the clock. This entailed feeding them, helping them with their toilet problems, and just helping any way we could.

I was frustrated watching these three men over the next two weeks. I pleaded every day to have them taken to a hospital, where they would at least have hospital beds and treatment by doctors and nurses, rather than the camp medics, who were obviously not well trained. The war was over. Why they didn't give these guys better medical treatment was beyond me. There were some prisoners with injuries far less serious than these guys that had been hospitalized for as long as a month or more. A hospital bed might have made a difference, but maybe the B-52 bombing caused all of the hospitals to be full. At any rate, my pleas went unanswered.

One morning several medics came to check on the wounded men. When they took the bandage off Madden's leg, we could see the bone sticking out of the flesh. They decided to set the bone. They carried him out into the courtyard and laid him on the ground, then they tied a piece of heavy rope around the ankle of his broken leg. Two men grabbed his shoulders, and another pulled the foot away from his body with the rope, hoping that the bones in his upper leg would line up together as he lay on the ground. As we watched the Vietnamese pull the foot, Madden screamed, and it made us all sick. It was obviously medicine in its most rudimentary form. Unfortunately, we could not offer anything better. And we did not even know if what the Vietnamese were doing to him might be causing more harm than good. We just hoped that these guys could get back home soon as possible.

Sgt. Cook, who was delirious most of the time, was from Georgia. He was shot down 26 December 1972. The co-pilot of the B-52, Bob Hudson, wrote this about him: The night we got bagged, as we taxied out our gunner got ill. I called for a replacement and was told we would get one before takeoff. At takeoff time a truck pulled up and a guy ran to the back of the plane (B-52 gunner sat in the rear). Cook came over the intercom and says I am ready. The crew never introduced themselves to him or got his name. We got hit after we dropped 108 bombs on the target. The first SAM killed the pilot of the plane. I ordered all to bailout. The nose pitched violently up so I assumed our gunner had jumped. I found out later that Cook had been knocked unconscious, got tangled up in his equipment and rode the plane down until a fourth SAM hit the aircraft around 20,000 feet and blew him from the "Buff," (Big Ugly Fat Fucker) affectionately called by B-52 airmen. Fortunately, his barometrically controlled parachute functioned properly and opened up at 14,000 feet and he was still unconscious when he hit the ground. He lost one leg below the knee shortly after release and the other leg about one year later. The co-pilot says his gunner's name was Papa Jim Cook, one of the bravest men I ever met.

I roomed with Fred Cherry, Render Crayton, Norlan Daughtrey, and John Pitchford, and we played bridge every night. The food improved, and we had virtually all the fruit we wanted. We got either canned garbage fish from Russia every day or a new kind of canned meat similar to Spam. Some of the guys got packages from home soon after we moved in. They were obviously old packages being passed out now to fatten us up. We had so much food that we could not eat it all.

Soon after we moved in, we set up a communications team, but we were so remote from the other part of the camp that it did us no good. We were receiving notes in our food, however. Starting in late November, the prisoners assisted in the preparation of the food. The communications team prepared notes and inserted them in plastic and then inserted each note in a string bean, potatoes, or any other piece of food that would act as a carrier. We had to examine our food closely before we ate it. We got some information off and on from Lt. Col. Jim Lamar on policy for going home, including how to act, what we could wear, etc.

Eugene Weaver, a CIA employee, moved into our building about three rooms down from our last room. The rooms in between were empty, and the door to his room opened on the opposite side of the building from where our door opened. We talked out the back window to him. We passed nothing secret between us, but he openly admitted he was from the CIA, so the Vietnamese apparently knew about his background, as well. We had never heard of him before and were surprised to find out how many other American prisoners about whom we knew nothing were in the North. Also, about one week after we moved into New Guy Village, Lt. Cdr. Phillip Kientzler moved into a room next to Weaver. Kientzler was shot down on 27 January, the day the agreements were signed. The Vietnamese apparently wanted to punish him a bit before they released him, so they kept him in solitary. It was no secret that we were talking out the back window to Kienzler and Weaver. So every day I asked the Vietnamese if they would allow those two guys to move in with us, or at least join us outside every day. But they refused.

The condition of the wounded B-52 crewmen remained unchanged the entire time we were in New Guy Village, despite the fact that we had as much food as we could eat, good vitamin pills, and even protein pills. Although two of the men were not all there mentally, they ate moderately well. Sgt. Madden, who had been a tail gunner on a B-52, however, was not eating very much. Although he was the guy whose leg the Vietnamese medics had tried to set by pulling the foot, he did not appear to be as bad off as the other two, because he had all of his mental faculties and appeared to be in good spirits. At any rate, he needed all the food he could get. We tried everything we could think of to influence him to eat, but he kept saying he wasn't hungry. I learned months later that the doctors in the U.S. had to amputate his leg because gangrene had set in. I felt really bad about it, because maybe in some way I had failed him. Maybe we should have force fed him or pressured him more to eat.

The good treatment continued. Although every day we heard on the radio of a multitude of problems that had arisen since the signing of the agreement, our optimism remained quite high. But we stayed somewhat cautious. Three days before the date of our scheduled release, which was fifteen days after the signing of the agreement, five new men moved into our compound. There were three junior officers, who had been shot down after the air war started again in 1971, and the other men introduced themselves as Cdr. Gene Wilbur and Lt. Col. Ed Miller. This was a shock. These guys had the worst reputations in the camp. They were said to have made numerous propaganda tapes for the Vietnamese, visited numerous delegations, accepted special favors, and for all practical purposes, gone over to the enemy's side. The senior ranking officer had warned them and threatened them about their conduct, and they continued to flagrantly violate the Code of Conduct and his direct orders. Rumor had it that they had participated in the torture of other prisoners and given prisoners' secrets to the Vietnamese. On top of all this, they had been given the opportunity to be forgiven for all of their bad conduct, if they would just join with the rest of us for the remainder of the time they were there. This was in accordance with a high command policy that we did not drag a repentant sinner to his grave. The Vietnamese told us that the new guys would live with us until we were released. The five of them were moved together into one of the vacant rooms.

As soon as the new men left our presence, three or four men from my group became upset. Everyone became involved in a heated discussion as to how this problem should be resolved. Within several hours, the position of our group had solidified: These guys should not be included in our group and released with us. In the first place, none of them was sick, wounded, or injured, nor were they shot down early in the war. Therefore, in accordance with the agreement on ending the war, they were not to be included in our group. Besides, if they were in the first group to be released, and their statements in support of the North Vietnamese war effort were among the first reports that the American public heard about our experience, it would not be fair to the other 99.999 percent of the prisoner who had not behaved the way this pair did.

The decision to have them move out of our group was an easy one, but how it should be done was more complicated and open to considerable debate. It became obvious that I couldn't handle this problem by discussing it with the entire group. So I met with Lt. Cdr. Render Crayton and Maj. Fred Cherry, who were the next two junior to me. We decided that the five new guys would have to voluntarily make every effort to be removed from the group, and if the Vietnamese refused to remove them from the group, then they would have to agree to obey all of the guidance and policy of Col. Flynn, and obey all my orders. If they did not agree to my conditions, then as previously agreed to by my group, all of the sick, wounded, and injured men would refuse release. This was not an easy decision. A.J. Meyers had walked painfully on the side of his ankle for years. Norlan Daughtrey had a shattered right elbow. John Pitchford had a useless left arm where he had been shot. Dale Osborne had a crippled right arm three inches shorter than his left arm. Two men had eating disorders and were as thin as rails. Another had a bleeding ulcer, and two or three men had severe cases of asthma. Ten other men were just as bad. And for the B-52 men, it was a matter of life and death. All of these men needed immediate medical attention. Nonetheless, every sick, wounded, and injured guy agreed to the proposal. If Wilbur and Miller had not agreed to my demands, then the sick, wounded and injured guys would have undoubtedly refused release. I would not, however, have kept the B-52 crewmen back, because they were in such bad physical condition.

The next morning, with Render Crayton and Fred Cherry at my side, I called in each of the five men individually and told them what had been decided. I told them everyone here except their group had tried to follow the Code of Conduct to the best of his ability. We felt that it was not right for Wilbur and Miller to go home in the first plane and possibly have the opportunity to misrepresent to the press and the free world what the rest of us had suffered for and stood for. I had no doubt that they could not refuse my ultimatum. They all accepted it. In addition, they had to agree to make no statements whatsoever until in the hands of the U.S. government authorities. Lt. Col. Miller didn't like what he heard, but he agreed to what I told him. He said he would not cause me any problems, but that he was senior to me and therefore not subject to my orders. I told him that he had been relieved of command by the SRO, and that he was subject to my orders. He still maintained that he was senior to me but said that he would not cause any difficulties. The others all agreed without any fuss.

The same morning I asked to see the camp commander and my request was granted. I told him the men were upset about Wilbur and Miller joining our group, because they were not supposed to be there in accordance with the already agreed upon Paris Peace Accords. He told me that there was nothing I could do about it, because his government and mine had already decided on it, and Wilbur and Miller would go home with our group. I asked how our governments could agree to something contrary to what had already been written and agreed upon. He said, "It has been decided, and that's it." Then he angrily sent me back to my room.

When I returned from the quiz, I told everyone what had been said. No one was pleased about what had happened, but there wasn't much else that we could do. Later that morning, I talked with Wilbur and Miller together, and they told me that when the Vietnamese informed them they would join our group, they had asked that it not be done. But they said the Vietnamese had forced them to join us. Later that morning, our officer in charge came into our compound, and both Wilbur and Miller went over to talk to him. Although we did not stand right next to them, they were in full view and could be heard by all of us. They both made as reasonably a strong request as possible to be removed from the group. But their request was again angrily denied on the spot. This act on their part was somewhat reassuring to the rest of us. We didn't want them with us, but they tried to leave, so that was at least an act of good faith on their part. There was a limit to what we could make the Vietnamese do. They were still the boss.

My major concern now was whether they would keep quiet about their views on the war until they were in the hands of our military authorities. I had envisioned both of them being handcuffed by the military police and separated from the rest of us as soon as we came under U.S. military control. At that time, my problems would finally be over. Reporters might meet us on arrival at our first stop, and Wilbur and Miller could give their views on the war. My fears were somewhat alleviated, however, after I talked to Wilbur and Miller for several hours that afternoon. Although I'd heard rumors that they had participated in the torture of U.S. prisoners and given POW secrets to the Vietnamese, I believed that these rumors were probably not true. I would not swear one way or the other, but after talking to them for a while, I got the feeling that they weren't the kind of men who would resort to behavior that base. It was just a feeling I had about them.

One thing was for certain, however. They had bought the Vietnamese version of the war, and as best I could tell, their behavior had apparently been completely voluntary. They didn't say, but I suspected that the Vietnamese got to these guys at the right time, and Wilbur and Miller bought their propaganda, and now they honestly believed the war was morally and ethically wrong, in the same way that McGovern, Fulbright, Morse, Spock, and others like them opposed the war. They were not the only guys who had fallen for the Vietnamese propaganda hook, line, and sinker. At the same time, their behavior could have resulted from their being afraid of the Vietnamese. Perhaps they were gutless, and they had done it for personal gain and better treatment for themselves, or it could have been a combination of factors.

Miller and Wilbur could have been forgiven for their behavior in accordance with the high command policy of not dragging a repentant sinner to his grave, and they were afforded the opportunity to be forgiven. But maybe they didn't really trust what Col. Flynn said about the forgiven thing, because they never got into the communications chain and, therefore, never really knew what had gone on over the years. Maybe they couldn't accept the forgiveness, because they had gone too far, and accepting the forgiveness would have been an admission that what they had done was a result of their weakness. But to continue in their opposition to the war on an intellectual and moral basis was the only hope they had to come out of this situation with some semblance of self-respect. They had to hope that punitive action would not be taken against them. Although I personally disagreed strongly with their anti-war views, I figured that both Wilbur and Miller still had a sense of honor as military men, and when they gave me their word that they would obey all of the orders of the high command, as well as my own, I believed them.

Twelve men had accepted early release, but their behavior was obviously self-serving, rather than from any sense of dedication to a higher belief as Wilbur and Miller had. Nonetheless, the conduct of Wilbur and Miller and the twelve men who were released could not be condoned. They could make excuses forever, but the fact was that once a man joined the military, he was obligated to defend the position of his government and show allegiance to it while he remained in the military. There might be examples where there should be exceptions to the rule, but if military men were ever allowed to choose when and where there should be an exception, there would be chaos in the military. Given the alternative, a military man must be bound to support his commander in chief at all times or pay the consequences.

The signs remained basically good up to the night before our release, but the radio broadcast evidence of small problems, such as accusations of the U.S. violating the agreement. Much was said about the monetary payoff to the DRV for reconstruction and to heal the wounds of war, but that payoff sounded like nothing more than a ransom to get the POWs released. They talked about Kissinger having to come to Hanoi to bring the money, and then we heard that he had come and left the day before our release.

On my last full day in Vietnam, I had a quiz with the Fox. At first, he talked about the war and how the Vietnamese had won. He said because the U.S. troops were now withdrawn from all of Vietnam, it would be just a matter of time before Vietnam would be one. I said, "If that's what you believe, that's okay by me." I wasn't in any mood to have an argument. Then he made threats about what would happen to me if I slandered the DRV after I was released. He said, "When you are released, don't think you are home free. There are many things we can still do, and if you tell lies about your treatment, we can slander you far beyond what you can do to us." The thought that they might keep me behind if I said the wrong thing entered my mind, but I found it hard to believe that after the signing of the Paris Peace Accords they would try any hanky panky like that, so I told him that when I came home, all I would do was tell the truth, and that seemed to satisfy him. In their eyes, their treatment of us was lenient and humane, whereas our view was the opposite.

After the threats, he reached behind him and put a gold wedding ring on the table and told me it was mine. I was quite surprised. I wasn't sure whether it was really mine, but I had had a gold ring that looked like it. There were no initials on the inside of the ring, and I couldn't remember whether my wife had had the ring initialed, but it fit my finger quite well, so I took it. The little boy who had pulled it off my finger almost eight years before must have given it to the authorities, or it was taken from him, and they kept it over the years. I thanked the Fox for it. He told me that I could leave. As I was going, he asked, "Why are all American rings size 14K?" I told him that to fly a plane, you had to have a size 14 finger.

The night before our release, each room went down to Heartbreak South, which was a room directly across from Heartbreak, itself. Clothes were piled all over the room. I found a pair of pants, a dress shirt, a wind beaker, and some underwear. There were shoes on the floor, but because I could use only one, I decided I would just wear the shower shoe they had given me years before.

The time for release was clearly coming close. They still hadn't said for sure that we would leave the next day, but from what we read in the agreement and what we heard on the radio, we figured tomorrow was probably the day. That night, we stayed up late. We had coffee from our packages, all the cigarettes we could smoke, and cans of Spam-like meat from Russia. We were excited and talked about how the release would take place. For the past week, men had been talking and joking about how their homecoming would be. We did not get much sleep that night.

We got up a little earlier than usual the next morning. The guard came to our door and told us to put on our civilian clothes. We got a piece of bread and some milk for breakfast. At around 0700, they told us to fall in out in the courtyard by date of shoot down. In my case, this worked out fine, because I was the first in the group and also the senior man. The high command had said that we were not to take anything home, because of the propaganda value that the Vietnamese might get. Some guys said the hell with that policy and brought a few souvenirs, such as cigarettes and old clothing. I cheated too. I brought two packs of cigarettes, the cigarette holder I had made, and a copy of the current camp regulations. Fred Cherry was offered all kinds of different Vietnamese works of art the day before we left, but he refused.

We marched out of New Guy Village by twos, through the courtyard outside Heartbreak, and then through the main gate of the prison. I felt wonderful. Outside the main gate, many buses were lined up along the sidewalk, and some were already filled with prisoners. We got to our bus and were allowed to sit anywhere. It was the first time in nearly eight years that I was outside the prison in the daytime without a blindfold, and it felt good. I looked at the prison wall, and it didn't look anything like I had imagined. I saw the building across the street, where guys had been taken in 1966 and tortured after the Hanoi March. The sidewalk was lined with Vietnamese people. They just stood there and stared at us. They exhibited no animosity toward us whatsoever. Then the buses started, and we drove in a long line through the city. People along the road waved and cheered as we went by. I had been driven through the city on numerous occasions, but always blindfolded. I had always heard the sounds of many people, a train, cars, trucks, and the trolley, and I'd had to visualize what it must look like. Now I could see it. People were all over the place, wherever we drove. I thought we would never have won this war if we had continued to fight the way we had before the B-52 bombing, because they had unlimited manpower. They had an inexhaustible supply of human beings. The only way to get them to bend was to take the stand we did with the B-52s and really show them some of the power and might of the U.S.

As we drove through the city, I felt great to experience freedom again. We crossed the Red River on a pontoon bridge. The river was low. We could see the precautions they had taken to prevent flooding from the river in the rainy season, with sandbags piled on their dikes. I could see the famous Lon Bin Bridge that I had read and heard about for many years. Two sections had been knocked down. When we reached the other side of the river, we could see large bomb craters scattered about. They obviously kept us away from the areas that had been most heavily bombed. When we got to the other side of the river, we were in the country. Rice paddies stretched as far as the eye could see. I found it fascinating to actually see the country I had lived in and heard about for nearly eight years, but had never seen close up before.

Finally, we arrived at the airport. We got out of the bus and fell in formation again. We marched two by two into a waiting room in the main terminal. Five or six buses had carried the first group of men to be released at the airport. The men had been divided into three groups and placed in separate waiting rooms. We were not allowed to go from one room to another, but we could talk to the men in the other rooms through a door. I talked to Col. Risner and informed him of the situation with Wilbur and Miller. He didn't seem very excited over what I told him. He seemed like he couldn't have cared less. But now I was off the hook with those guys, and I didn't give a hoot what happened to them either. I was on my way home to the good old U.S.A. We were given bottles of beer and pig fat sandwiches. They obviously were trying to impress us, but that was the best they could come up with. No one ate a thing. We waited about half an hour, and finally my group was told to get into the bus. We drove to the other side of the airport.

We could see two U.S. Air Force C-141 aircraft parked on the ramp, with the back part of the planes open. The bus stopped on the ramp, and we all climbed out. We got into formation again, and we were told to march up to where a large group of people stood about fifty yards away. As we marched along, we passed what seemed like at least forty or fifty photographers taking pictures of us. I saw an Air Force colonel who appeared to be in charge of the release for the American side. I stopped the group, walked up to the colonel on my crutches, saluted him, and said, "I report the return to the control of the United States, the sick, wounded, and injured group." The colonel saluted back and shook my hand. Then a U.S. civilian came over and introduced himself as Roger Shields from the Department of Defense, in charge of the Homecoming. I asked him how everything was, and he said, "You look great." We continued our march to the release point. Just before we got there, George Harris broke ranks and ran over to the colonel all by himself, saluted, and shook his hand. I yelled at him to get back into ranks. He had been told that we were to remain in a military formation, in order and with discipline during the release, and not as a group of undisciplined men. I knew George was emotional and excited, as all of us were, but what he did was wrong. After a few seconds, George returned to the formation, and we continued to march. Scotty Morgan, who was number 5 in order of shoot down, was by my side. As I approached the group of people ahead of us, I felt a swell of emotion come over me, and I told Scotty, "I'm going to cry. I can't hold it." But things were happening so fast, the feeling went away and fast as it had come. I was now beginning to believe that it was all over, and finally I was going home. When we got to the release point, hundreds of people crowded around, and many photographers were taking pictures. A guy put a microphone near us, so they might hear anything we said. But none of us said a word.

An imaginary line marked the release point, and on the left of the line stood the Rabbit, with a large group of Vietnamese people standing behind him. When we finally reached the line, we stopped. Then the Rabbit said, "Lt. Cdr. Raymond Vohden, shot down April 3, 1965." He indicated that I should walk across the line. I walked about four steps. Two Air Force colonels were standing there to accept my release. I saluted them and said, "I report my return to the custody of the United States." I was the first prisoner to cross the line and the first to be honorably released from Hanoi. I was very happy now. It seemed surreal, but I was truly on my way home.

The C-141 was about fifty yards away. It was the most beautiful plane I had ever seen in my life. As I walked away from the release point toward the plane, Roger Shields joined me. I told him immediately about the problem we had with Wilbur and Miller. I wasn't sure that Risner, Denton, and Guarino would be on the same plane. Although I felt reasonably sure that Wilbur and Miller would conform to the guidance and orders I had given them, I wasn't absolutely sure. He took in everything that I told him, but I was not sure he really understood our concern. I think he was just happy to get us back. Shields was pleasant. He told me that I had done a great job and said how glad he was to see us, as we walked towards the plane. As we approached the back ramp of the plane, some Air Force nurses came to greet me. When they saw me on crutches, they tried to help me walk up the ramp, but I didn't need or want any help. After walking on crutches for seven and a half years, I had become pretty good at it. They were perfectly dressed in their clean white uniforms. I had never seen women look so good in my whole life. In a few minutes, they brought me some U.S. made crutches. After walking on crutches without any padding for all this time, I really felt great to have crutches with padding on the armrests.

The aircraft had a fresh clean odor and already reminded me of the United States. The flight medics asked me if I wanted to lie down on one of the cots. I told them, "Hell, no." There were even clean white sheets on the cots. I wasn't on the plane for a half a minute, when a stewardess brought me a chocolate milkshake. It tasted unbelievably good. Then the other guys started to come aboard the plane, and everyone was talking, and excitement prevailed. Finally the plane was full, everyone was seated, we taxied out to the runway, and took off. We were going home. I still couldn't believe that this was actually happening to me. It was like a dream. Like the dream I'd had that I wasn't really a prisoner.

I finally met a few guys whom I knew but had never seen before. Larry Guarino was there, and I met Cdr. Denton personally for the first time. Since he was the senior man on the plane, I immediately informed him of the situation with Wilbur and Miller. They apparently were not going to be a problem. Shields gave us an idea of what would happen when we arrived at Clark Air Force Base in the Philippines, and it sounded like fun. Denton was in the process of writing a speech to give on our arrival. He asked others around him what we thought of his of speech, and it sounded good to all of us.

There were all the cigarettes I wanted, and I couldn't believe how good an American cigarette tasted. Because I had never smoked before I was shot down, I found it interesting to try the different brands that were available. They were all far better than what I had smoked in Vietnam. I talked to Roger Shields again, and he told me that he was in charge of the POW/MIA Organization in the Department of Defense.

We continued our flight. There were cups of coffee, milkshakes, cigarettes, ice cream, sandwiches, and all kinds of good things to eat. I looked out the window and could see white fleecy clouds and the ocean below us. One half hour out of Clark, we started our descent. The landing was normal, and the plane taxied in toward the ramp. We could see a large group of people waiting for our arrival. I couldn't believe so many people were out there. I never thought that it was going to be like this. The plane finally stopped, and we were told to leave in order of shoot down. Apparently each man's name would be announced over the loudspeaker as we left the plane, but the people on the ground didn't have the accurate release order. So we had a few minutes delay while that was straightened out.

A lot of the names were not correctly announced. The wounded men who had been on stretchers went off the back of the plane. We were all standing in line, and Bob Shumaker, who was the number two man shot down, asked me if I was sure that I didn't want go off the back of the plane, because the stairs might be dangerous. I said, "Hell, no. I'm going off the front, just like everybody else. I've walked up and down flights of stairs on crutches blindfolded, waited this long, I'm going to meet the people just like the rest of you guys." Denton went out first and made his speech. Then Alvarez, Shumaker, Lockhart, and I. Some guy tried to help me walk down the steps, but I didn't need his help. Once on the ground I walked on a red carpet, saluted and shook hands with an admiral and an Air Force general, saluted the American flag, and then went to a waiting bus. The whole thing was over in a few seconds. Those few seconds, however, were exhilarating. It was nice to be in the spotlight briefly and experience a little glory and appreciation for the eight years I had spent in Hanoi. And I was on my way home at last.

APPENDIX A:
CHRONOLOGY OF
NORTH VIETNAM POW HISTORY

5 August 1964 – First POW is captured.

1965-1973 – Hanoi Hilton is main POW prison in North Vietnam. All POWs are processed through this prison.

September 1965 – Camp Zoo opens. The Zoo is the major camp through September 1969. Other camps open and close through 1972.

29 June 1966 – First targets near Hanoi are bombed.

6 July 1966 – Fifty-two POWs are marched through Hanoi streets amidst violent throngs.

Spring 1967 – Camp Plantation opens. *Honor Bound* states, "Hanoi reaped substantial gains from ushering dignitaries and reporters through the camp, worldwide dissemination of Pilots in Pajamas and the early release of 12 POWs."

1 November 1968 – Rolling Thunder ends. Bombing halt lasts three and a half years, until April 1972. Only thirteen new POWs are captured in the north during this period.

10 May 1969 – Two men are recaptured within hours of escaping from the Zoo Annex. One of the men dies from punishment. Terror and torture are rampant throughout the entire POW population in

all camps in an effort to stem further attempts of escape, which in any case is impossible for westerners with no clothing or footwear. Prison life is set back years.

September 1969 – Ho Chi Minh dies. Treatment gradually improves throughout entire POW population. Torture essentially ends. The reason for improvement is debatable.

July – September 1969 – About 220 POWs are moved to Camp Faith in four compounds. Most POWs go from one- or two-man rooms to rooms holding five or more men. Isolation in individual compounds is eliminated at Camp Faith.

20 November 1969 – Fifty-nine men fly from Thailand to an empty Camp Sontay in an unsuccessful attempt to rescue POWs.

24 November 1969 – Unintended consequence of Sontay raid is that most of the POWs are moved to Hanoi Hilton in large 45- to 60-men rooms to avert further rescue attempts.

January 1970 – December 1972 – POWs wait for the war to end.

April 1972 – Limited bombing of Hanoi starts again in response to the North Vietnamese 1972 Easter offensive.

December 1972 – B-52s bomb Hanoi.

28 January 1973 – Paris Peace Accords to End War are signed.

12 February 1973 – First POWs are released.

APPENDIX B: COMMUNICATIONS

Communication was the most important part of the POW experience. If a man is isolated, he has no idea what is going on. This makes his situation far worse than it already is. It was not unusual for men to show signs of weakness when isolated but make complete turnarounds once they got into the system of communication. Knowing that isolation increased prisoners' vulnerability, the Vietnamese followed a policy of as much isolation as possible. They also used a divide and conquer strategy and tried to prevent men from linking up by moving them around from time to time.

Communicating was easy at first, but from early 1966 on, it was a far cry from the rapid and clear dissemination of information that some have purported it to be. Communicating from one room to the next became very risky because the punishment for being caught was severe. Men would get down on their knees and look out through the crack at the bottom of the door for hours at a time, clearing so that others might tap or talk on the wall. Sometimes a guard would continuously walk around the building, which made communication impossible. Contacting another building might take half a year, and even then the transfer of information might be limited. Months or even years elapsed before guidance could be promulgated to all of the men in the Zoo, even with the Vietnamese policy of moving POWs around frequently. When a new man moved into a building, the noise from the tapping was deafening. Communications took every conceivable form imaginable: sweeping a broom, coughing, morse code, notes on every kind of paper, hand signals, notes in beans or nuts, fingers under the door, and passing a stick through a hole in the roof, to name a few.

Communication allowed the guidance and orders from the senior officer, as well as news to keep up morale, to pass to the POWs. Communicating for even a few seconds a day was enough to help a man keep his sanity, and once he had the opportunity to communicate at length, prison life became bearable. Men had thick calluses on their knuckles from tapping. The tap code came from the Air Force. A man named Claude Watkins got the code from some RAF men while a POW in Stalag Luft 6 in World War II, and the code was passed on to some Air Force pilots at the survival school at Stead Air Force Base. Captain Smitty Harris is credited with introducing it in Hanoi. Captain Quincy Collins is credited with introducing the technique of talking through the wall.

APPENDIX C: LEADERSHIP

Leadership was the second most important thing for the POWS. In the beginning, Cdr. Denton and Lt. Col. Risner had time to assess the situation before they issued any guidance. The Code of Conduct was an excellent guide for a POW's behavior, but there was no substitute for guidance from the senior officers. Denton and Risner's policies spread slowly throughout the system in the Zoo and some outlying camps, because years elapsed before the big propaganda push began at the Plantation. In my opinion, other senior officers provided input over the years that influenced pockets of men, but for the most part, their words never had as much effect as Denton and Risner's guidance.

The Vietnamese spent about two years getting their act together. These were two of the roughest years for the POWs because they bore the brunt of the experimentation and mistakes as the Vietnamese slowly felt their way. Torture was used at the shoot-down, to procure the confession, and again to coerce the biography. Isolation was the rule in the early years.

In early 1967, the Vietnamese decided to seek the support of the American public. The Plantation was opened that year because the Vietnamese knew that propaganda from the prisoners would be of great value to them. They tried to get as much as they could at the least cost. They didn't bother with old-timers from the Zoo, because with time Denton and Risner's guidance had gotten around, men had learned to communicate and were wise to most of the camp authorities schemes. They had become acclimated to prison life and were on the team. Instead, they used the Plantation for fledgling POWs. Communicating was more difficult there than at the Zoo because the Vietnamese had learned from experience how to curb it.

Ray Vohden

Far less time was available to promulgate whatever resistance guidance there was. The unpopularity of the war was affecting the new prisoners. Leadership at best was shaky and it didn't take a rocket scientist to figure out that this was not a normal war. Honor Bound states, "at the Plantation, Hanoi reaped political gains from reporters being ushered through the camp, worldwide dissemination of Pilots in Pajamas and early releases." The POW's at the Plantation were no different from other POW's but conditions were different there. Nevertheless, this was a monumental victory for the Vietnamese.

The Vietnamese were also wise to remove many of the known leaders from the population by stashing them in a special camp. There is no question that they suffered unbelievable torture and lived in Hell while in Alcatraz but during the 2 years (Oct. 25,1967-Dec. 9, 1969) that the leaders were isolated and out of circulation (the hardest years for the POW's) the Vietnamese gained vital propaganda success at the Plantation. During another critical period, the aftermath of the failed escape of two POWs, the most effective leaders were not to be heard of.

During these critical years of captivity, while the senior officers who were the leaders of the resistance were out of circulation, and the remaining senior officers (05's) were isolated, the responsibility for the leadership of the majority of the men fell on the shoulders of mid-grade (04) Naval and Air Force Officers, and (03) Air Force Captains and Navy Lieutenants. The (04's) included Majors Makowski, Kasler, Stavast, Runyon, and LCDR's Crayton, Clower, Bell, Stafford, Mullens, Shuman and me. The senior ranking officers of many buildings and rooms were junior Air Force and Navy officers. The mid-grade officers were the company commanders who led large groups of men at such camps as Sontay, Faith, Briarpatch, Skid Row, and Dogpatch, and at large rooms at the Hanoi Hilton. This entire group of prisoners (mostly jet pilots) was the most elite group of POWs that had ever existed, but with every group of men, disputes had to be resolved. The mid-grade and junior officers were the men who made the day-to-day difficult decisions.

Denton and Risner had provided the seeds from which the resistance grew, but once they left, the mid-grade officers took over. A special note should be made about Major Larry Guarino. He was the senior 04 and provided the leadership for the majority of the POWs during the toughest years. He had a special knack of getting along with the Vietnamese while at the same time keeping his loyalty to the United States, and for that loyalty, he was tortured extensively. He was flexible, and that made him the most effective leader of all the POWs, but he offended many who disagreed with him.

AUTHOR BIOGRAPHY

Ray Vohden was graduated from Rutgers University in 1952 with a degree in business administration. He joined the U.S. Navy that year and went on active duty in January 1953. After earning his wings in 1954, he flew fighter jets for four years, and then served as a flight instructor for three years. He became a catapult officer on the U.S.S. Constellation in 1961 and jet-attack pilot on the U.S.S. Hancock in 1964. At the time of his capture in April 1965, he was a 34-year old lieutenant commander and operations officer of jet-attack squadron VA 216. After eight years as a POW, he attended the Industrial College of the Armed Forces, served three years as the head of the Pentagon's POW/MIA task force and another three years as Superintendent of the U.S. Naval Observatory in Washington, D.C. Having attained the rank of captain, he retired in 1985.

Made in the USA
Lexington, KY
21 December 2010